FIFTH EDITION

Issues and Trends in Literacy Education

Richard D. Robinson
University of Missouri—Columbia

Michael C. McKenna
University of Virginia

Kristin Conradi
University of Virginia

PEARSON

Boston   Columbus   Indianapolis   New York   San Francisco   Upper Saddle River
Amsterdam   Cape Town   Dubai   London   Madrid   Milan   Munich   Paris   Montreal   Toronto
Delhi   Mexico City   São Paulo   Sydney   Hong Kong   Seoul   Singapore   Taipei   Tokyo

*This book is dedicated to those teachers who have inspired an undying love
for reading and writing in their students and to future readers
Bailey Mychael and Alexis Ryan*

Editor in Chief: Aurora Martinez Ramos
Editorial Assistant: Meagan French
Executive Marketing Manager: Krista Clark
Senior Project Manager: Janet Domingo
Managing Editor: Central Publishing
Operations Specialist: Laura Messerly
Art Director: Jayne Conte
Cover Designer: Bruce Kenselaar
Cover Image: Shutterstock
Full-Service Project Management: Chitra Ganesan
Composition: PreMediaGlobal
Printer/Binder: Edwards Brothers
Cover Printer: Edwards Brothers
Text Font: Palatino

Credits and acknowledgments borrowed from other sources and reproduced, with permission, in this textbook appear on appropriate page within text.

Library of Congress Cataloging-in-Publication Data

Issues and trends in literacy education / [edited by] Richard D. Robinson, Michael C. McKenna, Kristin Conradi. — 5th ed.
  p. cm.
  Includes index.
  ISBN-13: 978-0-13-231641-5
  ISBN-10: 0-13-231641-2
  1. Language arts. 2. Reading. 3. English language—Composition and exercises.
4. Literacy. I. Robinson, Richard David. II. McKenna, Michael C. III. Conradi, Kristin.
IV. Title.

  LB1576.I87 2011
  372.6′044—dc22   2010052063

10 9 8 7 6 5 4 3 2 1 14 13 12 11

www.pearsonhighered.com

ISBN-10: 0-13-231641-2
ISBN-13: 978-0-13-231641-5

ABOUT THE AUTHORS

 **Richard D. Robinson** is Professor of Reading Education at the University of Missouri Columbia. He has published ten books on a range of literacy topics, and his research interests include content are reading instruction, adult literacy, and the history of literacy instruction. He was the 2007 winner of the University of Missouri's William H. Byler Distinguished Professor Award and the 1996 Albert J. Kingston Award from the National Reading Conference. His articles have appeared in *Educational Researcher, Journal of Reading Education, The Reading Teacher, Journal of Reading, Reading Psychology,* and others.

 **Michael C. McKenna** is Thomas G. Jewell Professor of Reading at the University of Virginia. He has authored, coauthored, or edited 16 books and more than 100 articles, chapters, and technical reports on a range of literacy topics. His books include *The Literacy Coach's Handbook, Differentiated Reading Instruction, Assessment for Reading Instruction, Help for Struggling Readers, Teaching through Text, The International Handbook of Literacy and Technology,* and others. His research has been sponsored by the National Reading Research Center (NRRC) and the Center for the Improvement of Early Reading Achievement (CIERA). His articles have appeared in *Reading Research Quarterly,* the *Journal of Educational Psychology, Educational Researcher, The Reading Teachers,* and others.

 **Kristin Conradi** is a doctoral candidate at the University of Virginia. She has taught literacy in kindergarten, second, and fourth grades in high-poverty, inner city schools, and she has worked as a reading specialist in grades K–3. She has served as a clinician in the McGuffey Reading Clinic, where she was worked extensively with young children and adolescents who suffer from severe reading problems. She has also served as mentor and coach to K–2 teachers, and she has planned and implemented extensive professional development programs in literacy for elementary faculty. Her articles have appeared in *Language Arts* and in several edited books.

TABLE OF CONTENTS

Preface   vi

1 Word Recognition   1

History of Phonics Instruction   6
Barbara J. Walker

2 Fluency   22

What Is Fluent Reading and Why Is It Important?   24
Melanie Kuhn

Teaching Reading Fluency to Struggling Readers: Method, Materials, and Evidence   37
Timothy Rasinski, Susan Homan, and Marie Biggs

One-Minute Fluency Measures: Mixed Messages in Assessment and Instruction   47
Theresa A. Deeney

3 Comprehension   62

Reading Through a Disciplinary Lens   66
Connie Juel, Heather Hebard, Julie Park Haubner, and Meredith Moran

Reading Comprehension Instruction: Focus on Content or Strategies?   72
Margaret G. McKeown, Isabel L. Beck, and Ronette G. K. Blake

Increasing Opportunities to Acquire Knowledge Through Reading   80
Gina N. Cervetti, Carolyn A. Jaynes, and Elfrieda H. Hiebert

4 Vocabulary   97

Vocabulary Development During Read-Alouds: Primary Practices   101
Karen J. Kindle

The Vocabulary-Rich Classroom: Modeling Sophisticated Word Use to Promote Word Consciousness and Vocabulary Growth   114
Holly B. Lane and Stephanie Arriaza Allen

Closing the Vocabulary Gap   125
Jane L. David

5 English Learners 130

Improving Achievement for English Learners 133
Claude Goldenberg

Supporting Content Learning for English Learners 153
Eurydice B. Bauer, Patrick C. Manyak, and Crystal Cook

6 Literacy Coaching 159

What Matters for Elementary Literacy Coaching? Guiding Principles for Instructional Improvement and Students Achievement 162
Susan L' Allier, Laurie Elish-Piper, and Rita M. Bean

Models of Coaching 175

7 Adolescent Literacy 189

The "Adolescent" in Adolescent Literacy 196
Thomas W. Bean and Helen Harper

The Literacy Needs of Adolescents in Their Own Words 210
Sharon M. Pitcher, Gilda Martinez, Elizabeth A. Dicembre, Darlene Fewster, and Montana K. McCormick

8 Technology 223

21st-Century Literacies 226

Rethinking Online Reading Assessment 233

9 Writing 241

What Is Happening in the Teaching of Writing? 243
Arthur N. Applebee and Judith A. Langer

Issues and Trends in Writing 256
Michael T. Moore

10 Response to Intervention 273

Response to Intervention (RTI): What Teachers of Reading Need to Know 275
Eric M. Mesmer and Heidi Anne E. Mesmer

Rethinking Response to Intervention (RTI) at Middle and High School 288
Lynn S. Fuchs, Donald Fuchs, and Donald L. Compton

Name Index 297
Subject Index 302

PREFACE

New To This Edition

The primary purpose of this book is to help you better study and understand the field of literacy education. What was once a rather limited discipline is today a vast and complicated body of knowledge and field of inquiry, frequently drawing on information from many diverse areas such as psychology, sociology, and linguistics. The individual wishing to investigate a question or topic in literacy today may find the experience a daunting one.

Because the field of literacy changes so rapidly, it is important to keep abreast of developments. The content of fifth edition of this book therefore bears little similarity to that of the first. The important changes in this most recent edition include the following:

- The content is completely revised to include all new, current articles—providing the latest information on a variety of literacy topics.
- Included in each chapter are references to the latest literacy research—providing current access to current research studies.
- The book offers references to the latest teaching practices and procedures—current information that teachers can put to use in their classrooms.
- The selections are altogether new and feature the work of the most respected authors in the field of literacy, bringing readers up to date on who's doing and saying what about teaching reading and writing.
- A new chapter is included on English as a second language, presenting the latest thinking in this important area.
- A new chapter on technology and literacy education is included, presenting the latest thinking in this rapidly evolving area.

We have assumed that most readers of this book have had at least some introduction to the study of literacy education. The book has been developed with practicing teachers in mind—practitioners interested in extending their own thinking about the important issues they face in classrooms. We have not attempted to produce an introductory text, but assume that the foundations of literacy instruction—its purposes, concepts, and methods—have already been laid by means of prior coursework and teaching experience.

Organization of the Text

One dimension of the book that has not changed is the overall organization. We believe that the structure of each chapter has proved useful to readers. Each chapter consists of six sections: (1) a brief introduction to the topic, (2) a guidance section that suggests important ideas to keep in mind while reading, (3) the articles themselves, (4) questions about classroom implications, (5) suggested print sources for further reading, and (6) a few key online sources.

Chapter Introductions

Each topic is first summarized in a brief section designed both to provide necessary background and to help stimulate thinking related to the topic. Many readers of this book will have—either through previous education classes or classroom teaching experiences—ideas and feelings about the topics discussed in this book. We challenge you to keep an open mind about what you currently believe concerning literacy instruction. In many literacy areas, either because of recent research or relevant classroom experiences, instructional strategies that were once considered appropriate are now being challenged by new ideas and pedagogy.

Each chapter introduction concludes with a list of important questions designed to guide your reading and organize your thinking. Actively considering them should give you a better understanding of your current knowledge, beliefs, and feelings about a particular literacy issue.

As You Read

This brief section in each chapter should provide you with some specific guidance as you read the individual articles. You might keep these ideas and suggestions in mind as you consider the material presented on these various literacy topics.

Articles

Following the introduction are the selections. Our intent is that this section will help familiarize you with important, though sometimes incompatible, views on the chapter topic. Of particular note is the presentation of differing points of view. For some topics, in which there is little disagreement or controversy, you will find a general discussion of the literacy trend. You should understand that the selections are never intended to be all-inclusive but rather to introduce the topic and encourage you to pursue further study on your own.

Classroom Implications

It is an important goal of this book to provide you with information that is applicable to the effective teaching of classroom literacy. In this section we present ideas and suggestions for the integration of the chapter content into your instruction. Although these thoughts are general in nature, they are provided in this format so that you can readily apply them to your own particular classroom setting and students.

For Further Reading

The materials presented here have been selected to support and in some cases challenge the ideas and thoughts of the articles in the chapter. If you would like to expand your thinking on a particular topic you might use these references for further reading. They also are good suggestions group study with colleagues.

Online Resources

In some of the chapters is a list of useful online references, where appropriate. These listings were current at the time this book was published but in many cases become obsolete relatively rapidly.

Acknowledgments

We wish to take this opportunity to thank the following reviewers for their helpful comments: Richard Bates, SUNY Potsdam; Dena G. Beeghly, West Chester University; Beverly J. Boulware, Middle Tennessee State University; Debby Deal, Loyola College of Maryland; Clarissa Gamble Booker, Prairie View A&M University; Terry H. Higgins, The Ohio State University at Newark; Michael Moore, Georgia Southern University; and Carolyn Ann Walker, Ball State University.

1

Word Recognition

*Instead of teaching the word as a whole and afterward subjecting it to phonic analysis,
is it not infinitely better to take the sounds of the letters for our starting point. . . .*

—Rebecca S. Pollard (1889)

*The ultimate goals in words perception are (1) to bring to the level of instantaneous
perception a maximum number of highly useful words that are common to different
types of materials that a child wants and needs to read and (2) to develop
understandings, skills, and abilities that enable him to attack unfamiliar words
independently and thus be on his own in reading.*

—William S. Gray (1960)

Perhaps of all the areas of literacy education, there is no more contentious issue than that of word recognition, particularly as it relates to phonics. Through the years this debate has been controversial and seemingly never ending. The following three statements regarding phonics instruction illustrate how this debate has unfolded over time. Horace Mann, writing in 1838 noted, "It can hardly be doubted therefore that a child would learn to name 26 unfamiliar words sooner than the unknown, unheard of letters of the alphabet" (Mann, 1838, p. 17). Rudolf Flesch, over a century later, took a much different approach to the teaching of phonics. He said, "if a child isn't taught the sounds of the letters, then he has absolutely nothing to go by when he tries to read a word. All he can do is guess. . . . Systematic phonics is *the* way to teach reading." (Flesch, 1955, pp. 21, 121). More recently, Allington and Cunningham (2007) have noted, "Phonics instruction is clearly important because one big task of beginning readers is figuring out how our alphabetic language works" (p. 68).

Adding to the current discussion of the role of word recognition in effective literacy instruction has been the report of the National Reading Panel (NICHHD, 2000). This research synthesis makes a strong case for the role of word recognition as one of the key aspects of literacy education.

While it is possible, in theory at least, to argue that reading instruction should be all phonics or no phonics, these are extreme positions that few would take very seriously. For most educators, there is a middle stance–namely, that phonics is an important aspect of a total classroom literacy program but that other aspects are crucial as well.

The Reading Wars

Why has word recognition instruction–and phonics in particular–occasioned such controversy. The situation has often been likened to warfare, with the two sides generally characterized as (1) those who believe that explicit instruction in decoding is profitable for most students and (2) those who believe that a meaning emphasis will lead naturally to proficient decoding. At the heart of the argument is what good readers do as they make their way through text. Educators who take the first view believe that virtually every letter of every word is recognized, even in the case of words known at sight. Those who subscribe to the second view believe that readers use context to predict each word and then merely sample the letters to test their predictions. Although there are several variations of these ideas, we can describe the first view as bottom-up because the letters of a word tell the brain how to identify it. We can describe the second view as top-down because the brain decides which portions of a word are useful for recognizing it. Let's look at these models in more detail.

As you read these words, you are not likely to be cognizant of exactly how it is happening. As a proficient reader, you merely take for granted that you can effortlessly bring meaning to any print you are likely to encounter. In recent decades, educators have taken a special interest in precisely how this process occurs and what subprocesses may be involved. Their interest goes beyond theoretical curiosity. Understanding how the mature reading process takes place can be very useful in addressing the problems experienced by some students. Now let's contrast the two competing models of how reading occurs.

The Top-Down Model *Processing*

A persuasive model of the reading process was proposed by Kenneth Goodman and Frank Smith in the late 1960s. It can be described as follows. The brain, they contended, is largely incapable of processing the huge volume of data contained in the letters on a page. Good readers therefore make this process as efficient as possible by continually forming hypotheses about the next word they will encounter. Consider the following partial sentence:

She combed her long blond _____.

When you reach the blank, you are able to form a reasonable guess about what the next word will be. The guess is based on all of the words that have gone before. That is, you used the context of the next word in order to help identify it. In real reading, of course, you are not faced with blanks but with actual words. This means that your guess can be aided by the letters of the word that you are trying to identify. To continue with our example, if you suspected that the next word was *hair*, you might simply notice that the first letter of that word was an *h*. This would be enough to confirm your prediction and allow you to keep reading quickly and efficiently.

She combed her long blond h___.

Goodman and Smith therefore viewed reading as a process of continually forming predictions about upcoming words and of confirming them–not by fully decoding those words but by merely sampling enough of the letters to confirm each prediction. In cases in which the reader's prediction is wrong, the reader would need to slow down and take a closer look at the actual letters of the word. What if the original sentence had been a bit different?

She combed her long blond tresses.

Expecting the word *hair*, the reader would sample one or more of the letters in the word *tresses* and realize that this prediction was incorrect. The reader would therefore need to slow down and take a closer look.

This model of reading is often called the "top-down" model because higher-level mental processes are very much in control of word recognition. The conscious thoughts of the reader are directing the lower-level process of letter and word recognition. In other words, the brain is telling the eye what to look for. Teachers tend to find this model very attractive because it gives a central role to comprehension. It is meaning oriented and is sometimes referred to as a "concept-driven" model.

The trouble with this model is that it is completely wrong, and a large number of studies have put it to rest. Let's look now at the model that has replaced it.

opinion/ bias? ✳

The Bottom-Up Model

The competing model that is now accepted as an accurate description of how reading takes place is often called the "bottom-up" model. At first, it may seem counterintuitive. According to this model, a proficient reader processes nearly every letter of every word. For the most part, this is done unconsciously and automatically. In fact, some psychologists have suggested that the process of recognizing words is conducted through an independent module of the mind. Like a conveyor belt, this module continually supplies a reader's conscious thoughts with the words encountered on the page. There is no need for the reader to make predictions about upcoming words because they are rapidly and efficiently supplied through the module. The brain does not need to tell the eyes what information is needed. Rather, this information is simply supplied when the reader needs it.

You may have had the experience of reading to a young child and allowing your mind to wander. Even though you were thinking about other matters, you were able to continue your oral reading, and the child may not have known the difference. You were able to do so because your word recognition module is capable of working automatically, and you are free to ignore the words it supplies.

The Role of Context

This is not to say that context plays no role in proficient reading. For one thing, when you came to the word *tresses* in our earlier example, studies show that you recognized it a few milliseconds more quickly having read the preceding context than if you had encountered the word *tresses* in isolation (on a flashcard, perhaps). However, this modest difference in time is merely the result of certain portions of your word memory (which psychologists call your lexicon) having been primed by the context. That priming is an unconscious process and is a far cry from making conscious predictions about what the next word will be. (Here's an example of priming. A friend makes a passing reference to *Gone with the Wind*. An hour later, as if out of nowhere, the theme from the movie runs through your mind.)

Context plays another important role in reading as well. Consider the following sentence:

The Braves scored a run in the first inning.

An unabridged dictionary gives more than 30 definitions of the word *run*. However, you had no difficulty choosing the right one, and you did so on the basis of context.

Without context, you would have been unable to arrive at the intended meaning of this word. Because most words have more than a single meaning, context utilization is a vital skill, one that all readers must acquire.

The bottom-up model (also called a "text-driven" model) suggests that context has no role in locating the word *run* in your lexicon. Instead, context comes in to play after the word *run* has been located. It is used to suppress all meanings of the word *run* except the one that makes sense in context. Again, you are scarcely aware that this process is occurring. When you read the sentence above, the idea that the word *run* might refer to a flaw in a woman's stocking did not enter your conscious thinking at all. Context was useful in suppressing this idea. And thankfully so. Imagine how cumbersome reading would be if it involved consciously sorting through all of the possible meanings of every word you encountered.

The Simple View of Reading

Phillip Gough and his colleagues have suggested that the best way of viewing the reading process is really quite simple. Reading entails two components: listening comprehension and word recognition. Anyone proficient in both of these areas is likely to be a good reader. While Stahl and Hayes have pointed out that it is also necessary to be motivated to read in the first place, it is generally accepted that these two components are a good way of reducing the reading process to its essentials. Of course, Gough and his colleagues were a bit tongue-in-cheek in suggesting that this view is simple. The catch is that each of these two components is highly complex. As an overview, however, a simple view is a good way of envisioning the process.

It is also a good starting point from which to assess the difficulties a child may have. For example, a child may be a weak decoder with strong comprehension skills. Another child may have achieved oral reading fluency and yet have limited capacity to understand what is read. Still another child may have deficiencies in both areas. Effective reading teachers must conduct the battle on two fronts: decoding and comprehension.

Stages of Reading Development

The bottom-up model provides an accurate depiction of proficient reading, but precisely how does an individual get to this point? A profitable way of viewing the process of learning to read is to describe a child's progress through discernible stages of development. The most widely accepted stage model is that of Jeanne Chall (1983/1996). Chall describes the following stages, and I have taken the liberty of updating her terminology slightly.

Emergent literacy.   During this stage, which begins in the preschool years, children acquire a foundation of oral language, learn the alphabet, and gain an early notion of how books and the print they contain are laid out. They also develop an awareness of the sounds of spoken language, an awareness that will serve them well as they learn to read.

Decoding.   Children learn next that letters and groups of letters represent the sounds they hear in spoken words. Instruction in letter-sound correspondences is what we call phonics. In an alphabetic language like English, children soon come to grasp a fundamental idea called the alphabetic principle. According to this principle, a limited number of letters are used to represent the basic sounds of spoken language. These basic sounds, called phonemes, are the building blocks of words. Of course, there are other decoding skills as well, including recognition of affixes, roots, and so forth. Depending on the curriculum the decoding stage may begin in kindergarten or first grade.

Fluency.   Children who have learned a great many specific decoding skills will be able to decode most unfamiliar words, but their oral reading is likely to be halting for a time and characterized by poor phrasing. This is because their decoding skills are not yet automatic. Their word recognition module is still in the formative stages. With practice, however, their oral reading will become more proficient and will sound more adult like. They will have attained oral reading fluency. Generally, this occurs during second grade.

Learning the new.   Once oral reading fluency is attained, a child's mental resources can be trained on comprehension. A reader who must devote conscious attention to too many words will not be able to adequately comprehend. But when word recognition becomes automatic, thinking about the content of what one reads becomes an attainable goal. There is a truism in reading: first, a child learns to read, and then the child reads to learn. When the child reaches the stage of learning the new, he or she is in a position to make reading a real tool. One of the dangers of an overemphasis on decoding in the primary grades, however, may be that some readers become excellent word callers but have only a limited ability (or inclination) to comprehend what they decode.

AS YOU READ

The single article in this chapter on word recognition (Walker, 2008) is an excellent review of the past history as well as the current state of this important aspect of literacy instruction. Pay particular attention to the various approaches to teaching phonics, such as analytic and synthetic. Make sure you can differentiate them. Note especially how many of the issues and procedures that are most often associated with word recognition have been debated by educators throughout our past literacy history. You might compare how these debates compare with today's discussion of the teaching of word recognition and how they have been resolved in the past.

REFERENCES

Allington, R. L., & Cunningham, P. M. (2007). *Schools that work: Where all children read and write* (3rd ed.). Boston, MA: Allyn & Bacon.

Camilli, G., & Wolf, P. (2004). Research on teaching: A cautionary tale. *Educational Leadership, 61,* 26–30.

Flesch, R. (1955). *What Johnny can't read and what you can do about it.* New York, NY: Harper.

Mann, H. (1838). *The Common School Journal, 1,* 7.

National Institute of Child Health and Human Development (NICHHD). (2000). *Report of the National Reading Panel. Teaching children to read: An evidence-based assessment of the scientific research literature on reading and its implications for reading instruction. Report of the subgroups* (NIH Publication No. 004754). Washington, DC: Government Printing Office.

Pollard, R. S. (1889). *Pollard's synthetic method: A complete manual.* Chicago, IL: Western Publishing House.

Walker, B. J. (2008). History of phonics instruction. In Mary Jo Fresch (Ed.), *An essential history of current reading practices,* (pp. 33–51). Newark, DE: International Reading Association.

History of Phonics Instruction

BARBARA J. WALKER

■ ■ ■ ■ ■

It was the early 1950s, and I slowly walked to my first school experience wondering what lay ahead in first grade. Public schools weren't really ready for the baby boomers. Large numbers of students in the classrooms made the easygoing curriculum of the past obsolete. For instance, there were 24 other students in my first-grade classroom. As all first-grade teachers did, Mrs. Railsback introduced us to Dick, Jane, and Sally basic readers. We had big charts of Dick and Jane in the front of the room where we could match the picture of Dick with his name. I can still remember the day we saw the picture of Spot, their dog. My dad really wanted a dog, so learning that word was important to me.

In the 1950s, teachers used the whole-word reading method, where they introduced the printed word along with a picture and then used the word in a meaningful sentence. We had to listen closely to what the teacher was saying and then look closely at the whole word and its form as we looked at a large chart. In second grade, the situation worsened. I had to do phonics workbook pages. What a nightmare! I could not then—and still cannot—synthesize sounds (blend the separate sounds to form a word). Therefore, phonics in isolation was difficult for me. However, synthesizing letter sounds is not the only way to figure out words. I used meaning, my experiences, and the pictures to figure out words.

Phonics is an important tool in reading, but there are different pathways to learning phonics. According to Chall (1992), learning phonics involves how the letters and sounds work together within a word. Hence, learning phonics means learning how words work. Word learning has many designations: word analysis, word attack, decoding, and the alphabetic principle, to name a few. In 1996, the International Reading Association position statement on phonics quoted Nila Banton Smith to demonstrate the early thinking about phonics. Smith (1963) wrote:

> When the child has reached the maturity level at which he can make the best use of formal instruction in phonics, certainly no time should be lost in launching an extensive and carefully organized program to promote the wide and independent use of phonics in attacking new words, regardless of the grade or the time in the school year when this occurs. (p. 213)

I still believe that statement.

This chapter describes the development of phonics instruction throughout the last five decades of the 20th century. Before the mid-1930s, teachers taught phonics through a mechanistic phonics approach (sounding out words by learning stringent rules and rigid procedures). In the last half of 1930, a backlash occurred. Scholars, publishers, and teachers banned phonics instruction. According to Beery (1949), phonics instruction was outdated and intrinsically wrong. By 1940, teachers did not teach phonics in schools.

Phonics—The Last Resort

By the early 1950s, teachers taught phonics as a last resort rather than banning it. Recognizing whole words was still the predominate approach for teaching words. Teachers taught whole words by providing an oral language context and having students look at the printed word on the chalkboard. Thus, they presented the words and discussed their meaning to encourage readers to remember the word in meaningful oral context. At this time, learning words mainly involved word perception. Gates (1951/2002), a leading researcher in reading, believed that young children should read naturally and instantly perceive words, as adults do when they read the morning newspaper. Furthermore, he believed that children spent three or more years in school without ever having read fluently. Rather, they had been painstakingly translating printed text, sounding out words letter by letter. He believed this approach developed word-by-word reading, which discouraged a love of reading. Teachers used intrinsic phonics instruction, phonics taught more gradually, in the context of meaningful reading, usually appearing in the second and third grades. Teachers were admonished to not "reinstate the old mechanical phonic drills," which would result in word-by-word reading (Gray, 1948, p. 28). During the 1950s, most reading professionals believed that if a student could recognize a large number of words instantly, he or she could use the sentence context to read unfamiliar words.

To learn words, children needed many repetitions before unfamiliar words became part of their sight word vocabulary. Through multiple repetitions of words, children would learn to read printed words and use context to promote learning new words. The basic readers, forerunner of the basal readers, included a lot of repetition, using phrases similar to the following:

See Max, said Jane.
See Max run.
Run, Max, run.

In fact, looking at whole words and repeating them frequently does work when children have to know only a small number of words.

Even though the reading program promoted word perception, Gray (1960) claimed that children needed other strategies, too. He suggested that as children read unfamiliar words, other clues might help readers. He suggested four major ways to aid word perception: "1) memory of word form, 2) context clues, 3) word analysis (structural and phonetic), and 4) the dictionary" (p. 16). He did include phonetic clues, but they were low on his list of what to use when encountering an unfamiliar word. The prevalent view was that basic readers provided enough repetitions so that children would learn to recognize words naturally. Dick, Jane, and Sally and their precursors would set the standard for reading instruction from the 1930s through the 1960s.

During the latter part of the 1950s, there was a growing concern that no strategies for analyzing unfamiliar words were being taught. Parents were getting anxious wanting their children to learn and use phonic knowledge. In 1955, when Rudolf Flesch published *Why Johnny Can't Read*, phonics instruction gained credibility. Flesch (1955) maintained children hesitated when they came to an unknown word. He advocated that children should learn to sound out words so they could recognize unknown words readily. The book sold over a half-million copies (see also chapters 1, 5, 7, and 9, this volume, for more discussion of Flesch's work). Parents and the public read the book and began to advocate for more phonics instruction. However, publishers maintained the whole-word approach in the basic reading programs. Thus, word perception by introducing the whole word within a meaningful oral context was still prevalent.

Phonics Makes a Comeback

During the 1960s, numerous basal reading series included a manual outlining how to teach each story. The manual included a program for analytical phonics instruction that recommended that the teacher use known words and ask children to analyze the phonetic elements in these words. In the latter part of first grade, the basal reading programs introduced analytic phonics, which taught letter–sound relationships using known sight words.

Analytic phonics relies on readers knowing a large number of words at sight. Drawing from known sight words, teachers directed students to make inferences about the phonic relationships within words containing the same letter combinations. In other words, the student matched the sounds in a known word with the sounds in the new word (Walker, 2008). This approach to phonics purported that after repeated exposures to words that contain consistent phonic relationships, students inferred phonic generalizations. For example, a reader might develop the understanding that short words that begin and end with a consonant usually have a short vowel in the middle. Often the teacher would ask questions to help students draw these kinds of inferences, such as "What sound of 'e' do you hear in the middle of *pet* and *met*. Is it a long or short sound?" The students might informally state the rule in vague terms, but they would intuitively understand and use this rule. Contextual or sentence analysis was still an important aspect of word learning. Workbooks required children to read a sentence with a blank and select one of three words to fit in the sentence. Thus, the new basal reading series published during the early 1960s contained an increased use of phonics instruction. The phonic instruction was predominately analytic phonics, which prevailed throughout the next decade.

However, in the 1960s, some reading programs differed from the mainstream basal readers that used analytic phonics. A few basal readers included instruction using linguistic units that had recurring patterns. The linguistics–phonics system used the idea that the English language had recurring written patterns that were systematic to develop their program. By pointing out the word patterns in common, Fries (1963) proposed to children to figure out words. Pictures, he believed, would distract students from focusing on the letters and word patterns. With these ideas, Fries and his colleagues (Fries, Wilson, & Rudolph, 1966) developed the Merrill Linguistic Readers. These readers contained very stilted language using words with the same graphic ending as the recurrent written pattern of /an/ in *man, ran,* and *fan*. Teachers introduced the words in a list. For example, a story using both the /at/ and /an/ patterns would read as the following:

> A fat man ran.
> Fan the fat man.
> Dan ran to the fat man.
> Dan can fan the fat man.

Other programs taught sound–symbol relationships at the onset of schooling. Following the thinking of the behaviorists, teachers introduced rules like short "a" and then the children read stories that had short "a" words.

The late 1960s was a time of great controversy. We, the children who learned to read with Dick, Jane, and Sally, were demanding change. We had learned that in the real world not all families were like Dick, Jane, and Sally. We wanted that changed! Therefore, some of us worked toward civil rights for all races; others demonstrated against the war; still others worked for more innovative views of learning and education. Learning to read also had its growing controversies. Several groups of professionals developed very different lines of thinking. Skinner (1958, 1965) developed the science of human behavior, or behaviorism, which viewed learning as a stimulus–response interaction (see also chapters 1 and 9, this volume, for further discussion of behaviorism). This view supported synthetic phonics instruction (sounding out words letter by letter) and the skills movement (teaching discrete parts of reading). The work of Gibson (1964, 1965) on word perception studied what students focused on when reading whole words. This research also supported the idea that there were subabilities, such as visual memory, that underlie reading; therefore, researchers continued the search for underlying aspects of reading. Holmes (1965) was working on the substrata theory of reading, which would identify other attributes that might underlie reading. Chomsky (1965) hypothesized that children were "wired" or biologically predisposed to acquire basic syntax or grammatical structures (see also chapters 1, 5, and 10, this volume, for further discussion of Chomsky's work). Even young children could produce an infinite number of novel sentences. Building on the syntax perspective, Goodman (1967) wrote the seminal piece "Reading: A Psycholinguistic Guessing Game." Other research in linguistics, psycholinguistics, and sociolinguistics segued into literacy instruction and later had a profound effect on beginning reading instruction (Pearson, 1997; see also Chapter 1, this volume). Symposiums sponsored by the Growth and Development Branch of the National Institute of Child Health and Human Development in 1968, 1969, 1971, and 1972 eventually led to the publication of the second edition of *Theoretical Models and Processes of Reading* (edited by Ruddell and Singer) by the International Reading Association (IRA) in 1977 (Kavanagh, 1977).

While those ideas were in their infancy, a great debate was growing about which method of beginning reading instruction was the best. Influenced by behaviorism, some programs employed an intensive, systematic, code-emphasis approach to learning phonics in which children learned sound–symbol relationships at the onset of first grade. Proponents of a code-emphasis approach (one of which is synthetic phonics) believed students would be able to read texts that are more complex earlier because they knew how to sound out unfamiliar words. Others believed that the conventional approach of analytical phonics was superior, because students learned to think independently by making inquiries about words. Others believed that by reading whole stories the children had dictated, students created their own system for learning words. The controversy grew. Therefore, the federal government commissioned the First Grade Studies to analyze what method for word learning was the "best" (see also chapters 1 and 5, this volume, for discussion of First Grade Studies). According to Bond and Dykstra (1967/1997), directors of the project, no "approach is so distinctly better in all situations and respects than the others that it should be considered the one best method and the one to be used exclusively" (p. 416). In a recent conversation, Carl Braun, who completed the statistical analysis of the studies, reiterated that there were no statistically different outcomes among the First Grade Studies (personal communication, May 2007). However, one interpretation that did influence the next decade was that a combination of approaches (basal plus phonics, phonic/linguistics and language experience, etc.) resulted in higher performance. That same year, Chall (1967) published her book *Learning to Read: The Great Debate*. Using her analysis of available studies, she maintained that a code-emphasis approach (intense phonics) was more effective than a meaning-emphasis approach (whole word). Chall (1967) wrote, "In summary, judging from the studies comparing systematic with intrinsic phonics . . . we can say that systematic phonics at the very beginning tends to produce generally better reading and spelling achievement than intrinsic phonics, at least through 3rd grade" (p. 114). From that year on, teachers taught reading using more and varied phonics instruction (see also chapters 1 and 5, this volume, for more discussion of Chall's influence).

Phonics: Anything Goes

Where should one begin when talking about phonics instruction in the 1970s? Due to the First Grade Studies and *Learning to Read: The Great Debate*, it appeared that many different approaches were acceptable, as long as teachers used some type of phonics instruction. The previous decade demonstrated that phonics instruction, whether it was intensive or gradual, improves students' word learning. Project Literacy occurred at the same time and focused on word perception and perceptual development. However, Gibson and the research team found that readers used distinctive features of word units rather than word configuration or recognizing the whole word (Gibson, 1965; Gibson & Levin, 1975). This marked the end of only teaching whole words. Additionally, Gibson along with her colleagues investigated the nature of the correspondence between written and spoken language; they found that invariable units (sound–symbol patterns) resulted in better perception for reading words (Gibson, Pick, Osser, & Hammond, 1962). The public believed the research endorsed all sound–symbol relationships. This misreading of Gibson's findings indirectly "endorsed decoding instruction" (Williams, 1984, p. 14). Taken together, these findings resulted in a plethora of basal reading programs in the early 1970s. The various basal reading companies worked to include more phonics instruction earlier; as a result, some publishers started analytic phonics instruction during kindergarten. For phonics instruction as well as reading processes, the research continued. Some researchers focused on the active role of the reader in the developing field of cognitive psychology, the study of how learners actively "build" knowledge.

However, the behaviorist viewpoint dominated instruction in the 1970s. The work of behavioral psychologists had a growing influence on reading instruction during this decade. Gagne (1970) purported that task analysis was important for learning complex tasks such as reading. The behaviorist view broke reading into its component skills; each skill had a determined sequence of subskills (discrete, small tasks of reading). Many educators and basal reading publishers jumped on this bandwagon. They dissected phonics instruction into minute subskills and sequenced them for reading instruction. Teachers taught certain consonants first, second, and so forth. The most interesting debate in classrooms was whether you taught the short "a" along with the long "a" or taught all the short vowel sounds first, then the long vowel sounds. Some reading professionals were convinced that an accumulation of subskills would produce a reader. Teachers used separate phonics workbooks in tandem with basal readers. Skills programs such as *Sullivan Programmed Readers*, in which children learned skills by filling in blanks in programmed workbooks, and the *Wisconsin Design for Reading*, which tracked skill development, were prevalent (Allington, 2002). However, no matter what the program, teachers measured the subskills of reading. These management systems seemed to take away teachers' decision-making power.

For example, while I was a reading specialist in the 1970s, a teacher who had been teaching first grade for 20 years asked, "What if everyone failed the 'ing' end of the unit test? Can I continue with the next story, or do I need to go back and reteach?" I asked her, "Can the students read the next story, and do they use 'ing' appropriately when they talk and read with you?" She answered, "Yes!" Therefore, I suggested that she teach the next story and slowly review the "ing" rule as she continued teaching stories. The class went on reading new stories, and they learned the "ing" rule at the same time. Even after 20 years, the teacher gave up her professional judgment because a textbook company mandated and tested skills in a prescribed order.

Rather than using basal readers and analytic phonics, other teachers chose synthetic phonics programs that taught phonics by analyzing sound–symbol relationships at the onset of reading. Various programs that taught "phonics first" were developed and used the synthetic approach to decoding, often referred to as explicit phonics or a code-emphasis approach. These synthetic phonics programs introduce the letter–sound relationships systematically. Next, students learned to blend the sounds together to decode an unknown word. The successive blending of sounds required the student to hold a sequence of sounds in their memory while blending them to form a word. For example, students learned letters and their sounds first. The teacher demonstrated how to blend sounds orally, and they practiced that skill. The students easily blended sounds. Next, the teacher taught consonant sounds in isolation. They readily learned the consonant sounds of /s/, /t/, /n/, /d/, and hard /c/. Next, the teacher taught some sight words (*in, on, the*) and the short /a/ sound. They also learned those quickly. At the end of that week, they read a simple story:

> Stan and Dan can stand on a mat. The cat can stand on the mat. The mat is in the sand. Stan and Dan sat on the mat in the sand. Stan tans on the mat and Dan can tan on the mat. A nat sat on Dan. A nat sat on Stan and the cat. Nats sat in the sand and on the mat. Nats! Nats! Nats!

As students learned other consonant and vowel sounds, the stories became more complex. They read each story, sounding out unfamiliar words.

Of these programs, Distar reading (currently known as Reading Mastery) consistently produced significant growth in word recognition (Bereiter & Engelmann, 1970). Distar introduced sounds slowly and demonstrated how to blend sounds. This improved phonemic synthesis (blending sounds). The program also used hand signals to direct attention to letters as students sounded out the words. Students spent a great deal of time learning to sound out words and then saying them fast. Teachers introduced stories later in the program. In spite of learning to blend sounds, the slow pace for learning words and reading stories, this program did not match how average students learned. Average students learn sound–symbol relationships more readily and move to longer stories much sooner.

The sequences of hierarchal skill development, as well as the systematic blending of sounds, were intrusive ways to develop phonic knowledge. Little actual reading occurred in classrooms because of the concentrated focus on skill instruction in phonics and the subsequent testing of phonic knowledge. This approach certainly had its opponents. Some believed that code instruction (learning letters and their sounds) had no place in a reading program.

Teachers using the Language Experience Approach, one of the methods used in the First Grade Studies, did not believe in direct instruction in letter–sound relationships. In this approach, children dictated a story and the teacher used the story to teach the children to read. A collection of the stories was the child's first reader. From the dictated language experience stories, the teacher selected initial consonants and simple vowel combinations to develop phonic knowledge. During the 1970s, with the work of Stauffer (1970) and Van Allen (1976), language experience gathered supporters for teaching reading this way.

The emerging cognitive revolution led to an increased focus on constructing meaning using readers' prior knowledge and text knowledge simultaneously

(Pearson & Stephens, 1994). Reading research shifted away from word learning and focused on meaning. Comprehension and constructing meaning were the foci of the federally funded research in the 1980s. At the same time, the concept of constructing meaning became the core of the whole-language movement. Thus, the whole-language movement would hold court against the skills approach and continue to grow throughout the 1980s and 1990s.

Phonics Drill Dies a Slow Death

During the 1980s, phonics-first programs and skill instruction decreased in use and basal readers included more literature-based stories because of the growing influence of whole language. In the mid-1980s, Anderson and his colleagues prepared a report for the United States government titled *Becoming a Nation of Readers* (Anderson, Hiebert, Scott, & Wilkinson, 1985). Their position on phonics instruction was clear. The researchers reiterated that young children needed to learn the "alphabetic principal" that letters in printed words represent the phonemes in speech. Further, they recommended teaching phonics as a strategic process of using familiar word patterns to figure out unknown words. This decoding-by-analogy strategy relies heavily on students' ability to segment words into sounds (phonemic segmentation) and match those sounds to letters or letter patterns. The research synthesis stated, "Classroom research shows that, on the average, children who are taught phonics get off to a better start in learning to read than children who are not taught phonics. This advantage is most apparent on tests of word identification" (Anderson et al., 1985, p. 37). Conversely, the researchers found that most phonics instruction consumed the entire elementary school years using an overwhelming number of workbook exercises, begging the best way to get children to refine and extend their knowledge of letter–sound correspondences is through repeated opportunities to read" (p. 38; see also chapters 4, 7, and 8, this volume for more discussion of *Becoming a Nation of Readers*). After this report was published, the debate between the whole-word approach and the phonics-first approach moved to a debate between those who believed students learned phonics naturally, advocating for a whole-language philosophy, and those who believed students refined phonic knowledge as they learned decoding strategies with explicit support.

Nevertheless, throughout the 1980s and into the 1990s, the whole-language movement was in full swing (see also Chapter 5, this volume, for more discussion of the whole-language movement). Whole language advocated trade books instead of basal readers and writing instead of phonics. Reading was a meaning-making process and was expected to develop naturally. Teachers read trade books aloud and talked about meaning and words; they invited students to chime in and encouraged students to write, accepting their invented spelling.

So where was the phonics instruction? The public, as well as many novice teachers, assumed there was none. Advocates of whole language encouraged phonics instruction to occur naturally as children and teachers shared stories and wrote together. For instance, first the teacher would read the story aloud several times while children chimed in. Finally, the children read stories independently with the teacher scaffolding unfamiliar words using prompts from the cueing system. According to Goodman and Goodman (1980), the cueing systems had three aspects: using meaning or what makes sense in the sentence or story (semantic cues); using the letters and their sounds (graphophonic cues), and the grammar of the sentence (syntactic cues). The teachers asked if what the student read made sense (semantic cue), asked what would make sense and start with the sound of the beginning letter (graphophonic cue), or asked if how the student read the sentence sounded like spoken English (syntactic cue). Prompts such as "Did that make sense and start with the sound you said?" helped students figure out how words work within the sentence rather than in isolation.

Additionally, advocates of whole language taught phonics instruction through writing. For instance, each day, first-grade teachers began the day with interactive writing, which involved the teacher and students jointly composing a written text. The teacher modeled writing words as students created a sentence or short story. The teacher began writing the story on a chart tablet, saying the letters and sounds as he or she wrote the words. Next, the teacher asked a student to take over writing the words as the other students spelled the words aloud. The teacher read the class-generated story aloud as the students chimed in. Interactive writing provided children with opportunities to hear sounds in words and connect those sounds with corresponding letters and words. Through writing, the reader can become sensitive to written conventions such as letter formation, phonics, and spelling.

Reading Recovery, an early intervention approach for reading, was developed by Clay (1979) during the 1970s in New Zealand and became prevalent in the United States in the 1980s. In Reading Recovery, teachers used writing for sounds to illustrate phonemic segmentation and phonemic synthesis (Clay, 1979). Using the troublesome word, the teacher would write boxes for the sounds in the words. The teacher slowly says the sounds, as the student writes the sounds in the Elkonin boxes (Elkonin, 1973). Then, the student writes this word in the sentence. This approach to phonics found its way into classrooms and helped students learn to use phonemic segmentation and phonemic synthesis to figure out words. Thus, children learned phonics as they wrote. Although the whole-language movement provided an environment rich in social interactions, discussions, high quality literature, student-centered learning, and integration of reading and writing, something more was needed.

Basic research on learning and thinking were paramount during the 1980s, which became the basis for a constructivist view of reading, that is, reading is an active process of building meaning (Pearson & Stephens, 1994; see also chapters 1, 5, 7, and 10, this volume, for more discussion of constructivism). Constructivism and the cognitive view involve an increasing understanding of the role of background knowledge to construct (build) meaning. Research began investigating how the process of constructing meaning worked. In a review of research on comprehension instruction, Pearson and Dole (1987) suggested that readers use strategies or processes to construct meaning and, often, readers need demonstrations in comprehension strategies so they can construct meaning. These theories helped professionals realize the importance of using background knowledge and strategy deployment when constructing meaning and word knowledge. However, during this decade, basic research on word learning slowed. Nevertheless, some professionals continued developing teaching approaches for word learning that would reflect the new constructivism view of learning.

Phonics: Multiple Pathways

According to IRA's (1996) position statement on phonics, readers learn phonics "by using many sources of information such as their experiences, illustrations in text, print on the page, and knowledge of language—including their knowledge of sound–symbol correspondences" (p. 4). This reflects the thinking of the 1990s, in which researchers and teachers were touting various phonic approaches be used simultaneously in the classroom.

During the late 1980s, word study investigations had influenced the way professionals thought about phonics. There was a growing consensus on several ideas related to phonics. Pearson (1996) suggested two that deal with linguistic understanding: "First, students must understand that oral and written language, while surely not identical, emanate from the common wellspring of language that resides deep in our being . . . and second, students must embrace the alphabetic principle . . . that English writing represents sounds" (p. 269). In Pearson's opinion, learning just the grapheme, as we had done in the 1950s, would make little sense "unless both the oral and written language units are accessible to children" (p. 270). These ideas formed a basis for phonics instruction drawing from cognitive theory; that is, even when decoding words, students use their own knowledge along with the text to construct the meaning and knowledge about the words.

In this decade, professionals realized that phonemic awareness was a critical aspect of learning to read (Goswami & Bryant, 1990). That same year, Adams (1990) published *Beginning to Read*. She wrote about the importance and inclusion of phonemic awareness and phonic instruction in all reading programs. The book explained the impacts of the alphabetic principle (using sound–symbol relationships) and phonemic awareness (using sound segmentation and sound synthesis) on learning to read. This tome laid out the growing knowledge of how words are learned. Although basic research on this topic had continued throughout the 1980s (Ehri, 1991), few syntheses had been compiled to give direction for instructional improvements. The debate started again; only this time, it appeared that debate was about the difference between whole language and explicit instruction (Ehri, 1998). The media used this book to rekindle and reformulate the debate in a dichotomous way. The growing debate challenged researchers to clarify multiple ways for teaching phonics. The increased attention set the stage for multiple variations on constructing a knowledge base for phonics. Stahl, Duffy-Hester, and Stahl (1998) declared, "Constructivism is not synonymous with discovery learning, since children can be guided in their constructions more or less explicitly" (p. 350). Thus, children are active learners who can construct a network of phonic knowledge about letters and sounds. Using the theory of constructivism, reading professionals have suggested multiple pathways to teaching phonics. Writing was emphasized, as were spelling-based approaches with teacher demonstration to make the procedures more strategic and explicit. Approaches for systematically teaching decoding by analogy were developed, as well. The following provide examples of the growing multiplicity of approaches to phonics instruction that were developed from a constructivist framework.

Writing

Writing is an important means to develop awareness of the individual sounds in words. As children write, they look closely at how letters are used to form words and construct a system for the spelling (phonic) conventions of written text. As with reading, lots of writing does improve phonic knowledge.

Spelling-Based Approaches

These approaches focused on having children look at the letters in the word and notice the spelling. Two examples follow.

Making Words

Cunningham and colleagues (Cunningham, Hall, & Defee, 1991) developed the Four Blocks Literacy Model, which uses Making Words as one of the key blocks in reading. Making Words is used to help readers develop the ability to spell words and apply this knowledge when decoding. In this procedure, young children learn to make a six- or seven-letter word and the smaller words using a limited number of letter cards. For example, the teacher asks students to take two letters and make the first word, for example an. The students make this word, and then the teacher asks them to add an *f*. The teacher says this new word is *fan*. In this way, readers learn to use their knowledge of letters and their patterns to figure out new words.

Word Study

Bear, Invernizzi, Templeton, and Johnston (1996) suggested word study as another approach to learning phonics. Word study gives children experience in examining patterns in English orthography. In word study, children sort word cards based on words' structure, including similarity of spelling. As students discuss how words are spelled alike, they construct knowledge of spelling and phonics.

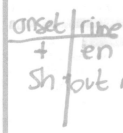

Analogy-Based Approaches

Decoding by analogy involves elements of the English syllable—the onset—and the rime. An onset is any consonant (or consonants) that comes before the vowel, and a rime is the vowel and any consonant that comes after the onset. A rime contains a pattern of letters that are always spelled the same and rhyme. Using onset and rime knowledge, readers can create analogies between known rime words and other words that use the same spelling pattern. During the 1990s, teachers began to demonstrate using decoding analogies. A few examples follow.

Word Detectives

In this approach, students use target words displayed in the classroom that represent specific letter patterns in words (Gaskins, Gaskins, & Gaskins, 1992). Young students learn the target word by stretching out the sounds and noticing the letter patterns. Then, teachers teach the strategic process of using key words to figure out unfamiliar words that use the same rime pattern.

Using Rime Analogies

In this approach, students learn key riming words to decode unknown words. Goswami's (1993) research found that rime analogies could be used to teach decoding strategies. Students learned a rime pattern and created a new word by changing the initial consonants. Greaney, Tunmer, and Chapman (1997) used this approach successfully with struggling readers, while Walton (1995) used this successfully with prereaders.

The 1990s ended with renewed emphasis on readers who struggle when learning to read. Consequently, another national report by the National Research Council (Snow, Burns, & Griffin, 1998) described ways to prevent reading difficulty. After reviewing reading research, the report emphasized using explicit instruction in phonics along with assorted other types of support including the "full array of early reading accomplishments: the alphabetic principle, reading sight words, reading words by mapping speech sounds to parts of words" (p. 6). Likewise, Stahl and colleagues (1998) found small differences in various phonics programs, but they believed that "it may not matter very much how one conduct(s) phonic instruction" because construction of "knowledge about words may explain why the differences among programs are small" (p. 350). The 1990s ended with a growing consensus that phonics in some way needs to be included in reading instruction. There was renewed support for multiple approaches to teach phonics.

A Brief Look at Phonics in the Early 21st Century

Early into the 21st century, the U.S. federal government enacted the No Child Left Behind (NCLB) Act of 2001, which funded the Reading First initiative (see also chapters 3, 7, 9, and 11, this volume, for further discussion of NCLB and Reading First). Grants became available for schools to purchase programs deemed "scientifically based" for reading instruction in grades K–3. Only programs claiming a "scientific base" defined by experimental studies could be used, which channeled more money into using explicit phonics instruction in beginning reading instruction, often to the exclusion of reading literature and reading information. The implementation of NCLB and Reading First focused on learning phonics by sounding out words letter by letter. Publishers repackaged their 1970s programs and touted them as explicit approaches to teaching phonics (Allington, 2002). There have been numerous investigations regarding the funding of programs. In fact, today there is a growing resistance to the structured one-way approach to phonics instruction that was adopted during the Reading First movement. The winds of change are blowing stronger: Large-scale studies are being conducted on programs such as the Four-Blocks Literacy Model, including Making Words (see page 45–46), to determine their effects on learning to read as well as learning the alphabetic principle. New research has supported a "more contextualized approach that allows teachers to differentiate instruction" (Craig, 2003, p. 38). Furthermore, it appears that writing instruction that encourages phonemic segmentation and invented spellings provides a rich context for developing alphabetic knowledge (Craig, 2003).

I hope that during this decade decoding by analogy and writing will gain greater support for teaching phonics. One program that focuses on using analogies begins with reading a predictable book with rime patterns. The teacher points out the onset and rime patterns in the story, then students rewrite the predictable book using new rimes (Smith, 2002; Walker, 2008). Research in using rime-analogy instruction is showing promising results. Two recent studies have demonstrated the success of using rime-analogy training (e.g., Walton, Walton, & Felton, 2001; White, 2005).

Using a multiplicity of approaches like writing, decoding by analogy instruction, word study, and so forth will allow teachers to meet students' individual needs for learning phonics. If this happens, we might start asking, What kind of information sources does a reader use? and How do we provide phonics instruction on that pathway?

QUESTIONS TO GUIDE THINKING

1. We need to rethink how to develop a phonics program that works for all learners. Is there only one way? How would a school or teacher manage multiple pathways to learning phonics? Is it even possible? Are there certain approaches to phonics instruction that teachers could combine to form a better system of phonics instruction in first and second grades?

2. Effective reading instruction includes some form of guided reading and a focus on skill development. How would you or any professional contextualize phonics instruction along with guided reading instruction?

3. Individual differences in learning phonics do exist. How would you explain phonics instruction? Can you describe two different ways teachers can teach phonics and then match these ways with individual learner patterns?

4. One suggestion for the future is to develop and honor multiple pathways for learning phonics. What new pathway might you design to teach phonics that is both meaningful and develops phonic knowledge?

5. Compare new ideas about decoding by analogy and rime analogy with synthetic phonics instruction. How might they be alike and how might they be different?

FINAL THOUGHTS

In closing, phonics instruction will continue to be a "hot topic" because the general public believes that phonics is the critical aspect when reading. The Essential Readings on Phonics Instruction listed in this chapter provide a good starting point for further study; in reviewing our past, we can find hints of the future. Certainly, we have learned that a single approach is not a valid approach for everyone. We have learned that phonics instruction is important but so is meaning and fluency. We have learned that decoding analogies are powerful ways to teach phonics, thus adding to our repertoire. Using rime analogy is another practice that promotes decoding analogies. Rather than a single pathway, multiple pathways seem an important consideration for dealing with individual differences in learning to decode words. Today, and in the future, professionals will teach phonics by having readers actively figure out words along with others, including the teacher, to create their own system for word learning.

Learning to read is a challenge for many children and should be a concern for all citizens. Conversely, for young children, figuring out words is often both mystery and magic. As professionals, we need to give young children clues to the mystery and celebrate the magic of learning words.

ESSENTIAL READINGS ON PHONICS INSTRUCTION

Anderson, R.C., Hiebert, E.H., Scott, J.A., & Wilkinson, I.A.G. (1985). *Becoming a nation of readers: The report of the Commission on Reading.* Washington, DC: National Institute of Education.

Goswami, U., & Bryant, P. (1990). *Phonological skills and learning to read.* Hillsdale, NJ: Erlbaum.

Juel, C., & Minden-Cupp, C. (2000). Learning to read words: Linguistic units and instructional strategies. *Reading Research Quarterly, 35,* 458–493.

Knapp, M.S. (1995). *Teaching for meaning in high-poverty classrooms.* New York: Teachers College Press.

Stahl, S.A., Duffy-Hester, A.M., & Stahl, K.A.D. (1998). Everything you wanted to know about phonics (but were afraid to ask). *Reading Research Quarterly, 33,* 338–355.

REFERENCES

Adams, M.J. (1990). *Beginning to read: Thinking and learning about print.* Cambridge, MA: MIT Press.

Allington, R. (2002). Troubling times: A short historical perspective. In R. Allington (Ed.), *Big brother and the national reading curriculum: How ideology trumped evidence* (pp. 3–46). Portsmouth, NH: Heinemann.

Anderson, R.C., Hiebert, E.H., Scott, J.A., & Wilkinson, I.A.G. (1985). *Becoming a nation of readers: The report of the Commission on Reading.* Washington, DC: National Institute of Education.

Bear, D.R., Invernizzi, M., Templeton, S., & Johnston, F. (1996). *Words their way: Word study for phonics, vocabulary, and spelling instruction.* Upper Saddle River, NJ: Prentice Hall.

Beery, A. (1949). Development of reading vocabulary and word recognition. In N. Henry (Ed.), *Reading in the elementary school* (48th yearbook of the National Society for the Study of Education, Part II, pp. 172–192). Chicago, IL: National Society for the Study of Education.

Bereiter, C., & Engelmann, S. (1970). *The Distar reading program.* Chicago: Science Research Associates.

Bond, G., & Dykstra, R. (1997). The cooperative research program in first-grade reading instruction. *Reading Research Quarterly, 32,* 348–427. (Original work published 1967)

Chall, J. (1967). *Learning to read: The great debate.* New York: McGraw-Hill.

Chall, J. (1992). The new reading debates: Evidence from science, art, and ideology. *Teachers College Record, 94,* 315–328.

Chomsky, N. (1965). *Aspects of the theory of syntax.* Cambridge, MA: MIT Press.

Clay, M.M. (1979). *Reading recovery: A guidebook for teachers in training.* Portsmouth, NH: Heinemann.

Craig, S.A. (2003). The effects of an adapted interactive writing intervention on kindergarten children's phonological awareness, spelling, and early reading development. *Reading Research Quarterly, 38,* 438–440.

Cunningham, P.M., Hall, D.P., & Defee, M. (1991). Non-ability grouped, multilevel instruction: A year in a first-grade classroom. *The Reading Teacher, 44,* 566–571.

Ehri, L. (1991). Development of the ability to read words. In R. Barr, M.L. Kamil, P.B. Mosenthal, & P.D. Pearson (Eds.), *Handbook of reading research* (Vol. 2, pp. 383–417). New York, NY: Longman.

Ehri, L. (1998). Research on learning to read and spell: A personal-historical perspective. *Scientific Study of Reading, 2,* 97–114.

Elkonin, D. (1973). USSR. In J. Downing (Ed.), *Comparative reading: Cross-national studies of behavior and process in reading and writing* (pp. 551–579). New York, NY: Macmillan.

Flesch, R. (1955). *Why Johnny can't read.* New York, NY: Harper & Row.

Fries, C.C. (1963). *Linguistics and reading.* Austin, TX: Holt, Rinehart and Winston.

Fries, C.C., Wilson, R., & Rudolph, M. (1966). *Merrill linguistic readers, Reader 1.* Columbus, OH: Merrill.

Gagne, R. (1970). *The conditions of learning* (2nd ed.). Austin, TX: Holt, Rinehart and Winston.

Gaskins, R.W., Gaskins, J.C., & Gaskins, I.W. (1992). Using what you know to figure out what you don't know: An analogy approach to decoding. *Reading and Writing Quarterly, 8,* 197–221.

Gates, A.I. (2002). What should we teach in reading? *Reading Psychology, 23,* 341–344. (Original work published 1951)

Gibson, E.J. (1964). On the perception of words. *The American Journal of Psychology, 77,* 667–669.

Gibson, E.J. (1965). Learning to read. *Science, 148,* 1066–1072.

Gibson, E.J., & Levin, H. (1975). *The psychology of reading.* Cambridge, MA: MIT Press.

Gibson, E.J., Pick, A., Osser, H., & Hammond, M. (1962). The role of grapheme-phoneme correspondence in the perception of words. *The American Journal of Psychology, 75,* 554–570.

Goodman, K.S. (1967). Reading: A psycholinguistic guessing game. *Journal of the Reading Specialist, 6,* 126–135.

Goodman, K.S., & Goodman, Y.M. (1979). Learning to read is natural. In L.B. Resnick & P.A. Weaver (Eds.), *Theory and practice of early reading* (Vol. 1, pp. 137–154). Hillsdale, NJ: Erlbaum.

Goswami, U. (1993). Toward an interactive analogy model of reading development: Decoding vowel graphemes in beginning reading. *Journal of Experimental Child Psychology, 56,* 443–475.

Goswami, U., & Bryant, P. (1990). *Phonological skills and learning to read.* Hillsdale, NJ: Erlbaum.

Gray, W.S. (1948). *On their own in reading: How to give children independence in attacking new words.* Chicago, IL: Scott Foresman.

Gray, W.S. (1960). *On their own in reading: How to give children independence in analyzing new words.* Glenview, IL: Scott Foresman.

Greaney, K.T., Tunmer, W.E., & Chapman, J.W. (1997). Effects of rime-based orthographic analogy training on the word recognition skills of children with reading disability. *Journal of Educational Psychology, 89,* 645–651.

Holmes, J. (1965). Basic assumptions underlying the substrata-factor theory. *Reading Research Quarterly, 1,* 5–28.

International Reading Association. (1996). *The role of phonics in reading instruction* (Position statement). Newark, DE: Author.

Juel, C. (1988). Learning to read and write: A longitudinal study of 54 children from first through fourth grades. *Journal of Educational Psychology, 80*, 437–447.

Kavanagh, J.F. (1977). Foreword. In R. Ruddell & H. Singer (Eds.), *Theoretical models and processes of reading* (2nd ed., pp. vii–viii). Newark, DE: International Reading Association.

Pearson, P.D. (1996). Reclaiming the center. In M.F. Graves, P. Van den Broek, & B.M. Taylor (Eds.), *The first R: Every child's right to read* (pp. 259–274). Teachers College Press: Newark, DE: International Reading Association.

Pearson, P.D. (1997). The first-grade studies: A personal reflection. *Reading Research Quarterly, 32*, 428–432.

Pearson, P.D., & Dole, J. (1987). Explicit comprehension instruction: A review of research and a new conceptualization of instruction. *The Elementary School Journal, 88*, 151–165.

Pearson, P.D., & Stephens, D. (1994). Learning about literacy: A 30-year journey. In R. Ruddell, M.R. Ruddell, & H. Singer (Eds.), *Theoretical models and processes of reading* (4th ed, pp. 22–42). Newark, DE: International Reading Association.

Ruddell, R., & Singer, H. (Eds.). (1977). *Theoretical models and processes of reading* (2nd ed.). Newark, DE: International Reading Association.

Skinner, B.F. (1958). Teaching machines. *Science, 128*, 969–977.

Skinner, B.F. (1965). *Science and human behavior*. New York, NY: Free Press.

Smith, M.L. (2002). *The effects of rhyme-rime connection training on second-grade reading performance*. Unpublished dissertation, Oklahoma State University, Stillwater.

Smith, N.B. (1963). *Reading instruction for today's children*. Upper Saddle River, NJ: Prentice Hall.

Snow, C.E., Burns, M.S., & Griffin, P. (Eds.). (1998). *Preventing reading difficulties in young children*. Washington, DC: National Academy Press.

Stahl, S.A., Duffy-Hester, A.M., & Stahl, K.A.D. (1998). Everything you wanted to know about phonics (but were afraid to ask). *Reading Research Quarterly, 33*, 338–355.

Stauffer, R.G. (1970). *The language-experience approach to the teaching of reading*. New York, NY: Harper & Row.

Van Allen, R. (1976). *Language experiences in communication*. Boston, MA: Houghton Mifflin.

Walker, B. (2008). *Diagnostic teaching of reading: Techniques for instruction and assessment* (6th ed.). Upper Saddle River, NJ: Merrill/Pearson.

Walton, P.D. (1995). Rhyming ability, phoneme identity, letter-sound knowledge, and the use of orthographic analogy by prereaders. *Journal of Educational Psychology, 87*, 587–597.

Walton, P.D., Walton, L.M., & Felton, K. (2001). Teaching rime analogy or letter recoding reading strategies to prereaders: Effects on prereading skills and word reading. *Journal of Educational Psychology, 93*, 160–180.

White, T.G. (2005). Effects of systematic and strategic analogy-based phonics on grade 2 students' word reading and reading comprehension. *Reading Research Quarterly, 40*, 234–255.

Williams, J. (1984). Reading instruction today. In A. Harris & E. Sipay (Eds.), *Readings on reading instruction* (3rd ed., pp. 12–19). New York, NY: Longman.

CLASSROOM IMPLICATIONS

1. Now that you have read our introduction to the topic and Barbara Walker's chapter, consider what you believe about this aspect of your classroom literacy instruction. How has your current definition of reading changed based on your beliefs concerning word recognition? Or has it?

2. What specific changes might you make in your classroom instructional program in literacy based on the material you have read in this chapter?

FOR FURTHER READING

Brady, S., Gillis, M., Smith, T., Lavallette, M.E., Liss-Bronstein, L., Lowe, E. . . . Wilder, T.D. (2009). First grade teachers' knowledge of phonological awareness and code concepts: Examining gains from an intensive form of professional development and corresponding teacher attitudes. *Reading and Writing Interdisciplinary Journal, 22*, 425–455. doi: 10.1007/s11145-009-9166-x

Cunningham, P.M. (2009). Polysyllabic words and struggling adolescent readers: The morphemic link to meaning, reading, and spelling. In K.D. Wood and W.E. Blanton (Eds.), *Literacy instruction for adolescents: Research-based practice*, (pp. 307–327). New York, NY: Guilford Press.

Ehri, L. C., Satlow, E., & Gaskins, I. (2009). Grapho-phonemic enrichment: Enrichment strengthens key-word analogy instruction for struggling young readers. *Reading & Writing Quarterly, 25*, 162–191.

Joseph, L. M., & Schisler, R. (2009). Should adolescents go "back" to the basics?: A review of teaching word reading skills to middle and high school students. *Remedial and Special Education, 30*, 131–147.

Nation, K., & Cocksey, J. (2009). The relationship between knowing a word and reading it aloud in children's word development. *Journal of Experimental Psychology, 103*, 296–306.

Palumbo, A., & Sanacore, J. (2009). Helping struggling middle school literacy learners achieve success. *Clearing House: A Journal of Educational Strategies, Issues and Ideas, 82*, 275–280.

Uribe, D. (2009). Rejecting the indiscriminate use of phonics. *Literacy Today, 58*, 10–11.

Yap, M. J., & Balota, D. A. (2009). Visual word recognition of multisyllabic words. *Journal of Memory and Language, 60*, 502–529.

ONLINE RESOURCE

The role of phonics in reading instruction. Position Statement of the International Reading Association. Available at
http://www.reading.org/General/AboutIRA/PositionStatements/PhonicsPosition.aspx

CHAPTER

2 Fluency

Give to each letter, to each syllable, and to each word its full, distinct, and appropriate utterance.

—William H. McGuffey (1866)

Deficiencies in fluency, phrasing , and expression are readily noted in oral reading . . . Jerkiness, hesitations, and repetitions are other defects in fluency that are easily detected.

—Albert J. Harris (1948)

The instructional importance of fluency cannot be understated, as fluency is strongly correlated with comprehension.

—Molly Ness (2009)

It has only been within the last decade that literacy educators have became interested in fluency as a basic component of an effective reading program. This interest is at least in part due to the National Reading Panel's decision to focus on fluency as a key area (Hudson, Pullen, Lane, & Torgesen, 2009; Kuhn, Schwanenflugel, & Meisinger, 2010). But although widely accepted, fluency is also widely misunderstood, making it important for us to be clear about exactly what is meant.

Technically, fluency can refer to any language skill that is so thoroughly learned that it can be applied with little conscious thought. A reader can be fluent in segmenting a spoken word into phonemes or in decoding regularly spelled words. In this chapter, we use the word *fluency* to denote fluent oral reading, but we note that this result is dependent on the reader's being able to fluently apply all of the specific word recognition skills that contribute to oral reading.

It is important to note that fluency has nothing to do with performance as one reads aloud. After all, the goal of fluency instruction is not to create newscasters. Reading is now seen as a limited resource system, one in which the reader's cognitive powers can only go so far. Dysfluent readers are forced to train their attention on word recognition, leaving little thinking capacity for comprehension. Fluent readers, by contrast, recognize words so rapidly that they are able to attend to meaning to a far greater extent (Kuhn, 2003; McKenna & Stahl, 2009). Moskal and Blachowicz (2006) describe fluent reading as "flowing, smooth, and effortless" (p. 3). We agree and would add that the more effortless word recognition is, the more effort can be directed toward understanding what one reads.

Fluent oral reading has three aspects:

1. word recognition accuracy,
2. word recognition speed, and
3. prosody (naturalness in terms of phrasing, pitch, etc.).

The idea that fluency comprises these three components extends back over a century (e.g., Huey, 1908). Although most agree on the importance of these three aspects the amount of importance placed on the different components varies considerably (Kuhn et al., 2010).

To put it somewhat differently, oral reading fluency can be described as the ability to read a text, both orally and silently, with appropriate speed, accuracy, and expression (Samuels, 2002; Rasinski, 2006). However, fluency does not guarantee comprehension. While the relationship between fluency and comprehension is not fully understood, it is probably reasonable to suggest at this point that fluency is necessary but not sufficient for comprehension to occur.

AS YOU READ

The three readings included in this chapter deal with teaching and assessing oral reading fluency in classroom settings. Melanie Kuhn outlines the path children follow as they progress toward fluency, and she briefly recounts the trends in fluency instruction over more than a century. She then identifies the issues concerning fluency, writing in accessible detail. Note in particular the three theories as to how prosody is related to comprehension, her four general principles of fluency instruction, and the three instructional approaches that reflect these principles. Tim Rasinski, Susan Homan, and Marie Biggs address fluency instruction for readers who struggle. They focus on the explicit instruction such children require. They recommend a variety of strategies, including modeling good fluency, coaching students as they read aloud, and others. They provide elaborate descriptions of several research-based approaches for struggling readers, including the Fluency Development Lesson (FDL) and Fluency-Oriented Reading Instruction (FORI). As you read, contrast the approaches these authors recommend with those suggested by Melanie Kuhn. Also, decide whether you agree with their reasoning that nonfiction is not appropriate for fluency practice. Last, Theresa Deeney warns that popular one-minute fluency screening measures risk reducing the concept of fluency to rate and accuracy. She argues that there is more to fluency and that focusing entirely on rate and accuracy can distort instructional goals. She also adds a fourth dimension to fluency—endurance—one that most writers do not address. See if you find her arguments persuasive.

REFERENCES

Harris, A. J. (1948). *How to increase reading ability*. Longmans, Green and Co.

Hudson, R. F., Pullen, P. C., Lane, H. B., & Torgesen, J. K. (2009). The complex nature of reading fluency: A multidimensional view. *Reading & Writing Quarterly, 25*, 4–32, doi: 10.1080/10573560802491208

Kuhn, M. R., Schwanenflugel, P. J., & Meisinger, E. B. (2010). Aligning theory and assessment of reading fluency: Automaticity, prosody, and definitions of fluency. *Reading Research Quarterly, 45*(2), 230–251, doi: 10.1598/RRQ.45.2.4

McKenna, M. C., & Stahl, K. A. D. (2009). *Assessment for reading instruction*. New York, NY: Guilford.

McGuffey, W. H. (1866). *McGuffey's new fifth electric reader: Selected and original exercises for schools*. Cincinnati: Wilson, Hinkle & Co.

Moskal, M. K. & Blachowiz, C. (2006). *Partnering for fluency*. New York, NY: Guilford, p. 3.

Nichols, W. D., Rupley, W. H., & Rasinski, T. (2009). Fluency in learning to read for meaning: Going beyond repeated readings. *Literacy Research and Instruction, 48*, 1–13, doi:10.1080/1938807080 2161906

National Institute of Child Health and Human Development (NICHHD). (2000). Report of the National Reading Panel. *Teaching children to read: An evidence-based assessment of the scientific research literature on reading and it implications for reading instruction: Reports of the subgroups*. (NIH Publication No. 00-4754). Washington, DC: U.S. Government Printing Office.

What Is Fluent Reading and Why Is It Important?

MELANIE KUHN

■ ■ ■ ■ ■

Instructional approach	Grade Levels	Grouping	Type of Text
Echo Reading	Any grade level	Any teacher-directed grouping (e.g., can be integrated into whole-class, small-group, or tutoring formats)	• Challenging texts
Choral Reading	Any grade level	Any teacher-directed grouping format (e.g., can be integrated into whole-class, small-group, or tutoring formats)	• Repeated reading of a longer, challenging text • Shorter instructional level texts (e.g., poems, speeches, passages from longer texts)
Partner Reading	Any grade level	Any grouping format (can be used as a whole-class, small-group, or tutoring formats; could also be used in centers)	• Challenging texts if previously read • Instructional level or independent level texts if previously unread

■ What is fluency's role in the reading process?
■ How has oral reading's role in the literacy curriculum changed?
■ Are there general principles of effective fluency instruction?

Where Does Fluency Fit in a Child's Reading Development?

A friend of mine recently mentioned that she was curious about the path her child's reading development had followed. When her daughter, Rebecca[1], was in kindergarten, she loved being read to and would listen to certain stories over and over. Eventually, Rebecca memorized her favorites, "reading" them to anyone who was willing to listen. What perplexed my friend was that her daughter sounded quite fluent when she shared these stories in kindergarten, but when she entered first grade, her reading suddenly became less fluent. Instead of reading smoothly, Rebecca grappled with words she didn't recognize in texts that were less predictable or familiar than her "old" favorites had been. It was only over the course of second and, now, third grade that Rebecca's reading began to sound fluent again. Rebecca is quite a good student; however, my friend was wondering if her daughter's experience was an unusual one. I assured her that it is quite common for learners to make such transitions and that students' reading development makes several qualitative shifts over the course of their schooling.

Unlike my friend, as an educator, you expect students' reading to move through different phases throughout their school years (Chall, 1996). Although the understanding and enjoyment of texts should always be the ultimate goal of reading instruction, students' comfort with written material varies widely depending on their development level. In general, **emergent readers** are developing **concepts** of print, familiarity with text (e.g., **book-handling knowledge**), and **phonemic awareness** (Teale & Sulzby, 1986; Yopp & Yopp, 2000). Having established this, the emphasis in first grade shifts to **word recognition** (Adams, 1990). As students develop familiarity with **letter-sound correspondence** and begin to build their **sight word** vocabulary, the focus in second and third grade shifts again to fluent reading. At this point, in addition to accuracy, readers should begin to develop automaticity and prosody, or the use of appropriate phrasing and expression (Kuhn & Stahl, 2003). By integrating fluency instruction into your literacy curriculum during these grades, you can help your learners make the transition from hesitant, word-by-word reading to reading that is smooth and expressive.

Beyond the primary grades, it is assumed that most readers have established a certain level of **fluency**, at least when it comes to reading grade-level material. Ideally, by the time students reach the fourth grade, they are making the transition from learning to read to reading to learn (Chall, 1996); their texts become increasingly complex, and there is a significant shift toward content-area literacy. Unfortunately, some learners never quite establish the transition to fluent reading; instead, their reading remains slow, choppy, and expressionless far past the third grade. This lack of fluency interferes with both the pleasure students derive from their reading and their ability to learn from text. If this is the case for some of your students, targeted fluency instruction is likely to help them become skilled readers. The chapters in this book address students at both ends of the spectrum; that is, students who are making the transition to fluency at what we consider to be a developmentally appropriate point (i.e., second and third grade) and students who have experienced difficulty with this transition (i.e., students in fourth grade and beyond). There will also be tables indicating the range of grade levels, grouping formats, and types of text that are appropriate for each strategy.

What Is Fluency and Why Is It Important?

Fluent readers share a range of characteristics; their **fluent reading** is smooth, effortless, and expressive (Kuhn & Stahl, 2003). In other words, fluent readers have developed the ability to recognize words automatically as well as accurately, and they can incorporate the use of appropriate phrasing and expression into their reading. All these elements indicate that the person reading is comfortable with the text at hand. As stated earlier, however, if fluency were simply a surface level issue, one that ensured automatic and expressive oral reading on the part of your students, it would be worth expending some class time on, but probably would not be worthy of your extensive instructional efforts. But fluency is actually considered by many to be a bridge between decoding and comprehension (Pikulski & Chard, 2005); its instruction deserves a significant role in the literacy curriculum (National Reading Panel, 2000).

So how, exactly, does fluency contribute to a reader's ability to comprehend text? I would argue that it does so in two ways, both of which build on its defining components: accurate, automatic word recognition, and the appropriate use of prosodic or expressive features such as stress, pitch, or suitable phrasing.

The Role of Accuracy

Component of Fluency

Accuracy is key to fluency. If students are to make sense of what they read, it is necessary that they accurately identify the vast majority of words they encounter in text (e.g., Chall, 1996; National Reading Panel, 2000). In order to do so, students must determine the relationship that exists between letters (or groups of letters, such as *sh*) and the sounds that those letters make. Similarly, they need to be able to identify **high-frequency words** without having to decode them (words that occur frequently in texts, such as *this*, *of*, and *when*). When students begin to read, they often appear to be overly focused on identifying every word they encounter, a process that makes their reading sound stilted and uneven. It is the role of decoding instruction[2], and of instruction in word recognition more broadly, to assist students in generalizing their understandings about letters, words, and word families, thereby allowing them to more easily recognize the words they encounter in print.[3] But, while such accuracy is critical to comprehension, it is not enough. In fact, students who are accurate but deliberate in their word recognition not only sound disfluent, they are unlikely to be able to construct meaning from text. In order to do so, it is critical that students develop their **automaticity** as well.

The Role of Automaticity

Component of Fluency

The significance of automatic word recognition in the reading process becomes clear when you visualize children's early attempts at reading. As mentioned earlier, first graders frequently expend significant amounts of effort trying to figure out the words that compose a given sentence, leaving them with little or no attention remaining to determine its meaning. As a result, by the time they have reached the end of a sentence, they have no idea what it was about—even though they would have easily understood it had someone read it to them. Unfortunately, older struggling readers who have yet to make the transition to automatic word recognition often experience the same difficulties.

The problems readers encounter as the result of slow word recognition can best be explained through *automaticity theory* (e.g., LaBerge & Samuels, 1974; Logan, 1997), which states that individuals have a limited amount of attention available for any complex task. When we encounter activities that are comprised of multiple components, it is difficult for us to focus fully on each aspect of these activities simultaneously. In order to deal effectively with such complex activities, it is necessary for certain aspects of those tasks to become effortless or automatic. In the case of reading, higher-order processes such as comprehension are underpinned by the need to correctly decode what is written.[4] So if we are to be able to focus on meaning, we need to make our decoding automatic.

The question becomes: How do learners go about developing such automatic decoding? The answer lies in practice. As with any new skill, from learning to play basketball to learning to play an instrument, the only way to progress from novice to expert is through practice. In terms of reading, this means ensuring that learners have extensive exposure to print in order to develop their comfort with the spelling patterns, or orthography, that comprise written English. In other words, in order to develop automatic word recognition, learners need to spend significant amounts of time reading. And, while word recognition instruction is an essential component of such practice, if students are to become fluent readers, it is critical that they also have the opportunity to apply their developing knowledge to the reading of **connected text** such as books, poems, or newspapers. Without such practice, there is no guarantee that what they have learned about how words work in isolation will transfer to their reading; on the other hand, when given plentiful opportunities to read—with appropriate support where necessary—the likelihood that learners will develop automaticity increases significantly.

The Role of Prosody   ↗ Component of Fluency

The final component of fluent reading has a more complex relationship to comprehension. **Prosody** incorporates those aspects of oral reading that allow it to sound expressive, including pitch or intonation, stress or emphasis, tempo or rate, and the rhythmic patterns of language (e.g., Erekson, 2003; Kuhn & Stahl, 2003). According to Lynn Truss (2004), prosodic elements in written text are regularly represented by punctuation. She argues that "punctuation directs you how to read, in the way musical notation directs a musician how to play" (p. 20). The importance of appropriate punctuation in the meaning of a sentence can be demonstrated by the joke that appears on the back cover of her book:

> A panda walks into a café. He orders a sandwich, eats it, then draws a gun and fires two shots in the air.
>
> "Why?" asks the confused waiter, as the panda makes towards the exit. The panda produces a badly punctuated wildlife manual and tosses it over his shoulder.
>
> "I'm a panda," he says, at the door. "Look it up."
>
> The waiter turns to the relevant entry and, sure enough, finds an explanation.
>
> "*Panda*. Large black-and-white bear-like mammal, native to China. Eats, shoots and leaves."

The degree to which this definition becomes muddled simply as the result of one incorrect comma is remarkable.

Unfortunately, many attributes that represent prosody in conversation, such as the fluctuation of a speaker's voice or the correct phrasing, don't directly translate to print. For example, while phrase units can sometimes be identified through the use of commas, this is not always the case (e.g., Miller & Schwanenflugel, 2006), and inappropriate breaks in a sentence can often interfere with a learner's understanding of the text. For example, if you were to read a sentence in two-word groupings, you would likely have to work harder to determine the meaning. Take a look at the following excerpt, taken from *Alice in Wonderland* (Carroll, 2006):

> Alice was beginning to get very tired of sitting by her sister on the bank and of having nothing to do: once or twice she had peeped into the book her sister was reading but it had no pictures or conversations in it, and "what is the use of a book," thought Alice, "without pictures or conversations?" (p. 1)

It is likely to be a bit difficult for you as a fluent reader not to jump over these breaks in order to make sense of the passage. However, such inappropriate phrasing often occurs in disfluent reading, and the lack of correctly phrased units, or **parsing**, can negatively impact comprehension. The good news is that many studies (e.g., Cromer, 1970; Casteel, 1988; Weiss, 1983) show that poor readers at all age levels demonstrate improved comprehension when text is presented in a manner that replicates speech; that is, when it has been organized into appropriate phrase units for them.

In order to tie these findings to fluent reading, I would argue that if fluent readers read aloud not only at a reasonable pace and with relatively few miscues but also with expression or in a manner that replicates oral language, they are also prosodic readers. And if, as the previous discussion indicates, prosodic readers are better able to comprehend text than their nonprosodic peers, then it seems reasonable to assert that fluent readers are better able to construct meaning from text than are disfluent readers. As such, by helping learners become fluent readers, we are aiding not only their ability to automatically decode and read with expression but also their ability to construct meaning from text.

Before leaving the issue of prosody, it is important to mention one caveat. While most researchers would agree that automaticity plays a role in a reader's comprehension, the exact relationship between prosody and comprehension is less clear (e.g., Kuhn et al., 2006). There are three possible explanations for this relationship: One is that readers need to have an understanding of what is being read before they can read it prosodically. The second is that readers must determine the prosodic elements of what is being read before they are able to understand it. And the third, which represents my position, is that prosody both reflects and contributes to readers' understanding of text. Ideally, as we learn more about fluency, we will better clarify this issue. In the meantime, whatever relationship exists between these two components of skilled reading, it is important to emphasize appropriate expression in the reading curriculum, both because a relationship between prosody and comprehension does exist and because the use of appropriate phrasing and expression are critical to a reader's enjoyment of a given text.

Oral Reading Then and Now

One issue that usually arises when discussing fluency has to do with the value of oral reading in the literacy curriculum. The value of this practice hinges, to a large extent, on what is meant by the term. If, by oral reading, you mean instruction that is comprised primarily or exclusively of round-robin reading or its virtual equivalents, popcorn, popsicle, or combat reading, then it is unlikely you will be able to further the reading development of your learners. If, on the other hand, you envision oral reading practice as involving a range of effective reading strategies—from repeated reading to Wide Reading Instruction—you will likely be successful at assisting your learners in becoming fluent readers. In the latter case, oral reading clearly deserves a place in your curriculum.

Round-Robin Reading— An All-Too-Common Experience

Given that round-robin reading and its equivalents are nearly omnipresent in our schools, it is necessary to discuss what constitutes these procedures, along with how and why they came to be the dominant forms of oral reading instruction. **Round-robin reading** requires that every student in a group or a classroom read a small portion of the material currently being covered, usually a few sentences or a paragraph. It is often used as part of the literacy curriculum, but is equally popular in the content-area classroom. There are a number of reasons touted for using this approach (Ash & Kuhn, 2006), including to make difficult material accessible, to ensure that each student reads at least a portion of the text, to assess students' oral reading development, to help with classroom management, and to develop students' fluency.

Despite the range of potential attributes that make round-robin reading look effective on the surface, the procedure fails on all counts. To begin with, while having each student read a section of the text in order to cover difficult material seems to make sense, it does little toward creating a unified rendering of a selection. Instead, it takes a single text and creates a number of dissonant parts. Further, since each reader is concentrating on part of a text rather than the text as a whole, such reading is likely to focus students away from the meaning of the passage and toward word identification instead.

While requiring each student to read a section of text ensures that everyone has covered at least a small portion of the material, this is unlikely to increase learners' reading ability—for two reasons: First, in terms of time expended, this format allows learners to read only between one and three minutes per day (Gambrell, 1984), not nearly enough time for students to become skilled readers (e.g., Allington, 1977; Shanahan, 2007). Second, if students are to read in front of their peers, it is important that they have the opportunity to practice the material beforehand so they can present themselves in the best possible light.

When students are forced to read an unpracticed text aloud, you will find that while some may perform well, many others will sound like disfluent or disengaged readers. And though this variation in reading ability seems to give you insight into your students' reading development, several factors may skew an accurate evaluation. For example, if students are nervous reading in front of their peers, their rendering may appear less skilled. Similarly, students may disengage with the text since they are only responsible for a small section of the material and, as a result, may not read as well. It is also possible that the material used for whole-class instruction is either too easy or too difficult for some of your readers, which may affect how fluent your students sound.

As for classroom management, it may seem that by asking each of your students to read a portion of the text you are helping them engage with the material, thereby increasing their time on task. In reality, it is more likely that this procedure actually decreases the amount of attention they pay to their reading. Some students will try to determine which passage they will be reading aloud and then practice that section to themselves in an attempt to sound competent in front of their peers. Once they have had their turn, they breathe a sigh of relief and proceed to tune out until they think their next turn is approaching. Other readers, who most need to practice identifying unfamiliar words, rarely get the opportunity to do so because their more skilled peers regularly "jump in" with the correct word—either in an attempt to be helpful or simply because they become impatient waiting. On the other hand, some students become so engaged with the text that they begin to read at their own pace rather than following along with the class, "losing their place" in the process. When their teacher discovers that they are not following along with the class, they are often reprimanded and asked to slow down in order to keep pace with their peers. Since it is extremely difficult for many readers to slow down their reading speed, these learners become bored with the entire process and disengage from the text.

Finally, there is the notion that round-robin reading helps learners develop fluency. But, since students are only responsible for reading small portions of connected text as part of this procedure, they do not have sufficient opportunities to develop into skilled readers.

Because of these negatives, round-robin reading has metamorphosed into three supposedly alternative approaches—popcorn, popsicle, and combat reading—that are designed to correct at least one of its failings: the lack of attention students pay to the text when it is not their turn to read. Students who participate in round-robin reading usually read in a predetermined order; as a result, they often spend time determining which passage they will be reading, practicing that passage, then tuning out once they have completed their turn. The three alternatives differ from the original in one notable way their approach to student selection. In **popcorn reading**, students are randomly selected and, as with kernels popping in a popper, it is uncertain who will be chosen next. In **popsicle reading**, students' names are written on popsicle sticks, which are then placed in a bag and selected at random by the teacher. In **combat reading**, students are assigned the task of selecting the next reader, with classmates who are not paying attention being the preferred target. However, despite the possibility that students may be somewhat more focused on the text as the result of these changes, the approaches do nothing to address the remaining issues and, overall, have similar results to round-robin reading.

The Changing Role of Oral Reading

Now you may wonder, why, given all these negatives, is round-robin reading so commonly used? To understand that, it is necessary to look at the history of reading instruction in the United States. According to Jim Hoffman (1987) and Tim Rasinski (2006), one of the primary purposes of reading instruction prior to the 1900s was to emphasize students' ability to recite a text expressively, either to share information or as a form of entertainment. The reason behind this was twofold. First, since many, if not most, jobs at this time required little reading or writing, education in America was not universal, and, where offered, was unlikely to be as comprehensive as it is today. As a result, far fewer individuals were literate. Second, written materials were not as plentiful as they are now, and those that did exist, especially books, were relatively expensive. In fact, the only book in many homes was the Bible, and many families could not even afford that. As a result, a limited number of individuals in any community, usually members of government, religious leaders, and professionals, were responsible for relaying text-based information to their less literate peers, often by reading a text aloud. Given the importance of conveying information to others in this manner, it was critical that literacy instruction stressed the oral interpretation of texts.

As universal education took hold and materials became increasingly available, reading for private purposes came to be regarded as the norm. Rather than reading aloud to family members in the parlor or to fellow citizens in the public square, individuals were likely to pick up a penny novel, comic book, or newspaper and read to themselves. This shift in reading led to a parallel shift in literacy instruction away from reading for oral performance and toward reading silently to meet individual needs and created a dilemma: when students are reading silently, it is difficult to determine whether they are learning what is being taught or even if they are reading at all.

In order to find out exactly what students were doing as they read a particular text, teachers began a process of randomly checking on students as they were reading silently to see whether they were developing word recognition, making progress in the text, and completing their assignment. Eventually, this random checking evolved into the procedure known as round-robin reading, and it became the norm. While originating from a set of valid concerns, this approach simply is not an effective way to help develop skilled readers. The question then becomes, what can you replace it with? While the rest of the book presents a range of instructional approaches that have been shown to be effective alternatives to round-robin reading, both in research and in practice (e.g., Kuhn & Stahl, 2003; National Reading Panel, 2000), I want to end this chapter by presenting four general principles (Rasinski, 2003) and three instructional approaches designed to support your students' fluency development and easily integrated into your day-to-day oral reading instruction.

What Makes for Effective Fluency Instruction?

As a teacher, you can easily incorporate four principles designed to promote fluent reading into your literacy instruction (Rasinski, 2003). The first is modeling expressive reading. This is perhaps one of the best ways to instill a love of reading in your students while providing them with a sense of what good reading should sound like. While this practice is quite common in the early primary grades, it becomes increasingly rare as students get older. Nevertheless, a substantial body of literature is best presented as spoken word, from poems and plays to highly descriptive narratives and gripping pieces of nonfiction. By taking five minutes or so each day to read a text, you are creating a shared experience for the class. You are also offering your students the chance to hear what fluent reading sounds like. And by making the effort to present a range of genres during this period, you are increasing the likelihood your students will recognize that reading provides something of interest for virtually everyone.

As positive an activity as this can be, it is important to stress that it should be only a small portion of your class's day. If too much of your class time is spent reading aloud to your students, they will not have the opportunities necessary to develop their own reading skills. And while it may seem as though this is an effective way of dealing with difficult material, it is important that your learners have the opportunity to read some challenging texts—especially those in the content areas—themselves, provided they are given sufficient scaffolding. Otherwise, they are unlikely to develop the ability to read this type of material—exactly the opposite of what you would want for them.

The second and third principles—offering learners extensive opportunities to practice reading connected text and providing sufficient support and assistance—help students make the transition to fluent reading by giving them a great deal of practice consolidating what they know about word recognition. Similarly, when learners are faced, with challenging material containing a high percentage of unknown words or new vocabulary or concepts, it is essential that support is available to aid them with their reading. This support can be as simple as integrating echo or choral reading into your literacy lessons, or it can entail a reworking of the shared reading component of your curriculum using an approach such as Fluency Oral Reading Instruction or the Wide Fluency Oral Reading Instruction (see Chapter 3 for a description).

The fourth principle is emphasizing appropriate phrasing as part of your oral reading lessons. This principle builds on the notions of modeling and support or **scaffolding** in effective instruction, as well as the importance of prosody in skilled reading. As was seen in the example from *Alice in Wonderland* earlier in this chapter when children's phrasing of text fails to follow the general flow of oral language, comprehension can suffer. By helping students recognize where appropriate breaks fall within a text, you are helping them see how attributes of oral language can and should be applied to written language. This can be done either indirectly, through the modeling of phrase breaks in your oral reading, or directly, by demonstrating to students exactly where those breaks lie within a written text.

The strategies that I discuss throughout this book incorporate these four crucial principles and are designed to help you integrate effective oral reading instruction into your literacy lessons. As such, they substantially increase the likelihood that all your students will become fluent readers.

Fluency Approaches to Support the Reading of Challenging Text in Multiple Settings

Three approaches to fluency instruction—echo, choral, and partner reading—can be implemented easily in a variety of grouping formats and can be used to support the reading of a range of challenging texts across a range of grade levels.

Echo Reading

The first of these fluency strategies is **echo reading**. It is a teacher-assisted approach to oral reading and provides the most scaffolding of the three strategies that comprise this section. As with all three strategies, the procedure is very simple. It involves your reading of a section of a text aloud while your students follow along in their own copy. Once you have completed a section, your children read back the same text to you as a group. This strategy offers your learners a great deal of modeling and a considerable amount of support. In fact, this simple procedure provides your children with a model of accurate word reading, phrasing, pacing, and use of expression. You can also adjust the amount of text that your students read at one time depending on the text's difficulty; in other words, you can read longer sections of text when your selection is easier and shorter sections of material when the passage is more challenging. It can also be used with texts from your literacy curriculum or from your content-area instruction.

Because echo reading provides your students with considerable scaffolding, it is an approach that should not be used with text at your students' independent levels. Similarly, text that is at your students' instructional level is unlikely to need the amount of support this procedure provides. Instead, I recommend echo reading for texts that are considered to be *challenging.* Since this procedure can be used whenever you encounter difficult text, you may find it effective to teach your students the process early in the school year so that they know what is expected of them. Then you can revert to it whenever they need support for a challenging selection.

LESSON SNAPSHOT

Despite the ease with which echo reading is conducted, certain elements are critical to its success:

- First, each student must have a copy of the text. Next, all your students need to know where you are beginning your reading so they can follow along from the correct point in their text. You can also ask them to track the material as you read to them to help them stay engaged. If you choose to, you can read the text to them in its entirety and discuss the selection prior to beginning the echo reading procedure. This will allow them to develop a sense of the text as a whole. If you decide to do this, have them follow along with your initial reading of the material as well.

- Second, it is important that your children understand the process they are about to engage in. Explain to them that their role is to listen and follow along when it is your turn to read, and to read aloud themselves, as a group, when it is their turn. During this procedure, consider walking around the room in order to ensure that students are keeping up with your reading and are actively engaged in reading back each section when it is their turn.

- Third, it is important that you build up the amount of reading that the children complete at one time. At first, it is likely that they will have difficulty echoing what you have just read to them, and it may take a while for them to get used to the process. However, because you do not want them relying on their auditory memory to respond correctly, it is essential that you increase the amount of text that they echo while reading. In order to assist them with this process, you may want to start by reading a sentence or two, but you should gradually build up to several paragraphs—or even a page—of text at a time, depending on your students' age, ability, and the amount of material on each page.

Choral Reading

The next teacher-assisted instructional approach is **choral reading**. While choral reading provides students with less scaffolding than echo reading, it still presents learners with a model for developing both their automaticity and their prosody. In this approach, the teacher and students simultaneously read a text or a section of a text aloud. Since you and your students are reading a selection at the same time, I recommend that you proceed in one of two ways. First, you could use it as a follow-up approach to the echo reading of a challenging text, providing the learners with an extra guided reading of the material; should you use it in this manner, you will be following a gradual release of responsibility model, such as is presented in Fluency-Oriented Reading Instruction and Wide Fluency-Oriented Reading Instruction approaches (see Chapter 3).

Alternatively, choral reading can be used with a text that is at the beginning of your students' instructional level; that is, material that requires a minimal amount of scaffolding before the students can work with it independently. For example, your students may be able to decode most of the words in a given selection, but need to work on their reading rate, or you may be working with a piece that calls for expression, such as a poem, a speech, or highly descriptive passages, provided they are not too long or too difficult. By reading such selections with your learners, you may find that their reading becomes more fluent not only when they are reading along with you but also when they next attempt to read the material on their own. Although choral reading does not provide the same degree of support that you find with echo reading, it is an enjoyable approach to fluency development and one that has an important role in bringing text alive.

LESSON SNAPSHOT

Choral reading is another straightforward approach, but students must be comfortable with the procedure if they are to benefit from its use in the curriculum:

- As with any of the fluency-oriented approaches, each of your students must have her own copy of the material you will be reading together. Be aware that when you are first introducing the approach, you may need to help your students locate where you are starting your reading. You likely will need to circulate around the room to ensure they are following along in their texts.

- Just as with echo reading, you will need to explain the process to your students. They should understand that they are going to be reading in unison with you and that you are going to be emphasizing the appropriate pace and use of expression with them and that it is their job to try to mimic you! Eventually, as they feel more comfortable with their reading of a particular text, they may want to develop their own interpretation, but for now they should try to read as a group.

- It is also important to build up the amount of text that your students can choral read with you. In order to do this, you may want to begin with short poems or passages from a longer text. Then, as students develop familiarity with the process, you can quickly build up to lengthier selections. However, you may want to continue circulating around the room to ensure that all the students are actively participating in the reading—with their eyes on the text—rather than simply repeating what they hear being said.

- Once the students are comfortable with this procedure, you can create variations. For example, you can select poems for two voices and ask the students to choral read based on:
  - their rows, tables, or by dividing the room into halves;
  - their first or last initials (A through L versus M through Z);
  - counting off as ones or twos; and
  - any other division you can think of that is good-natured and that the kids will enjoy.

Partner Reading

The final supplemental approach is that of **partner reading**. This is also a very simple yet effective strategy for developing reading fluency. As with echo and choral reading, partner reading significantly increases the amount of reading that students complete in a given period; however, it is not a teacher-assisted approach. Instead, students work in pairs to provide one another with support in the oral reading of a selection. The children take turns with one child reading approximately a page of text aloud while the child's partner follows along, listening and providing support and assistance. This support can consist of sounding out words, providing unknown words, and correcting misread words. The listener can also ask his partner if a word makes sense in a sentence, provide positive feedback or encouragement, or help the reader keep track of the reading. You may want to promote the use of these forms of assistance by modeling them for your students both in your own instruction and in demonstrations you conduct for your learners.

Of the three strategies discussed here, partner reading provides the least amount of scaffolding. As such, it should be used either to practice rereading a more challenging selection, perhaps one the students have previously echo or choral read with their teacher, or to read a text that is closer to the students' independent reading level. In partner reading, students alternate reading every other page throughout an entire selection. This allows the learners to read significant amounts of text with support from their partner. Rather than reading slightly over one minute for every thirty minutes of class time in round-robin reading, these students are each reading fifteen minutes during the same period of time. This simple shift in oral reading strategies allows students to increase their reading time by a factor of fifteen, a pretty powerful way of increasing their engagement with text! Although partner reading does not provide the learners with the same level of scaffolding as echo or choral reading, it is an effective way of ensuring that your students are spending significant amounts of time reading connected text in a supportive environment. And, because they provide students with support and extensive opportunities to read connected text; echo, choral, and partner reading are all effective aids to your students' overall reading development.

LESSON SNAPSHOT

Since partner reading requires the students to read a given text themselves, it is important that you present them with a clear understanding of the procedure:

- Before beginning partner reading, discuss the roles both students have in the process. First, the students each take turns reading and listening to one another read. Second, the listener should follow along in the text, paying attention to what the reader is reading. Third, the listener should also provide help and encouragement whenever the reader has difficulties with the text. As always, it is important that students have their own copies of the text, both to read from and to follow along in as their partners read.

- You can select partners for your students or they can self-select their pairs. If you are selecting pairs, the best method involves pairing readers across reading ability levels. But you do not want the differences between the learners to be so great that the partners get frustrated. The easiest way to accomplish this is by making two lists in which you place your most skilled reader at the top of the first list and the student who is experiencing the most difficulty with their reading development at the bottom of the second list. You should place your next most skilled reader on the first list and your reader who is having somewhat less difficulty on the second list. Continue with this process, working your way through your class, until every student is listed. Place the two groups side by side and match across the two lists. This should match your most skilled reader with a student who is an average reader and the student who is experiencing the greatest difficulty with a student who is also an average reader. Such pairings should increase the effectiveness of the process since the differences between the readers are substantial enough to maximize your learners' growth.

- Your role in this process is to circulate around the room, not only to help keep the students focused, but also to provide the partners with assistance as they need it.
- Until the learners become comfortable with the partner reading process, they should read short passages, say a paragraph or two, before switching off with their partner. As they develop stamina, readers can extend the amount of text they are reading, until they are able to cover about a page each (taking care to complete any sentence or paragraph that continues onto the next page).
- Should there be time available after reading through the selection once, students can complete a second reading with their partners; however, during their second turn, the partners should read the pages opposite to those they read initially (i.e., reading the odd pages if they read the even pages the first time through and the even pages if they initially read the odd pages).

This chapter provides you with a snapshot of fluency's role in the reading process and our education system, along with several principles and basic approaches for integrating effective fluency instruction into your classroom. The rest of the book will present a range of methods for use in specific classroom situations. I am certain you will find an instructional intervention that will work for you and your students, one that will enable you to integrate effective fluency instruction into your classroom and will assist your learners in their development as they become skilled, independent readers.

STUDY GUIDE QUESTIONS

- Do you envision integrating fluency instruction into your reading curriculum? If so, where do you feel there is a natural fit?

- Do you feel your students' reading development has followed the stages outlined at the beginning of the chapter? If so, do you feel they are on a trajectory to become skilled readers? If not, what instructional focus might assist them with their reading development?

- Why is it important that students' word recognition becomes automatic as well as accurate? Similarly, why is it important that students develop the ability to use appropriate phrasing and expression?

- Pick a chapter from the latter part of this book—or another book that you and your colleagues have not previously read—and go around the group reading aloud a paragraph each. What did you do and how did the process make you feel? Thinking back, both on your own experience with round-robin reading and the discussion in this chapter, what are some of the problems students' experience with the process? Given all the negatives associated with the approach, why do you think its use persists in many classrooms?

- How do you think the four principles outlined in the final section of the chapter help to support effective fluency instruction?

- Can you think of situations in which echo, choral, or partner reading could replace the oral reading instruction you are currently using in your literacy curriculum?

NOTES

1. All teacher and student names are pseudonyms.

2. While decoding instruction—and other word recognition instruction—are necessary if learners are to become fluent readers, it is beyond the focus of this book. Instead, the

instructional approaches included here assume that learners have established some degree of decoding ability and concentrate on the development of automaticity and the incorporation of elements such as appropriate expression and phrasing.

3. Since the preponderance of words used in early reading material fall within students' oral vocabulary once students have correctly identified a word, they are likely to know its meaning. This balance begins to shift as texts become more complex and the number of words that are decodable, but outside students' oral vocabulary, increases.

4. Clearly comprehension is multifaceted and much broader than word recognition, however, at this point in the discussion, I am focusing on the contribution automatic decoding makes to skilled reading.

Teaching Reading Fluency to Struggling Readers: Method, Materials, and Evidence

TIMOTHY RASINSKI

Kent State University, Kent, Ohio, USA

SUSAN HOMAN

University of South Florida, Tampa, Florida, USA

MARIE BIGGS

St. Petersburg College of Education, St. Petersburg, Florida, USA

■ ■ ■ ■ ■

Reading fluency has been identified as a key component in reading and in learning to read. Moreover, a significantly large number of students who experience difficulty in reading manifest difficulties in reading fluency that appear to contribute to their overall struggles in reading. In this article we explore the nature of effective instruction in fluency. We examine proven methods for teaching fluency and instructional routines that combine various methods into synergistic lessons. We also take issue with more mechanical approaches to fluency instruction that emphasize reading rate as the major goal of such instruction. Instead, we attempt to make the case for more authentic approaches to fluency instruction, approaches that employ texts meant to be practiced and performed.

On the surface James did not appear to be a poor reader. When he read grade-level material he was able to read all of the words accurately, and he knew the meanings of the words he read. His reading was full of effort; he labored over individual words and read them in a slow and unexpressive manner. He was significantly above average when tested for his overall intelligence and receptive vocabulary. When a passage was read to him, he understood it well. However, when he read it on his own, it was very likely that he would not understand much of what he had just read.

This type of student seems to defy conventional wisdom or explanation. Good word decoder, high verbal intelligence, good vocabulary, capable of listening and understanding, yet not very able to understand what he has read on his own. How could such a reader exist? Unfortunately, many students fit James's profile. Could it be that difficulty in reading fluency manifested in slow, labored, and unexpressive reading is the explanation for this difficulty?

For years reading fluency was the forgotten stepchild of the reading curriculum. Teachers and reading scholars were interested in readers' ability to decode words

Address correspondence to Timothy Rasinski, Kent State University, 404 White Hall, TLCS, Kent, OH 44242. E-mail: trasmsk@kent.edu accurately, not in readers' ability to decode words automatically and quickly. Teachers and reading scholars were more interested in moving students as quickly as possible into silent reading, not the level of expressiveness that expert readers embed in their oral reading. Slightly more than a decade ago, Rasinski and Zutell (1996) reported that mainstream reading instruction programs gave scant attention to direct or indirect instruction in reading fluency.

However, with the publication of the Report of the National Reading Panel (National Reading Panel, 2000) and other reviews of research on fluency (Kuhn & Stahl, 2000; Rasinski & Hoffman, 2003), reading fluency has emerged as an important component in effective reading instruction for elementary-grade students. In terms of assessment, research has found that measures of reading fluency, whether through reading speed or measures of students' prosodic oral reading, are significantly associated with measures of reading comprehension and other more general measures of reading achievement (Rasinski, 2004). Moreover, these research reviews have also noted that reading fluency instruction results in improvements in students' reading fluency and, more important, in their overall reading achievement (Kuhn & Stahl, 2000; Rasinski & Hoffman, 2003).

As a result of these efforts, fluency is now viewed alongside phonemic awareness, phonics and word decoding, vocabulary, and comprehension as a key element in any effective reading instruction program. Fluency may be a particularly salient factor when considering the achievement, or lack of achievement, of struggling readers. Rasinski and Padak (1998) found that among struggling elementary-grade readers referred for compensatory instruction in reading, reading fluency was a greater deficit than word recognition or comprehension. Similarly, Duke, Pressley, and Hilden (2004) noted that word recognition and reading fluency difficulties may be the key concern for upwards of 90% of children with significant problems with comprehension.

Thus, our current thinking on reading fluency is that it is indeed an important factor when considering effective reading programs for students. Moreover, it may be even more of a concern for those students who experience difficulty in learning to read and in comprehending what they read.

Why Direct Instruction in Reading Fluency?

Fluency in any activity is achieved largely through practice; the actor rehearses, the athlete talks about repetitious training drills, the musician spends time daily practicing pieces that will eventually be performed, and the novice driver spends as much time on the road as possible. Often, that practice involves the repetition of a particular line, skill, movement, or composition many times. So, too, is reading fluency achieved through practice—wide reading for some readers, repeated practice of particular pieces for others. Accomplished readers are often able to achieve and maintain their fluency through wide and independent reading. Even young successful readers can move toward higher levels of fluency through independent reading as found in sustained silent reading and its various permutations.

However, for many young and struggling readers of all ages, repeated readings seems to be an essential method for achieving fluency. Jay Samuels's (1979) seminal work on the method of repeated readings found that when students orally practiced a piece of text they improved on their reading of that text—rate, accuracy, and comprehension. Such an accomplishment is to be expected. However, he also found that when students moved to new passages, their initial readings of those new pieces were done with higher levels of fluency and comprehension than the initial readings of the previous passage, even though the new passages were as difficult as or more challenging than the previous piece. Since Samuels's work, other studies have demonstrated the value of repeated readings as an instructional tool for reading fluency and reading comprehension because reading fluency is related to text understanding (National Reading Panel, 2000; Rasinski & Hoffman, 2003).

Independent repeated readings might work for readers who are already sufficiently accomplished to be able to evaluate and monitor their own reading. However, for most younger and struggling readers repeated readings need to be under the guidance of a teacher or coach. This is where direct instruction in fluency comes in. In the same way that an actor is guided by an acting coach or director, the athlete by a trainer or coach, the musician by a teacher or conductor, the novice driver by a driving instructor or parent, the young or struggling reader involved in reading fluency instruction needs the assistance and guidance of a teacher. The reader's coach can select appropriate materials, model fluent reading, provide assistance while reading, evaluate progress within and between passages, give encouragement, and celebrate successes.

Although on the surface it may seem that the reader develops fluency simply by finding a quiet spot and practicing a text several times through, the reality is that there needs to be a coach to model, guide, and encourage in order to make that practice as valuable as possible. Below we identify the various direct instructional roles a teacher or coach can take in nurturing reading fluency.

Model Fluent Reading

Less fluent readers may not know what it means to read fluently. Readers need to develop an internalized model of fluent reading. In the current environment where reading speed has become the proxy for reading fluency, students may think that fluency is nothing more than reading fast. This is clearly a less than optimal conception of fluency, yet many students seem to have gotten it in their heads that fluency is reading fast, and they direct their reading efforts to reading as fast as they can. Reading speed may be an indicator or measure of the automaticity component of fluency, but reading speed is not automaticity, and it is not fluency.

The best way for a teacher, parent, or coach to counter the idea that reading speed is fluency and to help students develop the understanding that fluency is reading with meaningful expression and automaticity is to read to students regularly in a fluent manner and then to direct students' attention to how that reading was fluent—what made it fluent. Conversely, the teacher, parent, or coach could read to students in a nonfluent manner (monotone, staccato-like, excessively slow, or extremely fast) with a follow-up discussion that focuses on how such a reading was not as meaningful or satisfying as a more fluent rendering of the passage.

Act as a Fluency Coach

Students need to practice, through repeated readings, their own reading as well as listen to fluent readings by others. But practice without feedback may result in students reinforcing their errors or practicing to achieve the wrong goal (e.g., to increase reading speed without regard to expression). Teachers need to take on a direct coaching role as students read orally during fluency instruction. They need to listen to students read and give formative feedback on their reading. Teachers can note particular areas of concern in students' reading, give praise for strong efforts, and direct students to read in a particular manner (e.g., to read a passage with enthusiasm, with sadness, with boredom). This sort of coaching helps direct students' attention to areas that will allow them to develop their fluency and use it to increase text comprehension.

In the role of fluency coach, teachers can also monitor students' progress in reading fluency. On a regular and systematic basis, the teacher might record samples of students' oral reading and evaluate the recording for automaticity (reading speed) and prosody (reading expression). Progress or lack of progress can be shown through charting students' performance over time. Analysis of trends can lead to lesson planning that is aimed more precisely at students' needs.

Engage in Assisted Reading

Research into fluency has shown that assisted (also called paired, neurological impress, audio-assisted, or duolog) reading (Rasinski & Hoffman, 2003) can have a significantly positive effect on students' fluency. In assisted reading, an individual student reads a passage while simultaneously listening to a fluent reading of the same text. The fluent rendering of the text can be by a more fluent partner or can be a prerecorded version of the reading. In many classrooms teachers set aside a time of each day for students to engage in assisted reading with a coach or peer. In other cases, teachers create a listening center in which students are expected to spend some time each day reading while listening to an audiotaped recording of the book.

These are wonderful examples of how teachers can create classroom conditions and routines for supporting students. However, we think it is also important for the teacher to take on the specific role of fluent reading partner for students with particular needs in fluency. No doubt, the teacher is the most fluent reader in any elementary or middle school classroom. During the assisted reading period the teacher may pair up with an individual, pairs, or small groups of students and read orally with the students as they read orally on their own. Being integrally involved in such lessons allows the teacher to personally monitor each and every student in his or her classroom and to act as a personal model or trainer for students. Even more significantly, by being involved with students in this daily read-along routine, the teacher demonstrates firsthand to students that fluency is important—so important that he or she is willing to take time each day, time that could have been used for other duties, to read with students in the classroom. That is a very profound message indeed.

Collect Fluency Materials

Fluency instruction normally involves assisted, repeated (practice or rehearsal), and oral reading. (We must note, however, that fluency is also manifested in silent reading through the inner voice that only the reader hears.) These activities require resources that may not normally be available in a classroom. The informed fluency teacher, then, must take on the role of text collector and developer to make his or her classroom ready for fluency instruction.

For example, a teacher may decide to set up a listening center so that students can read books while listening to recorded versions of the book (assisted reading). The teacher needs to acquire the hardware necessary to play the recordings (e.g., tape recorders). More important, she will have to find or develop the recorded versions of the texts she wishes to stock in the listening center. Fortunately, more and more publishing companies are making recorded versions of texts. However, the teacher may also want to think about recording the passages herself or having some of her students (fluent readers as well as those still working on fluency) record passages after having practiced them to the point where they can be read fluently (Opitz & Rasinski, 1998). There is something special about reading a text while listening to a recorded version of the text produced by one's teacher or classmate.

Certain texts lend themselves to practice and oral performance, and these texts are not normally found in great quantities in basal readers and other textbooks. Poetry, songs and song lyrics, rhetoric, plays (usually in the form of readers theater scripts), and other texts written with a sense of the author's voice are among the texts that we find lend themselves most fittingly to fluency instruction. Not only can these texts be read orally and repeatedly, they also lend themselves to oral interpretation whereby the reader uses his or her voice to convey meaning and emotion.

Provide for Performance and Celebration

At its heart, fluency in any endeavor requires practice. Whether one is trying to become fluent with a musical instrument, a sport, writing, or reading, one needs to practice the craft in order to become fluent at it. In reading, the practice too often (and unfortunately) involves mundane repeated readings of dry passages that are often informational.

Informed teachers see practice as essential and attempt to find material that is meant to be performed. If the passage, whether it is a song, script, speech, or poem, is meant to be performed, it has to be rehearsed or practiced repeatedly. The performance of a passage makes the practice meaningful to students. They will want to perfect their reading so that the performance is as good as possible.

Teachers, then, need to think about how they can allow students to perform their material. Some teachers use Friday afternoons as a time for a "Poetry Cafe". During the last 45 min of every Friday, the lights are dimmed and the shades are drawn—low-level lighting is used to create a coffeehouse mood. A bar stool is set up at the front of the classroom and so is a microphone attached to a karaoke machine. Students are the main audience, but parents, teachers, the school principal, and other classrooms are invited to participate in the poetry readings. A parent may bring in popcorn, drinks, and other appropriate refreshments. Students love the authenticity of the performance, and it leads them to rehearse their readings even more diligently; they know they will be performing for an audience.

In a similar way, teachers can set up daily or weekly opportunities for students to perform their songs, scripts, or other performance texts. Imagine a weekly song festival, a daily poetry reading (done individually or chorally with groups of students), or a periodic readers theater festival for which groups of students plan and rehearse their scripts for performance for classmates.

Manifestations of Direct Instruction in Reading Fluency: Instructional Routines

Perhaps the central role of the teacher in direct fluency instruction is to develop and set in motion instructional routines in which reading fluency is the focus. An instructional routine is simply a set of instructional activities aimed at developing a particular skill in reading that is implemented on a regular schedule, usually on a daily or weekly basis.

Many commercial programs currently exist for teaching reading fluency and are based on the central instructional concept of practice or repeated readings. Most of these programs consist of informational texts that are meant to be practiced until a certain reading rate is attained. We think this is a corruption of effective instruction in reading fluency for several reasons. For one, the texts employed (i.e., informational texts) do not lend themselves easily to reading fluency development. They are meant to be read silently and are usually written in a third-person disembodied voice, one that does not lend itself to reading with expression (the voice that an author incorporates into his or her written text).

We are also concerned that such approaches to repeated readings give the goal of rereading mechanically until the passage can be read quickly. As we mentioned earlier, although speed in reading may be an indicator of automaticity in word recognition, speed is not reading fluency and should not be used as an explicit goal for instruction.

We argue again that repeated reading works best when the practice or repeated reading is aimed at recreating the voice of the author who wrote the text, reading with appropriate expression and meaning. Because informational texts do not necessarily lend themselves to expressive renderings, one needs to look for other genres of text that do tend to be written with voice. And to that end, we think of narrative, poetry, rhymes, scripts, dialogues, monologues, jokes, cheers, song lyrics, oratory, and other such texts as the appropriate materials for authentic and effective fluency instruction.

Given appropriate texts and teacher roles, what might direct authentic fluency instruction look like? The manifestations of direct fluency instruction can be as diverse as teachers and their styles of teaching. In this section we share several models of direct and authentic fluency instruction that have proven effective in working with struggling readers.

Fluency Development Lesson (FDL)

The FDL is a direct fluency instruction model developed by Rasinski, Padak, Linek, and Sturtevant (1994) for use with students experiencing difficulties in fluency and in learning to read. For 10 to 15 minutes per day, students and teachers work with a daily text. The teacher models reading the text for students and gradually releases responsibility for reading the text from himself or herself to the students. Eventually, the students perform the text and engage in word study and further practice of the passage at home. A detailed outline of the FDL is presented in Figure 1. In a year-long implementation of the FDL in urban second-grade classrooms where students were generally experiencing difficulty in learning to read, students doing the FDL regularly and with fidelity made substantial progress in reading fluency and overall reading achievement when compared with their previous year's progress and when compared with students not engaged in the FDL but doing other reading-related tasks during the time otherwise devoted to the fluency instruction (Rasinski et al., 1994).

Fast Start

Fast Start is an adaptation of the FDL and is intended for use by parents at home with their beginning readers (Padak & Rasinski, 2005; Rasinski, 1995; Rasinski & Padak, 2004). Parents and their children work with a daily fluency text (chosen by the teacher for its literary and poetry qualities, normally a nursery rhyme or poem). Parents are taught to read the poem to their children several times with their children looking on, read the poem with their children aloud several times, and eventually have their children read the poem to them several times. This repeated and assisted reading is then followed by a brief study of some of the words from the rhyme. Research has demonstrated the effectiveness of Fast Start in promoting early reading (Rasinski, 1995). One study in particular found Fast Start to be most beneficial among children who were struggling the most in acquiring early reading skills (Rasinski & Stevenson, 2005).

Rasinski and Stevenson (2005) reported that in a 12-week implementation of the program, the most at-risk students engaged in Fast Start at home made significantly more progress in word recognition and fluency than students not doing Fast Start at home but receiving the same reading instruction in school. In fact, the Fast Start students made nearly twice the gain in fluency (automaticity) of students not engaged in Fast Start.

The FDL employs short reading passages (poems, story segments, or other texts) that students read and reread over a short period of time. The format for the lesson is as follows:

1. Students read a familiar passage from the previous lesson to the teacher or a fellow student for accuracy and fluency.

2. The teacher introduces a new short authentic text *with voice* (meant for rehearsal and performance) and reads it to the students two or three times while the students follow along. The text can be a poem, a segment from a basal passage, a literature book, or so on.

3. The teacher and students discuss the nature and content of the passage.

4. The teacher and students read the passage chorally several times. Antiphonal reading and other variations are used to create variety and maintain engagement.

5. The teacher organizes student pairs. Each student practices the passage three times while his or her partner listens and provides support and encouragement.

6. Individuals and groups of students perform their reading for the class or other audience.

7. The students and their teacher choose three or four words from the text to add to the word bank and/or word wall.

8. Students engage in word study activities (e.g., word sorts with word bank words, word walls, flashcard practice, defining words, word games).

9. Students take a copy of the passage home to practice with parents and other family members.

10. Students return to school and read the passage to the teacher or a partner, who checks for fluency and accuracy.

FIGURE 1   The Fluency Development Lesson (FDL).

The teachers in the Fast Start program did play a critical role in teaching the parents the program, supplying the materials, and supporting and encouraging parents in their implementation of the program.

Fluency-Oriented Reading Instruction (FORI)

FORI (Stahl & Heubach, 2005) is an instructional fluency model that, like the FDL, incorporates repeated and assisted (partner) reading. Instead of the poetry or other short text selections used in the FDL, the texts employed in FORI are simply the basal reading stories that are part of the students' regular reading curriculum. This feature makes the identification and employment of texts for fluency practice simple for teachers. In FORI, a basal reading selection is read to the students by the teacher and is then followed by a brief discussion of the story. Students then read the story several times on their own at home and in school, in various modes (e.g., echo reading with the teacher, alternating pages while reading with a partner, reading alone, as a play). Following several readings of the passage students engage in worksheets and journal work related to the story that had been read under the direction of their teacher.

In a 2-year implementation study of FORI in 14 second-grade class-rooms, Stahl and Heubach (2005) found greater than expected growth in reading achievement in every classroom. The average growth in reading achievement was approximately 1.8 years for each year of the study. It should also be noted that a substantial number of students in the study were reading significantly below grade at the beginning of each year of the study. Yet by the end of the study, only two students were not reading at their assigned grade level. Despite the repetitive reading of basal texts, students and teachers had positive attitudes toward the lesson format.

Stahl and Heubach (2005) pointed out that the most pronounced effects of FORI were on struggling readers beginning their second-grade year reading above the primer level but below the second-grade level. Although most struggling readers tend to fall progressively further behind their normal-achieving classmates as time goes on, the students in this study, through fluency instruction manifested in various forms of repeated reading and using normal curriculum materials, were able to catch up and were, except for two students, reading at grade level by the end of second grade. The potential of a dedicated fluency component in the regular reading curriculum for accelerating reading progress is clearly evident.

Readers Theater

Lorraine Griffith is a fourth-grade teacher in Buncombe County, North Carolina. As in probably all fourth-grade classrooms around the country, Lorraine has her share of struggling readers. After having heard a presentation by Tim Rasinski on reading fluency, she decided to implement a fluency-oriented routine of her own in her classroom that focused on repeated reading and performance of readers theater scripts and other materials meant to be rehearsed and performed for an audience (e.g., speeches, poetry, dialogs; Griffith & Rasinski, 2004).

Students in Griffith's class would receive a script with appropriate parts highlighted early each week. The scripts were found and developed by the teacher. Many were thematically and topically connected to content students were studying in other areas of their fourth-grade curriculum. Students were expected to rehearse the script nightly at home for 10 min. On Fridays, before lunch, students would rehearse with the other members of their group. During this time Griffith would coach and encourage individual students and small groups. Her coaching emphasized the need to practice the passage in order to communicate meaning through oral expression, phrasing, pausing, and emphasis. On Friday afternoons students would perform their scripts for their classmates and other classroom visitors in a "dinner theater" atmosphere. The routine would begin again the following Monday with another set of scripts.

In only 10 weeks of implementation, Griffith noted remarkably positive results in students' reading achievement and in their interest in reading, well above normal expectations (Griffith & Rasinski, 2004). It was this initial success that led Griffith to continue working on and refining this model of authentic practice or authentic material for authentic reasons.

Singing as Reading

Singing lyrics to songs is a form of reading that is nearly ideal for fluency instruction. Songs are meant to be sung (read) orally, and they are meant to be sung (read) repeatedly. It is not unusual for friends to report to us that they have gotten a song into their head early in the morning and that they find themselves singing that very same song throughout the day, unable to clear their mind of the song—its melody and lyrics. This to us is a natural form of repeated exposure to text that will build reading fluency. In the reading clinic Rasinski directs at Kent State University, teachers and students sing and read songs repeatedly and regularly over the course of their instruction with very positive results.

Marie Biggs, Susan Homan, and their colleagues (2008) employed the notion of singing as a vehicle for teaching reading and reading fluency. The routine involved students using a software product that provides natural reinforcement of automaticity through the repeated readings of a song's lyrics. The software, Tune in to Reading (TIR), provides real-time, instant feedback for each child. The students used TIR for 30 min, three times a week. Through readability levels, songs were matched to each child's instructional reading level. The teachers initially directed the children to read the song lyrics silently. By silently reading the words to a song while they listened to the music, the students internalized the rhythm of the language for that particular song.

After the silent (repeated) readings of song lyrics, the students sang the song aloud and recorded their performance. Students were encouraged to sing the song aloud three times and then save the recording of their best rendition.

In the initial middle school study (Biggs et al., 2008), the treatment group gained more than a year and a half in overall reading achievement in 9 weeks. Even though students stopped using the program at the end of 9 weeks, the researchers conducted a sustainability assessment at the end of the school year (4 months after the study ended). The students who had used TIR experienced an additional 5-month gain in instructional reading level. Scores after 9 weeks and at the end of the school year demonstrated significant student improvement. Control students' scores evidenced no significant growth.

These results provided the impetus for an expanded study (2005–2006) involving 326 students in three school districts at elementary, middle, and high school levels (Homan, Biggs, Bennett, & Minick, 2007). The time frame and routines from the first study were continued in the expanded study. At all grade levels and at all sites, treatment students consistently made a minimum of a full year instructional-level gain in the 9-week implementation. Control students had alternative reading experiences, whereas treatment students used TIR. Again, all treatment gains were significant; however, control students at all levels and at all sites evidenced no significant growth.

The use of this interactive singing software not only significantly increased overall instructional reading level for students, it also provided significant improvement in fluency, word recognition, and comprehension.

As we previously mentioned, students need to develop the understanding that fluency is reading with meaningful expression and automaticity. TIR provides another positive example of how informed teachers can create classroom conditions and routines for supporting their students' fluency development. This software's use of singing for practice and performance is another example of authentic practice for authentic reasons.

DISCUSSION

In the quest to accelerate the progress of struggling readers, curriculum and materials developers have too often come up with approaches to instruction that do not even resemble authentic reading done outside of school. Students work on individual reading skills until a certain level of proficiency is achieved, at which time they work on the next reading skill, with little attention given to how these various parts come together in real-life reading. We see this mechanization of the reading process beginning to be applied to a great hope in reading—reading fluency. Although we are firm believers in direct and intensive instruction for students who need it, we continually ask the following question: Direct and intensive instruction in what form and for what purpose? Much too often we have seen the answer to that question in relation to fluency as reading informational text for the main purpose of reading it ever more quickly. For the first time in our careers, we now see children, mostly struggling readers, ask us if they should read an assigned text "as fast as they can."

Reading fluency has been identified as a key component in reading and in learning to read. Moreover, a large number of students who experience difficulty in reading manifest difficulties in reading fluency. The keys to the development of reading fluency include modeling fluent reading for students and providing students with repeated reading practice of written passages, while at the same time providing assistance and coaching in the repeated reading. Rather than have students involve themselves in a mechanical form of repeated readings for which the main goal is reading fast, we feel that a more authentic approach to repeated readings and fluency development is called for, especially for readers who struggle. This more authentic approach involves the use of materials that are meant to be read orally and performed for an audience. With such materials readers do not practice reading a text to improve their reading speed; rather, they practice reading a text to recreate the voice of the author so that an audience listening to the performance of the text read aloud will more fully appreciate the meaning that is embedded in the voice of the reader. Not only does such an approach to fluency instruction work, as the field-based research we have summarized in this article demonstrates, but the use of materials such as poetry, song, scripts, and the like will help students develop a love of and appreciation for the written language that is not always present in other forms of written discourse.

REFERENCES

Biggs, M. C., Homan, S. P., Dedrick, R., Minick, V., & Rasinski, T. V. (2008). Using an interactive singing software program: A comparative study of middle school struggling readers. *Reading Psychology, 29*, 195–213.

Duke, N. K., Pressley, M., & Hilden, K. (2004). Difficulties in reading comprehension. In C. A. Stone, E. R. Silliman, B. J. Ehren, & K. Apel (Eds.), *Handbook of language and literacy: Development and disorders* (pp. 501–520). New York, NY: Guilford Press.

Griffith, L. W., & Rasinski, T. V. (2004). A focus on fluency: How one teacher incorporated fluency with her reading curriculum. *The Reading Teacher, 58*, 126–137.

Homan, S. P., Biggs, M. C., Bennett, S., & Minick, V. (2007). *Singing and reading: How the bounce makes a big difference*. Unpublished manuscript.

Kuhn, M. R., & Stahl, S. A. (2000). *Fluency: A review of developmental and remedial practices* (CIERA Rep. No. 2-008). Ann Arbor, MI: Center for the Improvement of Early Reading Achievement.

National Reading Panel. (2000). *Report of the National Reading Panel: Teaching children to read. Report of the subgroups*. Washington, DC: U.S. Department of Health and Human Services, National Institutes of Health.

Opitz, M. F., & Rasinski, T. V. (1998). *Good-bye round robin: 25 effective oral reading strategies*. Portsmouth, NH: Heinemann.

Padak, N., & Rasinski, T. (2005). *Fast start for early readers: A research-based, send-home literacy program*. New York, NY: Scholastic.

Rasinski, T. V. (1995). Fast Start: A parental involvement reading program for primary grade students. In W. Linek & E. Sturtevant (Eds.), *Generations of literacy: Seventeenth yearbook of the College Reading Association* (pp. 301–312). Harrisonburg, VA: College Reading Association.

Rasinski, T. V. (2004). *Assessing reading fluency*. Honolulu, HI: Pacific Resources for Education and Learning.

Rasinski, T. V., & Hoffman, J. V. (2003). Theory and research into practice: Oral reading in the school literacy curriculum. *Reading Research Quarterly, 38*, 510–522.

Rasinski, T. V., & Padak, N. D. (1998). How elementary students referred for compensatory reading instruction perform on school-based measures of word recognition, fluency, and comprehension. *Reading Psychology, 19*, 185–216.

Rasinski, T. V., & Padak, N. (2004). *Effective reading strategies: Teaching children who find reading difficult* (3rd ed.). Columbus, OH: Merrill-Prentice Hall.

Rasinski, T. V., Padak, N. D., Linek, W. L., & Sturtevant, E. (1994). Effects of fluency development on urban second-grade readers. *Journal of Educational Research, 87*, 158–165.

Rasinski, T., & Stevenson, B. (2005). The effects of Fast Start reading, a fluency based home involvement reading program, on the reading achievement of beginning readers. *Reading Psychology, 26*, 109–125.

Rasinski, T. V., & Zutell, J. B. (1996). Is fluency yet a goal of the reading curriculum? In E. G. Sturtevant & W. M. Linek (Eds.), *Growing literacy: 18th yearbook of the College Reading Association* (pp. 237–246). Harrisonburg, VA: College Reading Association.

Samuels, S. J. (1979). The method of repeated readings. *The Reading Teacher, 32*, 403–408.

Stahl, S. A., & Heubach, K. M. (2005). Fluency-oriented reading instruction. *Journal of Literacy Research, 37*, 25–60.

One-Minute Fluency Measures: Mixed Messages in Assessment and Instruction

THERESA A. DEENEY

■ ■ ■ ■ ■

More and more school districts are adopting one-minute fluency assessments. Although valid and reliable, they may lead astray our understanding of struggling readers' reading development and instructional needs.

One-minute fluency measures are becoming prevalent, largely due to federal policies and initiatives such as the National Reading Panel's recommendation that "teachers should assess fluency regularly" (National Institute of Child Health and Human Development, 2000, pp. 3–4), and the reauthorization of the Individuals with Disabilities Education Act (IDEA), which mandates that states must permit a Response to Intervention (RTI) approach to identify students with specific learning disabilities, a subcategory of which is reading fluency skills. One-minute fluency measures do reliably identify students who are at risk for reading difficulty. However, they may not map onto current definitions of fluency. Because of this, they may generate misunderstanding about students' fluency, which, in turn, may lead to inappropriate instruction. Therefore, it is important to define reading fluency, determine which components are assessed in one-minute measures, and take note of what might be missing.

Reading Fluency

The Literacy Dictionary (Harris & Hodges, 1995) defines fluency as "freedom from word-identification problems that might hinder comprehension . . . automaticity" and a fluent reader as "any person who reads smoothly, without hesitation, and with comprehension" (p. 85). In this definition, fluency consists of four components: accuracy ("freedom from word-identification problems"), rate or speed ("automaticity," "without hesitation"), prosody ("smoothly"), and comprehension. This definition suggests that accuracy, rate, and prosody are vehicles to comprehension, so let's look at these more closely.

Accuracy

If students are to comprehend what they read, they must accurately identify the majority of words in a text. Misreading critical words, or a large percentage of words, can derail comprehension. Consider this example of Kenny's (all names used are pseudonyms), a seventh grader's, reading and think-aloud response for "The Mannerism" (de Maupassant, 1989; stricken words are the actual text, words in parentheses are Kenny's substitutions):

> Text: With my own hands I laid her in the coffin, and I went with it to the cemetery ~~where~~ (with) it was placed in the family vault. At my request, she was ~~buried~~ (burned) wearing all her jewelry—bracelets, necklaces, rings—and wearing a party dress. (p. 58)
>
> Kenny: "Well, like she, well, she died from this disease and he wants her to be burned and he's probably gonna, I don't know, maybe he's probably gonna try to kill himself or something 'cause he can't take it."
>
> Text: The ~~apparition~~ (appression) spoke again. 'Don't be afraid, father. I was not dead. Somebody came to steal my rings, and to get them they cut off one of my fingers'. (p. 61)
>
> Kenny: "Well, she said she's not dead, but they burned her or something."

Although Kenny's accuracy is within the instructional level (96%) for this text, his misreading of one crucial word ("burned" for *buried*) disrupts his understanding of the story. Even when we may think a miscue is not significant within the greater context of a story, such as mispronouncing someone's name, it can wreak havoc on comprehension. Kenny's retelling of "The Mannerism" suggested that his mis-pronunciation of a character's name caused him to create a misrepresentation of this text. He read,

> My old servant, ~~Prosper~~ (Prospector), who had helped me lay Juliette in her coffin . . . . (p. 60)

In this story, the servant, whose name is Prosper, cut off the girl's finger to steal her rings. Because Kenny read the servant's name as "Prospector," his retelling included a new character—a prospector who dug up the girl's grave to cut off her finger.

Rate

Rate includes both automaticity and speed of reading. Automaticity means getting words off the page quickly and effortlessly, without conscious attention. This is important because readers have limited attention available for complex tasks. If they need to use attention to get words off the page, they will have less attention available to devote to comprehension (LaBerge & Samuels, 1974; Stahl & Kuhn, 2002).

Reading speed similarly relates to comprehension. Although speed does require balancing components other than word recognition (e.g., phrasing, syntax, punctuation, prosody), automaticity is a significant contributor to speed. One reason we can read with acceptable speed is that we can get the words off the page without a great deal of effort, leaving more attention to devote to understanding. Although reading rate does not ensure comprehension (we have all come across students who read accurately and relatively quickly, but do not understand what they read), there is much research suggesting that higher rate is related to higher levels of comprehension (see among others Chard, Vaughn, & Tyler, 2002; Rasinski, 1989).

Prosody

Prosody refers to a reader's ability to read smoothly, with appropriate phrasing and expression. Prosody includes the expressive qualities of tone, inflection, and rhythm that make reading sound like oral language, speech, drama, or music. Prosody also includes phrasing or parsing text into appropriate segments. Readers use appropriate prosody through their understanding of the context of the text, and by using a variety of text cues such as signal words (cried, screamed, asked), typeface (That's *really* weird.), punctuation (He is here? He is here. He is here!), and syntax (Her office is/across the hall/on the left.).

The relationship between prosody and comprehension is unclear. Prosody may be the cause of comprehension (a reader understands what she's reading because she uses appropriate prosody) or the result of comprehension (a reader can use appropriate prosody because she understands what she's reading). Some researchers argue that there is a reciprocal relationship between the two (Kuhn, 2009). In a recent study of first and second graders, Miller and Schwanenflugel (2008) found inappropriate pauses negatively related to comprehension, but the study was not designed to offer further explanation. Although we may not understand the exact nature of the relationship between reading with appropriate prosody and understanding what one reads, it is clear that such a relationship exists (Miller & Schwanenflugel, 2008; Pinnell et al., 1995). From a practical standpoint, consider this fourth grader's reading of a passage about Tomie dePaola from the *Qualitative Reading Inventory* (Leslie & Caldwell, 2006):

> Tomie dePaola has illustrated over/200 books. He has also authored/over 100 of those/ he has/illustrated. Tomie was born in 19/34 in Connecticut, one/of four/children. Tomie's mother read to him as a young boy.

Although this student may understand the piece, I would be confused about how many books dePaola has written versus illustrated.

(Mis)Matching Definition and Assessment

Assessment choices should be based on our understanding of the construct being assessed. If we subscribe to the *Literacy Dictionary*'s (Harris & Hodges, 1995) definition of fluency as containing the four components of accuracy, speed, prosody, and comprehension, when assessing fluency we would naturally assess accuracy, speed, prosody, and comprehension. Yet this is not current practice, perhaps because there is not one universally agreed-upon definition of fluency. Kuhn and Stahl (2003) wrote, "There seems to be a consensus [in research literature] regarding the primary components of fluency: (a) accuracy in decoding, (b) automaticity in word recognition, and (c) the appropriate use of prosodic features such as stress, pitch, and appropriate text phrasing" (p. 5). Meyer and Felton (1999) similarly described fluency as "the ability to read connected text rapidly, smoothly, effortlessly, and automatically with little conscious attention to the mechanics of reading such as decoding" (p. 284). If we adopt this reduced view—accuracy, rate, and prosody—as our working definition of fluency, our assessment of fluency should incorporate accuracy, rate, and prosody. Yet even this is not current practice.

Torgesen (2000) argued that, although fluency is a complicated construct, we can only reliably measure two components, accuracy and rate, and in fact, many commercial assessments of fluency are assessments of accuracy and rate. Popular assessments such as AIMSweb *Standard Reading Assessment Passages* (Edformation, 2002) and the Oral Reading Fluency subtest (ORF) of the *Dynamic Indicators of Basic Early Literacy Skills* (DIBELS; Good & Kaminski, 2002) provide grade-level passages that the student reads for one minute as the teacher records the student's rate in words per minute (WPM; the number of words the student read in one minute), or rate and accuracy in words correct per minute (WCPM; the number of words the student read minus the number of errors the student made). Thus, we have now narrowed fluency to accuracy and rate.

Although we should choose assessments based on a solid understanding of the construct we want to assess, the opposite can happen. Widespread use of specific assessments can ultimately define the construct being assessed. What the measure assesses becomes the definition of the construct. This may be the case with reading fluency. The prevalence of one-minute fluency measures, which assess only two components of fluency, accuracy, and rate, has the potential to reduce fluency and redefine it as accuracy and rate. As Samuels (2007) stated,

> One criticism I have of the DIBELS tests is that, despite their labels, they are not valid tests of the construct of fluency as it is widely understood and defined. They only assess accuracy and speed . . . By attaching the term fluency to their tests, they create the false as-sumption that that is what the tests measure. (p. 564)

Fluency: A Deeper View

Although common assessment practice narrows fluency to rate and accuracy, our understanding of fluency should be broadened, rather than narrowed. Pikulski and Chard (2005) discussed a "deep" view of fluency, in which the development of accuracy, rate, prosody and, ultimately, comprehension is the result of a long line of component processes.

A deep view suggests that fluency begins well before a student is able to show that he or she can read connected text and extends far beyond what a student demonstrates in one minute. Fluent readers must develop accuracy (correctness) and automaticity (speed) with many small parts of the reading process—identifying letter sounds, using strategies for accurately decoding new words, identifying high-frequency words, and accessing word meanings (Wolf & Katzir-Cohen, 2001). Initially, then, readers are not fluent. Beginning readers read word-by-word, trying to coordinate all that is involved in figuring out the text. However, as children gain more experience with letters and words, they begin to identify them automatically, without consciously thinking about them. Automatizing letters, words, and strategies allows readers to move from word-by-word reading to grouping words together meaningfully and more quickly (Miller & Schwanenflugel, 2008).

Although Pikulski and Chard (2005) expanded fluency to include the many subprocesses that lead to accuracy, rate, prosody, and ultimately comprehension, their explanation does not explicitly capture another important aspect of fluent reading—endurance. I define endurance as the ability to continue reading with appropriate accuracy, rate, prosody, and comprehension over an extended period of time. Endurance can be a significant stumbling block for many struggling readers. Yet, endurance is rarely mentioned in fluency research or practice literature, or in reading research or practice literature.

Most research on the relationship between fluency and endurance comes from behavioral science and special education (Binder, 1996; Kubina, 2005), and suggests that endurance is a byproduct of accuracy and rate. When one increases the accuracy and rate with which one can perform a task, one is able to increase the length of time one can perform the task. Endurance is a necessary component of an even deeper view of fluency. In essence, it implies that *because* a reader has skill and control of the processes and subprocesses of reading, the reader can channel these to read and understand a variety of texts of a variety of lengths for a variety of purposes.

Comparing One-Minute Measures to a Deeper View of Fluency

One-minute fluency measures capture a reduced view of fluency—accuracy and rate—rather than a deeper view. I am not suggesting that one-minute measures are inappropriate, or that they do not accomplish their purpose. Measures such as AIMSweb and DIBELS are valid and reliable curriculum-based measures (CBM); that is, they measure how students are faring with respect to grade-level criteria (Deno, 1985). When used for their intended purpose, they are quick and provide useful information. Unfortunately, they are not always used in the way in which they were intended, perhaps due to the accountability pressures schools and teachers face.

In one district in which I work, students are placed into reading groups based on the results of one-minute assessments, which is not in keeping with the assessments' intent. Additionally, accountability pressure can confuse the measure with instruction. As Tierney and Thome (2006) pointed out, "DIBELS fails to separate outcomes from means. Accordingly, what DIBELS measures and what teachers teach become the same" (p. 52). If the outcome is increasing one-minute WCPM scores, more and more practice reading short pieces of connected text quickly and accurately will creep into the curriculum, which not only fails to capture the kinds of reading students do but paints a distorted picture of what reading is. Because continuous monitoring of fluency through accuracy and rate measures does not provide rich information, it may lead to inappropriate instructional decisions for students most in need of fluency instruction. These are issues of consequential validity (American Educational Research Association, American Psychological Association, & National Council on Measurement in Education, 1999)— indirect or unintended consequences of using an assessment on the overall educational program.

What We Don't Know From One-Minute Measures

One-minute measures help us identify students who cannot read accurately and quickly. This is useful information. Yet to focus instruction, we need additional information. Most important, we need to understand why students are dysfluent and the effects of time on students' reading.

Why Students Are Dysfluent

Because the goal of one-minute fluency measures is the quick and reliable assessment of oral reading accuracy and rate, administration procedures are streamlined. The number of errors and the speed of reading are the targets. Teachers strike out words the student misreads, count up the number of words read in one minute, and subtract the number of errors from the number of words read. This is all that is needed to identify *whether* a reader is up to expectations for accuracy and speed. It is not all that is needed to identify *why* a reader may not be achieving expectations, which is the critical issue in instruction for struggling readers. One-minute measures do provide a vehicle for understanding how students approach text-graded passages. Listening to a student read is a powerful way to gain critical information about his or her reading. Minimally, writing in miscues (errors) helps the teacher understand how the student is using lower level skills, such as alphabetic knowledge and word patterns, and which skills the student needs to develop. Yet some one-minute screens actually preclude this type of administration. Assessments that use handheld technologies may only allow strike-through recordings, losing critical information to help teachers understand how students are coordinating the many aspects of fluency.

The Effects of Time

Struggling readers may have reasonable rate and accuracy for limited periods of time. They can, in a one-minute snapshot, allocate their cognitive attention and resources to accuracy and speed—those components captured in one-minute screens—and to comprehension, which is not typically assessed in one-minute snapshots. Yet these students may not be able to maintain this reading over time. They lack endurance. Other students may struggle tremendously within the first minute, yet over time improve their accuracy and speed due to increased understanding of the context of the piece (cf. Jenkins, Fuchs, van den Broek, Espin, & Deno, 2003). Neither profile is captured in one-minute measures.

Let us take as examples of the effects of time students who attend an after-school literacy support program that I direct. Anna, Becky, and Peter are second graders who, despite reading intervention, read at a first-grade level. Jackie is a third grader who reads at a first-grade level, probably due to sporadic attendance in first and second grades. Jeffrey is also a third grader who, in first and second grades, was behind in the fall and caught up by the spring. Lily, Adam, and Miriam are fifth graders who read instructionally at a fourth-grade level, according to other assessments given. Because none of these students reads on grade level, a one-minute CBM benchmark easily captured their fluency difficulties. However, one-minute measures are also meant as progress monitoring tools. Monitoring struggling readers through grade-level text simply shows that they continue to be "deficient." Therefore, many districts monitor with grade-level prompts at specific points in the year and use prompts at students' instructional reading level as weekly or monthly checks. In this way, teachers can see students' progress in moving toward grade-level text. However, even with instructional-level text, one-minute may not represent struggling readers' actual accuracy and rate over time.

As shown in Table 1, these students in the after-school program all met the benchmark for their instructional level given a one-minute progress-monitoring assessment. Thus, they could be considered "fluent" at their instructional level. An implication of this might be that they are ready for an increase in text difficulty. Is that the appropriate next step? A closer look at Table 1 shows that none of the students maintains this level of fluency over time. Becky, Peter, Jeffrey, and Lily do not meet the same benchmark when reading for more than one minute, suggesting that, even at their instructional level, they are not truly fluent. Additionally, the relationship between accuracy and rate, something we may not see in reports of WCPM, is different for different students. For example, Jackie's accuracy and rate decline over time, whereas Peter maintains accuracy over time but decreases rate (see Figure 1).

Understanding *that* these readers have not truly developed fluency at their instructional level, despite the positive results of this one-minute measure, is critical to

TABLE 1   Examples of Struggling Readers' Reading Accuracy and Rate for One Minute and Whole Passage

Student	Grade placement	Instructional level	Recommended rate (WCPM)	WCPM: 1 minute	WCPM: >1 minute
Anna	2	1	30–60 (Spring)	55	56
Becky	2	1	30–60 (Spring)	43	21
Peter	2	1	30–60 (Spring)	48	29
Jackie	3	1	30–60 (Spring)	73	33
Jeffrey	3	2	70–100 (Spring)	71	41
Lily	5	4	70–110 (Fall)	90	67
Adam	5	4	70–110 (Fall)	93	85
Miriam	5	4	70–110 (Fall)	102	84

developing appropriate instruction, as is understanding *why* they have not yet developed fluency. Even within these limited examples of eight students, we can see differences that would warrant different instruction. Because Jackie's accuracy declines over time, she may need to solidify her word reading and decoding skills, whereas Peter, whose rate declines, may need to develop endurance.

Deeper Approaches to Fluency Assessment   DRÀS ?

[Fluency is far more than accuracy and rate.] Therefore, we need to take care with assessment practices and the language we use to describe them to ensure that we truly understand the information we gain and how it represents fluency. First and foremost, we should call assessments what they are. Rather than say AIMSweb and DIBELS are "fluency" assessments, we should say that they are assessments of accuracy and rate. They are what they are, and calling them what they are may avoid some of the misinterpretations that can arise from their results. Additional suggestions for deeper fluency assessment are as follows:

- Get the most from one-minute measures,
- Include fluency with other assessments,
- Tie assessment to instruction, and
- Assess endurance.

Get the Most from One-Minute Measures

Teachers who are mandated to use a one-minute accuracy and rate measure can obtain reliable information for typical and struggling readers. For typical readers, the administration procedures are appropriate as is, because they will quickly demonstrate that these readers are not at risk. For struggling readers, the teacher could gain the information required by the assessment, and information to inform instruction. First, the teacher

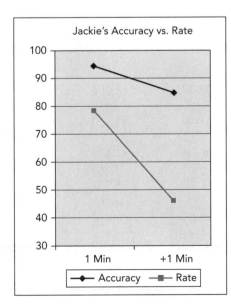
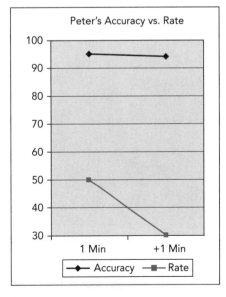

FIGURE 1   **Examples of Differences in Accuracy and Rate Over Time.**

should record students' miscues, rather than use a slash-through method of marking errors. This will provide the number of errors made, in keeping with the assessment requirements, and information about the lower-level skills that ultimately lead to fluency. Second, although the AIMSweb Training Workbook (Shinn & Shinn, 2002) states, "In the interest of time, don't let [students] finish the story" (p. 12), to gain information about endurance, the teacher could have students read the entire passage. The teacher can place a slash (/) in her copy of the text at the students' one-minute mark. That way, the teacher has a reliable rate for one-minute, as per the assessment requirements, and obtains the overall rate for the passage to assess endurance.

Include Fluency with Other Assessments

With good information about appropriate reading rate and accuracy, such as the recently developed oral reading fluency norms by Hasbrouck and Tindal (2006; see Table 2), and prosody, such as the Oral Reading Fluency Scale of the National Assessment of Educational Progress (NAEP, 1995; see Table 3), rather than adopt a separate fluency assessment, teachers can incorporate fluency assessment into any existing oral reading assessment. The 25th–75th percentile range of the oral reading fluency norms, and Levels 3 and 4 of the NAEP scale would indicate acceptable fluency.

Tie Assessment to Instruction

In an RTI approach, continual monitoring is essential. However, because instruction, rather than assessment, is the key to improving fluency, progress monitoring should be tied to instruction, rather than divorced from it. Some fluency intervention programs currently used in schools monitor accuracy and rate as a matter of course, so there is no need to use another measure of accuracy and rate. Other research-based fluency instruction techniques, such as repeated reading, also include accuracy and rate assessments.

TABLE 2   **Oral Reading Fluency Norms**

Grade	Percentile	Fall WCPM	Winter WCPM	Spring WCPM
1	50th		23	53
	25th—75th		12–47	28–82
2	50th	51	72	89
	25th—75th	25–79	42–100	61–117
3	50th	71	92	107
	25th—75th	44–99	62–120	78–137
4	50th	94	112	123
	25th—75th	68–119	87–139	98–152
5	50th	110	127	139
	25th—75th	85–139	99–156	109–168
6	50th	127	140	150
	25th—75th	98–153	111–167	122–177
7	50th	128	136	150
	25th—75th	102–156	109–165	123–177
8	50th	133	146	151
	25th—75th	106–161	115–173	124–177

Note. From Hasbrouck and Tindal (2006).

TABLE 3   National Assessment of Educational Progress (NAEP) Oral Reading Fluency Scale

Fluency Level	Description
4	Reads primarily in larger, meaningful phrase groups. Although some regressions, repetitions, and deviations from text may be present, these do not appear to detract from the overall structure of the story. Preservation of the author's syntax is consistent. Some or most of the story is read with expressive interpretation.
3	Reads primarily in three- or four-word phrase groups. Some smaller groupings may be present. However, the majority of phrasing seems appropriate and preserves the syntax of the author. Little or no expressive interpretation is present.
2	Reads primarily in two-word phrases with some three- or four-word groupings. Some word-by-word reading may be present. Word groupings may seem awkward and unrelated to larger context of sentence or passage.
1	Reads primarily word-by-word. Occasional two-word or three-word phrases may occur—but these are infrequent and/or they do not preserve meaningful syntax.

Note. From Pinnell et al. (1995).

In a repeated reading program, students' reading of a text is timed at the beginning of the week, then again at the end of the week after the student has practiced rereading the text throughout the week. These prereading and postreading rates can be used to document one kind of progress in accuracy and rate, progress with practice. Of course, generalization to other texts is critical, but any new text at that same grade level can be used to document generalization. Because many teachers monitor students' accuracy through running records, they can add rate and prosody to that assessment.

Assess Endurance

To understand what readers do over an extended period of reading, it is a good idea to have students read longer texts (text that take 4–5 minutes to complete). Most one-minute measures consist of short passages (250–300 words at grade 2 and up). At the second-grade level this length would provide sufficient reading to gauge endurance because it would take a fluent second grader approximately four minutes to read a 250-word passage. As a rule of thumb, each grade would need 100 additional words for a sufficient length to judge endurance (third graders would need approximately 350 words, fourth graders 450 words, and so on). If teachers need access to longer, graded texts, some informal reading inventories, such as the *Qualitative Reading Inventory* (Leslie & Caldwell, 2006), provide graded passages of varying lengths.

Instructing Fluency and Endurance

The overall goal of literacy instruction should be to help students flexibly use their literacy skills to accomplish a variety of literacy tasks for a variety of purposes. Flexibility necessitates fluency, and many reading tasks also necessitate endurance. Therefore, we need to be cognizant of both fluency and endurance in our instruction. If we understand that endurance is a byproduct of accuracy and rate, gaining fluency (accuracy, rate, prosody, and comprehension) will come before gaining endurance, and after gaining accuracy and automaticity in lower level processes. This has several implications for instruction. Of course, first and foremost is using assessment to gain the information necessary to design instruction, along with communication among those who work with struggling readers to ensure appropriate assessment and instruction.

Some suggestions for instructing the techniques for fluency and endurance are as follows:

- Increase automaticity,
- Decrease readability levels,
- Read interesting texts,
- Increase reading volume,
- Increase expectations,
- Reread books, and
- Engage parents and caregivers.

Increase Automaticity

Fluency is assessed in connected text; therefore, fluency instruction is often targeted toward connected text. Yet, considering a deep view of fluency, students' difficulties with fluency may stem from difficulties with lower level—beneath the paragraph—skills such as word reading, decoding, and letter–sound correspondence. If this is the case, instruction should target these skills. Good assessment will provide information about students' word recognition and decoding accuracy as well as automaticity. If accuracy is problematic, instruction may target decoding and word recognition accuracy in isolation. If students have good accuracy in lower level skills but have not established automaticity, instruction may include word and phrase reading to assist students in automatizing common elements of reading.

Decrease Readability Levels

We know that accuracy and automaticity pave the way for fluency by using less cognitive attention, and that endurance comes as a result of accuracy and automaticity. These imply that the level of text matters for developing fluency and endurance (see Hiebert & Fisher, 2005). To increase fluency to the point of en-durance, students need to spend time reading texts they can read *fluently* (accuracy, rate, prosody, and comprehension). Allington (2009) called this "high success reading," and suggested that it promotes not only fluency, but motivation.

Read Interesting Texts

Interest affects reading (Guthrie, Wigfield, Metsala, & Cox, 1999). Many struggling readers are not interested in reading books teachers recommend. Finding interesting text is not easy, but everyone is interested in *something*. For struggling readers, that something is often factual information. Having a variety of accessible texts (books, magazines, brochures, Internet), in terms of readability as well as availability, is critical for engaging students in reading.

Increase Reading Volume

If the texts struggling readers read are high success and interesting, we can increase students' reading volume, and increasing reading volume is related to fluency (Kuhn et al., 2006), and, I would argue, to endurance. Although many struggling readers need instruction in lower level skills, research suggests that intervention programs that include high success volume reading lead to reading achievement (Mathes et al., 2005).

Increase Expectations

Many struggling readers avoid reading, often for very good reasons. The cognitive effort and attention they need to expend coordinating the multiple processes involved in reading simply exhausts them. Although legitimate, this can contribute to reading avoidance. Breaking this mindset and increasing fluency and endurance for connected text first rests with lowering the text level, then with gradually increasing the expectations. Teachers can do this by setting an expectation for the number of pages to be read or some other "must-do" assignment and gradually extending it over time.

Reread Books

As we know from repeated reading research (Kuhn & Stahl, 2003), rereading assists with fluency. Because it assists with fluency, it can also assist with endurance. However, repeated reading instruction is typically done with short texts (200–300 words), so it will only help with endurance to that point. To use rereading to help with endurance, encourage students to reread longer texts, including books. What I have found helpful for students in the after-school program is for them to revisit books they read the previous year or heard read through teacher read-alouds. The students already have the background knowledge to understand the texts, and with a year's more literacy development, they read them with improved accuracy, rate, and prosody. Thus, they read for longer periods of time and are typically surprised and proud when they finish the book much sooner than they expected.

Engage Parents and Caregivers

Parents often have trouble either engaging reluctant readers in reading or choosing appropriate texts, particularly when the texts their children can read seem much easier than texts other students their age are reading. Recently, a teacher shared with me that she gave a seventh-grade struggling reader *Love That Dog* (Creech, 2001), written in short verse, to read for fluency. His parents refused to allow him to read it and took her to task for having their son read "baby books." Explain to parents the importance of reading easy texts at home, while assuring them that their children *do* read more difficult texts in school. One recommendation to help parents encourage their children to read, and at the same time avoid the parent–child reading wars that can occur in the homes of reluctant readers, is for parents to provide their children a wide choice of reading and allow them to read in bed at night. Staying up later is a good motivator, and if the books are easy enough and interesting enough, children usually comply.

Moving Beyond One-Minute Measures

One-minute accuracy and rate measures are reliable when used for their stated purpose, identifying which students may struggle with reading. However, because they are called "fluency" measures, they can lead astray our understanding of struggling readers' reading fluency. Fluency is more than accuracy and rate. Improving fluency begins with understanding dysfluency, which can begin with one-minute measures, but must extend to deeper fluency assessment. Through understanding *that* readers struggle and *why* they struggle, we can design appropriate instruction to support students' developing fluency.

REFERENCES

Allington, R.L. (2009). *What really matters in response to intervention*. Boston, MA: Allyn & Bacon.

American Educational Research Association, American Psychological Association, & National Council on Measurement in Education. (1999). *Standards for educational and psychological testing*. Washington, DC: American Educational Research Association.

Binder, C. (1996). Behavioral fluency: Evolution of a new paradigm. *The Behavior Analyst, 19*(2), 163–197.

Chard, D.J., Vaughn, S., & Tyler, B.J. (2002). A synthesis of research on effective interventions for building reading fluency with elementary students with learning disabilities. *Journal of Learning Disabilities, 35*(5), 386–407. doi:10.1177/0022219402 0350050101

de Maupassant, G. (1989). The Mannerism. In *The dark side: Tales of terror and the supernatural* (pp. 58–62). New York, NY: Carroll and Graf.

Deno, S.L. (1985). Curriculum based measurement: The emerging alternative. *Exceptional Children, 52*(3), 219–232.

Edformation. (2002). *AIMSweb standard reading assessment passages*. Eden Prairie, MN: Edformation.

Good, R., & Kaminski, R., (Eds.). (2002). *Dynamic indicators of basic early literacy skills* (6th ed.). Eugene, OR: Institute for the Development of Educational Achievement. Retrieved September 15, 2007, from dibels.uoregon.edu/

Guthrie, J.T., Wigfield, A., Metsala, J.L., & Cox, K.E. (1999). Motivational and cognitive predictors of text comprehension and reading amount. *Scientific Studies of Reading, 3*(3), 231–256. doi:10.1207/s1532799xssr0303_3

Harris, T.L., & Hodges, R.E. (1995). *The literacy dictionary: The vocabulary of reading and writing*. Newark, DE: International Reading Association.

Hasbrouck, J., & Tindal, G.A. (2006). Oral reading fluency norms: A valuable assessment tool for reading teachers. *The Reading Teacher, 59*(7), 636–644. doi:10.1598/RT.59.7.3

Hiebert, E.H., & Fisher, C.W. (2005). A review of the National Reading Panel's studies on fluency: The role of text. *The Elementary School Journal, 105*(5), 443–460. doi:10.1086/431888

Jenkins, J.R., Fuchs, L.S., van den Broek, P., Espin, C., & Deno, S.L. (2003). Accuracy and fluency in list and context reading of skilled and RD groups: Absolute and relative performance levels. *Learning Disabilities Research & Practice, 18*(4), 237–245. doi:10.1111/1540-5826.00078

Kubina, R.M., Jr. (2005). Developing reading fluency through a systematic practice procedure. *Reading & Writing Quarterly, 21*(2), 185–192. doi:10.1080/10573560590915987

Kuhn, M.R. (2009). *The hows and whys of fluency instruction*. Boston, MA: Allyn & Bacon.

Kuhn, M.R., Schwanenflugel, P.J., Morris, R.D., Morrow, L.M., Woo, D.G., Meisinger, E.B., et al. (2006). Teaching children to become fluent and automatic readers. *Journal of Literacy Research, 38*(4), 357–387. doi:10.1207/s15548430jlr3804_1

Kuhn, M.R., & Stahl, S.A. (2003). Fluency: A review of devel-opmental and remedial practices. *Journal of Educational Psychology, 95*(1), 3–21. doi:10.1037/0022-0663.95.1.3

LaBerge, D., & Samuels, S.J. (1974). Toward a theory of automatic information processing in reading. *Cognitive Psychology, 6*(2), 293–323. doi:10.1016/0010-0285(74)90015-2

Leslie, L., & Caldwell, J. (2006). *Qualitative reading inventory-4*. New York, NY: Addison-Wesley Longman.

Mathes, P.G., Denton, C.A., Fletcher, J.M., Anthony, J.L., Francis, D.J., & Schatschneider, C. (2005). The effects of theoretically different instruction and student characteristics on the skills of struggling readers. *Reading Research Quarterly, 40*(2), 148–182. doi:10.1598/RRQ.40.2.2

Meyer, M.S., & Felton, R.H. (1999). Repeated reading to enhance fluency: Old approaches and new directions. *Annals of Dyslexia, 49*(1), 283–306. doi:10.1007/s11881-999-0027-8

Miller, J., & Schwanenflugel, P.J. (2008). A longitudinal study of the development of reading prosody as a dimension of oral reading fluency in early elementary school children. *Reading Research Quarterly, 43*(4), 336–354. doi:10.1598/RRQ.43.4.2

National Assessment of Educational Progress. (1995). Oral Reading Fluency Scale. In G. Pinnell, J. Pikulski, K. Wixson, J. Campbell, P. Gough, & A. Beatty (Eds.), *Listening to children read aloud* (p. 15). Washington, DC: U.S. Department of Education, National Center for Education Statistics.

National Institute of Child Health and Human Development. (2000). *Report of the National Reading Panel. Teaching children to read: an evidence-based assessment of the scientific research literature on reading and its implications for reading instruction: Reports of the subgroups* (NIH Publication No. 00-4754). Washington, DC: U.S. Government Printing Office.

Pikulski, J.J., & Chard, D.J. (2005). Fluency: Bridge between decoding and reading comprehension. *The Reading Teacher, 58*(6), 510–519. doi:10.1598/RT.58.6.2

Pinnell, G., Pikulski, J., Wixson, K., Campbell, J., Gough, P., & Beatty, A. (1995). *Listening to children read aloud*. Washington, DC: U.S. Department of Education, National Center for Education Statistics.

Rasinski, T. (1989). Fluency for everyone: Incorporating fluency instruction in the classroom. *The Reading Teacher, 42*(9), 690–693.

Samuels, S.J. (2007). The DIBELS tests: Is speed of barking at print what we really mean by reading fluency? *Reading Research Quarterly, 42*(4), 563–566.

Shinn, M.R., & Shinn, M.M. (2002). *AIMSweb training workbook: Administration and scoring of reading curriculum-based measurement (R-CBM) for use in general outcome measurement*. Eden Prairie, MN: Edformation. Retrieved December 7, 2008, from www.aimsweb.com/uploads/pdfs/scoring_rcbm.pdf

Stahl, S., & Kuhn, M. (2002). Making it sound like language: Developing fluency. *The Reading Teacher, 55*(6), 582–584.

Tierney, R.J., & Thome, C. (2006). Is DIBELS leading us down the wrong path? In K.S. Goodman (Ed.), *The truth about DIBELS: What it is, what it does* (pp. 50–59). Portsmouth, NH: Heinemann.

Torgesen, J.K. (2000). Individual differences in response to early interventions in reading: The lingering problem of treatment resisters. *Learning Disabilities Research & Practice, 15*(1), 55–64. doi:10.1207/SLDRP1501_6

Wolf, M., & Katzir-Cohen, T. (2001). Reading fluency and its intervention. *Scientific Studies of Reading, 5*(3), 211–239.doi:10.1207/S1532799XSSR0503_2

LITERATURE CITED

Creech, S. (2001). *Love that dog*. New York: Harper Collins.

Deeney teaches at the University of Rhode Island, Kingston, USA; e-mail tdeeney@uri.edu.

CLASSROOM IMPLICATIONS

1. For many literacy educators the emphasis placed on fluency is a new aspect of their instruction. Based on what you have read in this chapter, what do you believe should be the role of fluency in your daily literacy instruction?

2. How can you implement the specific instructional practices described by these authors, especially those approaches that target struggling readers? Are they too involved and time consuming to be feasible?

3. How persuasive did you find the arguments against round-robin oral reading?

4. How persuasive did you find the arguments against using nonfiction to develop fluency?

FOR FURTHER READING

Applegate, M. D., Applegate, A. J., & Modla, V. B. (2009). "She's my best reader: She just can't comprehend": Studying the relationship between fluency and comprehension. *The Reading Teacher, 62,* 512–521. doi:10.1598/RT.62.6.5

Ash, E.A., Kuhn, M. R., & Walpole, S. (2009). Analyzing "inconsistencies" in practice: Teachers' continued use of round robin reading. *Reading & Writing Quarterly, 25,* 87–103.

Bashir, A. S., & Hook, P. E. (2009). Fluency: A key link between word identification and comprehension. *Language, Speech, and Hearing Services in Schools, 40,* 196–200.

Hicks, C. P. (2009). A lesson on reading fluency learned from the tortoise and the hare. *The Reading Teacher, 63,* 319–323. doi:10.1598/RT.63.4.7

Hudson, R. F., Pullen, P. C., Lane, H. B., & Torgesen, J. K. (2009). The complex nature of reading fluency: A multidimensional view. *Reading & Writing Quarterly, 25,* 4–32.

Lane, H. B., Hudson, R. F., Leite, W. L., Kosanovich, M. L., Strout, N. S., Fenty, N. S., & Wright, T. L. (2009). Teacher knowledge about reading fluency and indicators of students' fluency growth in Reading First Schools. *Reading & Writing Quarterly, 25,* 57–86. doi:10.1080/10573560802491232

Meisinger, E.B., Bradley, B.A., Schwanenflugel, P.J., & Kuhn, M.R. (2010). Teachers' perceptions of word callers and related literacy concepts. *School Psychology Review, 39*(1), 54–68.

Mesmer, H. A. E. (2010). Textual scaffolds for developing fluency in beginning readers: Accuracy and reading rate in qualitatively leveled and decodable text. Literacy Research and Instruction, 49, 20-39. doi:10.1080/19388070802613450

Musti-Rao, S., Hawkins, R. O., & Barkley, E. A. (2009). Effects of repeated readings on the oral reading fluency of urban fourth-grade students: Implications for practice. *Preventing School Failure, 54,* 12–23.

Ness, M. (2009). Laughing through rereadings: Using joke books to build fluency. *The Reading Teacher, 62,* 691–694. doi:10.1598/RT.62.8.7

Rasinski, T., Rikli, A., & Johnston, S. (2009). Reading fluency: More than automaticity? More than a concern for the primary grades? *Literacy Research and Instruction, 48,* 350–361. doi:10.1080/19388070802468715

Rasinski, T., Rupley, W. H., Nixholsa, W. D. (2009). Two essential ingredients: Phonics and fluency getting to know each other.*The Reading Teacher, 62,* 257–260.

Reutzel, D. R., Fawson, P. C., & Smith, J. A. (2009). Reconsidering silent sustained reading: An exploratory study of scaffolded silent reading. *Journal of Educational Research, 102,* 37–50.

Schwanenflugel, P.J., Kuhn, M.R., Morris, R.D., Morrow, L.M., Meisinger, E.B., Woo, D.G., et al. (2009). Insights into fluency instruction: Short- and long-term effects of two reading programs. *Literacy Research and Instruction, 48,* 318–336.

Young, C., & Rasinski, T. (2009). Implementing readers theatre as an approach to classroom fluency instruction. *The Reading Teacher, 63,* 4–13.

ONLINE RESOURCES

International Reading Association
www.org.reading

Florida Center for Reading Research
http://www.fcrr.org

3 Comprehension

The difficulty of making comprehension keep pace with utterances, has been experienced by every one who has superintended the education of children; and this difficulty must be carefully removed, or continue to present a powerful obstacle to good reading.

—W. Pinnock (1813)

In earlier days reading was often taught with emphasis on word recognition and oral reading.... Under this system children may have been 'barking at words' but they were not reading in the modern sense: that is in the sense of understanding and interpreting what is read.

—David Russell (1956)

Comprehension – thinking about and responding to what you are reading – is 'what it is all about!' Comprehension is the reason and prime motivator for engaging in reading . . . . Reading comprehension—and how to teach it—is probably the area of literacy about which we have the most knowledge and the most consensus. It is also probably the area that gets the least attention in the classroom.

—Patricia M. Cunningham & Richard L. Allington (2007)

To understand what one reads is the fundamental purpose for reading. Unhappily, this is one of the few statements about comprehension on which everyone agrees. Past debates have framed both the issues and trends in what comprehension is and how we can best foster it in children. Let's start by posing some of the central issues as a series of questions.

Is Comprehension the Construction or Reconstruction of Meaning?

A traditional view of reading comprehension is that the reader attempts to discern what the writer has attempted to convey through print. According to this view, reading is all about intended meaning. When the principal writes an email, the teacher's task is to infer the principal's thoughts. Clarity in writing will help, of course, but so will an understanding of the school context, an appreciation of the principal's philosophy of leadership, a knowledge of previous e-mails the principal may have sent, and so forth. Other teachers will be attempting to achieve the same goal; and while differences among teachers may occur as to what the principal intended to express, the comprehension process is a convergent one. But consider a different reading task. The following lines were written by William Blake, an English Romantic poet:

> *To see a world in a grain of sand*
> *Or a heaven in a wild flower,*
> *To hold infinity in the palm of your hand*
> *And eternity in an hour.*

Should comprehension of these lines also be viewed as an attempt to *reconstruct* in the reader's mind Blake's intended meaning? Or should we view the reader as free to *construct* any meaning that is based, however loosely, on the lines but filtered through one's own experience, cultural perspectives, emotional sensibilities, and aesthetic tastes? We believe that there is room for both views of comprehension but that the nature of the text and one's purpose for reading are considerations. Regardless of one's view, it is important for teachers to come to terms with the distinction.

Are There Levels of Comprehension?

The cognitive processes associated with comprehension range across the entire spectrum of thought from the simple remembering of facts to sophisticated dynamic processes such as critical reading and arriving at inferences about the contents of the text. What at first glance may seem a relatively easy process is in fact a complex and difficult undertaking that even today is not fully understood. E. L. Thorndike in a classic study now nearly a century old noted,

> It seems to be a common opinion that reading (understanding the meaning of printed words) is a rather simple compounding of habits . . . . In educational theory, then, we should not consider the reading of a textbook or reference as a mechanical, passive, undiscriminating task, on a totally different level from the task or evaluating or using what is read. While the work of judging and applying doubtless demands a more elaborate and inventive organization and control of mental connections, the demands of mere reading are also for the active selection that is typical of thought. It is not a small or unworthy task to learn "what the book says." (Thorndike, 1917, pp. 323, 332)

What are the implications of this complexity for teaching students to comprehend? Some authorities have argued that comprehension is profitably viewed as occurring at multiple levels. A popular approach has been to define at least three such levels: (1) the *literal* level, at which the reader extracts explicitly stated information; (2) the *inferential* level, at which the reader arrives at implicit facts by using prior knowledge and explicit information; and (3) the *critical* level, at which the reader makes value judgments about the text. The practicality of this view is that it facilitates activities and questioning strategies. It also helps guide test developers, who tend to be more interested in assessments at certain levels of comprehension, especially the inferential.

Should We Teach Skills or Strategies?

Another benefit of delineating comprehension into levels is that each level can be further subdivided into specific skills. For example, the inferential level is sometimes partitioned into skills like inferring the main idea, inferring cause-and-effect relationships, inferring a sequence of events, predicting an outcome, and so forth. This approach can make comprehension instruction seem concrete, manageable, and testable. It has grounded core reading programs for decades, as an inspection of any scope and sequence of comprehension skills will reveal. But does teaching isolated skills to mastery necessarily lead to proficient comprehenders? A more recent view is that these skills are like tools. One needs to be accomplished in how to apply them, to be sure, but it is also important to know when and how to use them to achieve a particular purpose. For example, a carpenter needs to know how to use a drill, a hammer, a saw, etc., but when the task is to install a window, the carpenter must be able to apply these skills strategically. Comprehension strategies therefore involve a variety of skills. Proficient readers are able to monitor their understanding as they read and to make repairs when they do not comprehend, by rereading, reading ahead, or seeking outside clarification. They can summarize what they read and make reasoned predictions before and during reading. Such strategies require more than a single skill, and their use will vary with the demands of the specific reading task. As educators have realized the importance of children becoming more strategic as they read, changes in what constitutes best practice have evolved (Shanahan, 2005). Strategy instruction, endorsed by the report of the National Reading Panel (NICHHD, 2000) has taken several forms, such as direct explanation (see Duffy, 2009) and transactional strategy instruction (Pressley et al., 1992).

AS YOU READ

The articles selected for this chapter represent recent research and commentary on this topic. Each has been included here to show the depth and breadth of this topic. Hopefully, these authors will stimulate you to read further in the extensive material that is currently available on the important task of fostering comprehension proficiency.

Connie Juel and her colleagues point out, through a series of persuasive examples, how important it is to read through the appropriate lens. Students are often in the habit of reading all texts in the same way, rather than in a manner that takes into account their sources and the practices used by professionals in particular areas. Next, McKeown, Beck, and Blake discuss two alternative approaches aimed at helping students grow as comprehenders of text-teaching specific strategies and focusing instead on making the content coherent. They describe studies that contrast the two approaches and conclude that one of them results in better recall. Cervetti, Jaynes, and Hiebert explore the reciprocal relationship between knowledge and comprehension. They make three arguments for a knowledge focus and in so doing discuss ways by which reading can become a tool to acquire knowledge, and how that knowledge will afterward be helpful in further reading. They also provide a summary of long-term trends in the merger of reading and content instruction and reading in the content areas.

As you read, consider the following questions, which address some of the primary issues in the role of comprehension in the reading process:

1. In what ways might a teacher's definition of the reading process shape the teaching of comprehension? For instance, if the teacher believes that "effective reading is saying all the words correctly," how would this belief influence that teacher's comprehension instruction?
2. Does meaning reside in the reader's background of experience or in what the author intended when writing the material? Are these views of comprehension the same or are they different? If the two perspectives differ, can they be reconciled?

3. Is it better to focus on general strategies or to help students connect the specific content of what they read?
4. Suggest some ways of jump-starting the reciprocal cycle of reading for knowledge building.

REFERENCES

Cunningham, P. (2006). What if they can say the words but don't know what they mean? *The Reading Teacher, 59,* 708–711.

Cunningham, P. M. & Allington, R. L. (2007). *Classrooms that work: They can all read and write* (3rd ed.). Boston, MA: Pearson, Allyn & Bacon.

Duffy, G. G. (2009). *Explaining reading: A resource for teaching concepts, skills, and strategies* (2nd ed.). New York, NY: Guilford Press.

National Institute of Child Health and Human Development (NICHHD). (2000). Report of the National Reading Panel. *Teaching children to read: An evidence-based assessment of the scientific research literature on reading and its implications for reading instruction: Reports of the subgroups.* (NIH Publication No. 00-4754). Washington, DC: U.S. Government Printing Office.

Pinnock, W. (1813). *The universal explanatory English reader.* Winchester, England: James Roberts.

Pressley, M., El-Dinary, P. B., Gaskins, I., Schuder, T., Bergman, J., Almasi, L., & Brown, R. (1992). Beyond direct explanation: Transactional instruction of reading comprehension strategies. *Elementary School Journal, 92,* 511–554.

Russell, D. H. (1956). *Children's thinking.* Boston, MA: Ginn & Company.

Shanahan, T. (2005). *The National Reading Panel report: Practical advice for teachers.* Naperville, IL: North Central Regional Educational Laboratory, Learning Point Associates.

Thorndike, E. L. (1917). Reading as reasoning. A study of mistakes in paragraph reading. *Journal of Educational Psychology, 8,* 323–332.

Reading Through a Disciplinary Lens

CONNIE JUEL

HEATHER HEBARD

JULIE PARK HAUBNER, AND

MEREDÏTH MORAN

■ ■ ■ ■ ■

Understanding how to think like a scientist, writer, or historian can provide students with new insights as they tackle a text.

Young faces are turned toward 8-year-old Elena. Their eyes are alert; they're waiting to hear what she has to say. Someone has just asked her why she really likes the book *One Tiny Turtle* (Candlewick, 2001) by Nicola Davies. Elena turns to page 6 and says, "Listen," as she reads the first sentence. "Far, far out to sea, land is only a memory, and empty sky touches the water." Her teacher, Ms. Ancova, can feel the magic of the sentence as Elena reads it.

Both Elena and Ms. Ancova anticipate the next question a student asks: "Why did you like that sentence?"

"I can see it in my mind," Elena replies, "the sky touching the water, and then, 'land is only a memory.' That really makes us understand how long it's been since that turtle has been on land."

Ms. Ancova is delighted that Elena is both visualizing images and appreciating writer craft. She makes a note to add a discussion of figurative language to her writing craft lessons and then goes back to listening to her students.

"I agree with you, Elena," states Jacob. "I like how the author makes us see the turtle's size. When the turtle is a baby, she says it's "not much bigger than a bottle top." And then when the turtle is about two, she says it's 'bigger than a dinner plate.'"

"And then," adds Kiah, "on page 21, when the turtle is over 30, the author says, "She's big as a barrel now.'"

Thinking Like a Scientist

"Do turtles get bigger than a barrel? How long do they live, anyway?" wonders Marcos.

"I want to know that, too," Elena adds. "And I wonder how we know that a turtle grows up and returns to lay its eggs on the *exact same* beach where it was born. I mean, was someone there on the beach when a baby turtle came out of the egg and then somehow followed the turtle for years in the sea?"

Not only is Elena looking at text through a literary lens, but she is also bringing a scientific eye to it. Ms. Ancova always seems to be short on time to devote to science and social science in her 3rd grade class, so when a text appears during language arts time dial can serve as a springboard to scientific or historical investigation, she seizes on that link. She says, "You know, both Marcos and Elena have a scientific inquiry. Marcos wonders how long loggerhead turtles live, and Elena wonders how we actually know that loggerheads return to the *exact same* beach where they were born to deposit their eggs. Both Elena and Marcos have turned their wondering into a scientific question."

"How will you go about answering your questions, Marcos and Elena?" queries Ms. Ancova.

"Well," says Elena. "I think I'm going to start by going to *National Geographic's* Web site . . . ."

In her research, Elena will discover that there is some doubt whether all loggerheads undertake this round-trip swim. She will be fascinated to learn that scientists track turtles by putting a beeping radio transmitter on their shells, which enables them to track the turtles by satellite. She may wonder whether they do this with other animals, and that will lead to new questions. She may wonder, too, whether the beeping is loud and bothers the turtles. She may imagine different tracking devices, maybe ones that she will invent someday.

Why a Disciplinary Lens?

Elena views text through disciplinary lenses. Such specific focusing and refocusing gives a depth to comprehension that more generic comprehension strategies may not provide. Although Elena can apply commonly taught strategies like visualization, prediction, or summarization, her deep engagement with the text comes from the disciplinary focuses of dunking like a scientist and thinking like a writer.

Much like a photographer changing lenses on a camera, Elena can home in on a specific literary device or question an author about his or her scientific evidence. Like the photographer, however, Elena, like all readers, can only focus well on one thing at a time. Ms. Ancova knows this, too, so she will often tell her students which lens they might consider for a specific text. When a text lends itself to a disciplinary view that they have discussed in class, she will encourage students to listen to or read the text with that focus in mind.

Before the class read *One Tiny Turtle,* Ms. Ancova explained that they were going to read a text written by a writer who uses lots of great images and that because the author is a zoologist, she includes scientific statements in her books as well. Ms. Ancova encouraged her students to think alternately like a scientist and like a writer as they read this book.

Viewing a text from a disciplinary perspective does not compensate for lack of vocabulary or conceptual knowledge that can quickly deter comprehension. It does, however, give the reader an idea of how to proceed when there is a roadblock. This is one reason that taking a disciplinary stance is recommended for teachers working with English language learners (Broek, Lapp, Salas, & Townsend, 2009).

Take Jenny, a 2nd grader, who could decode text considerably above grade level but whose reading comprehension was limited by her oral vocabulary (Juel, 1994). Jenny was interested in reading about rocks. Yet she was stymied when she encountered statements like, "There are various minerals in granite." She acknowledged, with considerable frustration. "I don't know much about rocks. I wouldn't know granite if I sat on it."

Jenny might not be so defeated if she had a way of thinking through this scientific subject matter. If she knew that observation might help her, she might seek out a photograph of granite or, better yet, find a rock sample. She might stare at a piece of granite and notice in it the shiny reflections of bits of translucent quartz, the flakes of black mica, and the creamy pink specks of feldspar. Even if she could not name these minerals, she could see how granite was composed of them. She might then wonder why these minerals adhere to one another.

What force in nature could twist and hold them together? What force creates that glass-like quartz? Wonder, question, observe, think, question. . . .

There are two crucial reasons to include disciplinary frames in our instruction. One relates to reading comprehension: Disciplinary habits of mind can extend students' reading comprehension by providing scaffolds for thinking. If a student knows that studying the natural world entails careful observation and thinking, then the student is more likely to observe and think about what he or she sees or to wonder about the causes of particular phenomena.

If a student knows that scientific claims involve careful collection of evidence, he or she is more likely to ask for evidence from those who make scientific claims rather than accept those claims at face value. Indeed, students who question and challenge one another for evidence in their text discussions typically acquire the habit of asking questions as well as the expectation that they will continually learn new things (Resnick & Nelson-LeGall, 1996). Of course, what counts as evidence depends on the discipline. In providing literary evidence, it is acceptable to say how words make you feel. But in science, feeling will not get you far.

The second reason to support a disciplinary stance is because of technology. No longer do students jump to a set of printed encyclopedias; rather, they jump on the Internet. To understand how to evaluate all the information that is readily available online, students need to know the standard for evidence in a given arena. How, for example, will a student judge whether an Internet entry about loggerhead turtles reflects someone's desire to save a given stretch of coastline (as admirable as that motive might be) or is based on scientific evidence? Understanding how to think like a scientist, to think like a writer, and to think like a historian can provide students with direction as they read particular texts.

Thinking Like a Writer

In Mr. Salazar's 2nd-grade classroom, the students have been studying narrative in their reading and writing. Today, as they think about how authors write their leads, their opening sentences, Mr. Salazar and his students revisit a read-aloud book, *Too Many Tamales* (Putnam, 1996), by Gary Soto. The class has already taken time to delight in the rich illustrations, feel the suspense of the dramatic plot, and respond to the texts as readers. Now the class rereads the lead, which Salazar has written on chart paper: "Snow drifted through the streets, and now that it was dusk, Christmas trees glittered in the windows." Students talk in pairs about what they notice and then share their comments with their classmates:

"You can tell what time of year it is and where you are," says Cerise.

"Yeah," says Robert, "it tells the setting."

"But it doesn't just say "It was Christmas,'" adds Maya. "You can see the place because he describes what it looks like."

The class reads the excerpt again, and students point out the descriptive language, such as the snow *drifted* and the trees *glittered.* Mr. Salazar then helps students connect their observations to the writer's purpose. "Why might Gary Soto have begun his book with this description?" Mr. Salazar wants his students to understand that writers make composing decisions all the time, and that they do this with their audience and their purpose in mind.

The students decide that beginning a story with a description of a setting helps readers know where the story takes place and enables them to imagine the scène. Next, Mr. Salazar asks the students to give this type of lead a name, they decide to call it a "descriptive setting lead." He knows that building a shared vocabulary for discussing craft will help his students talk about and use crafting techniques (Pritchard & Honeycutt, 2007). He also understands that although getting students to notice craft is a good start, he will need to provide more instruction to help these young writers use the techniques they notice (Hillocks, 1987).

In subsequent lessons, he will provide opportunities for students to try this kind of lead for their own purposes and audiences. He might organize inquiry activities to help students think about describing scènes using sensory detail (Smith & Hillocks, 1989). He might model the strategy of visualization to develop setting, thinking aloud as he visualizes the scène of a narrative he is writing. Or he might teach a technique, showing how he revises his lead to use vivid verbs, as Soto does (Graham, 2006).

As Mr. Salazar's class continues its study of narrative, the students will notice all kinds of things about texts. They will talk about the foreshadowing in the lead of Anthony Browne's *Piggybook* (Dragonfly Books, 1990); the short, suspenseful sentences in Donald Crews's *Shortcut* (Greenwillow Books, 1996); and the simile in Jane Yolen's *Owl Moon* (Philomel, 1987). They will map out the structures of the narratives they read and notice how characters often change through the events in the plot. And they will begin to notice the craft they study in other books they read.

Thinking like writers can support reading comprehension in a several ways. Students become more attuned to writing craft; craft that is closely tied to the meaning of the text. For example, students who have studied foreshadowing are more apt to notice it in their own reading and can use it to support their predictions. Moreover, when students learn how to read closely, they learn a whole new way to talk about and appreciate texts. They see the value of lingering with a text, rereading to appreciate its literary qualities.

Thinking like a writer also supports the development of critical literacy. Frequent discussions that speculate about the author's purpose and audience help students realize the intentionality behind the texts they read. For example, a 6th grade class might read and write feature articles. They might discover that authors of these articles frame their topics in persuasive ways. They might also learn some techniques of persuasion, such as the strategic use of an emotionally appealing anecdote or alarming statistics.

Young readers who are aware of such strategies are better equipped to critique the texts they encounter. As our students move into adolescence and adulthood, they are exposed to more and more texts that aim to persuade them to buy, vote, or think in a particular way. Thinking like a writer can help students critically navigate these texts.

Thinking Like a Historian

We often associate history with memorizing important dates in singsong rhymes, doing a project on a famous American, or enacting a fun simulation of Colonial days. But learning history can also be an opportunity to practice reading behaviors that can transfer into real-world situations.

Stacie, a 7th-grade language arts teacher who teaches a class period of history, is dismayed by the textbook's dry treatment of the U.S. Constitution. She wants her students to appreciate the importance and relevance of this document. So she finds stories of students denied their First Amendment rights and teaches a successful unit. Her students are emotionally invested in the tales of children who were affected directly by the Constitution.

Stacie values her students' personal responses and helps them relate their experiences to the texts, but she struggles with connecting her strengths in teaching reading to the discipline of history. What is new for Stacie, and for most of us who still think of history as learning about what happened in the past, is an understanding that the practice of history is a profoundly literate activity that has an important place in the school curriculum.

History is distinctive among the disciplines in seeking out many sources of information and wrestling with their contradictions and problems to tell a compelling narrative about a human event. Historians are experts at synthesizing huge amounts of texts. But how can the complex reading behaviors of a professional historian help improve a 7th grader's understanding of the world?

First, historians rarely learn from textbooks. We must acknowledge the limitations of the textbooks and non-fiction trade books that are the bulk of our school texts. The reality is that teachers can no longer control the amount or quality of information that students encounter. As Wineburg and Martin (2004) so vividly claim, "Ask any middle schooler with a research project how to spell the word *library*, and you'll get a six-letter response: G-O-O-G-L-E" (p. 43). And herein lies the danger. When a student searches for information on how Barack Obama got elected, for example, many of the Web sites listed contain varying degrees of bias and error. None of them even attempts to answer the question of how such a historic event happened. How can we even begin to help students decipher these results?

We can teach students that texts that deal with historical events often have real authors, as opposed to the faceless authors of textbooks, whose chief purpose is to write engaging, informative, and coherent text. Real authors have motivations for writing, and those motivations affect the credibility of their words. Consideration of the author's perspective, in historians' language, is called *sourcing*. Sourcing is the first and most instinctive reading move that historians make, and that students often *don't* make (Wineburg, 1991).

In this information age, students cannot wait until they are adults to acquire this skill. We can begin this conversation by providing even young students with texts that have a point of view and a visible author. Understanding who the author is and why he or she is taking this point of view is just as important as understanding what the author is saying.

In the instance of the student who searches online for information about how Barack Obama got elected, the historically minded student would make a point of noticing that one of the first Web sites retrieved, "Witness the death of journalism!" it exclaims, is authored by a filmmaker selling an inflammatory documentary about "media malpractice." When reading a textbook passage about the causes of the American Revolution or conflicting editorials about whether the United States should continue to fight in Afghanistan, the historically trained young reader would know that rarely are such complex events a simple story of good versus evil or right versus wrong. This reader would actively seek out more information to attain a more nuanced understanding.

It may be messy, long, and difficult, but the act of sifting through puzzling, conflicting, and biased texts should constitute at least part of a student's experience. This is the everyday work of the historian.

Of course, historians, like all good readers, also predict, reread, self-monitor, and so forth. But a distinctive trait of the discipline is the ability to synthesize vast amounts of text into a cohesive narrative, which is precisely the kind of critical thinking that we want our students to do. Historians are experts at corroborating information across different kinds of texts and perspectives. From them, we can learn how to help students think flexibly about multiple sources of information.

Start Young

We should cast a disciplinary lens over most texts, even when we're reading these texts with young children. Consider how a kindergarten teacher planted the seed for scientific reasoning, including the process of looking at data and forming hypotheses, while her students were reading the predictable text in Amy Casey's little book, *Can You Find It?* (Modern Curriculum Press, 1997).

On each page is a colored photo that shows an animal camouflaged in its natural surroundings. Underneath each photo appears the text, "Can you find the_____?" with the appropriate animal's name included (cat, frog, fox, and so forth). A striped house cat blends into the light and dark patterns of the foliage around it; a green frog perches on a green leaf; a white Arctic fox stands on snow. The teacher asks her students, "Why do you think the fox is white? Why do you think the frog is green? Why is the cat brown with black stripes? What is the big idea here?"

As a teacher, how might you decide which lens to adopt for a text? Take into account the message in the text and the vocabulary load. Think about what students might discuss. Clarify the discipline involved and the thinking specific to that discipline. Give students the opportunity to look at texts through the three useful lenses or science, writing, and history.

REFERENCES

Brock, C., Lapp, D., Salas, R., & Townsend, D. (2009). *Academic literacy for English learners.* New York, NY: Teachers College Press.

Graham, S. (2006). Strategy instruction and the teaching of writing: A meta-analysis. In C. A. MacArthur, S. Graham, & J. Fitzgerald (Eds.), *Handbook of writing research* (pp. 187–207), New York, NY:: Guilford

Hillocks, G., Jr. (1987). Synthesis or research on teaching writing. *Educational Leadership, 44(8)*, 71–82.

Juel, C. (1994). *Learning to read and write in one elementary school.* New York, NY:: Springer-Verlag.

Pritchard, R. J, & Honeycutt, R. L. (2007). Best practices in implementing a process approach to teaching writing. In S. Graham, C. A. MacArthur, & 3. Fitzgerald (Eds.), *Best practices in writing instruction* (pp. 287–49). New York, NY:: Guilford.

Restrick, L, & Nelson-LeGall, S. (1996). Socializing intelligence. In L. Smith, J. Dockrell, & P. Tomlinson (Eds.), *Piaget, Vygotsky, and beyond* (pp. 1457–158). London: Routledge.

Smith, M. W., & Hillocks, G., Jr. (1989). What inquiring writers need to know. *English Journal, 78(2)*, 587–63

Wineburg, S. S. (1991). Historical problem solving: A study of the cognitive processes used in the evaluation or documentary and pictorial evidence. *Journal of Educational Psychology, 83(1)*, 737–87.

Wineburg, S., & Martin, D. (2004). Reading and rewriting history. *Educational Leadership, 62(1)*, 42–45.

Reading Comprehension Instruction:
Focus on Content or Strategies?

MARGARET G. MCKEOWN,

ISABEL L. BECK, AND

RONETTE G. K. BLAKE

■ ■ ■ ■ ■

The importance of reading well has never been in dispute. Reading well not only provides practical tools for communication, for work, and, most importantly, for learning itself, it also helps citizens participate fully in the choices that govern communities and the nation. Yet, reports from research and the larger educational community suggest that too many students leave school without knowing how to read well.

Recent research on comprehension has certainly provided increased understanding of comprehension processes and broad and general knowledge of what makes for effective instructional practice. Knowing the effective practices at a general level may suffice to bring successful learning to many students. But helping readers who are struggling to achieve requires deep understandings of the kinds of instructional practices that affect students' comprehension.

A situation that raises the stakes on what goes on in schools is that struggling readers are least likely to spend time on reading outside of school (Cunningham & Stanovich, 1998). Further, students from lower socioeconomic status (SES) homes have the least amount of language interaction at home, providing them with less grist to enhance their language development (Hart & Risley, 1995; 1999). The consequence is that these students have little opportunity for development and practice of higher-level comprehension abilities, highlighting the need to provide the most effective school instructional practices.

Two Directions for Comprehension Instruction:
Strategies and Content

Presently, comprehension instruction research has come to focus on teaching explicit comprehensions strategies. A strategies approach is prominent in the literature on comprehension instruction and was featured in two major reports on reading: the National Research Council's (NRC) *Preventing Reading Difficulties in Young Children* (Snow, Burns, & Griffin, 1998) and the NICHD-sponsored report of the National Reading Panel (NRP) (2000). However, although a large body of research on strategies instruction has accumulated, a great deal remains to be explained. One reason that much is still unknown is that the studies have varied so widely in the kind of instruction offered, and little appears in the reports of studies about actual interactions with text. Thus, what is it about a strategies approach that has brought about the positive results?

Arguements against Strategies [handwritten annotation]

The issue of what makes strategy instruction effective seems to be reflected in comments that a number of reading scholars have made. The comments speak to the issue of what is essential for comprehension instruction. For example, Carver (1987) has suggested that the positive effects of strategies may spring from more time spent reading and thinking about text rather than from specific learning about strategies. Pearson and Fielding (1991) mused that strategies instruction might not be needed if student attention could simply be focused on understanding text content. Seeming to address this issue, Gersten, Fuchs, Williams, & Baker (2001) suggest moving from explicit strategies toward more fluid approaches to comprehension instruction, centered on getting students to read in a more thoughtful ways. Similarly, Sinatra, Brown, and Reynolds (2002) question whether it may be more effective to teach students to approach reading with a problem-solving perspective rather than to explicitly teach comprehension strategies.

The notion of approaching comprehension instruction as just getting students to focus on meaning is at the heart of an alternative instructional approach. This approach, which we have labeled a content approach, aims to direct students' attention toward the content of what they are reading and encouraging students to work through the text to make sense of it, connecting and integrating information as they proceed through the text. The goal of this process is a coherent mental representation of the ideas the text presents. In a content approach, working through text takes the form of an interactive discussion of text as reading proceeds.

What is it about a strategies approach that has brought about the positive results?

Relative to strategies instruction, fewer studies have been done that investigate a content approach, and none have compared strategies and content approaches. In this article, we report on a recently completed study in which we implemented standardized lessons on common texts for both a *strategies approach* and a *content approach* to comprehension instruction and compared their effects.

For a sense of how the two approaches operate, consider a group of students who have just finished reading a short segment of text. In a strategies approach, the teacher might ask the students to summarize the text and recall what kind of information goes into a good summary. She might follow up a student's summary by asking other students if it was a good summary and why or why not. In a content approach, the teacher might ask what the portion of text had been about, and as students respond, follow up by asking how pieces of information that students contributed fit in with what is being read or why the information is important.

Roots and Current Status of Strategies and Content Approaches

Strategies and content approaches have common features as well as distinctions. Both try to engender student engagement with reading and both approaches certainly intend that students understand the content of a text with which they are working. Both approaches can trace their roots to mental processing models: models of learning and thinking in the case of strategies and of text processing in the case of content.

The notion of providing instruction in strategies, individual routines for dealing with text, arose from work in developmental psychology that had established the active, strategic nature of learning that developed as children matured. Based on this developmental foundation, Brown and her colleagues researched strategies for general learning tasks, such as rehearsal, categorization, and elaboration (Brown, Bransford, Ferrara, & Campione, 1983), and followed by investigation of strategies for studying, such as note-taking and underlining (Brown, 1981; 1982b; Brown & Smiley, 1977). From their work, Brown and her colleagues surmised that strategies might be useful to improve comprehension of young or less able learners (Brown & Smiley, 1978). The eventual manifestation of this line of work in reading was Reciprocal Teaching, an approach that taught young students to apply strategies of summarizing, questioning, clarifying, and predicting (Palincsar & Brown, 1984).

Strategies instruction also finds roots in models of thinking. Pressley and his colleagues (Symons, Snyder, Cariglia-Bull, & Pressley, 1989) trace notions of strategy teaching to theories of Baron (1985) and Sternberg (1979; 1982), both of whom emphasize the role of efficient component processes in complex thinking such as problem solving. These subprocesses included identifying a goal, monitoring progress, and evaluating evidence. This line of thinking led researchers to provide young students with procedures they could employ while reading to facilitate comprehension. These roots led Pressley and his colleagues to develop Transactional Strategies Instruction, an approach in which the teacher explains and models strategies, and uses strategies to guide dialogue about text (Pressley, et al., 1992).

While models of thinking and general learning underlie strategies instruction, models developed to explain specifically how a reader processes text (see for example, Kintsch, 1974; Graesser, Singer, & Trabasso, 1994; Trabasso, Secco, & Van den Broek, 1984; Van den Broek, Young, Tzeng, & Linderholm, 1998) are the roots of a content approach to comprehension. Text processing models take the perspective that the mental processes in reading focus on the development of coherence based on organizing the meaningful elements of the text. From a text-processing perspective, a reader moves through text identifying each new piece of text information and deciding how it relates to information already given and to background knowledge (See Kintsch & van Dijk, 1978). The focus is on what readers do with text information to represent it and integrate it into a coherent whole. A text-processing perspective on comprehension suggests that comprehension enhancement might derive from a focus on continually striving for meaning as reading of the text moves along.

Overview of Study Comparing Strategies and Content Approaches

To conduct the study, we developed sets of standardized lessons for strategies and content around a common set of texts for fifth grade (McKeown, Beck, & Blake, 2008). The study ran for two consecutive years. In the first year the lesson materials were based on five narratives from the basal reader in use in the school district. In the second year, these same story lessons were used again, and we added three expository texts.

The study included all fifth graders from one school in a low-performing urban district. This involved six classrooms and their teachers, two classrooms in which teachers taught strategies lessons, two classrooms in which teachers taught content lessons, and two classrooms in which lessons using the basal reader material were taught, serving as our comparison group. In this article we will confine our discussion to the results from the strategies and content classrooms. The content lessons were based on an approach that Beck and McKeown and their colleagues developed, Questioning the Author (QtA) (Beck, McKeown, Sandora, Kucan, & Worthy, 1996; Beck & McKeown, 2006).

To develop the strategies lessons, we first needed to identify the strategies to use. We considered which strategies had been highlighted as showing positive effects in the NRC (Snow, Burns, & Griffin, 1998) and NRP (2000) reports. The NRC report focuses on summarizing, predicting, drawing inferences, and monitoring for coherence. The NRP report lists comprehension monitoring, summarization, question-generation, question-answering, cooperative learning, graphic and semantic organizers, and multiple-strategy teaching. To select among these strategies, we considered which of those procedures might be most naturally called on as a reader works through a text to understand the content. Our thinking was that readers tend to summarize important information as they move through text; they develop a sense of what may be coming next; they need to draw inferences to create connections; and they may well form questions to check that they are on track. Additionally, effective readers monitor their understanding and take steps to remedy the situation if they do not understand. We thus selected summarizing, predicting, drawing inferences, question-generation, and comprehension monitoring as the strategies for our lessons. We developed the strategies instruction in a three-tiered process of design and feedback, with input from strategies experts in the field.

For lessons in the two instructional and the comparison conditions we followed a similar format that we scripted for the teachers. We chose stopping places in the text, which were very similar across the approaches, and developed questions for the teacher to pose (in the case of content and the comparison) and procedures to prompt students to implement a specific strategy for the strategies condition. The scripts also included suggestions on following up student responses, in case students did not address key information in their initial responses.

A stop in a strategies lesson, for example, might begin with the teacher saying, "This is a good place to stop and summarize." After a student responds, follow-up prompts suggested for the teacher include: "Was that a good summary?" to have other students evaluate and add or revise, and "What do we do when we summarize?" to have students review the thinking that goes into summarizing. At a stop in a content lesson a teacher might ask, "What just happened?" with a follow-up provided in case key information was not elicited, such as, "Why might that be important?" The lessons were presented over nine weeks.

The strength of our design was that instructional conditions were held constant except for the issue of interest. Thus, both the strategies and content conditions featured whole-class, teacher-led instruction with interspersed reading and discussion. Text was read aloud and student responses were elicited, acknowledged, and dealt with by the teacher to help students focus on both the task at hand of understanding the text and encouraging students to internalize a way of dealing with text. The key difference in the approaches was the kind of prompts that the teachers posed to students during reading. In the strategies condition the teacher focused on getting students to interact with the text by applying strategies, and in the content condition, teacher prompts focused on getting students to grasp important ideas and events in the text and how they were connected.

Measures and Outcomes

We used a variety of measures to assess the outcomes of the lesson conditions that were aimed to capture different aspects of the comprehension process. This included a comprehension test for each lesson's text based on Royer's sentence verification technique (SVT) (Royer, Hastings, & Hook, 1979), recall of texts used in the lessons, recall of a transfer text, and a comprehension-monitoring task.

The SVT required students to discriminate sentence-level paraphrases and inferences of text content from false instances of the content. Thus, the measure was more text-bound and called for recognition and matching of text content with assessment items. The text recall called for a constructed response, which requires a reader to bring forth information from memory, decide which information to include in the recall, and put that information into language.

Recall of the transfer text had similar requirements but also assessed the degree to which students were able to take advantage of the scaffolding of the reading process provided for lesson texts when directing their own processing. This task was designed to follow a sequence of lessons in which the teacher gradually released responsibility for scaffolding comprehension to the students. The final two lessons in the sequence, the fourth and fifth, provided for no discussion at all, but simply teacher prompts for students to deal with the text as they had been doing in lessons. Recall was taken on the fifth and final text. Finally the comprehension-monitoring task measured a specific aspect of comprehension, the ability to identify potential obstacles to comprehension, by presenting texts to students individually that contained anomalies and asking students whether segments of the text made sense or presented any confusing information.

The outcomes of our analyses showed no differences between students in the instructional conditions on the comprehension-monitoring task or the sentence verification task. Differences were found, however, in recall of both lesson and transfer texts in favor of the content group for both years of the study. At first blush, these differences may seem like inconsistent results, but we see them as offering a meaningful pattern.

First, consider the measures applied to the lesson texts: sentence verification and recall. Sentence verification requires recognition, a less cognitively demanding task than recall, which, as a productive measure, is usually considered to capture a higher level of comprehension. Also consider that scores on the SVT were relatively high for both strategies and content groups. We take this to mean that instruction in both conditions prompted adequate comprehension from students. This was to be expected, given that both conditions provided high-quality lessons and scaffolding. As we discussed, both strategies and content instruction have been found to be successful, and in our study the lessons were carefully designed to provide faithful versions of that instruction.

The comprehension-monitoring task showed no differences between conditions. This measure was presented as a pretest/posttest comparison and did, however, show an overall pretest to posttest gain. Again, this would seem to reflect that students gained positive experiences in comprehension from both kinds of instruction, but the differences between conditions were not strong enough to bring about differential effects on texts that were well-removed from the classroom context of scaffolded lessons.

The differences in recall suggest that for higher levels of comprehension under conditions close to the learning condition, the kind of discussion fostered in the content lessons provided advantages for the students. Recall of lesson texts was directly influenced by the lesson discussion. The transfer task provided a measure of *proximal* transfer, in that it was not directly influenced by a structured lesson, but provided a similar but more generalized pattern of guidance.

Discussion

What are the roots of the benefits that occurred for the content group in text recall? An answer appears to lie in the nature of discussion prompted by the content lessons. Analysis of the discussions showed several features that may underlie the recall results. First, lesson discussions in the content classrooms included more information that was directly related to the text than the strategies discussions. Second, content students' contributions to discussions averaged twice as long as those in strategies classrooms.

Examination of transcripts of the discussions suggests how these differences may relate to the recall advantages. We consider aspects of discussions about two of the texts from one of the classrooms in each condition for that purpose. The first text is a story by Isaac Asimov, *The Fun They Had* (Asimov, 2005), about children in the future, the year 2157. In the first segment of the text, the children discover an old printed book and are stunned by it because "the words stand still" in contrast to the books they read on their television screens. In the strategies classroom, the teacher opens discussion of this segment by focusing on comprehension monitoring, asking if anything might be confusing. A student identifies a line of text that may offer confusion: "on the page headed May 17, 2157." When the teacher follows up by asking what the student could do to help herself understand 2157, the student replies with a strategic procedure: "Ask a question." Another student offers a way to address the confusion, but he frames it hypothetically: "Maybe you could, like, to tell if it's a date or what—just like if it's a date, you could see how many years from now it is."

Another student identifies a confusing aspect of the text, and when asked how he cleared up the confusion, the student also replies procedurally: "Ask a question, read on, reread." Although the students in this discussion select important concepts from the text, for the most part the concepts are not used for building meaning; rather they are treated as instances of how a strategy *could be* applied.

In the content classroom, the discussion for this segment begins with the teacher asking, "So what's this all about?" A student provides a ninety-six-word summary of the text segment in her own words, describing how the book the children found is different from those future children's experiences. Another student then weighs in, adding other relevant ideas, including that in this future time "They don't read books. They read, like, on television screens and they're shocked because the book is really old." As discussion proceeds, the teacher integrates student responses, and another student adds further elaboration.

In an example from another text, the classes are reading a story about a fifth-grade girl who is running for president of her class (*Off and Running*, Soto, 2005). In the segment in focus, the girl is looking for someone famous to endorse her campaign, and her mother tells her about a relative who was mayor of a Mexican town. The discussion in the strategies classroom begins with the teacher asking for a summary. When no student responds, the teacher asks what to do to form a summary. A student responds that it is the *who, what, when, where, why,* and *how* of the story. For the rest of the discussion the students respond to the teachers' prompts for the *who, what,* and *where* with brief, direct answers.

In the content classroom, the teacher asks, "What just happened?" A student begins to describe this new character who had been a mayor. Another student chimes in to clarify the woman's relationship to the girl. The first student continues, providing a fifty-five-word description of the events of the segment. The teacher then asks how this connects and a student responds appropriately and, again, at some length.

The discussions of the two texts show a similar pattern in that the strategies class focuses on aspects of strategy application while the content class focuses on text ideas and how they fit together. The pattern of discussion suggests that teacher questions that encourage students to express and integrate what they've understood from text supports the development of a coherent understanding, as evidenced by their higher quality recalls of text. As the foregoing examples typify, the discussions in the content classrooms seem to provide a kind of external model of comprehension, characterized by going through text, selecting what is important, and connecting those ideas to build understanding. Strategy prompts create a path that is not directly into the text, but once removed, going first through components of the strategy (e.g., *who, what, when, where*) or generalized ways to deal with text content and issues (e.g., ask a question, reread).

Strategy prompts create a path that is not directly into the text, but once removed. That is, rather than directing students' attention to the content of the text, strategy prompts may ask students to focus on components of a strategy, such as considering *who, what, when,* and *where* to create a summary. Or prompts may ask students to think about general ways to deal with text, such as that a reader might ask a question, or reread to resolve confusion.

The results of our study seem to bring into focus the question of what is the active processing that is at the heart of the rationale for both strategies and content instruction. For strategies instruction, active processing comprises conscious and deliberate attention to the process, while for content it is more of an active stance—consciousness that a process exists and that active effort is needed to bring about understanding. Our findings suggest that getting students to actively build meaning while reading does not necessitate knowledge of and focus on specific strategies, but rather it may simply require attention to text content in ways that promote selecting important ideas and establishing connections between them.

REFERENCES

Asimov, I. (2005). The fun they had. In *Trophies distant voyages* (pp. 584–592). Chicago, IL: Harcourt.

Baron, J. (1985). *Rationality and intelligence*. Cambridge, England: Cambridge University Press.

Beck, I. L., & McKeown, M. G. (2006). *Improving comprehension with Questioning the Author: A fresh and expanded view of a powerful approach*. New York, NY: Scholastic.

Beck, I. L., McKeown, M. G., Sandora, C., Kucan, L., & Worthy, J. (1996). Questioning the author: A year-long classroom implementation to engage students with text. *Elementary School Journal, 96*(4), 385–414.

Brown, A. L. (1981). Metacognition and reading and writing: The development and facilitation of selective attention strategies for learning from texts. In M. L. Kamil (Ed.), *Directions in reading: Research and instruction*. Washington, DC: National Reading Conference.

Brown, A. L. (1982b). Learning to learn how to read. In J. Langer & T. Smith-Burke (Eds.), *Reader meets author, bridging the gap: A psycholinguistic and social linguistic perspective*. Newark, NJ: Dell.

Brown, A. L., & Smiley, S. S. (1977). Rating the importance of structural units of prose passages: A problem of metacognitive development. *Child Development, 48*, 1–8.

Brown, A. L., & Smiley, S. S. (1978). The development of strategies for studying texts. *Child Development, 49*, 1076–1088.

Brown, A. L., Bransford, J. D., Ferrara, R. A., & Campione, J. C. (1983). Learning, remembering, and understanding. In J. H. Flavell & E. M. Markman (Eds.), *Handbook of child psychology* (4th ed., pp. 77–166). New York, NY: Wiley Press.

Carver, R. P. (1987). Should reading comprehension skills be taught? In J. E. Readance & R. S. Baldwin (Eds.), *Research in literacy: Merging perspectives* (Thirty-sixth yearbook of the National Reading Conference, pp. 115–126). Rochester, NY: National Reading Conference.

Cunningham A. E., & Stanovich, K. E. (1998). What reading does for the mind. *American Educator, 22*(1–2), 8–15.

Gersten, R., Fuchs, L., Williams, J. P., & Baker, S. (2001). Teaching reading comprehension strategies to students with learning disabilities. *Review of Educational Research 71*(2), 279–320.

Graesser, A. G., Singer, M., & Trabasso, T. (1994). Constructing inferences during narrative text comprehension. *Psychological Review, 101*, 371–395.

Hart, B., & Risley, T. (1995). *Meaningful differences*. Baltimore: Paul H. Brookes.

Hart, B., & Risley, T. (1999). *The social world of children learning to talk*. Baltimore, MD: Brookes Publishing Co.

Kintsch, W. (1974). *The representation of meaning in memory*. Hillsdale, NJ: Erlbaum.

Kintsch, W., & van Dijk, T. A. (1978). Toward a model of text comprehension and production. *Psychological Review, 85*(5), 363–394.

McKeown, M. G., Beck, I. L., & Blake, R. G. K., (in press). Rethinking reading com-prehension instruction: A comparison of instruction for strategies and content approaches. *Reading Research Quarterly*.

National Reading Panel (2000). *Teaching children to read: An evidence-based assessment of the scientific research literature on reading and its implications for reading instruction*. Washington, DC: National Institute of Child Health & Human Development.

Palincsar, A. S., & Brown, A. L. (1984). Reciprocal teaching of comprehension-fostering and comprehension-monitoring activities. *Cognition and Instruction, 2,* 117–175.

Pearson, P. D., & Fielding, L. (1991). Comprehension instruction. In R. Barr, M. Kamil, P. Mosenthal, & P. D. Pearson (Eds.), *Handbook of reading research* (Vol. 2, pp. 815–860). New York, NY: Longman.

Pressley, M., El-Dinary, P. B., Gaskins, I., Schuder, T., Bergman, J. L., Almasi, J., & Brown, R. (1992). Beyond direct explanation: Transactional instruction of reading comprehension strategies. *Elementary School Journal, 92*(5), 513–555.

Royer, J. M., Hastings, C. N., & Hook, C. (1979). A sentence verification technique for measuring reading comprehension. *Journal of Reading Behavior, 11,* 355–363.

Sinatra, G. M., Brown, K. J., & Reynolds, R. (2002). Implications of cognitive resource allocation for comprehension strategies instruction. In C. C. Block & M. Pressley (Eds.), *Comprehension instruction: Research-based best practices* (pp. 62–76). New York, NY: Guilford Press.

Snow, C. E., Burns, M. S., & Griffin, P. (1998). *Preventing reading difficulties in young children.* Washington, DC: National Academy Press.

Soto, G. (2005). Off and Running. In *Trophies distant voyages* (pp. 492–506). Chicago, IL: Harcourt.

Sternberg, R. J. (1979). The nature of mental abilities. *American Psychologist, 34,* 214–230.

Sternberg, R. J. (1982). A componential approach to intellectual development. In R. J. Sternberg (Ed.), *Advances in the psychology of human intelligence*, Vol. 1. Hillsdale, NJ: Erlbaum & Associates.

Symons, S., Snyder, B. L., Cariglia-Bull, T., & Pressley, M. (1989). Why be optimistic about cognitive strategy instruction? In C. McCormick, G. Miller, & M. Pressley (Eds.), *Cognitive strategy research: From basic research to educational applications.* New York, NY: Springer-Verlag.

Trabasso, T., Secco, T., & van den Broek, P. W. (1984). Casual cohesion and story coherence. In H. Mandl, N. L. Stein, & T. Trabasso (Eds.), *Learning and comprehension of text* (pp. 83–111). Hillsdale, NJ: Erlbaum.

Van den Broek, P., Young, M., Tzeng, Y., & Linderholm, T. (1998). The landscape model of reading: Inferences and the on-line construction of a memory representation. In H. van Oostendorp & S. R. Goldman (Eds.), *The construction of mental representations during reading* (pp. 71–98). Mahwah, NJ: Erlbaum.

Margaret G. McKeown, Ph.D., is a Clinical Professor of Education and Senior Scientist at the Learning Research and Development Center, University of Pittsburgh. Dr. McKeown's work focuses on reading comprehension and vocabulary. She received her PhD in education from the University of Pittsburgh. She is the codeveloper, with Isabel Beck, of Questioning the Author and robust vocabulary instruction. Before her career in research, Dr. McKeown taught reading in elementary school.

Isabel L. Beck, Ph.D., is Professor Emerita at the University of Pittsburgh. Dr. Beck has conducted extensive research on decoding, vocabulary, and comprehension, and has published many journal articles and several books on these topics. She received her PhD in education from the University of Pittsburgh. Her work has been acknowledged by awards from the National Reading Conference, the International Reading Association, and the American Federation of Teachers. Most recently she was elected to the National Academy of Education.

Ronette G. K. Blake is a Research Specialist at the Learning Research and Development Center at the University of Pittsburgh. She received a B.S. from Carnegie Mellon University and is currently working on a Master's degree in Applied Developmental Psychology at the University of Pittsburgh.

Correspondence may be sent to Margaret G. McKeown, Ph.D., Senior Scientist Learning Research and Development Center, Clinical Professor, School of Education, 3939 O'Hara St., University of Pittsburgh, Pittsburgh, PA 15260. e-mail: mckeown@pitt.edu

Increasing Opportunities to Acquire Knowledge Through Reading

GINA N. CERVETTI

CAROLYN A. JAYNES, AND

ELFRIEDA H. HIEBERT

■ ■ ■ ■ ■

The way in which students spend their time in American elementary classrooms has changed substantially over the past decade as a result of new educational policies (No Child Left Behind [NCLB], U.S. Department of Education, 2001). The nature and magnitude of these changes is evident in the findings of two recent studies that report that students are spending more time in reading/language arts and mathematics instruction than was the case a decade ago (Dorph et al., 2007; McMurrer, 2008). Whereas elementary teachers had previously been devoting an average of 2 hours a week to science instruction, 80% of the teachers studied by Dorph et al. (2007) reported allocating an hour a week to science, and another 16% reported spending no time in science. The gap between the literacy proficiencies of many American students and the complex literacy demands of the information age has resulted in a decade of policies that require that more time be spent in reading/language arts instruction for students not meeting standards. If students aren't reading well, policymakers reason, they should be spending more time learning to read. The phase of learning to read has been conceptualized as primarily a narrative experience that focuses on the learning of linguistic content (e.g., phonemes) and of reading strategies (e.g., summarizing main ideas).

The perspective that we will develop in this chapter is counter to this commonplace interpretation of what beginning and struggling readers need. We will argue that an important part of the reading experience for all students—but particularly struggling readers—is to read to acquire knowledge. We are not suggesting that beginning and struggling readers do not require exposure to and experiences with information about the alphabetic system; nor are we suggesting that narratives have no place in the early reading curriculum. But we will argue that acquiring knowledge is an important and currently neglected part of reading development. Acquiring information through text, we will demonstrate, serves as a powerful incentive for reading and writing. Increasing the amount of instructional time devoted to reading skills while decreasing opportunities to use reading and writing to learn about the physical and social world may serve to decrease involvement and expertise in reading. In addition, knowledge is critically important for continued reading, learning, and school achievement, and so reading instruction should be viewed as one context in which to build this knowledge. Delaying involvement with the compelling information of science and the social studies until students can "read well" may have the unintended consequence of making the poor even poorer while the rich get richer (Stanovich, 1986). We suggest that the integration of *page*

literacy and content-area instruction is a potentially effective way to create an engaging knowledge-supportive context for learning to read as well as necessary for students' acquisition of critical bodies of knowledge.

In this chapter, we develop a model of integrated content-area and literacy learning in three phases. First, we review scholarship to establish how knowledge acquisition affects comprehension and how it is affected, in turn, by reading experiences. The second section of the chapter presents prior efforts in which language and literacy processes have been integrated or combined with content-area learning goals. Finally, we present theory and research for integrated instruction where knowledge acquisition is in the foreground and reading processes are developed in the service of that knowledge acquisition.

Knowledge Building as a Goal of Literacy Instruction

The model in Figure 1 demonstrates the cyclical relationship between knowledge and comprehension. Comprehension depends on background knowledge. Since knowledge begets more knowledge, comprehending the information in texts serves as the context for obtaining and elaborating upon knowledge. This section of the chapter describes the research on the processes depicted in this model: the manner in which knowledge is developed through literacy and the manner in which knowledge supports comprehension. Underlying these processes is the relevance or authenticity of knowledge acquisition in students' learning.

Developing Knowledge

In the context of discussing the relationship between school funding and educational opportunity, Neuman and Celano (2006) argue the significance of the knowledge gap between low-income and middle-income children. They suggest not only that knowledge leads to more knowledge—those who have access to information read more, have higher-level conversations, and more continued educational opportunities—but also that the knowledge gap is associated with quality-of-life differences, including health and crime prevention.

We know a great deal about the strong relationship between background knowledge and school learning (e.g., Alao & Guthrie, 1999; Hailikari, Nevgi, & Komulainen, 2008): the more people know about something, the more likely they will learn something new about it. This work also suggests that learning that is not connected to existing knowledge is more likely to be forgotten. Dochy, Segers, and Buehl (1999) reported

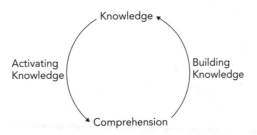

FIGURE 1　**Model of reciprocity between knowledge and comprehension.**

that more than 90% of the studies examining the contribution of prior knowledge to learning have found a positive effect and that prior knowledge generally explains 30–60% percent of the variance in performance on outcome measures of learning.

Given this relationship between background knowledge and academic achievement, Marzano (2004) suggests that enhancing knowledge should be at the top of any list of interventions to support students' academic achievement. The most obvious way to enhance students' world knowledge is to provide knowledge-enriching experiences in school; yet, literacy programs have long missed the opportunity to use reading, writing, and speaking as tools for developing knowledge (Marzano, 2004; Neuman & Celano, 2006). While literacy educators have suggested that reading instruction is enhanced by attention to content (Chall & Snow, 1988), literacy programs have largely emphasized the teaching of process (how) to the exclusion of content (what), distinguishing between learning to read and reading to learn (Palincsar & Duke, 2004). That is, literacy instruction often focuses on teaching students skills and strategies for decoding and comprehending text and pays less attention to the content of the texts. As Palincsar and Duke (2004) point out, one problem with this approach is that it deprives students of the information that they might use to read, write, and think.

Using discipline-based knowledge development as a context for literacy learning provides an opportunity for students to practice and apply their emerging literacy skills in the interest of developing understandings about the world that support their future learning. Knowledge, from this perspective, does not refer to a litany of facts, but rather to the discipline-based conceptual understandings that provide explanatory principles for phenomena in the world (Guthrie & Alao, 1997) and that engage students in becoming experts on the world around them. For example, in the project in which we have been involved over the past five years (Cervetti, Pearson, Bravo, & Barber, 2006; Cervetti, Pearson, Barber, Hiebert, & Bravo, 2007), science and literacy instruction are integrated in ways that invite students to become experts on important scientific topics. One unit develops the importance of shorelines as the habitat for innumerable fascinating organisms. Second- and third-grade students develop conceptual understandings that are likely to support their future learning, including the understanding that shoreline organisms have characteristics called adaptations that aid in their survival in a habitat. At the same time, students are learning facts about shoreline organisms such as that seagulls have webbed feet and that pismo clams have hard shells. These facts are grounded in the concept of adaptation, and it is this conceptual grounding that makes this information something more than a mere collection of fascinating facts or seductive details (Garner & Gillingham, 1991). The essential understanding that adaptations help organisms survive guides students in predicting that the webbed feet of gulls aid them in swimming in the shoreline habitat to escape predators and find food, or that clams have hard shells that serve as protection from predators and crashing waves. It is the discipline-based conceptual understanding about adaptation that becomes the readers' newfound prior knowledge that will support future learning—and reading—in this subject area.

Supporting Comprehension with Knowledge

There has been a strong emphasis in the research-and-practice literature in reading education on activating prior knowledge for reading (e.g., Harvey & Goudvis, 2007; Pressley et al., 1992; Spires & Donley, 1998) but less emphasis on finding ways to build knowledge to support reading comprehension. The problems with activating prior knowledge without building knowledge is that it privileges the students who have knowledge already and it depends on the knowledge that students bring to school.

Readers who have more knowledge of the topic of a text demonstrate better comprehension and recall (e.g., Tierney & Cunningham, 1984), particularly when reading texts that require more gap-filling inferences—those inferences that require a reader to fill in details that the author omitted (McNamara, Kintsch, Songer, & Kintsch, 1996). In their review of the contribution of factors such as knowledge, strategies, goals, and interest to constructing meaning from text, Jetton and Alexander (2001, page 19) suggest that nothing exerts a more powerful influence over what students understand and remember from reading a text than their existing knowledge. Prior knowledge has been shown to make a greater contribution to text comprehension than decoding or the reported use of strategies (Samuelstuen & Bråten, 2005) and to make a contribution to comprehension independent of topic interest (Baldwin, Peleg-Bruckner, & McClintock, 1985). Readers with more knowledge of the topic of a text also perform better on comprehension assessments than readers with less knowledge, independent of reading ability (e.g., Recht & Leslie, 1988).

Several decades ago, when schema theory was in the foreground, the research and pedagogical suggestions of researchers and teacher educators emphasized the reciprocal relationship between reading comprehension and knowledge. Schema theory (Anderson & Pearson, 1984) described the relationship of knowledge to comprehension as a cycle wherein knowledge supports comprehension and comprehension in turn builds new knowledge. This understanding of the relationship between comprehension and knowledge suggests that the new knowledge that students develop today, whether from a book or from an experience, is the prior knowledge they will bring tomorrow to another experience or another text. The vestiges of this understanding are still evident in the instructional focus on preparing children to read by activating text-relevant knowledge (Duke & Pearson, 2002).

We suggest, however, that the cognitive revolution's vision of knowledge as the basis of reading comprehension had been only partially realized. Literacy educators attended to activating prior knowledge and teaching students to bring this knowledge to bear on their comprehension of text. At the same time, the other half of the cycle—where comprehension builds new knowledge—was shortchanged as literacy educators moved to literature-based reading programs. While this movement had some positive outcomes (e.g., students got to read real literature), the expanded literacy curriculum has largely squeezed out content-area instruction and, consequently, attention to knowledge-building altogether (Kato & Manning, 2007).

While students acquire pockets of knowledge from wide reading, in-depth knowledge development may provide more benefits. As Jetton and Alexander (2001) point out, substituting superficial coverage of content for in-depth exploration of concepts can form a disjointed and only piecemeal basis for further text-based comprehension and learning. Broader disciplinary knowledge appears to be more powerful in supporting reading comprehension of content-area texts than knowledge of a specific topic. In their study of the role of subject matter knowledge on recall of and interest in science expository text, Alexander, Kulikowich, and Schulze (1994) found that college students who had more content-area knowledge, particularly in the form of domain knowledge, produced higher scores and gave higher interest ratings than those with less content-area knowledge.

Much has been written about the contribution of prior knowledge to comprehension (see, e.g., Stahl, Hare, Sinatra, & Gregory, 1991). A primary way in which prior knowledge supports comprehension is that students with more knowledge can assimilate additional information and distinguish between important and more peripheral information (Alao & Guthrie, 1999). Kintsch and Kintsch (2005) point out that readers must construct a situation model, a mental model of the situation described by the text, requiring an integration of text information with relevant prior knowledge and reader goals. As Garner and Gillingham (1991) point out, "If a topic is entirely unfamiliar, there is no way to relate new information in a text to existing knowledge structures."

In addition, knowledge is needed to understand the relationship between ideas in a text. Stahl et al. (1991) found that readers with low prior knowledge are able to recall as many facts as those with high prior knowledge, but readers with high prior knowledge are better able to infer an organization to those facts and selectively attend to different portions of the text (in particular information that is related to the themes of an article).

In recent years there has been a marked interest in nonfiction and informational text, driven in part by documentation of a genre imbalance in the early grades (Duke, 2000) and by concerns about reading achievement in the upper grades, particularly the drop-off in reading achievement at the fourth-grade level, when students are expected to handle nonfiction texts with increased independence (Gambrell, 2005). Students' struggles with reading and comprehending nonfiction texts have been documented across grade levels (McGee, 1982; Hidi & Hildyard, 1983), and their performances have been found to be poorer with expository than narrative texts (Dreher, 1999). These difficulties, it has been argued, reflect the lack of significant exposure to informational texts in the early grades (Yopp & Yopp, 2000) and little instruction in the structures and functions of informational texts (Duke & Bennet-Armistead, 2003). Students may also lack the knowledge that would make these content-rich texts accessible.

We do not wish to minimize the importance of skills and strategies associated with decoding, fluent oral reading, and reading comprehension. Instead, we want to suggest that knowledge and skills are mutually supportive. Kintsch and Kintsch (2005) suggest that the goal of reading comprehension instruction is to assist students in constructing good situation models from texts in order to understand and retain information. In this view, comprehension requires a combination of knowledge and strategies/skills. In addition, these processes are supported when reading instruction is situated in a meaningful knowledge-building context that fuels literacy development by providing background knowledge for future reading and future learning and that inspires literacy development by engaging students in becoming experts on the world around them. As we describe below, reading about something compelling in the natural world from an increasingly informed knowledge base can provide greater ease of reading as well as a motive for continued reading. In our own work, we connect students' firsthand investigations—of the solar system, energy, and ecosystems—to the texts they read so that they are mutually informing and together build sustained engagement in a set of ideas, yielding opportunities for rich discussions, complex forms of writing, and, indeed, instruction in the skills and strategies of reading.

Building Authenticity with Knowledge

Many arguments for integration of literacy and content instruction stem from notions of increased authenticity and engagement (Guthrie, Wigfield, & Perencevich, 2004a). From this perspective, instruction that situates conceptual understandings or knowledge as the ends of instruction and that positions reading, writing, and discourse as tools to achieve these ends creates the kind of need to know that can motivate engaged reading and propel literacy development ahead.

Reading for Real Reasons.   Several studies have offered compelling evidence that growth in reading engagement and reading comprehension is accelerated when students are involved in authentic reading activity (e.g., Knapp, 1995; Purcell-Gates,

Reading w/ a Purpose

Duke, & Martineau, 2007). By "authentic," we mean reading real texts for real purposes—that is, where the goal of reading is understanding the material well enough to use it for other purposes, such as making an argument, applying a concept in some way, or engaging in a firsthand investigation. Hiebert (1994) similarly defines authentic tasks as "ones in which reading and writing serve a function for children" and "involve children in the immediate use of literacy for enjoyment and communication" (p. 391). Authentic literacy tasks focus on student choice and ownership, extend beyond the classroom walls, involve a variety of reading and writing opportunities, promote discussion and collaboration, and build upon students' interests, abilities, background, and language development (Hiebert, 1994).

Purcell-Gates et al. (2007) examined student growth in reading-and-writing informational text genres. The project infused second- and third-grade classrooms with the target text genres and monitored, among other things, the degree of authenticity of literacy activities in these classrooms. Authentic literacy activity was defined as (1) the reading and writing of text genres that serve a communicative purpose that can occur *outside of* a learning-to-read-and-write context and purpose (e.g., reading for information that one wants or needs to know, such as reading instructions to complete a task); and (2) the match between the genres that students read in school and the actual tasks that those genres might be used for in the world outside of school. Purcell-Gates and her colleagues reported that student growth in reading and writing the target genres did not relate to the amount of time spent reading and writing the genres alone or even explicit teaching of genre features. The crucial ingredient was the nature of the interaction with the text. Students in classrooms with more authentic reading and writing of science informational and procedural texts (that is tied to authentic communicative purposes and an authentic need to know) grew in reading ability at a faster rate than those using texts with less authenticity.

more motivated

An Emphasis on Deep Understanding. A number of studies, including the CIERA School Change study (Taylor, Pearson, Peterson, & Rodriguez, 2003), have found that reading achievement is higher the more that teachers emphasize deep understanding of text rather than literal comprehension or recall. Readers who are driven by a learning goal and engaged in deep processing of information are more likely to recall information from text (Graham & Golan, 1991). Participation in knowledge building, or reading with a knowledge goal, demands a level of involvement in text and a level of meaning making that might not be demanded of reading isolated texts. A knowledge goal provides opportunities for deep processing of textual information, for connecting ideas across texts, and for making meaning of information through writing and, in science, through subsequent investigations.

D. P

In addition, Guthrie et al. (2004a) suggest that conceptual goals for reading increase interest and enjoyment. They point out that it is motivating to develop expertise: to know about something, to learn more about it, to connect it to other learning, and to be able to explain it. Jetton and Alexander (2001) similarly conclude that, while the skills and strategies of reading are important, readers "also need a commitment or will to explore text in a deep or meaningful way." Ongoing investigations of the natural and social world provide reasons to persist in the reading of challenging texts. Learning what others have discovered about the world and sharing one's own discoveries can be powerful motivators for learning to read, write, and speak effectively.

There is some evidence that students are more strategic when reading and writing are associated with a learning goal that extends beyond the particular text at hand. Examining the role of a learning goal orientation in reading, Also and Guthrie (1999) found that, after controlling for prior knowledge, a learning goal orientation accounted for thirty-four percent of the total variance in students' use of higher-level reading strategies, such as monitoring and elaboration. In fact, in the Also and Guthrie study, learning goals was a better predictor of strategy use than prior knowledge. A large body of research demonstrates the association between learning goal orientations and learning outcomes.

Both of these principles—reading for real purposes and reading for deep understanding—are supported by knowledge goals. Approaches to reading in contexts where the learning goals emphasize acquiring the knowledge or skills of another discipline may tend toward a more functional view of literacy, that is, one that emphasizes employing reading, writing, and discourse as a set of tools and processes that people use to acquire knowledge in other domains. Not only do content-area disciplines create a setting in which students can "practice" applying their discrete reading and writing strategies, they also foster opportunities for sophisticated and dynamic enactment of these strategies in the service of learning about the world. When a knowledge goal is positioned as the "end" of instruction, even discrete skills can be taught in the context of meaningful reading rather than out-of-context reading. That is, even when one is teaching skills, knowledge goals keep the focus on meaning and render transparent the relationship between the skills and the goal of constructing meaning from text. As Goodlad and Su (1992) point out, an integrated curriculum can build close relationships among concepts, skills, and values so that they are mutually reinforcing.

The Evolving Relationship of Reading and Content

Having put forth three arguments for focusing on knowledge in reading instruction, we shift our attention to the attempts that schools have made to explore and implement this relationship. Over the past hundred years, a number of educational movements have embraced the idea of combining the development of reading, writing, speaking, listening, and viewing processes with content-area learning goals. In essence, we want to distinguish the approach we advocate—an integrated approach to literacy and content-area instruction—from related instructional approaches that have come before, making sure to emphasize both their commonalities and differences.

Origin in the Progressive Movement

The origin of integrated approaches to reading and content-area instruction is often associated with the progressive movement in education that started in the first half of the twentieth century. The progressive tradition did not separate reading instruction from subject matter instruction (Zirbes, 1918). Rather than isolating literacy skills instruction, many progressive educators believed that reading was to be "organically bound up" with all of the other content-based learning work of the school (Thorne-Thomsen, 1901). Progressive educators such as Francis parker and John Dewey argued that all reading should be focused on the study of subject matter. In this way, the learning of reading, writing, speaking, listening, and viewing was necessarily integrated with and *in the service of* content-area learning. Characteristic of this movement was Parker's (1894) declaration that "in the school all the reading should be a direct means of intensifying, enhancing, expanding, and relating the thought evolved by the study of the subjects. . . . Reading in botany, in zoology, in history—in fact, all reading—should be concentrated upon the study of the central subjects" (p. 220).

In 1925, the National Committee on Reading stressed the importance of *reading for a reason*, characterizing the relationship between reading and subject matter as follows: "The difficulty which constantly confronts the teacher is to keep the reading skills sufficiently in the foreground that they may be improved and refined, yet at the same time make them subservient to the real interests and larger purposes for which pupils read" (Whipple, 1925, p. 140).

While the initial basis for this integrated approach to reading and content-area instruction was largely theoretical rather than empirical, this element of the progressive movement underpinned the Eight-Year Study from the 1930s. The study found that college students who had attended progressive high schools with integrated instruction across disciplines as one of its foundations outperformed students from traditional high schools on standardized tests (Chamberlin, Chamberlin, Drought, & Scott, 1942). Nevertheless, by the middle of the twentieth century, many of the principles guiding the progressive movement in education, including those associated with integrated instruction, were subjected to serious criticism. Some held the movement responsible for producing citizens who were underprepared for careers in science and technology, advocating a return to instruction that emphasized more traditional disciplinary lines. As a result, instruction shifted to more a reductionist and behavioristic view of reading (Moore, Readance, & Rickelman, 1983).

Theme

Thematic Instruction

In the last part of the twentieth century, integrated instruction reemerged in different forms, including thematic instruction. Thematic instruction commonly refers to instruction organized around broad topics in order to facilitate connection making across academic domains (Lederman & Niess, 1997). Some educators distinguish thematic instruction from other forms of integrated instruction that organize different subject areas around narrower real-world problems to form a "seamless whole" wherein distinctions among academic disciplines melt away. We use *thematic instruction* to refer to a broad set of approaches that uses themes as a framework on which to merge language and literacy learning with content-area learning.

While thematic instruction invited subject matter topics back into language arts instruction, its focus was on supporting literacy more than serving knowledge development or content-area learning. In the 1970s and 1980s, the emergence of whole language brought with it a form of instruction designed to make literacy learning more meaningful and authentic by centering reading and writing activities around content-relevant themes (Morrow, 2001). In her review of how thematic instruction found a comfortable home in the whole-language movement, Morrow explains that whole language, with its focus on teaching literacy skills as needed depending on what the children were reading or writing, freed teachers to use different kinds of organizing heuristics for literacy instruction, including themes. With these early forms of whole-language thematic units, literacy instruction remained the primary goal, and eventually thematic language arts basal programs followed suit.

While many basals have been organized thematically since this time, the lack of attention to subject matter-relevant content has long been noted (e.g., Flood & Lapp, 1987; Stotsky, 1997). Even as basals have included more expository text in recent years, attention has not been paid to substantial knowledge development (Walsh, 2003). Possibly in part as a reflection of this, the latest rendering of thematic instruction as it is embodied in basal programs and implemented in language arts instruction often incorporates themes as loose umbrellas for literacy instruction. These themes (e.g., "bears", "water", and "change") allow teachers and publishers to identify materials and activities that are topically related, but the latter probably do not realize the potential of integrated instruction for disciplinary knowledge development.

negative

While contemporary thematic instruction is often a testament to teachers' creativity and ability to build connections across domains, the possibility remains that the connections may be tenuous (Holdren, 1994). Because the focus is squarely on supporting literacy development, activities are typically chosen based on their link to the theme rather than their potential to deepen students' knowledge of the domain. And although classroom experiences centered on a unifying theme may provide students with multiple exposures to related academic vocabulary, such instruction does not guarantee that this is done is any systematic way. Indeed, some research suggests that students engaged in thematic instruction develop less conceptual understanding than they would with more scaffolded approaches (Lederman & Niess, 1997). Although the instructional approach we propose in this chapter centers around topics or themes in particular domains, it considers the goal of instruction to be not only connection making but also building deep conceptual knowledge of the domain.

Reading Instruction in the Content Areas

Reading instruction in the content areas most commonly refers to content-area teachers' providing students with explicit instruction on various "good reader strategies" to facilitate word identification, vocabulary development, and comprehension while reading content-area texts. As early as the 1920s, major figures in education were calling for reading instruction that included specific skills needed for content-area study (Moore et al., 1983). It was Gray (1925) who popularized the slogan "Every teacher a teacher of reading." Recent attention to content-area reading came about in response to research that has documented that students across grades struggle with reading and understanding content-area and other expository texts and the recognition that different reading strategies may be needed, depending on the nature of the reading material and the purpose (Dreher, 1999; Hidi & Hidyard, 1983; McGee, 1982; Moore et al., 1983).

Content-Area Reading Instruction

neg. to content Area reading

It is reasonable to expect that strategic reading can enhance content-area learning; however, it is important to bear in mind that text is typically operationalized as traditional textbooks rather than the broad range of nonfiction genres that readers are likely to encounter beyond the classroom. Consequently, it may be the case that the notion of text in content-area reading instruction is not rich enough to help students acquire a wide range of understandings about content and literacy (Beck & McKeown, 1991).

Alternatively, some curricular embodiments of content-area reading programs commonly take the form of more traditional content-area instruction, augmented by the use of nonfiction trade books (Palmer & Stewart, 1997). As Palmer and Stewart point out, "Increasing numbers of teachers are supplementing or supplanting textbooks with nonfiction trade books" (p. 630). Important to take into account, however, is the fact that making effective use of nonfiction trade books may require supplemental support for both teacher and student so that these new texts are not simply treated as another textbook (Palmer & Stewart, 1997). We suggest that true integration of literacy and content-area instruction can provide the opportunity for students to deepen their learning of the content as they broaden their understanding of, and facility with, the skills and strategies of nonfiction reading and writing.

Use of Nonfiction or Informational Texts

As Duke (2000) pointed out nearly a decade ago, students in many classrooms get much smaller doses of informational texts than the narrative fiction texts that often dominate much of their home and early school literacy experiences. This research, in combination with research documented in the report *Reading for Understanding* (RAND Reading Study Group. 2002), calls into question the decades-long assumption that text is text— that students can and will transfer generic reading skills from fictional literature to other genres of text. The research summarized in the Rand report indicates that, for students to use nonfiction text effectively, teachers need to instruct students directly on how to navigate and extract information from text. Such instruction on the part of teachers, Palmer and Stewart (1997) stress, depends on adequate training in using such texts, especially content-area teachers who may have more limited text-based pedagogical knowledge.

In the intervening years there has been a strong resurgence of interest in nonfiction and informational text. Further, evidence has verified that many students are genuinely interested in reading nonfiction texts (Duke & Bennett-Armistead, 2003; Edmunds & Bauserman, 2006; Mohr, 2006). As a result, many teachers have expanded the number of nonfiction texts in their classroom libraries, basal programs have boosted the proportion of nonfiction selections, and publishers have increased their selections of nonfiction trade books. Most educators will agree that it makes sense to provide students with exposure to a broader range of the nonfiction text structures and features that they are likely to encounter outside the classroom. Even so, simply giving students nonfiction texts—especially ones that superficially address various topics—may be an insufficient means of developing bodies of background knowledge and engaged reading. As we discuss further in the next section, evidence is mounting that experiences with nonfiction texts can be most powerful when they are related to and situated within content-area instruction that has the potential to build students' skills with, and extend their conceptual understandings of several *different* genres of text.

Integrated Instruction that Foregrounds Knowledge

The instruction in reading that we envision is more than the opportunity to read—it is the opportunity to learn *something meaningful* through text and related activities around text (i.e., discussion and also hands-on learning experiences). McRae and Guthrie (Chapter 3, this volume) have described this phenomenon as "beyond opportunity to read." Our way of conceptualizing the phenomenon is "opportunity to learn"—something that we believe is best achieved through the integration of content-area learning and literacy learning. The instruction we envision integrates content-area learning with an emphasis on reading and writing in the context of knowledge development and with a related emphasis on the cultivation of shared and reciprocal processes across domains. In our work on science—literacy integration, we have often used the word *synergistic* to describe this relationship (Cervetti et al., 2006).

In many respects, this synergistic approach harkens back to the earlier forms of integrated instruction from the progressive era in education. In this approach, reading skills and strategies are taught and learned in a context that supports the development of disciplinary knowledge and skills with high level of integrity. Scientific inquiry, reading, writing, and discussing are woven together in mutually reinforcing ways and always in the interest of important scientific understandings. In this approach, the concepts and skills of science are in the foreground. The content provides an engaging and enriching context for teaching the skills, strategies, and dispositions of literacy.

To provide a concrete example, consider an astronomy unit for fourth and fifth graders that we developed recently for the Seeds of Science/Roots of Reading program that manifests our approach (Seeds of Science/Roots of Reading, 2009). In this unit, students investigate the ways that scientists and engineers use technology to learn about distant solar system objects (mainly planets and moons). Having studied many of these solar system objects earlier in the unit, students read about space scientists and space missions and engage in the activity of designing a spacecraft that might be successful in landing on and gathering data about a solar system object characterized by specific environmental conditions and surface features. Students write scientific explanations about how their spacecraft design and mission goals are suited to the conditions on the solar system object they intend to study. They learn about the models that scientists use to study their designs in advance of the missions. They learn about the determination and persistence that are necessary to engage in the challenging enterprise of space exploration. They learn a great deal about the solar system in which they live and the conditions, features, and movement of many of its objects. In the meantime, they learn about and engage in reading and writing scientific genres of text, learn the language and structures of scientific argumentation, and engage in rich discussions of the nature of science, scientific design, and our solar system.

Research CAR

Approaches to the integration of literacy and content-area instruction that foreground knowledge development are not simply intuitively appealing; their efficacy is increasingly borne out by rigorous research studies. This research is providing increasingly compelling evidence that these instructional approaches result in greater growth in literacy and disciplinary knowledge development than isolated instruction (Gavelek, Raphael, Biondo, & Wang, 2000). Two programs have particularly impressive records of research: Concept-Oriented Reading Instruction (CORI) and In-Depth Expanded Application of Science (IDEAS). Each program has accumulated a record of learning outcomes across a number of studies using a variety of literacy measures, including standardized measures.

John Guthrie, Alan Wigfield, and their colleagues developed CORI to integrate inquiry-based science and reading strategy instruction in order to enhance elementary students' use of reading strategies, motivation to read, and conceptual knowledge in science and social studies (see Guthrie, Wigfield, & Perencevich, 2004b). The CORI program uses content goals for reading instruction and creates a highly collaborative learning environment that engages students in hands-on activities and the reading of interesting texts related to the content goal.

The IDEAS project (Romance & Vitale, 1992, 2001) is an instructional model that integrates science and literacy instruction by providing students with opportunities to access and build upon their prior knowledge; do hands-on science activities; read, write, and journal about science; and use a variety of instructional tools to build meaningful connections and increase their conceptual science understandings. Romance and Vitale (1992, 2001) have reported that what seemed to make the IDEAS model effective with students was the fact that it provided them with an opportunity to pursue an in-depth understanding of conceptually meaningful structured knowledge, not just simple or superficial connections.

Similarly, while the objective of CORI is to increase the amount of engaged reading students do, CORI situates direct instruction of reading strategies within a context that allows students to develop in-depth knowledge on a science or social studies topic with a high degree of disciplinary integrity. In both programs, students construct meaningful knowledge and then use that knowledge to support future learning. An important characteristic of both programs is what CORI researchers call "coherence," or the linking of activities and content in ways that enable students to make connections between experience and reading, strategies and content, and among different texts.

While other forms of thematic instruction in reading allow for connection making, the repetition of vocabulary and possibly the development of some background knowledge, both of these programs pursue substantive knowledge goals within the domain of science and use reading, writing, speaking, concept mapping, strategy instruction, and so on to further these goals. CORI and IDEAS not only use the context of science to build on students' curiosity about the world and allow that curiosity to drive reading instruction, but they also establish knowledge goals and a context of developing expertise that drives students' literacy development.

Conclusion

The schism between learning to read and reading to learn has been extensive and long-standing. We suggest that it is time to reconsider this schism. There are many reasons to believe that knowledge development may be the necessary next frontier in reading education. Progress has been made over the past decade in students' fundamental capacity to read, but the gains have not been commensurate in students' ability to comprehend and remember critical information. And the knowledge gap between wealthier students and lower-SES students persists. Knowledge is a necessary and natural outcome of reading, and evidence is beginning to demonstrate that reading instruction is more potent when it builds and then capitalizes upon the development of content knowledge.

Equally important, though, is the potential of knowledge goals to engage students in reading (and writing and speaking). If we want students to persevere through the challenges of learning to read, we need to provide a motive for reading that makes it worth the effort. If we want to inspire students to love reading, we need to give them opportunities to experience firsthand reading's power to expose them to amazing new ideas and communities, to help them explore and explain the world around them, and to answer their questions. Knowledge goals provide motives for reading that go beyond getting the words straight or reading through to the end of the text. Children should be learning real things for real reasons as they read. We should not deliberately delay students' involvement in reading to learn until they necessarily have all of the skills of reading in place. Practicing for years on end without ever getting to play the game is no fun. And there is compelling evidence that those students who view reading as important are also those who like it best (Scholastic, 2008). To ensure that our students develop the skills to participate in the complex literacy experiences of the digital age and to help assure that they become truly engaged as readers, the first priority of literacy educators is to make reading genuinely important to students.

REFERENCES

Alao, S., & Guthrie, J. T. (1999). Predicting conceptual understanding with cognitive and motivational variables. *Journal of Educational Research, 92(4)*, 243–254.

Alexander, P. A., Kulikowich, J. M., & Schulze, S. K. (1994). How subject-matter knowledge affects recall and interest. *American Educational Research Journal, 31(2)*, 313–337.

Anderson, R. C., & Pearson, P. D. (1984). *A schema-theoretic view of basic processes in reading comprehension.* In P. D. Pearson, R. Barr, M. L. Kamil, & P. B. Mosenthal (Eds.), *Handbook of reading research* (pp. 255–291). New York, NY: Longman.

Baldwin, R. S., Peleg-Bruckner, Z., & McClintock, A. H. (1985). Effects of topic interest and prior knowledge on reading comprehension. *Reading Research Quarterly, 20(4)*, 497–504.

Beck, I. L., & McKeown, M. G. (1991). Social studies texts are hard to understand: Mediating some of the difficulties (Research Directions) *Language Arts, 68(6)*, 482–90.

Cervetti, G. N., Pearson, P. D., Barber, J., Hiebert, E., & Bravo, M. (2007). Integrating literacy and science: The research we have, the research we need. In M. Pressley, A. K. Billman, K. Perry, K. E. Refitt, & J. M. Reynolds (Eds.), *Shaping literacy achievement: Research we have, research we need* (pp. 157—174). New York, NY: Guilford Press.

Cervetti, G., Pearson, P. D., Bravo, M. A., & Barber, J. (2006). Reading and writing in the service of inquiry-based science. In R. Douglas, M. Klentschy, & K. Worth (Eds.), *Linking science and literacy in the K–8*. Arlington, VA: NSTA Press.

Chall, J. S., & Snow, C. E. (1988). Influences on reading in low-income students. *Education Digest, 54,* 53–56.

Chamberlin, D., Chamberlin, N., Drought, E., & Scott, W. E. (1942). *Did they succeed in college?* New York, NY: Harper.

Dochy, F., Segars, M., & Buehl, M. M. (1999). The relation between assessment practices and outcomes of studies: The case of research on prior knowledge. *Review of Educational Research, 69*(2), 145–186.

Dorph, R., Goldstein, D., Lee, S., Lepori, K., Schneider, S., & Venkatesan, S. (2007). *The status of science education in the Bay Area*. Berkeley, CA: Lawrence Hall of Science, UC-Berkeley.

Dreher, M. J. (1999) Motivating children to read more nonfiction. *The Reading Teacher, 52(4),* 414–417.

Duke, N. K. (2000). 3.6 minutes per day: The scarcity of informational texts in first grade. *Reading Research Quarterly, 35,* 202–224.

Duke, N. K., & Bennett-Armistead, V. S. (Eds.). (2003). *Reading and writing informational text in the primary grades: Research-based practices*. New York, NY: Scholastic.

Duke, N. K., & Pearson, P. D. (2002). Effective practices for developing reading comprehension. In A. E. Farstrup & S. J. Samuels (Eds.), *What research has to say about reading instruction* (3rd ed., pp. 205–242). Newark, DE: International Reading Association.

Edmunds, K. M., & Bauserman, K. L. (2006). What teachers can learn about reading motivation through conversations with children. *The Reading Teacher, 59(5),* 414–424.

Flood, J., & Lapp, D. (1987). Forms of discourse in basal readers. *The Elementary School Journal, 87(3),* 299–306.

Gambrell, L. (2005). Reading literature, reading text, reading the Internet: The times they are a'changing. *The Reading Teacher, 58(6),* 588–591.

Garner, R., & Gillingham, M. G. (1991). Topic knowledge, cognitive interest, and text recall: A micro-analysis. *Journal of Experimental Education, 59(4),* 310–319.

Gavelek, J. R., Raphael, T. E., Biondo, S. M., & Wang, D. (2000). Integrated literacy instruction. In M. L. Kamil, P. B. Mosenthal, P. D. Pearson, & R. Barr (Eds.), *Handbook of reading research* (Vol. III). Mahwah, NJ: Erlbaum.

Goodlad, J. I., & Su, Z. (1992). The organization of the curriculum. In P. W. Jackson (Ed.), *Handbook of research on curriculum* (pp. 327–344). New York, NY: Macmillan.

Graham, S., & Golan, S. (1991). Motivational influences on cognition: Task involvement, ego involvement, and depth of information processing. *Journal of Educational Psychology, 83,* 187–194.

Gray, W. S. (1925). *Summary of investigations relating to reading*. Supplementary Educational Monograph, No. 28. Chicago, IL: University of Chicago Press.

Guthrie, J. T., & Alao, S. (1997). Designing contexts to increase motivations for reading. *Educational Psychologist, 32(2),* 95–105.

Guthrie, J. T., Wigfield, A., & Perencevich, K. C. (Eds.). (2004a). Scaffolding for motivation and engagement in reading. In J. T. Guthrie, A. Wigfield, & K.C. Perencevich *(Eds.), Motivating reading comprehension: Concept-Oriented Reading Instruction (pp. 55–86)*. Mahwah, NJ: Erlbaum.

Guthrie, J. T., Wigfield, A., & Perencevich, K. C. (Eds.). (2004b). *Motivating reading comprehension: Concept-Oriented Reading Instruction*. Mahwah, NJ: Enbaum.

Hailikari, T., Nevgi, A., & Komulainen, E. (2008). Academic self-beliefs and prior knowledge as predictors of student achievement in mathematics: A structural model. *Educational Psychology, 28*(1), 59–71.

Harvey, S., & Goudvis, A. (2007). *Strategies that work: Teaching comprehension for understanding and engagement* (2nd ed.). Portland, ME: Stenhouse.

Hidi, S., & Hildyard, A. (1983). The comparison of oral and written productions of two discourse types. *Discourse Processes, 6,* 91–105.

Hiebert, E. H. (1994). Becoming literate through authentic tasks: Evidence and adaptations. In R. Ruddell & M. R. Ruddell (Eds.), *Theoretical models and processes of reading* (4th ed.). Newark, DE: International Reading Association.

Holdren, J. (1994). Is "interdisciplinary" better?: The limits of thematic instruction. Common Knowledge, 7(4). Available at *www.coreknowledge.org/ck/about/print/thematic.htm*.

Jetton, T. L., & Alexander, P. A. (2001, July/August). Learning from text: A multidimensional and developmental perspective. *Reading Online, 5(1).* Available at *www.readingonline.org/articles/art_index. asp ?HREF=/articles/handbook/jetton/index.html*.

Kato, T., & Manning, M. (2007). Content knowledge—the real reading crisis. *Childhood Education, 83(4),* 238.

Kintsch W., & Kintsch, E. (2005). Comprehension. In S. G. Paris & S. A. Stahl (Eds.), *Current issues in reading comprehension and assessment* (pp. 71–92). Mahwah, NJ: Erlbaum.

Knapp, M. S. (1995). *Teaching for meaning in high-poverty classrooms.* New York, NY: Teachers College Press.

Lederman, N. G., & Niess, M. L. (1997). Integrated, interdisciplinary, or thematic instruction?: Is this a question or is it questionable semantics? *School Science and Mathematics, 97,* 57–58.

Marzano, R. J. (2004). *Building background knowledge for academic achievement: Research on what works in schools.* Alexandria, VA: Association for Supervision and Curriculum Development.

McGee, L. M. (1982). Awareness of text structure: Effects on children's recall of expository text. *Reading Research Quarterly, 17,* 581–590.

McMurrer, J. (2008). *Instructional time in elementary schools: A closer look at changes for specific subjects.* Washington, DC: Center on Education Policy. Retrieved July 15, 2008, from www.cep-dc.org.

McNamara, D. S., Kintsch, E., Songer, N., & Kintsch, W. (1996). Are good texts always better?: Interactions of text coherence, background knowledge, and levels of understanding in learning from text. *Cognition and instruction, 14,* 1–43.

Mohr, K. A. J. (2006). Children's choices for recreational reading: A three-part investigation of selection preferences, rationales, and processes. *Journal of Literacy Research, 38(1),* 81–104.

Moore, D. W., Readance, J. E., & Rickelman, R. J. (1983). An historical exploration of content area reading instruction. *Reading Research Quarterly, 18,* 419–438.

Morrow, L. M. (2001). *Literacy development in the early years: Helping children read and write.* Boston, MA: Allyn & Bacon.

Neuman, S. B., & Celano, D. (2006). The knowledge gap: Implications of leveling the playing field for low-income and middle-income children. *Reading Research Quarterly, 41(2),* 176–201.

Palincsar, A. S., & Duke, N. K. (2004). The role of text and text-reader interactions in young children's reading development and achievement. *The Elementary School Journal, 105(2),* 183–197.

palmer, R. G., & Stewart, R. A. (1997). Nonfiction trade books in content area instruction: Realities and potential. *Journal of Adolescent and Adult Literacy, 40(8),* 630–641.

Parker, F. W. (1894). *Talks on pedagogics: An outline of the theory of concentration.* New York, NY: Kellogg.

Pressley, M., El-Dinary, P. B., Gaskins, I., Schuder, T., Bergman, J. L., Almasi, J., et al. (1992). Beyond direct explanation: Transactional instruction of reading comprehension strategies. *The Elementary School Journal, 92(5),* 513–555.

Purcell-Gates, V., Duke, N. K., & Martineau, J. A. (2007). Learning to read and write genre-specific text: Roles of authentic experience and explicit teaching. *Reading Research Quarterly, 42(1),* 8–45.

RAND Reading Study Group. (2002). *Reading for understanding: Towards an R&D program in reading comprehension.* Retrieved November 16, 2007, from *www.rand.org/multi/achievementforall/reading/ readreport.html*.

Recht, D. R., & Leslie, L. (1988). Effect of prior knowledge on good and poor readers' memory of text. *Journal of Educational Psychology, 80(1),* 16–20.

Romance, N. R., & Vitale, M. R. (1992). A curriculum strategy that expands time for in-depth elementary science instruction by using science-based reading strategies: Effects of a year-long study in grade four. *Journal of Research in Science Teaching, 29(6),* 545–554.

Romance, N. R., & Vitale, M. R. (2001). Implementing an in-depth expanded science model in elementary schools: Multi-year findings, research issues, and policy implications. *International Journal of Science Education, 23(4),* 272–304.

Samuelstuen, M. S., & Braten, I. (2005). Decoding, knowledge, and strategies in comprehension of expository text. *Scandinavian Journal of Psychology, 46(2)*, 107–117.

Scholastic. (2008). *2008 kids and families reading report*. New York: Author. Seeds of Science/Roots of Reading. (2009). *Planets and moons*. Nashua, NH: Delta Education.

Spires, H., & Donley, J. (1998). Prior knowledge activation: Inducing engagement with informational texts. *Journal of Educational Psychology, 90(2)*, 249–260.

Stahl, S. A., Hare, V. C., Sinatra, R., & Gregory, J. F. (1991). Defining the role of prior knowledge and *vocabulary* in reading comprehension: The retiring of number 41. *Journal of Reading Behavior, 23(4)*, 487–508.

Stanovich, K. E. (1986). Matthew effects in reading: Some consequences of individual differences in the acquisition of literacy. *Reading Research Quarterly, 21*, 360–380.

Stotsky, S. (1997). Why today's multicultural basal readers may retard, not enhance, growth in reading. In L. R. Putnam (Ed.), *Readings on language and literacy; Essays in honor of Jeanne S. Chall*. Cambridge, MA: Brookline Books.

Taylor, B. M., Pearson, P. D., Peterson, D. S., & Rodriguez, M. C. (2003). Reading growth in high-poverty classrooms: The influence of teacher practices that encourage cognitive engagement in literacy learning. *The Elementary School Journal. 104*, 3–28.

Thorne-Thomsen, G. (1901). Reading in the third grade. *The Elementary School Journal and Course of Study, 2*, 227–229.

Tierney, R. J., & Cunningham, J. W. (1984). Research on teaching reading comprehension. In P. D. Pearson, R. Barr, M. L. Kamil, & P. Mosenthal (Eds.), *Handbook of reading research* (pp. 609–655). New York: Longman.

U.S. Department of Education. (2001). No Child Left Behind. Retrieved September 16, 2008, from *www.ed.gov/policy/elsec/leg/esea02/index.html*.

Walsh, K. (2003). Basal readers: The lost opportunity to build the knowledge that propels comprehension. *American Educator, 27(1)*, 24–27.

Whipple, G. M. (1925). Report of the National Committee on Reading. In *Twenty-fourth yearbook, part 1, National Society for the Study of Education*. Bloomington, IL: Public School Publishing.

Yopp, R. H., & Yopp, H. K. (2000). Sharing informational text with young children *The Reading Teacher, 53(5)*, 410–423.

Zirbes, L. (1918). Diagnostic measurement as a basis for procedure. *Elementary School Journal, 18*, 505–512.

CLASSROOM IMPLICATIONS

1. How has your conceptualization of reading comprehension changed by your having read this chapter? In what specific ways might you modify your current approach to teaching comprehension?

2. The readings in this chapter detail a number of teaching strategies. Which of these do you think might be most important in your own instruction? What problems might you need to consider before these changes could be effectively implemented?

FOR FURTHER READING

Allen, K., & Ingulsrud, J. E. (2005). Reading manga: Patterns of personal literacies among adolescents. *Language and Education, 19,* 265–280.

Cragg, L., & Nation, K. (2006). Exploring written narrative in children with poor reading comprehension. *Educational Psychology, 26,* 55–72.

Cris, T. (2005). The power of purposeful reading. *Educational Leadership, 63*(2), 48–51.

Dieterich, S. E., etc. (2006). The impact of early maternal verbal scaffolding and child language abilities on later decoding and reading comprehension skills. *Journal of School Psychology, 43,* 481–494

Ehren, B. J. (2005). Looking for evidence-based practice in reading comprehension instruction. *Topics in Language Disorders,* Oct. –Dec. 310–321.

Manning, M. (2005). Celebrations in reading and writing: An end to pseudo-reading. *Teaching Pre K-8, 35,* 78–79.

Pearson, P. D., Ferdig, R. E., Blomeyer, R. L., & Moran, J. (2005). *The effects of technology on reading performance in the middle-school grades: A meta-analysis with recommendations for policy.* Naperville, IL: North Central Regional Educational Laboratory.

Salinger, T., & Fleischman, S. (2005). Teaching students to interact with text. *Educational Leadership, 63*(2), 90–92.

Walker, B. J. (2005). Thinking aloud: Struggling readers often require more than a model. *The Reading Teacher, 58,* 688–692.

Vaughn, S., & Edmonds, M. (2006). Reading comprehension for older readers. *Intervention for School & Clinic, 41,* 131–137.

Wolf, M. K., Crossen, A. C., & Resnick, L. B. (2005). Classroom talk for rigorous reading comprehension instruction. *Reading Psychology, 26,* 27–53.

ONLINE RESOURCES

RAND Reading Study Group. (2002). *Reading for understanding: Toward an R&D program in reading comprehension.* Santa Monica CA: RAND. Downloadable at **http://www.rand.org/pubs/monograph_reports/MR1465/**

Reading Comprehension (Southwest Regional Development Laboratory) **http://www.sedl.org/reading/framework/nonflash/reading.html**

Text Comprehension Instruction (National Institute for Literacy) **http://www.nifl.gov/partnershipforreading/publications/reading_first1text.html**

CHAPTER

4   Vocabulary

We don't just borrow words; on occasion English has pursued other languages down alleyways to beat them unconscious and rifle their pockets for new vocabulary.

—Booker T. Washington

Perhaps one of the most important reasons why teachers need to pay attention to vocabulary is that vocabulary knowledge is cumulative. The more words you know, the easier it is to learn yet more words.

—Stahl & Nagy (2005)

For I am a Bear of Very Little Brain and long words Bother me.

—Winnie the Pooh

It might have been more appropriate to call this section "vocabularies," for indeed there are many. We can use the word *vocabulary* with respect to the four basic language processes (speaking, listening, reading, and writing vocabularies) or to the domain associated with words (general and technical vocabularies). We also speak of sight and word recognition vocabularies. A global term often used to refer to all of the word meanings an individual knows is *meaning vocabulary*. This is the subject of this chapter.

No one would deny that vocabulary is crucial to the development of proficient readers. Oral vocabulary at the end of first grade is a significant predictor of comprehension ten years later (Cunningham & Stanovich, 1997). The gap in word knowledge between the best and worst readers starts early and grows larger over time (Hart & Risley, 1995), with little being done to narrow it. Biemiller (2004) puts the matter bluntly: "Vocabulary levels diverge greatly during the primary years, and virtually nothing effective is done about this in schools" (p. 29).

One reason it is so difficult to bridge this gap is that reading widely helps build vocabulary. Stanovich (1986) and others have suggested that the relationship between vocabulary knowledge and reading comprehension is reciprocal. On the one hand, knowing more words makes one a better reader. On the other hand, being a better reader generally means that one reads more; and if much of a person's vocabulary is gained through reading, one would expect better readers to develop larger vocabularies. We can think of this relationship as a cycle: Having a bigger vocabulary makes you a better reader, being a better reader makes it possible for you to read more, and reading more gives you a bigger vocabulary. This circular relationship tends to increase differences over time. On the positive side, better readers tend to read more, acquire bigger vocabularies, and become even better readers. On the negative side, poorer readers tend to read less, fail to develop large vocabularies, and find reading increasingly difficult as the vocabulary demands of the texts they have to read increase.

Stahl and Nagy (2005) suggest four obstacles to building a large vocabulary:

1. The number of words in English is very large;
2. Academic English differs from the kind of English used at home;
3. Word knowledge involves far more than learning definitions; and
4. Sources of information about words are often hard to use or unhelpful.

The first obstacle alone is quite formidable. At this writing, the third edition of the Oxford English Dictionary has compiled some 600,000 words, and the number grows each month (www.oed.com). No one could possibly learn or teach this many words. In fact, estimates of the number of words children learn each year are far more modest, in the neighborhood of 3,000 words during each year of school. The arithmetic quickly suggests that not all of these words are explicitly taught. Given a 180-day school year, this would mean teaching 16 new words each day. The answer to this riddle is that many new word meanings are learned incidentally, through exposure in conversation, reading, and other media.

In that case, you might well ask, why bother teaching vocabulary at all? Why not provide children with opportunities to bump into new words through reading and conversation? Wouldn't that be enough? Ironically, there are persuasive arguments on both sides of this issue. On the wide reading side, we can argue (1) that vocabulary size and the amount a child reads are correlated and (2) direct instruction cannot possibly account for the number of word meanings children acquire. On the other side of the issue are two arguments why wide reading is not enough: (1) context is generally unreliable as a means of inferring word meanings, and (2) most words occur too infrequently to provide the number of exposures needed to learn them. Marzano (2004) has suggested that teachers really don't have to make a choice. They can do both. "There is no obvious reason why direct vocabulary instruction and wide reading cannot work in tandem" (p. 112).

In the case of technical vocabulary (science, math, and social studies terms), direct instruction is clearly desirable. But what other words should be taught? We might start by ruling out those that should not be taught. Beck and McKeown (2004) suggest two characteristics that make a word inappropriate for teaching:

1. we can't define it in terms that the students know; and
2. the students are not likely to find the word useful or interesting.

These rules are often violated. We observed a fourth-grade teacher as she violated the first rule. She anticipated that her students might not know the word *scrubbed*, which appeared in the story they were reading. So she wrote the dictionary definition of *scrub* on the board prior to reading: "to wash vigorously." The second rule is routinely violated as well. Some teachers feel they must preteach every unknown word, even rare ones. Biemiller and others recommend ignoring such words.

Perhaps the most productive way to look at the vocabulary challenge is to frame the problem, as Beck, McKeown, and Kucan (2002) have, in terms of three tiers of words. The first tier includes the most familiar words, about 8,000 word families[1] in all. These words are known by the average third grader and are learned incidentally, without formal instruction. Examples of tier-one words are *happy* and *go*. Tier-two words include about 7,000 word families. These words, such as *fortunate* and *ridiculous*, are important to aca-

---

[1]A family is a convenience for counting words. It includes the base word and all derivatives and variants. The family for the word *history*, for example, includes words such as *historian* and *prehistoric*.

demic success. They are not limited to one content area. Tier-three words are relatively rare and comprise an additional 73,500 word families that students might encounter between kindergarten and grade 12. These include content area words, such as *isotope* and *estuary*. Beck, McKeown, and Kucan recommend a two-part strategy for choosing which words to teach. First, content-specific words must be taught even though they are tier three. Second, general vocabulary instruction should focus on tier-two words. This strategy makes vocabulary instruction reasonable. However, one difficulty lies in the fact that there is no list of tier-two words. Teachers must use their own judgment in identifying them. Another problem is coordinating efforts across grade levels.

It is important to note that vocabulary instruction should not be solely relegated to the teaching of key words. Vocabulary instruction also comprises a broader focus on academic language in general.

Academic language refers both to the words and syntactic structure found in school settings and texts. Academic language is decidedly distinct from the language most of us use in everyday conversations. Snow (2010) suggests thinking about it this way: "There is no exact boundary when defining academic language; it falls toward one end of a continuum (defined by formality of tone, complexity of content, and degree of impersonality of stance), with informal, casual, conversational language at the other extreme" (p. 450).

How, then, do we become familiar with academic language? It is unlikely that many of us encounter academic language at home at the dinner table or outside, talking with friends. Instead, familiarity and fluency with academic language requires both wide reading of, and deliberate discussion surrounding, academic texts. Unfortunately, those of our students who most need assistance are least likely to be engaging in these activities. Academic language varies for each discipline and requires that teachers be knowledgeable about how such language is typically used in particular subject areas.

AS YOU READ

These three articles do a good job of distilling the key issues involved with addressing the vocabulary problem. Jane David succinctly frames these issues and presents some of the conflicting opinions that are often expressed today. Karen Kindle discusses what we believe to be one of the most promising approaches, the interactive read-aloud. Although much has been written in recent years about read-alouds, Kindle orients her discussion principally around their potential for building vocabulary. Holly Lane and Stephanie Allen look at vocabulary instruction through a wider lens and offer an abundance of research-based ways that teachers might stimulate growth. As you read these articles, we encourage you to fashion a coherent view of the problem, one that incorporates a knowledge of the challenge with an understanding of the approaches most likely to make a difference.

REFERENCES

Baumann, J.F., & Kame'enui, E.J. (2004). *Vocabulary instruction: Research to practice*. New York, NY: Guilford.

Beck, I.L., McKeown, M.G., & Kucan, L. (2002). *Bringing words to life: Robust vocabulary instruction*. New York, NY: Guilford Press.

Biemiller, A. (2004). Teaching vocabulary in the primary grades. In J.F. Baumann & E.J. Kame'enui (Eds.), *Vocabulary instruction: Research to practice* (pp. 28–40). New York, NY: Guilford.

Cunningham, A.E., & Stanovich, K.E. (1997). Early reading acquisition and its relation to experience and ability 10 years later. *Developmental Psychology, 33,* 934–945.

Marzano, R.J. (2004). The developing vision of vocabulary instruction. In J.F. Baumann & E.J. Kame'enui (Eds.), *Vocabulary instruction: Research to practice* (pp. 100–117). New York, NY: Guilford.

Stahl, S.A. (1999). *Vocabulary development.* Cambridge, MA: Brookline Books.

Stahl, S.A., & Kapinus, B.A. (2001). *Word power: What every educator needs to know about teaching vocabulary.* Washington, DC: NEA.

Stahl, S.A., & Nagy, W.E. (2005). *Teaching word meanings.* Mahwah, NJ: Lawrence Erlbaum.

Vocabulary Development During Read-Alouds: Primary Practices

KAREN J. KINDLE

■ ■ ■ ■ ■

The read-aloud context has proven to be an effective vehicle for vocabulary instruction, but teachers need to recognize the practices that optimize word learning and determine the most effective manner of adding elaborations and explanations during story reading without detracting from the pleasure of the reading itself.

Reading storybooks aloud to children is recommended by professional organizations as a vehicle for building oral language and early literacy skills (International Reading Association & National Association for the Education of Young Children, 1998). Reading aloud is widely accepted as a means of developing vocabulary (Newton, Padak, & Rasinski, 2008), particularly in young children (Biemiller & Boote, 2006). Wide reading is a powerful vehicle for vocabulary acquisition for older and more proficient readers (Stanovich, 1986), but since beginning readers are limited in their independent reading to simple decodable or familiar texts, exposure to novel vocabulary is unlikely to come from this source (Beck & McKeown, 2007). Read-alouds fill the gap by exposing children to book language, which is rich in unusual words and descriptive language.

Much is known about how children acquire new vocabulary and the conditions that facilitate vocabulary growth. Less is known about how teachers go about the business of teaching new words as they read-aloud. The effortless manner in which skilled teachers conduct read-alouds masks the complexity of the pedagogical decisions that occur. Teachers must select appropriate texts, identify words for instruction, and choose strategies that facilitate word learning. This study sheds light on the process by examining the strategies that teachers use to develop vocabulary as they read-aloud to their primary classes.

What We Know About Vocabulary and Read-Alouds

Reading aloud to children provides a powerful context for word learning (Biemiller & Boote, 2006; Bravo, Hiebert, & Pearson, 2007). Books chosen for read-alouds are typically engaging, thus increasing both children's motivation and attention (Fisher, Flood, Lapp, & Frey, 2004) and the likelihood that novel words will be learned (Bloom, 2000). As teachers read, they draw students' attention to Tier-2 words—the "high frequency words of mature language users" (Beck, McKeown, & Kucan, 2002, p. 8). These words, which "can have a powerful effect on verbal functioning" (Beck et al., 2002, p. 8), are less common in everyday conversation, but appear with high frequency in written language, making them ideal for instruction during read-alouds. Tier 1 words, such as *car* and *house*, are acquired in everyday language experiences, seldom requiring instruction. Tier 3's academic language is typically taught within content area instruction.

During read-aloud interactions, word learning occurs both incidentally (Carey, 1978) and as the teacher stops and elaborates on particular words to provide an explanation, demonstration, or example (Bravo et al., 2007). Even brief explanations of one or two sentences, when presented in the context of a supportive text, can be sufficient for children to make initial connections between novel words and their meanings (Biemiller & Boote, 2006). Word learning is enhanced through repeated readings of text, which provide opportunities to revise and refine word meanings (Carey, 1978). These repetitions help students move to deeper levels of word knowledge—from *never heard it*, to *sounds familiar*, to *it has something to do with*, to *well known* (Dale, 1965).

Incidental Word Learning Through Read-Alouds

Carey (1978) proposed a two-stage model for word learning that involves *fast* and *extended mapping*. Fast mapping is a mechanism for incidental word learning, consisting of the connection made between a novel word and a tentative meaning. Initial understandings typically represent only a general sense of the word (Justice, Meier, & Walpole, 2005) and are dependent on students' ability to infer meaning from context (Sternberg, 1987).

Extended mapping is required to achieve complete word knowledge, because "initial learning of word meanings tends to be useful but incomplete" (Baumann, Kame'enui, & Ash, 2003, p. 755). Through additional exposures, the definition is revised and refined to reflect new information (Carey, 1978; Justice et al., 2005).

Adult Mediation in Read-Alouds

The style of read-aloud interaction is significant to vocabulary growth (Dickinson & Smith, 1994; Green Brabham & Lynch-Brown, 2002) with reading styles that encourage child participation out-performing verbatim readings. Simply put, "the way books are shared with children matters" (McGee & Schickedanz, 2007, p. 742).

High-quality read-alouds are characterized by adult mediation. Effective teachers weave in questions and comments as they read, creating a conversation between the children, the text, and the teacher. To facilitate word learning, teachers employ a variety of strategies such as elaboration of student responses, naming, questioning, and labeling (Roberts, 2008).

Analysis of the literature on vocabulary learning through read-alouds leads to two conclusions. First, adult mediation facilitates word learning (i.e., Justice, 2002; Walsh & Blewitt, 2006). Biemiller and Boote (2006) concluded that "there are repeated findings that encouraging vocabulary acquisition in the primary grades using repeated reading combined with word meaning explanations works" (p. 46).

Second, the relative effectiveness of different types of mediation remains less clear. Adult explanations are clearly linked to greater word learning, but it is not evident which aspects of the explanations are the critical components: the context, a paraphrased sentence, or even the child's interest in the story (Brett, Rothlein, & Hurley, 1996; Justice et al., 2005). It is also possible that active involvement in discussions is more salient than the type of questions posed (Walsh & Blewitt, 2006).

Setting for the Study

This study was conducted at a small private school in the south central United States. Westpark School (pseudonym) is located in an ethnically diverse, middle class neighborhood in a suburb of a large metropolitan area. Four of the six primary teachers at

Westpark agreed to participate in the study: one kindergarten, one first-grade, and two second-grade teachers. Cindy, Debby, Patricia, and Barbara (all pseudonyms) varied in their years of experience. Debby, who had previously retired from public school teaching, was the most experienced with more than 20 years in the classroom. Barbara was also a veteran with 10 years of experience. At the other end of the spectrum, Patricia was in her third year of teaching, and Cindy was in her internship year of an alternative licensure program.

Observations and Interviews

To determine the teachers' practices for developing vocabulary within read-alouds, the teachers' "own written and spoken words and observable behavior" (Bliss, Monk, & Ogborn, 1983, p. 4) provided the best sources of data. By constructing detailed, extensive descriptions of teacher practice within a single site, patterns of interaction and recurring themes can be identified (Merriam, 2001).

Carspecken's (1996) critical ethnography methodology was adapted and used to collect and analyze data. Observations were conducted to identify patterns of teacher–student interactions within read-alouds. Following preliminary coding, individual interviews were conducted. The combined data provide a rich description of the pedagogical context of vocabulary development during read-alouds.

Each teacher was observed four times over a six-week period. The teachers were asked to include a read-aloud during each observation and were informed that vocabulary development was the focus of this study. They were encouraged to "just do what they normally would do" when reading to their classes. The hour-long observations, scheduled at the teachers' convenience, were audiotaped and transcribed. Additional data, such as gestures, actions, and descriptions of student work, were recorded in field notes. Transcriptions and field notes were compiled in a thick record for analysis.

Following the observations and preliminary data coding, semistructured individual interviews were conducted. An interview protocol was developed and peer-reviewed. Topics for discussion included teaching experience, understanding of vocabulary development, use of read-alouds, and instructional strategies. Lead-off questions and possible follow-up questions were generated to ensure that key areas were adequately addressed in the interview. Transcripts of the interviews were coded and the observation data were re-analyzed and peer-reviewed.

Vocabulary Instruction During Read-Alouds

The determination that a particular word in a read-aloud is unfamiliar to students triggers a series of decisions. The teacher must decide both the extent and intent of instruction. How much time should be spent? What do students need to know about this word? Also, the teacher must select an appropriate instructional strategy from a wide range of possibilities. Which strategy will be most effective? What is the most efficient way to build word knowledge without detracting from the story? The teachers at Westpark used a variety of instructional strategies and levels of instructional foci in their read-alouds.

Instructional Focus

Categories of instructional focus emerged during data coding. Interactions centered on vocabulary differed in both extent and intent. The extent, or length, of interactions varied greatly. Typically, more instructional time was spent on words that were deemed

TABLE 1   Levels of Instruction

Level of instruction	Example	Explanation
Incidental exposure	I don't know what I would have done. *Curiosity* might have gotten the better of me.	Teacher infuses a Tier-2 word into a discussion during the read-aloud.
Embedded instruction	And he's using a stick—an oar—to help move the raft [pointing to illustration].	Teacher provides a synonym before the target term *oar*, pointing to the illustration.
Focused instruction	Let's get *set* means let's get ready [elicit examples of things students get ready for].	Teacher leads a discussion on what it means to get *set*, including getting set for school and Christmas.

critical to story comprehension or that students would be using in a subsequent activity. Pragmatic issues of time seemed to impact the extent of the interactions as well. The frequency and length of interactions tended to decrease through the course of the read-aloud as the time allotted came to an end or children's attention began to wane.

As seen in Table 1, three different levels of instruction were identified in the data: incidental exposure, embedded instruction, and focused instruction. Incidental exposure occurred during the course of discussions before, during, and after reading and resulted from teachers' efforts to infuse rich vocabulary into class discourse. For example, during one discussion, Cindy commented that the character was *humble*; in another that she came *bearing gifts*. Even though no direct instruction was provided for these terms, the intent is instructional since Cindy deliberately infused less common words to build vocabulary knowledge through context clues.

Embedded instruction is defined as attention to word meaning, consisting of fewer than four teacher–student exchanges. The teachers used embedded instruction when the target word represented a familiar concept for the students or when it was peripheral to the story. Information was provided about word meaning with minimal disruption to the flow of the reading. Typically, teachers gave a synonym or a brief definition and quickly returned to the text.

Focused instruction occurred when target words were considered important to story comprehension or when difficulties arose communicating word meaning. These interactions varied greatly in length from 4 to 25 teacher–student exchanges. Focused instruction often took place before or after reading. In most cases, the teachers had identified keywords that they felt were important for students to learn, warranting additional time and attention. Other times, focused instruction appeared to be spontaneous, triggered by students' questions or "puzzled looks" during the reading.

Instruction also varied in its intent. Teachers sought to develop definitional, contextual, or conceptual word knowledge (Herman & Dole, 1988) based on the specific situation. The learning goal shaped the nature of the interactions.

The definitional approach was used when the underlying concept was familiar to the students or when the goal of instruction was to simply provide exposure to a word. Teachers either provided or elicited a synonym or phrase that approximated the meaning of the target word. This approach can be quite efficient, requiring little investment of time (Herman & Dole, 1988), thus allowing attention to be given to many words during the course of the read-aloud.

Teachers developed contextual knowledge when they referred students back to the text to determine word meaning. In such cases, the teacher might refer students back to the text or reread the sentence in which the target term occurred, helping students to confirm or disconfirm their thinking as in this example from *Sarah, Plain and Tall* (MacLachlan, 1985):

CINDY: Wooly ragwort. Where is that? [looks through text] What was wooly ragwort? Do you remember? It was part of Caleb's song.

STUDENT: Yeah.

CINDY: It said—or Sarah said [reads from the text], "We don't have these by the sea. We have seaside goldenrod and wild asters and wooly ragwort."

Cindy's intent was for students to gain contextual knowledge using the information in the text to draw a tentative conclusion about word meaning. This example highlights one of the problems inherent with contextual strategies. Students, perhaps misled by the word *sea* in the text, suggested that *wooly rag-wort* might be a seal, a bird, or a stone. Since they were unfamiliar with goldenrod and asters, they were unable to use these clues effectively to conclude that wooly ragwort was a plant. In this case, reminding students that the characters were picking wildflowers might have helped.

Learning a definition is seldom enough for children to develop deep word knowledge. Students need conceptual knowledge to make connections between new words, their prior experiences, and previously learned words and concepts (Newton et al., 2008). Cindy relayed an incident that taught her the importance of building conceptual knowledge when working with unfamiliar words. She had instructed her students to look up the word *pollinate* in the dictionary, write two or three sentences using the word, and then draw a picture illustrating its meaning. Unfortunately, the definition contained many words that the children did not know such as *pistil* and *stamen*. It was obvious when she reviewed their work that her students "didn't get it." Cindy realized that the definition was not sufficient for them to understand the concept of pollination.

Instructional Strategies

Within the constructs described above, teachers employed a variety of instructional strategies. Nine categories of instructional strategies were identified during the observations:

1. Questioning
2. Providing a definition
3. Providing a synonym
4. Providing examples
5. Clarifying or correcting students' responses
6. Extending a student-generated definition
7. Labeling
8. Imagery
9. Morphemic analysis

Each of these strategies is described along with examples from the observation data.

Questioning.   The most commonly used strategy was questioning. As the teachers read and encountered a word that they thought might be unfamiliar, they would simply stop and ask about it. This strategy usually occurred at the beginning of an instructional exchange. For example, after reading a section of *Sarah, Plain and Tall* (MacLachlan, 1985), Debby paused to ask her students about the word *bonnet*.

> **DEBBY:**   What's a bonnet? Do you all know what a bonnet is? What's a bonnet?

It is interesting to note that most of the teachers repeated the question several times in their initial utterance. This practice gives students time to formulate a response and also helps to establish a phonological representation of the new word, which is linked to word learning (Beck & McKeown, 2001).

Questioning was also used to assess the students' existing word knowledge and to determine if students had effectively used context clues. Once a correct response was given, the exchange ended and the teacher resumed reading, as seen in the following sequence.

> **DEBBY:**   [reads from *The BFG*, Dahl, 1982] "So I keep staring at her and in the end her head drops on to her desk and she goes fast to sleep and snorkels loudly." What is that?
>
> **STUDENT:**   Snores.
>
> **DEBBY:**   [resumes reading] "Then in marches the head teacher."

Alternatively, the teacher might provide the definition and ask students to supply the term. For example, in an after-reading discussion, Patricia asked students to recall the meaning of *research* to review or assess word learning.

> **PATRICIA:**   And what was it called when they look in the encyclopedia for information? What was that word, John?

This strategy can prove difficult. John and several of his classmates made incorrect responses before the correct answer was given.

Providing the Definition.   At times, teachers chose to provide a definition of a word. Word learning is enhanced when the explanation is made in simple, child-friendly language and the typical use of the word is discussed (Beck et al., 2002). This strategy was more commonly used in embedded instruction, as seen in the following example.

> **BARBARA:**   [reading *Duck for President* (Cronin, 2008)] "On election day, each of the animals filled out a ballot and placed it in a box." Filled out a piece of paper. Wrote down who they wanted to vote—or who they wanted to win the election.

Barbara thought it unlikely that her students would be familiar with the word *ballot*, so she simply provided the definition in terms that kindergartners could understand.

Providing Synonyms.   An expedient means of providing word meaning is to state a synonym for the word. This method was used often in conjunction with recasting. That is, the teacher repeated a sentence, replacing the target word with a synonym, as seen in this example.

> **BARBARA:**   Let's get ready. Let's get set.

This strategy was used extensively by Barbara to reinforce word meanings. For example, in a postreading discussion, she went back and reviewed key events in the story, simultaneously reinforcing the meaning of the phrase *a bit*. Although her focus was comprehension, the students heard the target word alongside a recasting with a synonym many times.

BARBARA: So remember, a bit of blue means—how much is she going to add?

STUDENT: Um—a little bit?

BARBARA: A little bit, right. Just a small amount.

BARBARA: So what happened here? They mixed red, they mixed blue—but it's still red. But why? Why is that Sarah?

STUDENT: Because Sal adds a bit of blue.

BARBARA: Right, just a little bit of blue. Just a tiny small amount. But that wasn't enough to change the color, was it?

STUDENT: No.

BARBARA: Just a little bit, right.

Providing Examples. Word knowledge can be extended and clarified through examples that may be provided by the teacher or elicited from the students. Students learn how the target word is related to other known words and concepts and are given opportunities to use the target words, further strengthening word learning (Beck et al., 2002). Teachers help students make their own connections when they ask for examples of how or where students have heard the word used, or remind them of situations in which they might have encountered a specific word.

As Patricia introduced a folk tale, she wanted her students to be prepared for the regional language they would hear. Although she did not use the word *dialect*, she explained that the language in the story would sound different to them and asked them for examples from their own experiences.

PATRICIA: This is a story from Appalachia and they use a different kind of language. Uh, they speak in English, but they kind of talk—what do you call it—country. Have you ever heard people talk like that?

STUDENT 1: Yeah.

STUDENT 2: My grandma.

PATRICIA: They use different little sayings and maybe have a different accent to their voice.

STUDENT 3: But they're still speaking English.

STUDENT 4: Like New York?

STUDENT 5: England, England!

STUDENT 6: Kind of like cowboys?

Two students demonstrated their understanding of the concept as they generated their examples of New York and English accents. Another student made the connection between dialect and the cowboy lingo the class had learned during a recent unit of study.

Clarification and Correction. Teacher guidance is an important part of the instructional process (Beck et al., 2002). At times, students suggest definitions for target words that reflect misconceptions or partial understandings. The teacher must then either correct or clarify students' responses. When Patricia asked her students for the meaning of the word *glared*, a student gave a response that was partially correct, but missed the essence of the meaning. Patricia's additional question helped the students to refine their understandings.

PATRICIA: What does it mean to glare at somebody?

STUDENT: Stare at them?

PATRICIA: Yeah. Is it a friendly stare?

STUDENT: No—like [makes an angry face].

Extension.   Due to the gradual nature of word learning, students may provide definitions that are correct but simplistic. The teacher may elect to extend the definition, providing additional information that builds on the student's response. For example, when a student stated that a bonnet was something you wear on your head, Debby extended the definition by providing some historical information and describing its function or use.

DEBBY: They wore it a lot on in the prairie days because they traveled a lot and they got a lot of you—those wagon trains and the stage-coaches and all were kind of windy. And so they would keep their bonnets on—to keep their head—their hair from blowing all over the place. Very, very common to use—to wear bonnets back then.

Labeling.   Labeling was most often used with picture book read-alouds. As the teacher named the unfamiliar item, she pointed to the illustration, connecting the word with the picture. Debby used this strategy while reading *Leonardo and the Flying Boy* (Anholt, 2007) to her second graders, pointing to the depictions of various inventions mentioned in the text. Thus, without interrupting the flow of the reading, word meaning was enhanced as children related novel terms with the visual images.

Barbara used the strategy extensively with her kindergartners. While reading *Duck for President* (Cronin, 2008), she pointed to the picture of the lawn-mower as she described how a push mower is different from the more familiar power mowers. In another text, she reversed the process, providing the unfamiliar word *raft* for the boat pictured in the illustration.

Imagery.   At times, teachers used facial expressions, sounds, or physical movements to demonstrate word meaning during the course of read-alouds. Gestures of this type occurred more frequently when the teachers were reading aloud from chapter books, perhaps due to the lack of illustrations to provide such visual support. In some cases, imagery appeared to be intrinsic to expressive reading, rather than a deliberate effort to enhance word meaning. For example, Debby lowered her head and looked sad as she read about a character hanging his head in shame. Although her intent was to create a dramatic reading, the addition of the simple actions would also serve to facilitate word learning if that particular expression was unknown to students. In the following example, Debby provided two imagery clues as she read the text.

DEBBY: [reads text] "There was a hiss of wind." [extends /s/ to create a hissing sound] "A sudden pungent smell." [holds her hand up to her nose]

The use of imagery was more common with embedded instruction than with the longer focused instructional exchanges. Typically, imagery was used to enhance students' understanding of the text without impeding the flow of the story, although in some instances, imagery was used after discussion as a means of reinforcing the stated definition.

At times, however, the use of imagery was a more integral part of instruction and was even used by the children when they could demonstrate a word meaning more easily than put it in words. When Patricia asked her students about the meaning of the word *pout*, several responded nonverbally, sticking out their lower lips and looking sad. Cindy used the strategy to help her students understand the meaning of the word *rustle*. Although a student provided a synonym, Cindy used imagery to extend word learning.

> CINDY: What does *rustle* mean?
>
> STUDENT: Moves?
>
> CINDY: Movement. OK. What's a rustle sound like? Somebody rustle for me. [students begin moving their feet under their desks] Maybe like [shuffles her feet], like really soft sounds. Like a movement. They're not meaning to make a noise, but they are just kind of moving around in the grass and stuff.

Morphemic Analysis.   Even young children need to become aware of how word parts are combined to make longer, more complex words. Children can be taught to "look for roots and/or familiar words when trying to figure out the meaning of an unfamiliar word" (Newton et al., 2008, p. 26). Instructional strategies that draw children's attention to structural analysis are an appropriate choice when the meaning of the root word is familiar. In the exchange that follows, Barbara drew attention to the prefix *re-*, affixed to the familiar word *count*.

> BARBARA: [reads text] "Farmer Brown demanded a recount." A recount is—do you know what a recount is, Jeremy?
>
> JEREMY: Uh, no.
>
> BARBARA: A recount is—he said he wanted the votes to be counted *again*.

Multiple Strategies.   Teachers often employed more than one strategy during focused instruction. Although questioning was commonly used to initiate instruction, the target word must be either partially known or appear in a very supportive context for this strategy to be effective. Questioning can lead to guessing, so "it is important to provide guidance if students do not quickly know the word's meaning" (Beck et al., 2002, p. 43). In cases where questioning yielded either an incorrect response or no response at all, teachers added additional strategies, such as providing the definition, examples, or imagery.

Discussion

The practices of the teachers at Westpark are both unremarkable and remarkable. They are unremarkable in that their practices are consistent with the descriptions of read-alouds in the literature. The teachers selected appropriate texts, words for instruction, and strategies to teach unknown words. They engaged in discussions before, during, and after reading the texts. Practitioners and researchers alike will find familiarity in the descriptions of the read-alouds.

At the same time, their practices were remarkable. The intricate series of interactions between teacher, students, and text in a read-aloud reflects countless instructional decisions, underlying pedagogical beliefs, and the unique quality of the relationship that has been built between teacher and students. The data obtained from the observations and interviews provide a window into the processes of the read-aloud, providing brief but significant glimpses that have important implications.

There were many similarities noted in the read-aloud practices of the teachers in this study. With the exception of one performance-style reading, read-alouds were interactive with the children actively engaged. Attention to word meaning occurred in every read-aloud, providing evidence of the importance placed on vocabulary by the teachers.

At the same time, individual differences were noted in the way the teachers went about developing word meaning. They varied in their use of incidental exposure, embedded instruction, and focused instruction. Cindy felt it was important for her students to be able to independently figure out word meaning from context. Consistent with that conviction, she most frequently used focused instruction with questioning and incidental exposures, with relatively few incidences of embedded instruction. In contrast, Barbara's pattern of interaction seems to reflect a preference for adult mediation over incidental learning, perhaps stemming from a belief that kindergarten children require more support to learn words during read-alouds than their older schoolmates.

In addition to variance in the level of instruction used by the teachers, they also exhibited differences in their use of instructional strategies. Some differences were directly related to the type of book being read. For example, labeling was common when reading picture books, but was seldom used with chapter books. Differences in strategy use may also reflect the teachers' perceptions of appropriate practice for a specific grade. Both second-grade teachers stressed the importance of context clues in teaching vocabulary. This conviction was evident in their frequent use of questioning and context strategies. Other strategies were only used when an adequate response was not obtained, or when a more extensive definition was required for comprehension. The increased use of multiple strategies seen in kindergarten and first grade may reflect the teachers' beliefs that vocabulary development was an important goal apart from story comprehension.

There may be a more pragmatic explanation as well. When reading chapter books, the teachers seemed to have a set stopping point in mind each day. Completing a chapter on time appeared to take precedence over vocabulary instruction. Shorter picture books seemed to afford teachers more time to develop words and employ more strategies within instructional sequences. This would suggest that text selection impacts strategy use in addition to word selection.

Individual differences in read-aloud practice are significant because they impact word learning. Even when scripts were used for read-alouds, Biemiller and Boote (2006) found that "some teachers were more effective than others in teaching vocabulary to children" (p. 51). They concluded that intangible qualities such as the teachers' attitudes about and enthusiasm for word learning could be a factor in the number of words children learn. Given the degree of variance in word learning, evident when teachers were constrained by a script, it would certainly be expected that differences would only increase when teachers are free to conduct read-alouds in their own manner.

Recommendations for Practice

Read-alouds are instructional events and require the same advance planning as any other lesson. Although the teachers in this study used many strategies identified in the literature as effective, additional time and thought in advance of the reading would have decreased confusions, used time more efficiently, and ultimately increased learning. Books should be selected with vocabulary in mind, previewed, and practiced. Attention to student questions about word meaning that arise during reading is important but may result in extended discourse on words that are not critical to comprehension and can detract significantly from the read-aloud experience. Teachers should select target words in advance and plan instructional support based on those particular words. To increase word learning potential, the following five steps are recommended.

1. *Identify words for instruction.* To maximize learning, words targeted for instruction should be identified in advance. Examine the text for words that are essential for comprehension and Tier-2 words (Beck et al., 2002) that will build reading vocabulary. Look for words that are interesting or fun to say. Narrow the list down to four or five words to target for more in-depth instruction, giving priority to those needed for comprehension.

2. *Consider the type of word learning required.* Does the target word represent a new label for something familiar or an unfamiliar concept, or is it a familiar word used in a new way? Is the word critical for comprehension? These questions determine the appropriate level of instruction (incidental, embedded, or focused); whether instruction should occur before, during, or after reading; and strategy selection.

3. *Identify appropriate strategies.* Select strategies that are consistent with your instructional goals. When the novel word represents a new label for a familiar term, a synonym, or a gesture may be adequate. Providing examples and questioning might be used to develop a new concept prior to reading, with a simple definition included during the reading to reinforce learning.

4. *Have a Plan B.* If a strategy proves ineffective, be prepared to intervene quickly and provide correction or clarification. Have an easy-to-understand definition at the ready. Be able to provide a synonym or an example.

5. *Infuse the words into the classroom.* Find opportunities for the new words to be used in other contexts to encourage authentic use and deepen word learning.

Final Thoughts

Read-alouds can be viewed as microcosms of balanced instruction. This balance does not result from adherence to a prescribed formula but rather from countless decisions made by teachers. These instructional decisions affect the balance of direct and incidental instruction, between planning in advance and seizing the teachable moment, the quantity and quality of vocabulary instruction within the read-alouds, and ultimately student learning. Teachers' perceptions of an appropriate balance are evident in their uses of read-alouds, styles of reading, text selection, and in the way that vocabulary is developed.

The read-aloud context has proven to be an effective vehicle for vocabulary instruction, but further research is needed to clarify the conditions that optimize word learning and to determine the most effective manner of adding elaborations and explanations during story reading without detracting from the pleasure of the reading itself. Identifying the practices that are commonly used by primary classroom teachers provides researchers with valuable information that can lead to the development of effective instructional strategies, inservice teachers' staff development, and preservice teacher training.

REFERENCES

Baumann, J.F., Kame'enui, E.J., & Ash, G.E. (2003). Research on vocabulary instruction: Voltaire redux. In J. Flood, D. Lapp, J.R. Squire, & J.M. Jensen (Eds.), *Handbook of research on teaching the English language arts* (pp. 752–785). Mahwah, NJ: Erlbaum.

Beck, I.L., & McKeown, M.G. (2001). Text talk: Capturing the benefits of read-aloud experiences for young children. *The Reading Teacher, 55*(1), 10–20.

Beck, I.L., & McKeown, M.G. (2007). Different ways for different goals, but keep your eye on the higher verbal goals. In R.K. Wagner, A.E. Muse, & K.R. Tannenbaum (Eds.), *Vocabulary acquisition: Implications for reading comprehension* (pp. 182– 204). New York, NY: Guilford.

Beck, I.L., McKeown, M.G., & Kucan, L. (2002). *Bringing words to life: Robust vocabulary instruction.* New York, NY: Guilford.

Biemiller, A., & Boote, C. (2006). An effective method for building meaning vocabulary in primary grades. *Journal of Educational Psychology, 98*(1), 44–62. doi:10.1037/0022-0663.98.1.44

Bliss, J., Monk, M., & Ogborn, J. (1983). *Qualitative data analysis for educational research: A guide to uses of systematic networks.* Croon Helm, Australia: Croon Helm.

Bloom, L. (2000). The intentionality model of word learning: How to learn a word, any word. In R.M. Golinkoff, K. Hirsh-Pasek, L. Bloom, L.B. Smith, A.L. Woodward, N. Akhtar, et al. (Eds.), *Becoming a word learner: A debate on lexical acquisition* (pp. 19–50). New York, NY: Oxford University Press.

Bravo, M.A., Hiebert, E.H., & Pearson, P.D. (2007). Tapping the linguistic resources of Spanish/English bilinguals: The role of cognates in science. In R.K. Wagner, A.E. Muse, & K.R. Tannenbaum (Eds.), *Vocabulary acquisition: Implications for reading comprehension* (pp. 140–156). New York, NY: Guilford.

Brett, A., Rothlein, L., & Hurley, M. (1996). Vocabulary acquisition from listening to stories and explanations of target words. *The Elementary School Journal, 96*(4), 415–422. doi:10.1086/461836

Carey, S. (1978). The child as word learner. In M. Halle, J. Bresnan, & G.A. Miller (Eds.), *Linguistic theory and psychological reality* (pp. 359–373). Cambridge, MA: MIT Press.

Carspecken, P.F. (1996). *Critical ethnography in educational research: A theoretical and practical guide.* New York, NY: Routledge.

Dale, E. (1965). Vocabulary measurement: Techniques and major findings. *Elementary English, 42,* 82–88.

Dickinson, D., & Smith, M.W. (1994). Long-term effects of pre-school teachers' book readings on low-income children's vocabulary and story comprehension. *Reading Research Quarterly, 29*(2), 104–122. doi:10.2307/747807

Fisher, D., Flood, J., Lapp, D., & Frey, N. (2004). Interactive read-alouds: Is there a common set of implementation practices? *The Reading Teacher, 58*(1), 8–17. doi:10.1598/RT.58.1.1

Green Brabham, E., & Lynch-Brown, C. (2002). Effects of teachers' reading-aloud styles on vocabulary comprehension in the early elementary grades. *Journal of Educational Psychology, 94*(3), 465–473. doi:10.1037/0022-0663.94.3.465

Herman, P.A., & Dole, J. (1988). Theory and practice in vocabulary learning and instruction. *The Elementary School Journal, 89*(1), 42–54. doi:10.1086/461561

International Reading Association & National Association for the Education of Young Children. (1998). *Learning to read and write: Developmentally appropriate practices for young children.* Newark, DE: International Reading Association.

Justice, L.M. (2002). Word exposure conditions and preschoolers' novel word learning during shared storybook reading. *Reading Psychology, 23*(2), 87–106. doi:10.1080/027027102760351016

Justice, L.M., Meier, J., & Walpole, S. (2005). Learning words from storybooks: An efficacy study with at-risk kindergartners. *Language, Speech, and Hearing Services in Schools, 36*(1), 17–32. doi:10.1044/0161-1461(2005/003)

McGee, L.M., & Schickedanz, J.A. (2007). Repeated interactive read-alouds in preschool and kindergarten. *The Reading Teacher, 60*(8), 742–751. doi:10.1598/RT.60.8.4

Merriam, S.B. (2001). *Qualitative research and case study applications in education* (2nd ed.). San Francisco, CA: Jossey-Bass.

Newton, E., Padak, N.D., & Rasinski, T.V. (2008). *Evidence-based instruction in reading: A professional development guide to vocabulary.* Boston, MA: Pearson Education.

Roberts, T.A. (2008). Home storybook reading in primary or second language with preschool children: Evidence of equal effectiveness for second-language vocabulary acquisition. *Reading Research Quarterly, 43*(2), 103–130. doi:10.1598/ RRQ.43.2.1

Stanovich, K.E. (1986). Matthew effects in reading: Some consequences of individual differences in the acquisition of literacy. *Reading Research Quarterly, 21*(4), 360–406. doi:10.1598/ RRQ.21.4.1

Sternberg, R.J. (1987). Most vocabulary is learned from context. In M.C. McKeown & M.E. Curtis (Eds.), *The nature of vocabulary acquisition* (pp. 89–105). Hillsdale, NJ: Erlbaum.

Walsh, B.A., & Blewitt, P. (2006). The effect of questioning style during storybook reading on novel vocabulary acquisition of preschoolers. *Early Childhood Education Journal, 33*(4), 273–278. doi:10.1007/s10643-005-0052-0

LITERATURE CITED

Anholt, L. (2007). *Leonardo and the flying boy: A story about Leonardo da Vinci.* Hauppauge, NY: Barron's Educational Books.

Cronin, D. (2008). *Duck for president.* New York, NY: Atheneum.

Dahl, R. (1982). *The BFG.* New York, NY: Puffin.

MacLachlan, P. (1985). *Sarah, plain and tall.* New York, NY: Harper-Trophy.

Kindle teaches at the University of Missouri, Kansas City, MO; e-mail kindlek@umkc.edu.

The Vocabulary-Rich Classroom: Modeling Sophisticated Word Use to Promote Word Consciousness and Vocabulary Growth

HOLLY B. LANE, AND

STEPHANIE ARRIAZA ALLEN

■ ■ ■ ■ ■

Promoting incidental learning and word consciousness through frequent and deliberate modeling of sophisticated vocabulary can add substantial breadth to students' vocabularies.

The Weather Watcher

In Ms. Barker's (all names are pseudonyms) kindergarten classroom, just like in so many other kindergarten classrooms, the day began with "circle time." During circle time, Ms. Barker led her students through a series of routines designed to teach basic skills and help students acquire fundamental knowledge. They sang songs that helped them remember the letters of the alphabet and their numbers in sequence. The students spent time on calendar activities that helped them learn the months of the year and the days of the week.

Ms. Barker assigned classroom jobs during circle time, too, and guided the students in carrying out their duties. The "zookeeper" was in charge of feeding and watering the classroom pets (a pair of hamsters). The "cleanup helper" made certain that all scraps of paper were picked up off the floor throughout the day. The "line leader" got to be first in line to lunch and anywhere else the class went, and the "caboose" was in charge of bringing up the rear of the line. Finally, the "weather watcher" reported the day's weather to the group, so they could discuss how to prepare for such weather: what to wear, whether to carry an umbrella, and so forth.

The weather watcher activity also illustrated how Ms. Barker carefully guided her students' vocabulary development. One early September day, Ms. Barker announced, "Sarah, you're our weather watcher today. Go outside and watch the weather and come back and tell us what it's going to be like outside today." Sarah dutifully jumped up and walked to the classroom door that opens to the outside. She opened the door and, standing in the doorway, looked up and around her and said quietly to herself, "Sunny." As she made her way back to the circle, she repeated to herself in a whisper, "Sunny. Sunny. Sunny." It was all Sarah could do to keep this important word in her head for the 30 seconds she needed it there. When Ms. Barker asked Sarah for her weather report, Sarah blurted out, "Sunny!" Sarah was obviously relieved. Ms. Barker smiled at Sarah and continued with the discussion, "That's right, it's sunny outside today. Does that mean it will be warm or cool?"

Given the time of year, only three weeks into the school year, Sarah's response was exactly what could be expected. The choices of words to describe the weather at that time were *sunny*, *cloudy*, and *rainy*. The children were learning the difference between these basic terms and what they meant to them. Should they wear shorts or long pants? Should they wear a raincoat? Will they be able to play outside? They were getting what they needed at that point in their development.

Fast forward to February in Ms. Barker's class. Circle time looked much like it did in September, but there were subtle differences. Instead of simply reciting the days of the week, the students were able to tell Ms. Barker what day it was yesterday and what day it will be three days from then. Instead of simply reciting the months of the year, the children identified the holidays that occur in February, how many days there are in the month, and in what season it falls.

Perhaps the biggest difference became evident when Ms. Barker was going over the duties of the class jobs. The zookeeper had become the "animal nutrition specialist." The cleanup helper had become the "custodian". The line leader was the "class movement coordinator", whereas the caboose was still the caboose. The weather watcher had become the "meteorologist."

Ms. Barker explained, "Jared, you're our meteorologist for today. Go outside and observe the weather conditions, then bring us back your weather forecast." Jared did as directed and returned to the circle. When Ms. Barker asked for his forecast, he announced, "It's going to be rather brisk today." Ms. Barker smiled and went on with the discussion about how to prepare for brisk weather.

The observer in this classroom, a bit startled at a 5-year-old's use of the words *rather brisk*, approached Jared later to ask him about his choice of words. Jared explained, "Well, it's colder than cool, but it's a long way from frigid." Even more surprised that Jared not only used the word appropriately but also seemed to have a strong command of its meaning, the observer asked Ms. Barker how Jared came to know such sophisticated ways to describe the weather.

Ms. Barker explained that it was all part of the design of her circle time. At the beginning of the year, children learned the basic concepts through repetition and practice. Her challenges at that point were to keep the concepts understandable and engaging. As the children mastered the basics, her efforts turned to building on this solid foundation of knowledge. She used the classroom jobs to expand her students' vocabulary. Although at the beginning of the year the zookeeper "feeds the hamsters," by midyear the animal nutrition specialist "provides nutritional sustenance to our rodent friends."

The kindergartners in Ms. Barker's class were all comfortable using words that we do not typically expect to hear 5-year-olds using. Their comfort came from their teacher's careful approach to developing their vocabularies through modeling and meaningful practice. Their well-developed vocabularies will undoubtedly serve them well as they learn to read.

Affable Annie

In Ms. Rivas's fourth-grade class, everyone looked forward to "morning meeting" (Kriete & Bechtel, 2002). The routine was a critical piece of her classroom management plan, but more importantly, it served as a catalyst for building her classroom community and for learning in engaging ways. The first segment of the morning meeting routine was the "greeting." The greeting ensured that each student was recognized daily and made to feel like a part of the group. The greeting activity changed from day to day, but one of the favorites was generating positive words to describe classmates as they were greeted. Each student was directed to say hello to the person sitting to his or her left and to say something to describe this person in a positive way. Each greeting was said aloud for the whole class to hear.

When the school year started, this type of greeting was limited to simple descriptive words: "Hi, Annie! You are always nice;" "Hello to the very happy Fernando;" "Good morning, Tyran, you are so talented." As the year progressed, Ms. Rivas encouraged students to think of more original ways to describe their classmates. At first, students were reluctant to stretch their vocabularies too far, and *nice, happy,* and *talented* became *friendly, jolly,* and *creative*—an improvement, albeit a small one.

To push her students a bit further, Ms. Rivas took over the greeting one day, replacing words she had used to describe children before with substantially more sophisticated synonyms. The words she chose were mostly words the children had never heard before, but they were words that related to the ideas already expressed about each student. Annie was affable, Fernando was jovial, and Tyran was virtuous.

These new words sent the children scrambling to their dictionaries to find out what exactly Ms. Rivas was saying about them. The students each learned at least their own descriptive word, and most remembered a few more. This simple step nudged the students to work harder to generate better, more sophisticated descriptors the next time this greeting routine was used. Each time, the student who used the new word and the student the word described were virtually assured to learn and remember the word. Everyone in the class heard each word, however, and associated the word with a classmate, helping them understand its meaning. The students soon became comfortable with a large collection of descriptive words.

Before long, Ms. Rivas started to notice these descriptive words being used during class discussions and even during casual conversations among students. She was thrilled to see the words turning up in writing assignments, as her students described characters in stories or the historical figures they were learning about in social studies. The students owned these words.

The Role of Vocabulary Learning

Vocabulary is a critical factor in the development of reading skills. Vocabulary knowledge has long been identified as one of the best predictors of reading comprehension (Davis, 1972; Thorndike, 1917), reading performance in general, and school achievement (Beck, McKeown, & Kucan, 2002, 2008). Receptive vocabulary is also a predictor of decoding skills (Ouellette, 2006). The more words the reader knows, the easier it will be to read and understand what is read (Blachowicz, Fisher, Ogle, & Watts-Taffe, 2006; Kamil, 2004; National Institute of Child Health and Human Development [NICHD], 2000).

Unfortunately, not every student comes to school with an adequate level of vocabulary knowledge to support reading success, and the diversity of vocabulary knowledge among children entering school is great (Blachowicz et al., 2006). Among students from different socioeconomic groups or with different learning abilities, there is a marked difference in vocabulary knowledge (Beck et al., 2002; Hart & Risley, 1995). Furthermore, these differences can be observed throughout the school grades (Beck et al., 2002; White, Graves, & Slater, 1990). Unless vocabulary becomes an integral part of everyday literacy instruction, the gap among groups will continue to widen, making it harder for low-performing groups to catch up to their peers. Vocabulary instruction is particularly critical for students with reading difficulties, as their improvements in comprehension as a result of vocabulary instruction are even greater than for students without reading difficulties (Elleman, Lindo, Morphy, & Compton, 2009).

Thus, vocabulary instruction should be "robust—vigorous, strong, and powerful in effect" (Beck et al., 2002, p. 2). To have an effect on reading comprehension, vocabulary instruction should include multiple exposures to a word, teach both definitions and contexts, and engage students in deep processing (Beck et al., 2008).

What Does It Mean to Know a Word?

Vocabulary refers to the "knowledge of words and word meanings" (Honig, Diamond, Cole, & Gutlohn, 2008, p. 407). Different types of vocabulary are used in different circumstances. According to Kamil and Hiebert (2005), there are four types of vocabulary: oral, print, receptive, and productive. Oral vocabulary refers to those words we understand when we communicate orally or when someone reads aloud to us. Print vocabulary refers to words we know when we read or write. Receptive vocabulary includes words we understand when we listen or read. Productive vocabulary encompasses words that are used during speaking and writing. According to Kamil and Hiebert (2005), words in the receptive vocabulary are "less well known" and "less frequent in use" (p. 3) when compared with productive vocabulary. Words used in speaking and writing tend to be "well known, familiar, and used frequently" (p. 3). Overall, receptive vocabulary is larger than productive vocabulary and plays a key role in the early years when children learn to read. As they encounter text and decode words, they use their knowledge of words to understand what they read. If the words they encounter are not part of their vocabulary, the readers will not comprehend their meaning (Kamil, 2004). Therefore, developing children's vocabulary is extremely important.

When we talk about developing children's vocabulary, we are not only talking about knowing a high number of words but also about how well they know those words. According to Beck et al. (2002), "knowing a word is not an all-or-nothing proposition: it is not the case that one either knows or does not know a word" (p. 9). That is, an individual may know a little bit or a lot about a word. Dale (1965) was one of the first to explain the importance of differences in levels of word knowledge and to classify these levels: (a) never saw or heard the word before; (b) heard the word, but does not know its meaning; (c) recognizes the word in context as having something to do with _____ ; and (d) knows the word well. Beck, McKeown, and Omanson (1987) also identified the quantity of word knowledge along a continuum of levels: (a) no knowledge; (b) general sense of the word; (c) narrow, context-bound knowledge; (d) some knowledge of a word, but not being able to recall it readily enough to use it in appropriate situations; and (e) rich, decontextualized knowledge of a word's meaning.

So what should our goal for instruction be? Some researchers (e.g., Beck et al., 2002; Coyne, 2009) suggested that knowing fewer words well is more important than knowing many words superficially. According to Beck et al., teachers should strive to help students use the words they have learned not only during reading but also during writing and speaking. This means that they need a "deep kind of knowledge" (p. 11). Other researchers (e.g., Biemiller & Boote, 2006) promoted breadth of vocabulary knowledge acquisition. Those who emphasize vocabulary breadth assert that knowing many words is critical to understanding a variety of text. No matter which they emphasize, most researchers would agree that both breadth and depth of vocabulary knowledge are important.

Selecting Words to Teach

Although recent research tells us more about how to teach words, determining which words to teach remains a challenge (Coyne, Simmons, Kame'enui, & Stoolmiller, 2004). Nagy and Anderson (1984) found that a typical third grader knows about 8,000 words, and a high school student knows between 25,000 and 50,000 words, or even more. A student typically will learn between 3,000 and 4,000 new words each year (Graves & Watts-Taffe, 2002). Knowing this, Beck and colleagues (2002, 2008) argued that not all unfamiliar words in a text should be the focus of classroom instruction. They developed a three-tier model for selecting words to teach, based on each word's level of utility. The first tier includes basic words that most children already know and that seldom require direct instruction in school. Words like *house, mom, car,* and *toy* are examples of tier-1 words. Tier-2 includes words that are key to comprehension and are frequently used by "mature language users" (p. 16). Examples of tier-2 words include *curious, gazing, mysterious, stingy, scrumptious,* and *drowsy.* Tier-3 encompasses low-frequency words that are associated with specific domains or content areas. This tier includes words like *morpheme, peninsula, similes, nucleus,* and *protons.* Tier-3 words should be taught as they are encountered, usually during content area instruction. However, the focus of most vocabulary instruction should be on tier-2 words—those words that adults use with ease in everyday conversation, reading, and writing.

Beck and McKeown (2007) maintained that sophisticated words are particularly appropriate for instruction, because these words are not likely to be encountered or learned through typical interaction with academic materials or everyday conversation. Selecting for instruction words that are more sophisticated labels for familiar concepts expands both vocabulary breadth and depth. Vocabulary breadth is expanded, because these sophisticated words add to the number of words a child knows. Vocabulary depth is increased because each of the new words can be linked to familiar words, which enhances understanding of both the new and familiar words.

Promoting Word Consciousness

Considering the number of new words a child encounters each year, vocabulary instruction becomes a titanic task. Based on this knowledge, Graves (2000) identified four key components of vocabulary instruction: wide reading, instruction of individual words, word learning strategies, and development of word consciousness. Word consciousness involves being aware and interested in words and word meanings (Anderson & Nagy, 1992; Graves & Watts-Taffe, 2002) and noticing when and how new words are used (Manzo & Manzo, 2008). Individuals who are word conscious are motivated to learn new words and able to use them skillfully. Helping students become word conscious is a crucial endeavor for teachers across grade levels, especially teachers working with students whose prior vocabulary exposure may be limited.

By mid-kindergarten, Ms. Barker's students were eager to learn new words for familiar concepts. Their enthusiasm stemmed from the success they had learning new words all year, with Ms. Barker's support, in a word-rich environment. They noticed unfamiliar words when others used them and asked what the words meant. They also recognized new words they had learned as they heard them used in different contexts, allowing them to deepen their understanding of the words and make more connections between the new words and other words. By mid-kindergarten, these children had already developed sharp word consciousness. Similarly, the fourth-grade students Ms. Rivas taught moved beyond finding sophisticated words to describing their classmates and applying their word consciousness to classroom assignments and even to their conversations with their peers.

Both teachers worked in high-poverty schools with large populations of English-language learners. Ms. Barker's school is a rural school, where many of the students are children of migrant farm workers. Ms. Rivas teaches in an urban school, where nearly 100% of the students participate in the free and reduced-price lunch program. These teachers recognized the need for their students to learn as many words as they can during the school day, because their home environments provided little opportunity for word learning. Despite these challenges, their students became word conscious and were anxious to add words to their lexicons.

According to Graves and Watts-Taffe (2002), this positive disposition for words greatly facilitated the challenging task of learning thousands of words each year, especially since most of the learning happens incidentally in the context of reading and listening (NICHD, 2000). Incidental learning from context has been identified as a main cause of vocabulary growth among children. Children are remarkably skilled at learning new words from unstructured contexts (Akhtar, Jipson, & Callanan, 2001; Nagy, Herman, & Anderson, 1985; Rice, Buhr, & Oetting, 1992). This effortless acquisition of word knowledge happens through oral communication and casual reading without direct instruction (Nagy et al., 1985; Oetting, Rice, & Swank, 1995).

Because incidental learning is an authentic medium for expanding children's vocabulary, and word consciousness is key for this learning to happen, teachers can take advantage of adult–children interactions in the classroom to model the use of sophisticated language (Beck et al., 2002; Graves & Watts-Taffe, 2002). Incorporating these words into daily routines and classroom conversations creates a learning atmosphere where children become motivated and competent in word usage. Graves and Watts-Taffe (2002) suggested that teachers should promote "adept diction" (p. 145) as a way of developing word consciousness. Teachers who model and encourage adept diction foster curiosity and interest about words in their students.

In addition to a general atmosphere of promoting adept diction, we need to consider other conditions that are necessary to ensure learning. One of the main findings of the National Reading Panel (NICHD, 2000) regarding vocabulary instruction was that repetitious and diverse exposures to vocabulary are vital. The more children hear, see, and engage with words, the better they will learn them (Armbruster, Lehr, Osborn, & Adler, 2001). According to Beck et al., (2008), frequent encounters help students not only remember the meaning of words but also access word meanings more efficiently. This has a significant implication for reading, because when readers access word meanings quickly, more cognitive resources are available to be allocated to the comprehension of connected text (Beck et al., 2008; Beck, Perfetti, & McKeown, 1982).

Modeling Sophisticated Vocabulary Use

Multiple encounters are important in word learning, but they are not enough. For children to actually learn and use the new words, teachers need to make sure that those encounters allow children to make connections with their prior knowledge and experiences (Armbruster et al., 2001). There are many different strategies we can use to foster the acquisition of new and more sophisticated words, but one of the simplest and most powerful approaches is Ms. Barker's method of frequently modeling sophisticated labels for familiar concepts. Several aspects of her method likely contributed to its effectiveness.

First, she planned carefully which words she would introduce. She spent a good deal of time thinking about the words she used throughout the school day. She made lists of words that were related to classroom routines and to different areas of the curriculum. For each word on each list, she searched for more sophisticated substitutes and culled these lists of synonyms to a list of words she believed to be manageable for her students. She selected words that related to the most familiar concepts first and began introducing more sophisticated terms for those words. For example, the children already knew what it meant to feel *happy*, so Ms. Barker began using synonyms such as *glad, cheerful,* and *delighted*. They already knew what nice meant, so she began to use *kind, pleasant,* and *thoughtful*. Most importantly, she helped the children understand when one of those words might be a more appropriate choice than another. For other words, she taught the concept and the simpler word first, then only after allowing the children to become comfortable with the simple word, she introduced the more sophisticated synonym. Her circle time routine was replete with this type of introduction.

Although her students' learning of the words may have been incidental, Ms. Barker's teaching was not. The introduction of new words was deliberate but natural. With some words, the instruction was somewhat implicit. For example, she asked for a volunteer to pass out paper for an art activity to each table. When they were finished, as she started directions for the activity, she said, "Thank you, Angelo, for distributing the paper." She continued casually linking *pass out* with *distribute* in this way for a few more days until one day when she asked for a volunteer to help "distribute our snacks," and all the children knew what this meant.

With other words, instruction would be more explicit. For example, Ms. Barker explained to her students, "Everybody knows now what the weather watcher does, right? Today, we're going to learn a new word for weather watcher. From now on, we'll call the weather watcher our meteorologist. A meteorologist watches the weather. Can everyone say that word with me? Meteorologist." All the children practiced saying the word with help from Ms. Barker. By saying the word themselves, the children created a phonological representation of the word in their heads that will make it easier to recall the word later (Beck, 2004). Ms. Barker followed up at the end of the lesson by asking again, "What is our new name for the weather watcher?," and the children said the new word again, further strengthening the associations they were forming.

With older children, Ms. Rivas was able to delegate more of the responsibility for learning new words to her students. She first made them comfortable with the greeting routine during the morning meeting. She then provided a clear and compelling example for them to follow. Finally, she encouraged their attempts to follow her example as the students used sophisticated words on their own.

Ms. Barker and Ms. Rivas both made decisions about how direct their teaching needed to be to ensure students learned the words they intended. Their decisions to use either implicit or explicit means to introduce new words were based on (a) their familiarity with their students' word knowledge and (b) their careful thought about the complexity of the words (Mercer, Lane, Jordan, Allsopp, & Eisele, 1996). Any teacher at any grade level can follow these procedures for generating a list of words to teach through modeling. Familiarity with a particular group of students and what they know is the best gauge to use when selecting words. Table 1 contains sophisticated words that might be used to substitute for the more mundane words we typically use during classroom routines. When a teacher shifts from asking the class to line up *next* to the wall to suggesting they line up *adjacent* to the wall, she is expanding her students' vocabularies. Table 2 contains words to use when describing students' behavior or academic performance.

Sophisticated words can also be used during content instruction. For example, beyond the content vocabulary in a unit on plants (e.g., stamen, pistil, germinate), the teacher can find mature words to describe plant growth in general (e.g., flourish, thrive) or a particular plant (e.g., a *meandering* vine). Table 3 contains examples of words that might be connected to specific content areas.

TABLE 1   Sophisticated Words to Use During Classroom Routines

Classroom Supplies	Walking in Line	Group Time
accumulate	adjacent	articulate
allocate	approach	ascertain
allot	disorderly	assemble
amass	efficiently	coherent
arrange	file	contribute
collect	halt	converse
deplete	linger	convey
dispense	orderly	cooperate
distribute	parallel	deliberate
dole	pause	determine
gather	perpendicular	disband
hoard	proceed	disperse
issue	procession	elaborate
replenish	proximity	elucidate
reserve	queue	express
stockpile	rapidly	lucid
	remain	oblige
	swiftly	partake
	vicinity	participate
		portray
		verbalize

TABLE 2   Sophisticated Words to Use When Discussing Classroom Behavior or Performance

Satisfactorily	Conflict	Impolite	Correct	Wrong
affable	amends	boorish	accomplished	awkward
agreeable	bicker	coarse	appropriate	erroneous
amiable	quarrel	discourteous	exemplary	flawed
compassionate	rectify	offensive	masterful	inaccurate
considerate	resolve	uncouth	precise	inadequate
courteous	squabble	vulgar	proficient	incorrect
decorous			proper	invalid
gracious			superior	
pleasant			suitable	
respectful				
sympathetic				

TABLE 3   Sophisticated Words That Are Related to Specific Content Areas

Science: Plant Life	Science: Space	Social Studies: Civilizations
abundant	celestial	cooperation
burgeoning	existence	customary
dwindling	globe	dominant
fertile	immeasurable	hardy
flourish	infinite	hierarchy
lush	miniscule	nomadic
meandering	orb	obligation
neglect	remote	prosperity
sow	trajectory	resistant
tend	universe	resourceful
thrive	vast	stability

Avoiding the Temptation to "Dumb Down" Our Language for Children

One of the biggest barriers to vocabulary growth in school is the simplistic way many teachers talk to children. We have all been guilty at one time or another of using words beneath our students' level of understanding. Simplistic vocabulary may be appropriate for initial instruction, as a support for students' understanding of a new concept. But once students develop a basic understanding, it is time to elevate our instructional language to enhance our students' vocabularies.

For example, at the beginning of first grade, teaching students to put a list of words in "ABC order" may help them better understand the concept of alphabetizing. However, even first graders can understand that *alphabetical* order is the same thing as ABC order, and using the more sophisticated term as soon as students understand the concept is appropriate. Continuing to use the simplistic term limits our students' vocabulary growth. Likewise, using phrases such as *take away* in place of *subtract* or *same as* in place of *equal* beyond initial instruction is limiting. If we listen carefully to our own words during instruction, most teachers can find many examples of unnecessarily simplistic language use. Avoiding oversimplification and exposing students to more mature terminology helps them be more confident as they progress to more complex content.

Be a Word-Conscious Teacher

Incidental learning is the method by which we acquire knowledge of most new words throughout our lives. It is important to note, however, that incidental learning is necessary but not sufficient for the vocabulary learning that must occur during the school years. We know that children learn words best through extended instruction over time (Coyne, 2009), and explicit instruction is the best way to ensure that children learn word meanings and, especially, subtle differences between words (Scott & Nagy, 2004). That said, promoting incidental learning and word consciousness through frequent and deliberate modeling of sophisticated vocabulary can add substantial breadth to children's vocabularies.

Being a word-conscious teacher is the best way to promote word consciousness among students. Ms. Barker's kindergarten class is a prime example of well-developed word consciousness. By linking new words with familiar concepts, introducing the words clearly and matter-of-factly during classroom routines, having the children say the word repeatedly, and then continuing to use the word in place of the familiar word, Ms. Barker optimized conditions for word learning—and it showed. Likewise, by beginning with words that described her students, Ms. Rivas hooked her students immediately, because they all wanted to know what she was saying about them.

The students in both teachers' classes used language far beyond what might otherwise be expected for their age and grade level, and they used this language effortlessly. They enjoyed learning and using new words. As the kindergartners move into reading independently, their advanced vocabularies will support their reading comprehension. As the fourth graders face more challenging assignments and high-stakes assessments in reading and writing, their expanded vocabularies will become a support to them. Any teacher can accomplish what Ms. Barker and Ms. Rivas did by creating a word-rich classroom environment with more sophisticated models for students to follow.

REFERENCES

Akhtar, N., Jipson, J., & Callanan, M.A. (2001). Learning words through overhearing. *Child Development*, 72(2), 416–430. doi:10.1111/1467-8624.00287

Anderson, R.C., & Nagy, W.E. (1992). The vocabulary conundrum. *American Educator*, 16(4), 14–18, 44–47.

Armbruster, B.B., Lehr, F., Osborn, J., & Adler, C.R. (2001). *Put reading first: The research building blocks for teaching children to read, kindergarten through grade 3.* Washington, DC: National Institute for Literacy, U.S. Department of Education.

Beck, I.L. (2004, April). *Igniting students' knowledge of and interest in words.* Presentation at the Florida Middle School Reading Leadership Conference, Orlando, FL.

Beck, I.L., & McKeown, M.G. (2007). Different ways for different goals, but keep your eye on the higher verbal goals. In R.K. Wagner, A.E. Muse, & K.R. Tannenbaum (Eds.), *Vocabulary acquisition: Implications for reading comprehension* (pp. 182– 204). New York, NY: Guilford.

Beck, I.L., McKeown, M.G., & Kucan, L. (2002). *Bringing words to life: Robust vocabulary instruction.* New York, NY: Guilford.

Beck, I.L., McKeown, M.G., & Kucan, L. (2008). *Creating robust vocabulary: Frequently asked questions and extended examples.* New York, NY: Guilford.

Beck, I.L., McKeown, M.G., & Omanson, R.C. (1987). The effects and uses of diverse vocabulary instructional techniques. In M.G. McKeown & M.E. Curtis (Eds.), *The nature of vocabulary acquisition* (pp. 147–163). Hillsdale, NJ: Erlbaum.

Beck, I.L., Perfetti, C.A., & McKeown, M.G. (1982). Effects of longterm vocabulary instruction on lexical access and reading comprehension. *Journal of Educational Psychology*, 74(4), 506–521. doi:10.1037/0022-0663.74.4.506

Biemiller, A., & Boote, C. (2006). An effective method for building meaning vocabulary in primary grades. *Journal of Educational Psychology*, 98(1), 44–62. doi:10.1037/0022-0663.98.1.44

Blachowicz, C.L.Z., Fisher, P.J.L., Ogle, D., & Watts-Taffe, S. (2006). Vocabulary: Questions from the classroom. *Reading Research Quarterly*, 41(4), 524–539. doi:10.1598/RRQ.41.4.5

Coyne, M.D. (2009, April). *Closing the vocabulary gap: Current issues in vocabulary intervention and research.* Paper presented at the annual meeting of the Council for Exceptional Children, Seattle, WA.

Coyne, M.D., Simmons, D.C., Kame'enui, E.J., & Stoolmiller, M. (2004). Teaching vocabulary during shared storybook readings: An examination of differential effects. *Exceptionality*, 12(3), 145–162. doi:10.1207/s15327035ex1203_3

Dale, E. (1965). Vocabulary measurement: Techniques and major findings. *Elementary English*, 42, 895–901, 948.

Davis, F.B. (1972). Psychometric research on comprehension in reading. *Reading Research Quarterly, 7*(4), 628–678. doi:10.2307/747108

Elleman, A.M., Lindo, E.J., Morphy, P., & Compton, D.L. (2009). The impact of vocabulary instruction on passage-level comprehension of school-age children: A meta-analysis. *Journal of Research on Educational Effectiveness, 2*(1), 1–44. doi:10.1080/19345740802539200

Graves, M.F. (2000). A vocabulary program to complement and bolster a middle-grade comprehension program. In B.M. Taylor, M.F. Graves, & P. van den Broek (Eds.), *Reading for meaning: Fostering comprehension in the middle grades* (pp. 116–135). New York: Teachers College Press; Newark, DE: International Reading Association.

Graves, M.F., & Watts-Taffe, S.M. (2002). The place of word consciousness in a research-based vocabulary program. In A.E. Farstrup & S.J. Samuels (Eds.), *What research has to say about reading instruction* (3rd ed., pp. 140–165). Newark, DE: International Reading Association.

Hart, B., & Risley, T.R. (1995). *Meaningful differences in the everyday experience of young American children.* Baltimore, MD: Paul H. Brookes.

Honig, B., Diamond, L., Cole, C.L., & Gutlohn, L. (2008). *Teaching reading sourcebook: For all educators working to improve reading achievement.* Novato, CA: Arena; Berkeley, CA: Consortium on Reading Excellence.

Kamil, M.L. (2004). Vocabulary and comprehension instruction: Summary and implications of the National Reading Panel findings. In P. McCardle & V. Chhabra (Eds.), *The voice of evidence in reading research* (pp. 213–234). Baltimore: Paul H. Brookes.

Kamil, M.L., & Hiebert, E.H. (2005). Teaching and learning vocabulary: Perspectives and persistent issues. In E.H. Hiebert & M.L. Kamil (Eds.), *Teaching and learning vocabulary: Bringing research to practice* (pp. 1–23). Mahwah, NJ: Erlbaum.

Kriete, R., & Bechtel, L. (2002). *The morning meeting book.* Greenfield, MA: Northeast Foundation for Children.

Manzo, U.C., & Manzo, A.V. (2008). Teaching vocabulary-learning strategies: Word consciousness, word connection, and word prediction. In A.E. Farstrup & S.J. Samuels (Eds.), *What research has to say about vocabulary instruction* (pp. 80–105). Newark, DE: International Reading Association.

Mercer, C.D., Lane, H.B., Jordan, L., Allsopp, D.H., & Eisele, M.R. (1996). Empowering teachers and students with instructional choices in inclusive settings. *Remedial and Special Education, 17*(4), 226–236. doi:10.1177/074193259601700405

Nagy, W.E., & Anderson, R.C. (1984). How many words are there in printed school English? *Reading Research Quarterly, 19*(3), 304–330. doi:10.2307/747823

Nagy, W.E., Herman, P.A., & Anderson, R.C. (1985). Learning words from context. *Reading Research Quarterly, 20*(2), 233–253. doi:10.2307/747758

National Institute of Child Health and Human Development. (2000). *Report of the National Reading Panel. Teaching children to read: An evidence-based assessment of the scientific research literature on reading and its implications for reading instruction* (NIH Publication No. 00-4769). Washington, DC: National Institutes of Health.

Oetting, J.B., Rice, M.L., & Swank, L.K. (1995). Quick incidental learning (QUIL) of words by school-age children with and without SLI. *Journal of Speech and Hearing Research, 38*(2), 434–445.

Ouellette, G.P. (2006). What's meaning got to do with it: The role of vocabulary in word reading and reading comprehension. *Journal of Educational Psychology, 98*(3), 554–566. doi:10.1037/0022-0663.98.3.554

Rice, M.L., Buhr, J., & Oetting, J.B. (1992). Specific-language-impaired children's quick incidental learning of words: The effect of a pause. *Journal of Speech and Hearing Research, 35*(5), 1040–1048.

Scott, J.A., & Nagy, W.E. (2004). Developing word consciousness. In J.F. Baumann & E.J. Kame'enui (Eds.), *Vocabulary instruction: Research to practice* (pp. 201–217). New York, NY: Guilford.

Thorndike, E.L. (1917). Reading as reasoning: A study of mistakes in paragraph reading. *Journal of Educational Psychology, 8*(6), 323–332. doi:10.1037/h0075325

White, T.G., Graves, M.F., & Slater, W.H. (1990). Growth of reading vocabulary in diverse elementary schools: Decoding and word meaning. *Journal of Educational Psychology, 82*(2), 281–290. doi:10.1037/0022-0663.82.2.281

Lane teaches at the University of Florida, Gainesville, FL; e-mail hlane@ufl.edu. Arriaza Allen teaches at the University of Florida; e-mail satienza@ufl.edu.

Closing the Vocabulary Gap

JANE L. DAVID

■ ■ ■ ■ ■

Vocabulary size predicts comprehension, but learning new words is especially hard for students who come to school with small vocabularies or limited knowledge of English.

What's the Idea?

Students who enter school with limited vocabularies, especially English language learners, often struggle to understand what they read because they are unfamiliar with many of the words they encounter. This barrier hampers their learning in all the subjects they study. The consensus of researchers and educators today is that such students need explicit vocabulary instruction.

What's the Reality?

Now, as in past decades, most teachers devote little time to explicit vocabulary instruction. Teachers are already under the gun to cover more material than time permits, and they are stymied by the need to devote extra time to vocabulary. Moreover, teachers face the challenge of identifying which words are most important for their students to learn, especially given the large gap in vocabulary size between students with poorly educated or non-English-speaking parents and their more advantaged peers.

What's the Research?

The research shows a strong relationship between vocabulary size and reading comprehension level; moreover, that relationship grows stronger as students progress through school (Snow, Porche, Tabors, & Harris, 2007). Because students who know many words can comprehend what they read, they continue to increase their vocabularies and content knowledge through reading. The opposite holds true for students with limited vocabularies, especially English language learners (Blachowicz, Fisher, Ogle, & Watts-Taffe, 2006).

Building vocabulary is more difficult than it might seem. Vocabulary signifies more than a list of words, it is a proxy for content knowledge. Learning new words often involves learning new ideas and information; memorizing definitions is not the same thing (Stahl & Fairbanks, 1986). Researchers concur that to "own" a new word for the long term, the learner must see and use the word multiple times in several contexts. The question is, How can teachers accomplish this goal efficiently?

Researchers have studied a variety of strategies to help students expand their vocabularies. In one such study, Beck and McKeown (2007) exposed kindergarten and

1st grade students to read-aloud trade books chosen because they included sophisticated words that struggling readers would be unlikely to learn on their own. The students had opportunities to discuss the books, hear the words explained in the context of the story, and hear the words used over the next few days. They learned more words than students in the comparison group, who participated in traditional read-alouds.

Carlo and colleagues (2004) tested the effects of a vocabulary enrichment intervention in which engaging texts and activities were used to teach fifth grade students strategies for analyzing new words using context clues and knowledge of root words and cognates. Students read newspaper articles, diaries, and histories about immigrants' experiences followed by daily work in small groups on such tasks as filling in missing words, making word associations, and playing charades. In classes randomly assigned to the intervention, both English language learners and native English speakers outscored comparison students on several measures of vocabulary development, including depth of knowledge and understanding of multiple meanings.

No one strategy can do the job alone, however. Because different kinds of words require different approaches—and students' needs vary by age, background knowledge, native language, and motivation—teachers must know and be adept in selecting among multiple strategies (Blachowicz et al., 2006).

Students at the secondary level need to expand their vocabularies rapidly to comprehend the multiple subjects they are learning. This challenge is especially intense for English language learners. Even those labeled as fluent English speakers, whose gaps in English may not be readily apparent, often struggle to develop the academic vocabulary they need to be successful (Butler & Hakuta, 2006).

Across grade levels, teachers get conflicting advice about which words to focus on. Some researchers argue that struggling students should be introduced early on to interesting, sophisticated words, partly to engage their interest and partly to help them catch up to their more advantaged peers (Beck & McKeown, 2007). Some argue for subject-specific academic words, such as *circumference* and *pollination* (Marzano & Pickering, 2005), and others for words that cut across disciplines, such as *synthesize* or *infer* (Coxhead, 2000).

According to one synthesis of best practices for English language learners, the core reading program is a good place to begin choosing words for instruction in the elementary grades (Gersten et al., 2007). Others, however, point out that most basal reading books have little informational text and are therefore of limited help in building vocabulary or background knowledge (Walsh, 2003).

Whichever words teachers choose to teach, researchers agree that they need to provide a variety of structured opportunities for students to encounter and use new words in authentic and engaging contexts. The essential strategy is providing opportunities for students to practice using new words through reading, writing, speaking, and especially conversations led by teachers (Carlo et al., 2004).

What to Do?

Students grasp the full meaning of words gradually, with repeated use and varied contexts that illustrate how meanings can change. Whether the word is *of* or *revolution*, students cannot understand its meanings and usage without repeated practice and feedback. Conversations with teachers and peers that home in on vocabulary are one key element. Other elements include associating new words with pictures, creating semantic maps that show relationships among words, playing word games, and when appropriate, linking new words to students' native languages.

Devoting sufficient time to these activities can happen only if all teachers come on board and integrate vocabulary development into their instruction throughout the day. For example, elementary teachers might pick informational texts and stories with rich vocabulary as opportunities to learn new content and new vocabulary, along with careful attention to strategies that support learning the new words. Secondary teachers might use science experiments and movies, as well as written text, as sources for zeroing in on vocabulary development.

Without such concerted, schoolwide efforts, the achievement gap between students with limited vocabularies and their peers will continue to expand.

REFERENCES

Beck, I. L., & McKeown, M. G. (2007). Increasing young low-income children's oral vocabulary repertoires through rich and focused instruction. *The Elementary School Journal, 107*(3), 251–271.

Blachowicz, C. L. Z., Fisher. P. J. L., Ogle, D., & Watts-Taffe, S. (2006). Vocabulary: Questions from the classroom. *Reading Research Quarterly, 41*(4), 524–539.

Butler, Y. G., & Hakuta, K. (2006). Cognitive factors in children's L1 and L2 reading. *Academic Exchange Quarterly, 10*(1), 23–27.

Carlo, M., August, D., McLaughlin, B., Snow, C., Dressler, C., Lippman, D., Lively, T., & While, C. (2004). Closing the gap: Addressing the vocabulary needs of English language learners in bilingual and mainstream classrooms. *Reading Research Quarterly, 39*(2), 188–206.

Coxhead, A. (2000) A new academic word list. *TESOL Quarterly, 34*(2), 213–238,

Gersten, R., Baker, S.K., Shanahan, T., Linan-Thompson, S., Collins, P., & Scarcella, R. (2007). *Effective literacy and English language instruction for English learners in the elementary grades: A practice guide* (NCEE 2007-4011). Washington, DC: Institute of Education Sciences, U.S. Department of Education. Available: http://ies.ed.gov/ncee/wwc/pdf/practiceguides/20074011.pdf

Marzano, R. R., & Pickering, D. J. (2005). *Building academic vocabulary: Teacher's manual.* Alexandria, VA: ASCD.

Snow, C. E., Porche, M. V., Tabors, P. 0., & Harris, S. R. (2007). *Is literacy enough? Pathways to academic success for adolescents.* Baltimore, MD: Paul H. Brookes.

Stahl, S., & Fairbanks, M. (1986). The effects of vocabulary instruction: A model-based meta-analysis. *Review of Educational Research, 56*(1), 72–110.

Walsh, K. (2003). Basal readers: The lost opportunity to build the knowledge that propels comprehension. *American Educator, 21*(1), 24–27.

CLASSROOM IMPLICATIONS

1. In what ways are interactive read-alouds more likely to produce more word learning than a program of direct instruction? Or would you argue the opposite?

2. What steps can you take in your own classroom to improve your students' word consciousness?

3. Can you suggest approaches other than those described by these three authors for alleviating the gap in vocabulary?

FOR FURTHER READING

Beauchat, K.A., Blamey, K.L., & Walpole, S. (2009). Building preschool children's language and literacy one storybook at a time. *The Reading Teacher, 63,* 26–39. doi: 10.1598/RT.63.1.3

Lesaux, N.K., Kieffer, M.J., Faller, S.E., & Kelley, J.G. (2010). The effectiveness of implementation of an academic vocabulary intervention for linguistically diverse students in urban middle schools. *Reading Research Quarterly, 45,* 196–228. doi: 10.1598/RRQ.45.2.3

Manyak, P.C., & Bauer, E.B. (2009). English vocabulary instruction for English learners. *The Reading Teacher, 63,* 174–176. doi: 10.1598/RT.63.2.11

McCutchen, D., Logan, B., & Biangardi-Orpe, U. (2009). Making meaning: Children's sensitivity to morphological information during word reading. *Reading Research Quarterly, 44,* 360–376. doi: 10.1598/RRQ.44.4.4

Neuman, S.B., & Dwyer, J. (2009). Missing in action: Vocabulary instruction in pre-k. *The Reading Teacher, 62,* 384–392. doi: 10.1598/RT.62.5.2

Nichols, W.D., Rupley, W.H., Kiser, K. (2009). How can vocabulary instruction be made an integral part of learning in middle and high school classrooms? In J. Lewis (Ed.). *Essential questions in adolescent literacy: teachers and researchers discuss what works in classrooms* (pp. 175–200). New York, NY: Guilford Press.

Snow, C.E., Lawrence, J.F., & White, C. (2009). Generating knowledge of academic language among urban middle school students. *Journal of Research on Educational Effectiveness, 2,* 325–344.

Stahl, K.A.D., & Bravo, M.A. (2010). Contemporary classroom vocabulary assessment for content areas. *The Reading Teacher, 63,* 566–578. doi: 10.1598/RT.63.7.4

Townsend, D. (2009). Building academic vocabulary in after-school settings: Games for growth with middle school English-language learners. *Journal of Adolescent & Adult Literacy, 53,* 242–251. doi: 10.1598/JAAL.53.3.5

Winters, R. (2009). Interactive frames for vocabulary growth and word consciousness. *The Reading Teacher, 62,* 685–690. doi: 10.1598/RT.62.8.6

English Learners

A central way for teachers to assess the learning and understanding of their ELLs is to give them myriad opportunities to write and talk during lessons. When ELLs are silent during extended periods of lesson times, it is not possible to know if or how much they are learning from lessons.

—Brock & Raphael, 2005, p. 51

The presence of English learners (ELs) in American classrooms has increased dramatically in recent years. The challenges they pose are considerable, and straightforward solutions do not exist. There are two major approaches to helping these children attain proficiency in English. Students of limited English proficiency (LEP) may be taught in a context of *bilingual education*, in which instruction in both English and the native language occurs in the same classrooms. During one period, instruction might be conducted in the native language while during another it might be conducted in English. In contrast, the *ESL approach* (English as a second language) is one in which intense instruction in basic English is conducted in separate classrooms so that students can become proficient as quickly as possible; for the remainder of the day, students are immersed in English-only classes.

The relative merits of these approaches have been hotly debated. Some research indicates that bilingual education can be effective in helping students evolve in their personal language acquisition to the point that they are capable of learning from written materials and oral presentations in English. However, many Hispanic parents object to instruction in Spanish because they believe that their children may be disadvantaged. In 1998, this sentiment led to passage of Proposition 227, the English for the Children Initiative, in California. This proposition called for an end to bilingual education and reliance instead on total immersion of California schoolchildren in English-speaking classrooms. Proponents of the proposition pointed to increases in the test scores of immigrant children as evidence that immersion works better than bilingual education. In 2005, on the other hand, the National Literacy Panel on Language Minority Children and Youth concluded that the available evidence casts doubt on the effectiveness of English-only instruction. The U.S. Department of Education, however, declined to publish the Panel's report, perhaps for political reasons (see *Reading Today*, October/November 2005, *23*(2), 1,3). The report was then published privately (August & Shanahan, 2006). The debate continues.

While no quick fix exists, suggestions for helping teachers contend with language-diverse classrooms are numerous. Fitzgerald and Graves refer to "scaffolding reading experiences" for these children (Fitzgerald & Graves, 2004; Graves & Fitzgerald, 2009). They define a scaffolded reading experience (SRE) as "a set of prereading, during-reading, and postreading activities specifically designed to assist English-language learners in successfully reading, understanding, and learning from a particular selection" (Fitzgerald & Graves, 2004, p. 15) The best activities are often those that research has shown to be beneficial to native speakers as well. Many options are available for use before, during, and after reading. You must be selective. Consider the nature of the selection and the needs of your ELs.

Suggested prereading SREs include: using motivational approaches; pointing out links to students' lives; building or activating prior knowledge; providing text-specific knowledge; preteaching vocabulary; preteaching concepts; prequestioning, predicting, and direction setting; suggesting strategies; using students' native language; and involving ELL communities, parents, siblings

Suggested SREs for use during reading include: silent reading, reading aloud to students, supported reading, oral reading by students, and modifying the text

Suggested postreading SREs include: questioning; discussion; writing; drama; artistic, graphic, and nonverbal activities; application and outreach activities; building connections; and reteaching. If these approaches seem familiar, it reinforces the axiom that good teaching for ELs involves the skillful, focused use of techniques that are effective with all learners.

In content areas, another popular approach in content teaching is sheltered instruction (Echevarria & Graves, 2010). There is very little difference between the general concepts in sheltered instruction and good content area instruction. In sheltered instruction, however, content and language objectives are interwoven. Sheltered instruction is commonly applied at grades four and higher and stresses the use techniques designed to prepare and support ELs. Some of these approaches include:

- visual aids
- modeling and demonstrations
- graphic organizers
- vocabulary overviews
- predictions
- cooperative learning
- peer tutoring
- multicultural content

Finally, a note on terminology. The field of instructing English learners is filled with a confusing array of acronyms. The following chart may help you navigate this alphabet soup.

Common Acronyms

EL	English learner
ESL	English as a second language
ELL	English-language learner
LEP	Limited English Proficiency
EFL	English as a Foreign Language
ESOL	English for Speakers of Other Languages
TESOL	Teacher of English to Speakers of Other Languages
TESL	Teaching English as a Second Language
TOEFL	Test of English as a Foreign Language

AS YOU READ

These two articles shed light on the challenging issues of meeting the instructional needs of ELs. Claude Goldenberg provides an excellent overview of the topic, including a current research review. From the numerous studies currently available, he extracts three principal conclusions and discusses their implications for instruction. Eury Bauer, Patrick Manyak, and Crystal Cook examine the needs of ELs during content instruction and stress the necessity of having both content and language objectives. They describe the importance of small-group work to increase engagement and facilitate differentiation. They then recommend strategies to help reach these students, including learning as much as possible about the culture and language of the ELs. As you read, judge whether you think their advice can be applied in regular classrooms that serve a small number of ELs.

REFERENCES

Brock, C.H., & Raphael, T.E. (2005). *Windows to language, literacy, and culture: Insights from an English-language learner*. Newark, DE: IRA.

Drucker, M. J. (2003). What reading teachers should know about ESL learners. *The Reading Teacher, 57,* 22–29.

Echevarria, J., & Graves, A. (2010). *Sheltered content instruction: Teaching English language learners with diverse abilities* (4th ed.). Boston, MA: Allyn & Bacon.

Fitzgerald, J., & Graves, M.F. (2004). *Scaffolding reading experiences for English-language learners*. Norwood, MA: Christopher-Gordon.

Graves, M.F., & Fitzgerald, J. (2009). Implementing scaffolding reading experiences in diverse classrooms. In J. Coppola & E. Primas (Eds.), *One classroom, many learners: Best literacy practices for today's multilingual classrooms* (pp. 121–139). Newark, DE: International Reading Association.

Helman, L.A. (2004). Building on the sound system of Spanish: Insights from the alphabetic spellings of English-language learners. *The Reading Teacher, 57,* 452–460.

Helman, L.A. (2005). Using assessment results to improve teaching for English-language learners. *The Reading Teacher, 58,* 668–677.

Herschel, J. (1833). Address at the opening of Eton Library, Windsor, England.

Hickman, P., Pollard-Durodola, S., & Vaughn, S. (2004). Storybook reading: Improving vocabulary and comprehension for English-language learners. *The Reading Teacher, 57,* 720–730.

Shanahan, T., & August, D. (Eds.). (2006). *Developing literacy in English-language learners*. Mahwah, NJ: Lawrence Erlbaum.

Tabors, P.O., & Snow, C.E. (2002). Young bilingual children and early literacy development. In S.B. Neuman & D.K. Dickinson (Eds.), *Handbook of early literacy research* (Vol. 1, pp. 159–178). New York, NY: Guilford.

Improving Achievement for English Learners

Conclusions from Recent Reviews and Emerging Research

CLAUDE GOLDENBERG

■ ■ ■ ■ ■

This chapter will:

1. Present key findings from two major syntheses of research published in 2006 on the education of English language learners (ELLs),
2. Identify and summarize relevant recent research published after the years reviewed by the research syntheses,
3. Explain how instruction and support in ELLs' primary language can help them develop literacy skills (and possibly other academic skills) in English, and
4. Compare and contrast "generic" effective instruction with instruction that has been adjusted to the needs of ELLs.

Imagine that you are a second-grade student. During reading and language arts you will be faced with be an ambitious agenda. It will likely include irregular spelling patterns, diphthongs, syllabication rules, regular and irregular plurals, common prefixes and suffixes, or what we have traditionally called structural analysis. It also includes how to follow written instructions, to interpret words with multiple meanings, to locate information in expository texts, and to use comprehension strategies and background knowledge to understand what you read, cause and effect, and features of texts, such as theme, plot, and setting. You will be expected to read fluently and correctly at least 80 words per minute, adding approximately 3,000 words to your vocabulary each year from different types of texts. And you'll be expected to write narratives and friendly letters using appropriate forms, organization, critical elements, capitalization, and punctuation, revising as needed.

You will have a similar agenda in math. And if you are fortunate enough to attend a school where all instruction has not been completely eclipsed by reading and math, you'll be tackling topics such as motion, magnetism, life cycles, environments, weather, and fuel; the physical attributes of objects; family histories and time lines; labeling continents and major landmarks on maps; and learning how important historical figures made a difference in the lives of others. The expectations created by state and district academic standards can be a bit overwhelming both for students and teachers.[1]

If you don't speak English very well, your job will be to learn what everyone else is learning—and learn English as well. And not just the kind of English you will need to talk with your friends and teacher about classroom routines, what you like to eat, what you are having for lunch, where you went over the weekend, or who was mean to whom on the playground. You will also need what is called *Academic English,* a term that refers to more abstract, complex, and challenging language that will eventually permit you to participate successfully in mainstream classroom instruction. Academic English involves things such as relating an event, or a series of events, to someone who was not present; being able to make comparisons between alternatives and to justify a choice; knowing different forms and inflections of words and their appropriate use; and possessing and using content—specific vocabulary and modes of expression in different academic disciplines, such as mathematics and social studies. As if this were not enough, you eventually need to be able to understand *and produce* Academic English, both orally and in writing (Scarcella, 2003). If you don't, there is a real chance of falling behind your classmates, making poorer grades, getting discouraged, falling further behind, and having fewer educational and occupational choices.

This is the situation faced by millions of students in U.S. schools who do not speak English fluently. Their number has grown dramatically just in the past 15 years. In 1990, 1 of every 20 public school students in grades K–12 was an English language learner (ELL), that is, a student who speaks English either not at all or with enough limitations that he or she cannot fully participate in mainstream English instruction. Today the figure is 1 in 9. In 20 years demographers estimate that it might be 1 in 4. The ELL population has grown from 2 to 5 million since 1990, a period when the overall school population increased relatively little. States not typically associated with non-English speakers—South Carolina, Tennessee, Georgia, Indiana—each saw an increase in the ELL population of at least 400% between 1993 and 1994 and 2003 and 2004.

ELL students in the United States come from over 400 different language backgrounds; however, by far the largest proportion—80%—is Spanish speakers. This is an important fact to bear in mind, since Spanish speakers in the United States tend to come from lower economic and educational backgrounds than either the general population or other immigrants and language-minority populations. Consequently, most ELLs are at risk for poor school outcomes because of not only language but also socioeconomic factors. Speakers of Asian languages (e.g., Vietnamese, Hmong, Chinese, Korean, Khmer), who generally, although certainly not uniformly, tend to be of higher socioeconomic status, comprise the next largest group—about 8% of the ELL population.

In what sort of instructional environments are these students included? The question is difficult to answer, partly because of definitional and reporting inconsistencies from state to state (U.S. Department of Education, 2005; Zehler et al., 2003). The most recent national data come from a 2001–2002 school year survey (Zehler et al., 2003). To the extent that the portrait is still accurate 9 years later, a majority of English learners—approximately 60%—are in essentially all-English instruction. Beyond this, it is impossible to say what is typical. If anything, the picture has gotten more complex. Three states have over the past decade enacted laws that curtail bilingual education: California in 1998, Arizona in 2000, and Massachusetts in 2002; the number of students receiving bilingual education has steadily declined in those states. But even in states that require bilingual education—New Jersey, Texas, Illinois, New York, and New Mexico—the trends vary. In Texas, the number of students in bilingual education has gone up a bit; in Illinois, it has stayed about the same; in New York and New Jersey, it has gone down (Zehr, 2007a).

The shifting landscape is partly due to the accountability requirements of No Child Left Behind Act of 2001 (particularly in basic skills such as reading and math) and how individual states interpret them. No Child Left Behind permits assessment of ELLs in their primary language for up to 3 years and in some cases for an additional 2 years. But most states do not take advantage of this flexibility. The pressures on educators to immerse students in English are thus nearly overwhelming (Zehr, 2007a). This is ironic, since the best evidence we have shows that instruction in the primary language makes a positive contribution to academic achievement (particularly in reading) *in the second language.* I discuss this point at length in the following section.

About 12% of ELLs apparently receive no services or support at all related to their limited English proficiency. This might be a violation of the 1974 Supreme Court decision in *Lau v. Nichols* (414 U.S. No. 72–6520, pp. 563–572), requiring schools to teach ELLs so that they have "a meaningful opportunity to participate in the public educational program" (p. 563). Somewhat fewer than half of ELLs receive all-English instruction with some amount of "LEP services." (ELLs were formerly called LEP, or *limited English proficient*; the term is sometimes still used.) LEP services can include aides or resource teachers specifically for ELLs, instruction in English as a second language (ESL), and/or content instruction specially designed for students with LEP. The remaining ELLs—about 40%—are in programs that make some use of their primary language. Here, again, there is a wide range, with nothing being typical. In some cases, the native language is used extensively; and students are taught academic skills in that language, for example, how to read and write in Spanish. In other cases, students are taught academic skills in English, but their primary language is used only for "support," for example, to translate, explain, or preview material prior to an all-English lesson (Zehler et al., 2003). There is no way to know the amount of support students receive or, most critically, the quantity of the instruction and whether it is helpful for student achievement.

There are numerous program models that states report using with ELLs (U.S. Department of Education, 2005; see Genesee, 1999, for a description of the different program alternatives for ELLs, ranging from all-English instruction to different forms of bilingual education). Variability is again the rule. All 50 states (plus Washington, DC, and Puerto Rico) report some type of ESL instruction, but no state uses only one program model. Some states have as many as eight or nine different programs; New Mexico reports 10 (U.S. Department of Education, 2005). Clearly, it is difficult to generalize about the varied and complex instructional landscape for ELLs.

Regardless of the instruction ELLs are receiving, however, we have not done a particularly good job of promoting high levels of achievement among this fast-growing segment of the K–12 population. On state and national tests, students who are learning English consistently underperform in comparison to their English-speaking peers. In California, for example, approximately 50% of students who are fluent in English score as proficient or advanced on the California Standards Test in English language arts (the actual percentage of proficient or advanced students ranges from a high of 68% in grade 4 to a low of 46% in grade 11). In Contrast, among ELLs *who have been enrolled in school for 12 months or more*, the percentage that is proficient or advanced in English language arts ranges from a high of 28% in second grade to a dreadfully low 4% in 10th and 11th grades (data are from the California Department of Education Web site *cde.ca.gov*). The national picture shows the same discrepancies. On the 2005 National Assessment of Educational Progress (NAEP; *nces.ed.gov/nationsreportcard*), fourth-grade ELLs scored 35 points below non-ELLs in reading, 24 points below non-ELLs in math, and 32 points below non-ELLs in science. These are very large gaps—on fourth-grade NAEP, 10 points is roughly equivalent to a grade level. Similar gaps have also been found in reading, math, and science among eighth graders.

These discrepancies should be no surprise, of course, since ELLs—even if they have been in the United States for a year—are limited in their English proficiency, and the tests cited here are *in* English. This points, again, to the important and very complex question of how and particularly in what language ELLs should be assessed. If ELLs are assessed in English, we are almost certain to underestimate what they know and put them at even greater risk of poor achievement. This is problematic both from a policy perspective and instructionally: How can we design effective policies and practices if we systematically misjudge the knowledge and skills of a large number of students? There is no way to know whether ELLs tested in English score low because of lagging content knowledge and skills or because of limited English proficiency or some other factor, or a combination of factors. Unfortunately, many states do not take advantage of even the modest provisions in the No Child Left Behind Act that permits assessing ELLs in their primary language for up to 3, possibly 5, years. Recently a group of school districts sued to force the state of California to allow Spanish-speaking ELLs to take state-mandated test in Spanish. Plaintiffs in *Coachella Valley Unified School District v. California* argued that state "violated its duty to provide valid and reliable academic testing" (King, 2007). However, in a preliminary ruling, the judge indicated that the court lacked the jurisdiction to decide the case (Zehr, 2007b).

Whatever the explanation for these achievement gaps, they bode ill for English learners' future educational and vocational options. They also bode ill for the society as a whole, since the costs of large-scale underachievement are very high (Natriello, McDill, & Pallas, 1990). Passage of No Child Left behind in 2001 raised the stakes higher than ever for educators. Schools cannot meet their adequate yearly progress (AYP) goals unless all major subgroups at the school—including ELLs—meet achievement targets. Teachers of ELLs, as well as their site and district administrators, are thus under tremendous pressure. It is imperative that teachers, administrators, other school staff, and policymakers understand the state of our knowledge regarding how to improve the achievement of these students.

Unfortunately, the state of our knowledge is very modest. This is true for several reasons, among them that debates over language of instruction—the so-called "bilingual education" question—have historically dominated this field and, as a result, there has been relatively little solid research on many other important topics. *Bilingual education* is a term used to describe any instructional approach that teaches academic skills, such as reading, in the native language, in addition to teaching students academic skills in English. (For descriptions of the various approaches that fall under the bilingual umbrella, see Genesee, 1999.) The preeminent question in the education of ELLs has historically been whether student achievement is better when students are in some form of bilingual education or whether achievement is superior when students are taught using only English.

Research and policy affecting ELLs have historically been fueled by ideological and political considerations (Crawford, 1999), often with less attention to coherent programs of research that could shed light on ways to improve these students' educational outcomes. The net result has been an inadequate research base for informing comprehensive policies and practices, including, very critically, guidelines for determining the skills and knowledge teachers need to be effective with ELLs. As if this were not enough, the research is practically nonexistent at the secondary level. Almost all the research we have is at the element level, with a handful in middle school. But the issues change as children go through school, so findings from elementary school might not be particularly useful in high school. In higher grades, the learning is more complex and the achievement gaps are wider. Adolescence ushers in questions of identity, motivation, peer groups, and a wide range of other factors that change in fundamental ways what teachers and parents must address. Although the picture is slowly changing, the research we have precious little guidance.

Studies Agree on Key Findings

Two major reviews of the research on educating English learners were completed in 2006, one by the National Literacy Panel (NLP; August & Shanahan, 2006), the other by researchers associated with the Center for Research on Education, Diversity and Excellence

(CREDE; Genesee, Lindholm-Leary, Saunders, & Christian, 2006), The NLP comprised 18 researchers with expertise in literacy, language development, education of language-minority students, assessment, and quantitative and qualitative research methods. The NLP, whose work took nearly 3 years, identified over 3,000 reports, documents, dissertations and publications, produced from approximately 1980 to 2002, that were candidates for inclusion in its review. Fewer than 300 met the criteria for inclusion: They were *empirical* (that is, they collected, analyzed, and reported data rather than stated opinions, advocated positions, or reviewed research) and dealt with clearly identified language-minority populations, and studied children and youth ages 3–18. The CREDE report was produced over 2 years by a core group of four researchers (and three coauthors), all of whom had been engaged in language-minority and language research for many years. Like the NLP, the CREDE panel conducted literature searches to identify candidate empirical research reports on language-minority students from preschool to high school, but their searches were not as extensive as the NLP's. Approximately 200 articles and reports comprised the final group of studies the CREDE panel reviewed and upon which they based their conclusions. The studies the CREDE panel reviewed were published during approximately the same period as the studies the NLP reviewed.

Although they covered a lot of the same terrain, the CREDE and NLP reports differed in some ways. For example, the CREDE report only examined research conducted in the United States and only took into consideration outcomes in English; the NLP included studies conducted anywhere in the world (as long as they were published in English) and took into consideration outcomes in children's first or second language. The CREDE panelists only included quantitative studies (experiments or correlational research) almost exclusively, whereas the NLP also included quite a few qualitative studies.[2] The CREDE panel reviewed research that addressed children's English language development, literacy development, and achievement in the content areas (science, social studies, mathematics). In contrast, the NLP only looked at influences on literacy development (and aspects of oral language that are closely related to literacy; e.g., phonological awareness and vocabulary). A final and very important difference between the two reports was the criteria used to determine whether to include studies of bilingual education. The NLP used more stringent criteria, resulting in a difference in the two reports' findings about how long ELLs should receive bilingual instruction. I describe this difference in the section that follows.

These two reviews used various methods to synthesize the research and draw conclusions that would be helpful to educators and that would also identify areas for additional future study.[3] In doing their reviews, both sets of panelists paid particular attention to the quality of the studies and the degree to which reported findings were adequately supported by the research undertaken. The reports warrant our attention, since they represent the most concerted effort to date to identify the best knowledge available and set the stage for renewed efforts to find effective approaches to help English learners succeed in school. It would be impossible to summarize fully the reports here, and educators are encouraged to obtain and study them. But their key conclusion can help us forge a new foundation for improving the education of children from non-English-speaking homes. The findings can be summarized in three major points, which I discuss in the sections that follow:

1. Teaching students to read in the first language promotes higher levels of reading achievement in *English*.
2. What we know about good instruction and curriculum in general holds true for English learners as well.
3. English learners require instructional modifications when instructed in English.

Teaching Students to Read in the First Language Promotes Higher Levels of Reading Achievement in English

To date, five meta-analyses[4] have concluded that bilingual education promotes academic achievement in students' *second* language (Greene, 1997; August & Shanahan, 2006; Rolstad, Mahoney, & Glass, 2005; Slavin & Cheung, 2005; Willig, 1985). This finding most clearly applies to learning to read. Findings for other curricular areas are much more equivocal. Nonetheless, this is an extraordinary convergence. To appreciate the strength of the finding, readers should understand how unusual it is even to have five independent meta-analyses on the same issue conducted by five independent researchers from diverse perspectives. The fact that they all reached essentially the same conclusion is noteworthy. With the exception of one, none of the meta-analysts have or had any particular investment, professionally or otherwise, in bilingual education. They were completely nonpartisan, methodologically rigorous, and independent researchers. (The one exception, Willig, was also rigorous, but had worked in the field of bilingual education, so skeptics might suspect a probilingual education agenda.) I know of no other finding in the entire educational research literature that can claim to be supported unanimously by five independent meta-analyses conducted over a 20-year span. In fact, this might be one of the strongest findings in the entire field of educational research. Although many questions remain about the role of primary language in educating English learners, the role of primary language in educating English learners, the consistent finding from these meta-analyses should put to rest the idea that English-only instruction is preferable.

Approximately two or three dozen experiments conducted and reported over the past 35 years have compared reading instruction that uses students' primary and secondary languages with second-language immersion (which in the United States would, of course, be English). The NLP conducted a meta-analysis of 17 of these studies—the others did not meet their stringent methodological criteria—and concluded that teaching ELLs to read in their primary language, compared with teaching them to read in their second language only, boosts their reading achievement *in the second language.* In other words, students' second language reading achievement will be higher if they are first taught to read in their home language, compared to being taught to read in the second language right off the bat. And the higher-quality, more rigorous studies showed the strongest effects of all.

Although there are other possible explanations, the key to explaining how a primary language instruction results in higher achievement in English is probably what educational psychologists call "transfer." Transfer is one of the most venerable and important concepts in education. With respect to English learners, a substantial body of research reviewed by both CREDE and NLP researchers suggests that literacy and other skills and knowledge transfer across languages; that is, if you learn something in one language, such as decoding, comprehension skills, or a concept such as "democracy," you either already know it in (i.e., transfer it to) another language, or you can more easily learn it in another language. Transfer also explains another important finding first pointed out in the meta-analysis by Slavin and Cheung (2005), published a year before the NLP report appeared[5]: ELLs can be taught to read in their primary language and in English simultaneously (at different times in the school day), with mutual benefit to literacy development in both languages. Teachers cannot assume that transfer is automatic, however. Students sometimes do not realize what they know in their first language (e.g., the cognates *elefante* and *elephant* or *ejemplo* and *example*). Jiménez (1997) puts it this way: "Less successful bilingual readers view their two languages as separate and unrelated and they often see their non-English language backgrounds as detrimental" (p. 227). It is necessary that teachers be aware of what students know and can do in their primary language, so they can help them apply these skills and knowledge to tasks in English.

Transfer of reading skills across languages appears to be true even if languages use different alphabetic systems, although the different alphabets probably diminish the degree of transfer. For example, studies of transfer between English and Spanish find relatively high correlations on measures of word reading and spelling. Some studies of English and non-Roman alphabets (e.g., Arabic or Persian) in contrast find much lower correlations. However, comprehension skills appear to transfer readily between languages with different alphabets, such as English and Korean.

"Transfer" is a critical point, since opponents of primary language instruction often argue that time spent in the first language is wasted from the standpoint of promoting progress in the second. The opposite is actually true: Productive learning in one language makes a positive contribution to learning in the second language. Since academic learning—with which schools and teachers must be most concerned—is most efficient and productive in the language one knows best, the clear conclusion from this research is that teaching academic skills (keeping in mind that research is strongest with respect to teaching reading) in the learner's stronger language is the most efficient approach to take.

The effects of primary language instruction are modest—but they are real. Researchers gauge the effect of a program or an instructional practice in terms of an *effect size* that tells us how much improvement can be expected from using the program or practice. The average effect size of primary language reading instruction over 2 to 3 years (the typical length of time children in the studies were followed) is around 0.35–0.40; estimates range from about 0.2 to about 0.6, depending on how the calculation is done. What this means is that teaching students to read in their home language can boost achievement in the second language by a total of about 12–15 percentile points (in comparison to students who do not receive primary language instruction) over 2–3 years. This is not a huge amount, but neither is it trivial. These effects are reliable, and they apply to both elementary and secondary school students (although only two of the 17 studies the NLP included in the meta-analysis were with secondary school students, both produced positive effects). To provide some perspective, the National Reading Panel (2000), which reviewed experimental research on English speakers only, found that the average effect size of phonics instruction is 0.44, a bit larger than the likely average effect size of primary language reading instruction. Primary language reading instruction is clearly no panacea, just as phonics instruction is no panacea. But, relatively speaking, it makes a meaningful contribution to reading achievement *in English.*

Beyond the finding that primary language instruction promotes achievement in English, however, there are a great many unknowns: Is primary language instruction more beneficial for some learners than for others (e.g., those with weaker or stronger primary language skills? Weaker or stronger English skills?) Is it more effective in some settings than others? What should be the relative emphasis between promoting knowledge and skills in the primary language and developing English language proficiency? What level of skill in the students' primary language does the teacher need to possess to be effective? In an English immersion situation, what is the most effective way to use the primary language to support children's learning? We cannot answer these questions with confidence. Individual studies might point in certain directions, but we lack a body of solid studies that permit us to go beyond the general finding about the effects of primary language instruction on achievement in English.

We also cannot say with confidence how long students should receive instruction in their primary language. On the one hand, the CREDE synthesis concluded that more primary language instruction over more years leads to higher levels of ELL achievement in English. On the other hand, the NLP's meta-analysis of language of instruction did not support any conclusion about optimal number of years of primary language instruction. The reason for the discrepancy lies in the different criteria CREDE and NLP researchers used for including studies in their syntheses: The CREDE report included studies and evaluations of *two-way bilingual education*. Two-way models involve some combination of first (e.g., Spanish) and second language (e.g., English) instruction throughout elementary school; some go through middle and high school. Their goal is bilingualism and biliteracy for all students in the program. Evaluations have been very positive, but these studies do not control for preexisting differences or population differences between students in the two-way programs and students in comparison programs. Because of this limitation in the research designs, the NLP did not include two-way programs in its meta-analysis. The NLP included only programs of relatively short duration—l to 3 years—among which there were no differences in student outcomes in relation to years in primary language instruction.

Despite these many unknowns, there is another reason to consider bilingual instruction for English learners. And that is the inherent advantage of knowing and being literate in two languages. It should come as no surprise that the meta-analyses found that in addition to promoting achievement in the second language, bilingual instructions also promotes achievement in the primary language. In other words, it helps students become bilingual. Knowing two languages confers numerous obvious advantages—cultural, intellectual, cognitive (e.g., Bialystock, 2001), vocational, and economic (Saiz & Zoido, 2005), although readers should note that the populations studies to support these conclusions are different from the population of ELLs addressed in this chapter. Regardless, many would argue that bilingualism and biliteracy ought to be our educational goal for English learners (see, most recently, Gándara & Rumberger, 2006). I would agree but take it a step further: It should be a goal for all students.

Questions of how long and to what extent bilingual instruction should be used and the benefits of bilingual instruction do not even arise in many schools. Instruction in the primary language is sometimes not feasible, either because there are no qualified staff or because students come from numerous language backgrounds or, sadly, because of uniformed policy choices or political decision, such as California's Proposition 227. English learners can still be helped to achieve at higher levels. Although the research here is not as solid as the research on primary language instruction, which itself is incomplete in many respects, educators have two other important principles, supported by research to varying degrees, on which to base their practice. We turn to them now.

What We Know about Good Instruction and Curriculum in General Holds for ELLs

Both the CREDE and NLP reports conclude that ELLs learn in much the same way as non-ELLs (although modifications are almost certainly necessary, as discussed in the next section). Good instruction for students in general tends to be good instruction for ELLs in particular. If instructed in the primary language, the application of effective instructional models to English learners is transparent; all that differs is the language of instruction. But even when instructed in English, effective instruction for ELLs is similar in important respects to effective instruction for non-ELLs.

As a general rule, all students tend to benefit from clear goals and learning objectives; meaningful, challenging, and motivating contexts; a curriculum rich with content; well-designed, clearly structured, and appropriately paced instruction; active engagement and participation; opportunities to practice, apply, and transfer new learning;

feedback on correct and incorrect responses; periodic review and practice; frequent assessments to gauge progress, with reteaching as needed; and opportunities to interact with other students in motivating and appropriately structured contexts. Although these instructional variables have not been studied with ELLs to the degree they have with English speakers, existing studies suggest that what is known about effective instruction in general ought to be the foundation of effective teaching for English learners. There are, of course, individual or group differences: students might require or benefit from more or less structure, practice, review, autonomy, challenge, or any other dimension of teaching and learning. This is as likely to be true for English learners as it is for English speakers.

The NLP found that ELLs learning to read in English just like English speakers learning to read in English, benefit from explicit teaching of components of literacy (e.g., phonemic awareness, phonics, vocabulary, comprehension, and writing). Particularly with respect to phonological and decoding skills, ELLs appear to be capable of learning at levels comparable to those of English speakers, if they are provided with good, structured, explicit teaching. Some of the studies supporting this conclusion were conducted with ELLs in Canada, so we must be cautious in interpreting them for the U.S. context. The ELL population in Canada is very different from the ELL population in the United States. Because of highly restrictive immigration laws, the Canadian ELL population is from families with higher income and education levels. Nonetheless, the NLP reviewed five studies that, as a group, showed the benefits of structured direct instruction for the development of these early literacy skills. A study in England, for example, found that Jolly Phonics had a stronger effect on ELLs' phonological awareness, alphabet knowledge, and their application to reading and writing than did a Big Books approach.

Other studies also showed similar effects of directly teaching the sounds that make up words, how letters represent those sounds, and how letters combine to form words. In fact, studies published since the NLP and CREDE reports completed their reviews continue to show the positive impact of structured, explicit instruction on beginning reading skills. Vaughn et al. (2006) have shown the benefits of small-group, explicit instruction for at-risk first-grade readers. The intervention was conducted in either English or Spanish, depending on children's instructional language. In both languages, the intervention consisted of explicit phonological and phonics (decoding) instruction, fluency, oral language, vocabulary, and comprehension. Compared to children who received their school's existing intervention, children in the Vaughn et al. program scored higher on multiple measures of reading and academic achievement. In a study conducted solely in English, Roberts, and Neal (2004) also showed that ELLs were more likely to learn what they were explicitly taught: Preschool children in a "comprehension-oriented" group learned more vocabulary and print concepts than children in a "letter/rhyme-focused" group. In contrast, children in the letter/rhyme-focused group learned more letter names and how to write letters.

Studies of vocabulary instruction for ELLs also show that students are more likely to learn words when they are directly taught. Just as with English speakers, ELLs learn more words when the words are embedded in meaningful contexts and students are provided ample opportunities for their repetition and use, in contrast to looking up dictionary definitions or presenting words in single sentences. In a preschool study, Collins (2005) showed that explaining new vocabulary helped Portuguese-speaking children acquire vocabulary from storybook reading. Although children with higher initial English scores learned more words, explaining new words was helpful for all children, regardless of how little English they knew. Similarly, a study reviewed by the NLP involving fifth-graders showed that explicit vocabulary instruction, using words, from texts appropriate for and likely to interest the students, combined with exposure to and use of the words in numerous contexts (reading and hearing stories, discussions, posting target words, and writing words and definitions for homework) led to improvements in word learning and reading comprehension (Carlo et al., 2004). These principles of effective vocabulary instruction have been found to be effective for English speakers (e.g., Beck, McKeown, & Kucan, 2002).

Other types of instruction that the NLP review found to be promising with ELLs include *cooperative learning* (students working interdependently on group instructional tasks and learning goals), encouraging reading in English, discussions to promote comprehension *(instructional conversations)*, and mastery learning. A *mastery learning study* reviewed by the NLP was particularly informative because the researchers found this approach (which involves precise behavioral objectives permitting students to reach a "mastery" criterion before moving to new learning) more effective in promoting Mexican American students' reading comprehension than an approach that involved teaching to the students' supposed "cultural learning style."

The CREDE report concludes that "the best recommendation to emerge from our review favors instruction that combines interactive and direct approaches" (Genesee, 1999, p. 140). *Interactive* refers to instruction with give-and-take between learners and the teacher, where the teacher is actively promoting students' progress by encouraging higher levels of thinking, speaking, and reading at their instructional levels. Examples of interactive teaching include structured discussions *(instructional conversations)*, brainstorming, and editing/discussing student or teacher writing. *Direct approaches* emphasize explicit and direct teaching of skills or knowledge, for example, letter–sound associations, spelling patterns, vocabulary words, and mathematical algorithms. Typically, direct instruction uses techniques such as modeling, instructional input, corrective feedback, and guided practice to help students acquire knowledge and skills as efficiently as possible. The CREDE report notes that "direct instruction of specific skills" is important to help students gain "mastery of literacy-related skills that are often embedded in complex literacy or academic tasks" (Genesee, 1999, p. 140).

In contrast to interactive and direct teaching, the report found at best mixed evidence supporting what it termed *process approaches,* in which students are exposed to rich literacy experiences and literacy materials but receive little direct teaching or structuring of learning. In one study, for example, students were exposed to alternative reading and writing strategies on wall charts, but this was insufficient to ensure the strategies would be employed. In another study, Spanish-speaking ELLs who received structured writing lessons outperformed students who received extended opportunities to do "free writing." The CREDE report concludes that process strategies are "not sufficient to promote acquisition of the specific skills that comprise reading and writing . . .

[F]ocused and explicit instruction in particular skills and subskills is called for if ELLs are to become efficient and effective readers and writers" (Genesee, 1999, pp. 139–140).

English Learners Require Instructional Modifications

The NLP review showed that in the earliest stages of learning to read, when the focus is on sounds, letters, and how they combine to form words that can be read, English learners can make comparable progress to that of English speakers, provided that the instruction is clear, focused, and systematic. In other words, when the language requirements are relatively low, as they are for learning *phonological skills* (the sounds of the language and how words are made up of smaller constituent sounds), letter–sound combinations, decoding, and word recognition, it is possible for ELLs to make the sort of progress we expect of English speakers, although they still probably require some additional support due to language limitations. But as content gets more challenging and language demands increase, more and more complex vocabulary and syntax are required, and the need for modifications to make the content more accessible and comprehensible increases accordingly.

ELLs' language limitations begin to slow their progress as vocabulary and content knowledge become more relevant for continued reading (and general academic) success, around third grade. Learners who know the language can concentrate on the academic skills they are to learn. But learners who do not know the language, or do not know it well enough, must devote part of their attention to learning the skills, and part of their attention to learning and understanding the language in which those skills are taught. This is why it is critical that teachers work to develop ELLs' English oral language skills, particularly vocabulary, and their content knowledge from the time they start school, even before they have learned the reading "basics." Vocabulary development is, of course, important for all students; but it is particularly critical for ELLs. There can be little doubt that explicit attention to vocabulary development—everyday words, as well as more specialized academic words—needs to be part of English learners' school programs. What constitutes effective vocabulary instruction for ELLs, and how does it differ from effective instruction for English speakers?

As I have already discussed, there are probably many similarities. Collins (2005), cited earlier, found that preschool English learners acquired more vocabulary when the teacher explained words contained in a storybook read to them. ELLs benefit from clear explanations, just as English speakers do. But Collins also found that children who began with lower English scores learned less than children with higher English scores; that is, knowing less English made it harder to learn additional English. What might have helped the children with lower initial English proficiency gain more English vocabulary? Another preschool study (Roberts & Neal, 2004) revealed that pictures helped children with low levels of oral English learn story vocabulary (e.g., *dentist*, *mouse*, *cap*). The *visual representation* of concepts, not just a language-based *explanation*, provided children with additional support in learning the vocabulary words. There is scant research on this topic, but we would also expect that songs, rhymes, chants, and additional opportunities to use and repeat words would help build vocabulary among young English learners.

It is a good bet that effective strategies for English speakers will involve some sort ✖ of modifications or adjustments to make them as effective as they are with English learners. Roberts and Neal (2004) provide an example related to the critical issue of assessment, which I mentioned earlier in the chapter. Roberts and Neal attempted to teach preschool ELLs rhyming skills, an important aspect of phonological awareness. The way they assessed rhyming skills was by prompting the children with a word and asking them to provide a word that rhymed. If the tester said *lake*, the child would be expected to produce, for example, *cake*. As it turned out, regardless of instructional group, *all* the children did very poorly on the assessment. The average score on the rhyming test was less than 1, meaning that a lot of children simply did not respond. Why? Probably because the task demand was simply beyond the children; they were unable to *produce* a rhyming word, since their vocabularies were so limited. The children were, in essence, given a test that measured their productive vocabularies as much as it measured their rhyming skills. The study would probably have obtained different results if the researchers had presented pairs of words and asked the children to distinguish between rhyming and non rhyming pairs, or else had children select the rhyming word from several possible choices.

This example suggests two things: First, it is essential that ELLs be assessed in a way that uncouples language proficiency from content knowledge; language limitations can obscure an accurate picture of what children actually know and can do. Second, and directly following from this, an important instructional modification for ELLs might be to tailor task demands to children's English language proficiency. Teachers should not expect children to produce language beyond their level of English proficiency; conversely, they should provide language-learning and language-use tasks that challenge children and stretch their language development.

What about older children? Some clues for vocabulary instruction are offered in a study, also cited earlier, by Carlo et al. (2004), who examined the effects of a vocabulary instruction program on Spanish-speaking ELL and English-speaking fifth graders. Their approach was based on principles of vocabulary instruction found to be valid for children who already speak English (e.g., explicit teaching of words, using words from texts likely to interest students, multiple exposures to and uses of the words in numerous contexts). The researchers included additional elements: activities such as charades that got learners actively involved in manipulating and analyzing word meanings; writing and spelling the words numerous times; strategic uses of Spanish (e.g., previewing lessons using Spanish texts, providing teachers with translation equivalents of the target words, using English–Spanish cognates, such as *supermarket* and *supermercado*); and selection of texts and topics on immigration that were expected to resonate with the Mexican and Dominican immigrant students. Overall, the experimental program produced relatively strong effects in terms of students learning of the target vocabulary. It produced much smaller, but still significant, effects on reading comprehension. Particularly noteworthy is that the effects of the program were equivalent for ELLs and English-speaking students. Thus, although the researchers acknowledged that they could not determine which of the extra ELL supports explained the program's impact on these students, their demonstration that, with additional support, a program can have a similar impact on both ELLs and English speakers is very important.

Below is a possible list of supports or modifications for ELLs receiving English-only instruction. Some of these are only now starting to be investigated empirically; others have data from studies that fail to control for important variables, therefore limiting our conclusions; still others have no supporting data.

Modifications Using Students' Primary Language

The first group of modifications involves use of the primary language. Readers should note the contrast between the use of the native language in bilingual instruction and in an English immersion context. In bilingual education, students are taught language arts, and sometimes math and other subjects, such as social studies, in their primary language. In contrast, when the primary language is used as an instructional modification in an English immersion context, instruction is basically in English, but the primary language is used to make the instruction more meaningful or comprehensible. This does not involve teaching children academic skills in their primary language or attempting to promote primary language development per se. Instead, the primary language is used as a bridge, or "scaffold," to learning the content in English. There are several possible examples of using the primary language as a support for ELLs:

- Use of the primary language for clarification and explanation. This can be done by the teacher, classroom aide, a peer, or a volunteer in the classroom. While this approach makes intuitive sense, I know of no research that actually gauges its effectiveness. It is easy to see how explaining or clarifying concepts in the home language can help provide ELLs with access to what is going on in the classroom. But it is also not difficult to imagine downsides; for example, if anyone but the teacher provides the explanations (e.g., a peer), he or she might not be accurate; or students can become dependent on a "translator," who provides a crutch for them and as a result do not exert themselves to learn English; or if translations or periodic explanations in the primary language are offered throughout lessons, students can "tune out" during the English part.

- Introducing new concepts in the primary language prior to the lesson in English, then reviewing the new content again in the primary language (sometimes called *preview–review;* see Ovando, Collier, & Combs, 2003). This is different from clarification and explanation since what this does is "front-load" the new learning in the student's primary language, then review it after the lesson. There is no ongoing explanation or translation. When the real lesson is delivered in English, the student already is somewhat familiar with the content, but he or she has to concentrate to get the message as it is delivered in English. Because of the previewing, the language used in the lesson should be more comprehensible and, in principle at least, the student will walk away knowing more content *and* more language (vocabulary, key phrases). Then, by reviewing lesson content afterward, the teacher checks to see whether students accomplished the lesson objective. The NLP reviewed a study that provided some support for the effectiveness of this approach. Prior to reading a book in English, teachers previewed difficult vocabulary in the primary language (Spanish), then reviewed the material in Spanish. This produced better comprehension and recall than the control conditions: reading the book in English and doing a simultaneous Spanish translation while reading.

- Other primary language support. One can imagine numerous variations on the "primary language support" theme. A study not included in the NLP provides a creative example. Fung, Wilkinson, and Moore (2003) found that introducing reciprocal teaching strategies in students' primary language improved reading comprehension in the second language. *Reciprocal teaching* is a technique for promoting reading comprehension. Students are taught four strategies: asking questions about the text, summarizing what they have read, clarifying the text's meaning, and predicting what will come next. This set of strategies has been found to promote reading comprehension among students who are adequate decoders but poor comprehenders. Fung et al. taught middle school ELLs reciprocal teaching strategies in their primary language and in English. They then found that students used more reading comprehension and monitoring strategies, *and* their reading comprehension improved when they read in English. Although the authors suggest that teaching reading strategies in students' home language can be an effective form of primary language support, the study did not compare home-language-assisted reciprocal teaching with English-only reciprocal teaching; thus, we do not really know the role that primary language support itself played in improving student comprehension.

- Another type of primary language support consists of focusing on the similarities—difference between English and students' native language (e.g., if using the Roman alphabet, letters represent the same sounds in English and other languages, but others do not). In addition, languages have *cognates,* that is, words with shared meanings from common etymological roots (e.g., *geography* and *geografía*). Calling students' attention to these cognates could help extend their vocabularies and improve their comprehension. However, we do not know the effect of cognate instruction per se. The Carlo et al. (2004) vocabulary program described earlier used cognates as one strategy to help ELLs develop their vocabularies and improve comprehension; but, as previously discussed, the intervention comprised many elements, and it is impossible to know the effect of any single element. Nonetheless, there are a number of useful sources of Spanish–English cognates that teachers of ELLs can consult (e.g., Calderon et al., 2003). Nash (1999) offers an exhaustive, book-length list, but also see Prado (1996) for false cognates that can cause problems, such as (my personal favorite) *embarrassed* and *embarazada*. The latter means "pregnant." When put in the masculine form, *embarazado*, it can really light up a classroom of Spanish-speaking adolescents.

Modifications Using Only English

In addition to modifications that make use of students' primary language, a number have been suggested that use only English. All of the following appear to be "generic" scaffolds and supports; that is, there is little obviously tailored to ELLs. They might, in fact, be effective strategies for many students, particularly those who need more learning support than is typically provided in teaching–learning situations where verbal exchanges of information predominate. These modifications include the following:

- Predictable and consistent classroom management routines, aided by diagrams, lists, and easy-to-read schedules on the board or on charts, to which the teacher refers frequently.
- Graphic organizers that make content and the relationships among concepts and different lesson elements visually explicit.
- Additional opportunities for practice during the school day, after school, or for homework.
- Redundant key information (e.g., visual cues, pictures, and physical gestures) about lesson content and classroom procedures.
- Identifying, highlighting, and clarifying difficult words and passages within texts to facilitate comprehension and, more generally, greatly emphasizing vocabulary development.
- Helping students consolidate text knowledge by having the teacher, other students, and ELLs themselves summarize and paraphrase.
- Giving students extra practice in reading words, sentences, and stories to build automaticity and fluency.
- Providing opportunities for extended interactions with teacher and peers.
- Adjusting instruction (teacher vocabulary, rate of speech, sentence complexity, and expectations for student language production) according to students' oral English proficiency.
- Targeting both content and English language objectives in every lesson.
- Use of reading materials that take into account students' personal experiences, including relevant aspects of their cultural background, which aids their reading comprehension (although proficiency in the language of the text has a stronger influence on comprehension than familiarity with passage content).

The modifications that students need will probably change as they develop increased English proficiency. Students who are beginning English speakers will need a great deal of support, sometimes known as *instructional scaffolding*. For example, at the very beginning levels, teachers have to speak slowly and somewhat deliberately, with clear vocabulary and diction; use pictures or other objects to illustrate the content being taught; and ask students to respond either nonverbally (e.g., by pointing or signaling) or in one- or two-word utterances. As they gain in proficiency, students need less modification; for example, teachers can use more complex vocabulary and sentence structures, and expect students to respond with longer utterances; visual information can be presented in written form, as well as in pictures. On the other hand, more modification may be needed when completely new or particularly difficult topics are taught. It might also be that some students in some contexts require more modifications than others. We utterly lack the data necessary to offer such guidelines. In any case, proficiency in Academic English (as distinct from conversational English, which can be acquired to a reasonably high level in approximately 2–3 years) can require 6 or more years (Genesee et al., 2006), so some degree of support is probably required for a substantial portion of ELLs' schooling.

Why does proficiency in Academic English take 4–5 or more years than proficiency in conversational English? There are several possible reasons. Conversational English is probably used more and is fairly limited in the vocabulary and forms of expression it requires. It is also almost always contextualized by gestures, intonation, and references to familiar and concrete situations. In contrast, Academic English is generally not used outside of school and tends to present new vocabulary, more complex sentence structures, and rhetorical forms not typically encountered in nonacademic setting. "Academic" forms of the language are also used to refer to abstract and complex concepts in subject-matter disciplines (science, literature, mathematics, social studies, the arts), particularly as students progress through the grades. Knowing conversational English obviously helps in learning Academic English, but the latter is clearly a more challenging task.

English Language Development and Other Considerations

It should be apparent that providing English language development (ELD) instruction to ELLs is critically important. Unfortunately, and surprisingly, the CREDE report reveals that research can tell us very little about how or even whether we can accelerate progress in oral English language development. Studies have shown that specific aspects of language can be taught at least in terms of short-term learning effects (e.g., vocabulary, listening comprehension, grammatical elements; see meta-analysis on second-Language teaching in Norris & Ortega, 2000), but we do not really know how to accelerate the overall process of language learning.

A study that appeared after the CREDE report was published, however, suggests that a comprehensive and structured approach to teaching English directly and explicitly can help accelerate young children's English language development. Tong, Lara-Alecio, Irby, Mathes, and Kwok (2008) found that providing kindergarten and first-grade students with an "English-oracy intervention" resulted in accelerated ELD growth (as measured by tests of vocabulary and listening comprehension. The intervention was equally effective with students in English immersion and bilingual education. Some of the elements it comprised included: daily tutorials with a published ELD program; storytelling and retelling with authentic, culturally relevant literature and questions leveled from easy to difficult; and an academic oral language activity using a "question of the day." Students with lowest levels of English proficiency received 10–20 minutes of instruction in addition to the 75–90 minutes/day of the base intervention program. Because the experimental group received more ELD instructional time than the control group, it is impossible to rule out the effects of additional time. In addition, the measures of oral language used were very limited and did not gauge many important dimensions of language proficiency. Nonetheless, the study is important in demonstrating the possibility of accelerating English language development, at least in the early grades and on some aspects of language, through intensive, organized instruction.

Based on descriptive studies of ELLs in the United States, the CREDE report concluded that it takes at least 6 years for most students to go from being a nonspeaker to having native-like proficiency (e.g., from kindergarten to grade 5 or later). Even students in all-English instruction do not begin to show advanced intermediate levels—which are still short of native-like proficiency—for at least 4 years (i.e., grade 3 or later). The idea that children will quickly become fluent in English if immersed in all-English instruction is contradicted by the research literature. Certainly, exceptions can be found, but fluency within a year of English immersion in school is not the norm among the ELL population in the United States. Can the process be meaningfully sped up so that ELLs can benefit from mainstream English instruction earlier in their educational careers? We don't really know. The near absence of such research, combined with the obvious need to develop English proficiency as students acquire knowledge and skills across the curriculum, places a huge burden on both students and teachers.

One question that frequently arises is whether ELD should be taught separately or integrated with the rest of the curriculum. A recent study suggests that English language achievement is somewhat enhanced by a separate ELD period. Saunders, Foorman, and Carlson (2006) found that when a separate ELD block was used, teachers spent more time on oral English, and were more efficient and focused in their use of time. The ELD block, by design, targeted ELD, and students who received a separate ELD block scored somewhat higher than students who did not. When there was no ELD block, less time was spent focusing on English per se and more on other language arts activities, such as reading. It is important to bear in mind that this study was limited to kindergarten, and the effect was small. But if the findings are accurate, the cumulative effect of a separate block of ELD instruction over many years could be substantial. At the moment, however, this is speculation.

Some educators have also suggested that instruction for ELLs must also be tailored to students' culture. This suggestion is based on the observation that because different cultural groups speak, behave, and interact differently, educators should use instructional approaches that are "culturally compatible" (that build upon or complement students' behavioral and interactional patterns). Many readers will be surprised to learn that the NLP concluded that there is little evidence to support the proposition that culturally compatible instruction enhances the actual achievement of English learners (although materials that take into account students' background knowledge and personal experiences can aid in reading comprehension and development of literacy skills; see "Modifications Using Only English"). In fact, as mentioned earlier, a study reviewed by the NLP found that a mastery learning-direct instruction approach produced better effects on Mexican American students' reading comprehension than did an approach tailored to their "cultural characteristics." Some studies, most of which are methodologically very weak, have indicated that culturally accommodated instruction can promote engagement and higher-level participation during lessons. This is a meaningful finding, but it is not the same as establishing a connection between culturally accommodated instruction and measured achievement. The hypothesis is certainly plausible, and future research might establish such a connection. But for now it appears that developing lessons with solid content and clearly structured instruction is a better use of teachers' time.

Another proposition with dubious research backing is that grouping ELLs and English speakers during instruction will, in itself, promote ELLs' oral English proficiency. (Simply grouping or pairing students together should not be confused with well-implemented "cooperative learning," for which we have evidence of positive effects on ELLs' learning, discussed earlier.) Teachers sometimes assume that pairing ELLs and English speakers will provide ELLs with productive language learning opportunities, but the CREDE synthesis casts doubt on this. One study described the case of an ELL whose teacher relied almost exclusively on classmates to support the student's classroom participation. Because the assignments were far beyond this child's language and academic skills, her peers "were at a loss as to how to assist her" (Genesee, 2006, p. 28). Another study, an examination of cooperative learning in one 6th-grade classroom, found that English speaking students and ELLs rarely engaged in interactions that we might expect to promote learning. More typically, English speakers cut the interactions short in order to finish the assignment, as did this student: "Just write that down. Who cares? Let's finish up." (p. 28). If teachers use cooperative or peer learning activities, they must ensure that English speakers be grouped with ELLs who are not so lacking in English skills that meaningful communication and task engagement become problematic. In addition, tasks that students engage in must be carefully designed to be instructionally meaningful and provide suitable opportunities for students to participate at their functional levels. Simply pairing or grouping students together and encouraging them to interact or help each other is not sufficient.

Implications for Improving Instruction

Practically, what do these findings and conclusions mean? The following is the sort of instructional framework to which our current state of knowledge points:

- If feasible, children should he taught reading, and possibly other basic skills, in their primary language. Primary language instruction (1) develops first-language skills, thereby promoting bilingualism and biliteracy; (2) promotes learning (particularly learning to read) in English; and (3) can be carried out as children also learn to read (and learn other academic skills) in English. We lack definitive studies on whether there are optimal lengths of time for ELLs to receive primary language instruction; however, the answer to this question will partly depend upon our goals for the education of ELLs.
- As needed, students should be helped to transfer what they know in their first language to learning tasks presented in English; teachers should not assume that transfer is automatic.
- Teaching in the first and second languages can be approached similarly; in fact, what we know about effective instruction in general should be the foundation for how we approach instruction of ELLs; direct and explicit instruction is probably especially helpful. However, . . .
- Adjustments or modifications will be necessary, probably for several years and at least for some students, until students reach sufficient familiarity with Academic English to permit them to be successful in mainstream instruction; more complex learning might require more modifications.
- ELLs need intensive ELD instruction (especially targeting Academic English), but we have little data on how, or even whether, the process of English language acquisition can be accelerated.
- ELLs also need academic content instruction, just as all students do; although ELD is crucial, it should not completely supplant instruction designed to promote academic content knowledge.[6]

Local or state policies, such as those in California, which block use of the primary language and limit instructional modifications for English learners, are simply not based on the best scientific evidence. Moreover, these policies make educators' jobs more difficult, which is unconscionable under any circumstance but especially egregious in light of increased accountability pressures they and their students face. Despite many remaining questions, we have useful starting points for renewed efforts to improve the achievement of this fastest growing segment of the school-age population. If educators and their students are to be held accountable, practice and policy must be based on the best evidence we have. Otherwise, claims of "scientifically based practice" are simply hollow slogans.

ENGAGEMENT ACTIVITIES

1. In your own words, identify and explain what you think are the key findings from the CREDE and National Literacy Panel reports.

2. Explain how ELLs' primary language can help them develop literacy skills (and possibly other academic skills) in English. Discuss primary language *instruction* and primary language *support* separately.

3. Describe how instruction that has been adjusted to the needs of ELLs differs from "generic" effective instruction.

4. Describe (in about a paragraph) a lesson for English speakers that uses elements of effective instruction identified in this chapter. Discuss the adjustments you would incorporate into the lesson if you were to teach it to a class with ELLs (assume approximately intermediate English proficiency).

ACKNOWLEDGMENTS

This chapter is adapted with permission from Goldenberg, C. (2008). Improving achievement for English language learners. In S. Neuman (Ed.), *Educating the other America: Top experts tackle poverty, literacy, and achievement in our schools* (pp. 139–162). Baltimore: Paul H. Brookes Publishing Co., Inc.; and Goldenberg, C. (2008). Teaching English language learners: What the research does—and does not—say. *American Educator, 32*(2), 8–23, 42–44.

NOTES

1. Most of the preceding list is derived from content standards for second grade adopted by the California State Board of Education available at *www.cde.ca.gov*. The reading fluency figure is from Behavioral Research and Teaching (2005); vocabulary from Lehr, Osborn, and Hiebert (n.d.).

2. Experimental studies are considered the "gold standard" if one wants to determine the effect of a particular program or type of instruction. Experiments include treatment and comparison groups, as well as other controls designed to ensure that any impacts found can be attributed to the treatment (e.g., as opposed to differences between two groups of students). Corelational studies can establish that there is a relationship between two things (e.g., an instructional method and student achievement), but they cannot indicate that one thing caused another. Qualitative studies generally attempt to describe and analyze rather than measure and count. Precise and highly detailed qualitative studies can establish causation (e.g., a part of a lesson that led to student learning), but because the number of subjects in a qualitative study is typically low, they are not good for establishing generalizability.

3. Readers should be aware of the dramatic discrepancy between the research base for English speakers and English learners. For example, the National Reading Panel (2000) synthesized findings from over 400 experimental studies of instruction in phonological awareness, phonics, vocabulary, reading fluency, and reading comprehension. In contrast, the NLP could identify only 17 experimental studies of instructional procedures, even though the NLP considered more topics and used looser inclusion criteria.

4. A *meta-analysis* is a statistical technique that allows researchers to combine data from many studies and calculate the average effect of an instructional procedure. It is useful because studies often reach conflicting conclusions. Some find positive effects of a program; others find negative effects of the same type of program, and still others find no effects. Even among studies that report positive findings, the effects can be small or large. The questions a meta-analysis addresses are these: Taking into account all the relevant studies on a topic *overall,* is the effect positive, negative, or zero? And if overall it is positive or negative, what is the magnitude of the effect: large, and therefore meaningful; small, and therefore of little consequence; or something in between? Are there additional factors (e.g., student characteristics) that influence whether effects are large or small?

5. Robert Slavin was a member of the NLP and worked on the meta-analysis of instructional language. He resigned to publish his review before the Panel's work was completed.

6. Starting in fall 2007, ELLs in Arizona spend 4 hours per day learning English exclusively (Kossan, 2007; Small, 2010). This virtually guarantees they will not receive instruction to promote academic content knowledge, which is no less necessary than English proficiency for school success.

REFERENCES

August, D., & Shanahan, T. (Eds.). (2006). *Developing literacy in second-language learners: Report of the National Literacy Panel on language-minority children and youth.* Mahwah, NJ: Erlbaum.

Beck, I., McKeown, M., & Kucan, L. (2002). *Bringing words to life: Robust vocabulary instruction.* New York, NY: Guilford Press.

Behavioral Research and Teaching. (2005, January). Oral reading fluency: 90 years of assessment (BRT Technical Report No. 33). Eugene, OR: Author. Available online at *www.jhasbrouck.com.*

Bialystock, E. (2001). *Bilingualism in development: Language, literacy, and cognition.* New York: Cambridge University Press.

Calderon, M., August. D., Duran. D., Madden, N., Slavin. R., & Gil, M. (2003). *Spanish to English transitional reading: Teacher's manual.* Baltimore: Success for All Foundation. Adapted version available online at *www.ColorinColorado.org.*

Carlo, M. S., August, D., McLaughlin, B., Snow, C. E., Dressler, C., Lippman, D., et al. (2004). Closing the gap: Addressing the vocabulary needs of English language learners in bilingual and mainstream classrooms. *Reading Research Quarterly. 39,* 188–215.

Collins, M. (2005). ESL preschoolers' English vocabulary acquisition from storybook reading. *Reading Research Quarterly, 40,* 406–408.

Crawford, J. (1999). *Bilingual education: History, politics, theory, and practice* (4th ed.). Los Angeles: Bilingual Education Services.

Fung, I., Wilkinson, I., & Moore, D. (2003). L1–assisted reciprocal teaching to improve ESL students' comprehension of English expository text. *Learning and Instruction, 13,* 1–31.

Gandara, P., & Rumberger, R. (2006). *Resource needs for California's English learners.* Santa Barbara, CA: UC Linguistic Minority Research Institute. Available online at *www.lmri.ucsb.edu/publications/jointpubs.php.*

Genesee, F. (Ed). (1999). *Program alternatives for linguistically diverse students* (Educational Practice Report 1). Santa Cruz, CA: Center for Research on Education, Diversity and Excellence.

Genesee, F., Lindholm-Leary, K., Saunders, W., & Christian, D. (2006). *Educating English language learners.* New York, NY: Cambridge University Press.

Greene, J. (1997). A meta-analysis of the Rossell and Baker review of bilingual education research. *Bilingual Research Journal, 21,* 103–122.

Jiménez, R. (1997). The strategic reading abilities and potential of five low-literacy Latina/o readers in middle school. *Reading Research Quarterly, 32,* 221–243.

King, M. (2007, May 22). English-only tests, judge rules. Available at *www.santacruzsentinel.com/archive/2007/May/22/local/stories/04local.html.*

Kossan, P. (2007, July 14). New learners must spend 4 hours a day on English. Available at *www.azcentral.com/arizonarepublic/news/articles/0714english0714.html.*

Lehr, F., Osborn, J., & Hiebert, E. (n.d.). *A focus on vocabulary.* Honolulu: Pacific Resources for Education and Learning.

Nash, R. (1999). *Dictionary of Spanish cognates thematically organized.* Sylmar, CA: NTC.

National Reading Panel. (2000). *Report of the National Reading Panel—Teaching children to read: An evidence-based assessment of the scientific research literature on reading and its implications for reading instruction* (Report of the subgroups). Washington, DC: National Institute of Child Health and Human Development. Available at *www.nichd.nih.gov/research/supported/nrp.cfm.*

Natriello, G., McDill, E., & Pallas, A. (1990) *Schooling disadvantaged students: Racing against catastrophe.* New York, NY: Teachers College Press.

Norris, J., & Ortega, L. (2000). Effectiveness of L2 instruction: A research synthesis and quantitative meta-analysis. *Language and Learning, 50,* 417–528.

Ovando, C., Collier, V., & Combs, M. C. (2003). *Bilingual and ESL classrooms: Teaching in multicultural contexts* (3rd ed.). Boston, MA: McGraw-Hill.

Prado, M. (1996). *Dictionary of Spanish false cognates.* Sylmar, CA: NTC.

Roberts, T., & Neal, H. (2004). Relationships among preschool English language learners' oral proficiency in English, instructional experience and literacy development. *Contemporary Educational Psychology, 29,* 283–311.

Rolstad, K., Mahoney, K., & Glass, G. (2005). The big picture: A meta-analysis of program effectiveness research on English language learners. *Educational Policy, 19,* 572–594.

Saiz, A., & Zoido, E. (2005). Listening to what the world says: Bilingualism and earnings in the United States. *Review of Economics and Statistics, 87,* 523–538.

Saunders, W., Foorman, B., & Carlson, C. (2006). Do we need a separate block of time for oral English language development in programs for English learners? *Elementary School Journal, 107,* 181–198.

Scarcella, R. (2003). *Academic English: A conceptual framework* (Technical Report 2003–1). Santa Barbara, CA: Linguistic Minority Research institute. Available at *lmri.ucsb.edu.*

Slavin, R., & Cheung, A. (2005). A synthesis of research on language of reading instruction for English language learners. *Review of Educational Research, 75,* 247–281.

Small, J. (2010, February 1). Unanimous vote moves ELL opt-out bill through committee. AzCapitolTimes.com. Retrieved February 17, 2010, from *azcapitoltimes.com/blog/2010/02/01/unanimous-vote-moves-ell-opt-out-bill-through-committee/*

Tong, F., Lara-Alecio, R, Irby, B., Mathes, P., & Kwok, O. (2008). Accelerating early academic oral English development in transitional bilingual and structured English immersion programs. *American Educational Research Journal. 45,* 1011–1044.

U.S. Department of Education. (2005). *Biennial evaluation report to Congress on the implementation of the State Formula Grant Program. 2002–2004: English Language Acquisition, Language Enhancement and Academic Achievement Act (ESEA, Title III, Part A).* Washington, DC: Author.

Vaughn, S., Mathes, P., Linan-Thompson, S., Cirino, P., Carlson, C., Pollard- Durdola, S., et al. (2006). Effectiveness of an English intervention for first grade English language learners at risk for reading problems. *Elementary School Journal. 107,* 154–180.

Willig, A. (1985). A meta-analysis of selected studies on the effectiveness of bilingual education. *Review of Educational Research, 55,* 269–317.

Zehr, M. (2007a, May 8). *NCLB seen a damper on bilingual programs.* Retrieved April 30, 2007, from *www.edweek.org.*

Zehr, M. (2007b, May 23). Another take on Coachella Valley Unified School District v. California. *Learning the language.* Blog available at *blogs.edweek.org/edweek/learning-the-language.*

Zehler, A. M., Fleischman, H. L., Hopstock, P. J., Stephenson, T. G., Pendzick, M. L., & Sapru, S. (2003). *Descriptive study of services to LEP students and LEP students with disabilities: Vol. I. Research report.* Arlington, VA: Development Associates.

Supporting Content Learning for English Learners

EURYDICE B. BAUER, PATRICK C. MANYAK, AND CRYSTAL COOK

■ ■ ■ ■ ■

In each of our previous columns, Patrick and I have written about topics that we believe are relevant to classroom teachers and have provided suggestions based on our collective research and classroom experiences with teachers of English learners (ELs). In this column, we include another perspective by adding the voice of an English as a Second Language (ESL) classroom teacher, Crystal Cook (third author). Specifically Patrick, Crystal, and I address (a) the difference between having language and content objectives, (b) using small-group work to maximize involvement, and (c) including beginning English speakers in the learning process.

Having Language and Content Objectives

To address language and content objectives in class, Crystal uses her experience teaching a unit on recycling and caring for the earth to engage all of her students regardless of their language ability. The need to engage all EL students in academic learning regardless of language skills is important, because the literature of the last two decades suggests that students who are in greater need of quality instruction are often offered vocabulary-controlled material, which limits the amount of engaging content they are exposed to. According to Stanovich (1986), this type of instructional structure reinforces the context where the "rich-get-richer" (p. 381) and the poor get poorer.

If the goal is to reduce the gap between native English speaker and ELs—according to the National Assessment of Educational Progress, there is a 36-point gap between these students—it is important to examine the nature of instruction provided to EL students. According to Echevarria, Vogt, and Short (2008), a good starting point is to have clear content and language objectives. When asked how she addressed content and language objectives, Crystal offered the following:

> As part of my recycling unit, a major content objective is to realize that certain materials can be recycled or conserved (according to the Tennessee state performance indicators in Life Science for third graders). This is communicated to the students in writing and through discussion in the classroom.

In addition to the content objectives, one of Crystal's language goals is to have her students identify cause and effect relationships in text. To achieve that goal, she engages in language objectives such as identifying keywords in cause and effect texts (e.g., *this happened because* and *therefore*). Ideally, Crystal wants the language objectives explicitly taught to empower her students. Specifically, students are taught signal keywords, then they are asked to use the keywords in their writing, and finally students are asked to write a cause and effect piece. Throughout this process, Crystal and the students discuss the importance of recycling and identify positive effects of recycling on their environment as well as negative effects if people do not recycle.

Although the unit on recycling is more encompassing than the content and language objectives presented, Crystal ensures that there are content and language objectives that increase the students' chances for not only learning the content but also developing the academic language that is necessary for success.

Using Small-Group Work to Maximize Involvement

At any point in the year, Crystal has students who are at the very beginning of learning English, those who have a good base, and those who are becoming more fluent. To meet all of her students' academic and language needs, Crystal encourages students to work in pairs and small groups.

As part of the recycling unit, students engage in as many recycling activities as possible. Students learn from the content objectives such as discovering the reason it is important to recycle and the process that is involved. As part of their learning, the EL students actively encourage the rest of the school to engage in recycling by using posters to communicate their message. A central goal of the unit is helping students become more aware of the small things that they do that can waste or save energy. Students work alone or in pairs to write journal entries that document ways in which their school could better recycle or save energy.

Crystal engages in an ongoing dialogue via writing with the students as the unit unfolds. As students write their entries, Crystal highlights grammatical elements that are relevant and specific to their needs, which makes the language itself a central point of discussion. For example, when writing in English, adjectives are placed before the noun (e.g., The big dog is cold.). In Spanish, however, the adjective is placed after the noun (e.g., El perro grande esta frío). Crystal remembered how she and a student worked on a letter the student had written to the city, asking for them to pick up the recycling from school:

> During one of our interactions as she was composing, we talked about reasons the city should collect our recycling from school. I encouraged the student to think of legitimate reasons and add them to an idea web, which seemed to help her with what she was doing. The student maintained focus and generated details relevant to the topic. With the help of *Michael Recycle* by [Ellie] Bethel [2008, Worthwhile Books] and discussions held during time in EL, the student and I were able to complete a letter the student understood and felt proud of! Upon completing the letter, the student was excited because she saw herself as a writer with a voice!

Being explicit when the students need you to be is very important as an EL teacher. Timing is everything!

Including Beginning English Speakers in the Learning Process

When working with new ELs, Crystal focuses on a couple of important goals: engaging students in the lessons by making the student comfortable enough to participate and work with others, and on encouraging them to use their new language with her in the EL classroom with their regular classroom teacher, and with peers at school. Crystal described her actions this way:

> To work with students who are beginning English learners, I first learn about their culture. I do this by using books and the Internet, searching for info about their language, native foods and mannerisms. I also engage in constant communication with bilingual/bicultural mentors in the district that share the same cultures as my students. I attempt to learn about their language and use it with the students in a way to show I want to learn more about them. Each time I attempt to learn more about their culture, students seem more comfortable with me in the EL classroom. I encourage classroom teachers to do the same, and my experience at our school suggests that the teachers are generally excited about learning about their students' cultures.
>
> With new English learners, I focus on vocabulary by using their language as a bridge. For example, as part of the unit on recycling we discussed the concept of taking care of our earth. Some students struggled with understanding of how to take care of the earth. However, after students discussed (sometimes using their native language) the topic among themselves, and created a list of ways that caring for the Earth applies in their own personal experiences in their native language, they then used their English to explain it to me. In this way, students see their language as an asset (or bridge) that can assist them as they are learning a new language.
>
> Beyond the group activities, I also have the new English speakers meet with me in addition to their regular, daily EL class. In these individual sessions with the ELs, we work on specific skills, which are then communicated with the classroom teacher. One activity that I have found beneficial is to have them create picture dictionaries of the important words and ideas that we are studying as part of a particular unit. In the case of the recycling unit, words such as *recycling* can be shown pictorially as a series of steps that explain the concept of recycling. Other words such as *environment*, *Earth*, *protect*, *natural resources*, *reduce*, and *reuse* are also worthy of attention. I do some of this with students individually, because it gives me an opportunity to really understand and support their emerging English language skills. My experience is that the personal content dictionaries help students better understand new vocabulary.
>
> At my school, another EL teacher, a bilingual/bicultural mentor and myself work with ELs in an after-school program. The last three years, I have participated in the after-school program that meets twice a week for an hour each day. During that time, we work with the students on vocabulary building and encourage students to interact with each other using the English language. All English learners in our school speak Spanish as their first language. The additional attention given to just 20 students in the after-school program is a way for us to assist students as they build their vocabulary among each other for social purposes and academic learning.

An advantage for many students at Crystal's school is that most EL teachers are bilingual in both Spanish and English. All the EL students are Spanish speakers. Teachers use their Spanish when they sense that students do not understand the content presented to them. Crystal hopes that, by using her Spanish when students need it, the students learn that they too can use what they know in Spanish to assist them in learning English.

REFERENCES

Echevarria, J., Vogt, M., & Short, D. (2008). *Making content comprehensible for English learners: The SIOP Model* (3rd ed.). Boston: Pearson/Allyn & Bacon.

Stanovich, K.E. (1986). Matthew effects in reading: Some consequences of individual differences in the acquisition of literacy. *Reading Research Quarterly*, 21(4), 360–407. doi:10.1598/ RRQ.21.4.1

Bauer teaches at the University of Illinois, Urbana-Champaign, USA; e-mail ebbauer@uiuc.edu. Manyak teaches at the University of Wyoming, Laramie, USA; e-mail PManyak@uwyo.edu. Cook teaches for Memphis City Schools, Tennessee, USA; e-mail perkinscrystald@ mcsk12.net

The department editors welcome reader comments. Patrick C. Manyak teaches at the University of Wyoming, Laramie; e-mail PManyak@uwyo.edu. Eurydice Bouchereau Bauer teaches at University of Illinois at Urbana-Champaign; e-mail ebbauer@uiuc.edu.

CLASSROOM IMPLICATIONS

1. Reexamine your personal views on the education of English learners, particularly as related to your own teaching.

2. How do you interpret the research finding that "process" approaches do not seem to be as effective with ELs as explicit instruction?

3. Goldenberg separates the political issues of language instruction from the instructional questions. But are they that easy to disentangle? In what ways do the recommendations of researchers present problems of implementation due to the views of stakeholders?

4. What problems do you foresee if regular classroom teachers were to try to merge content and language objectives?

5. Interview the ESL teacher(s) in your school and district noting what they consider to be the most important issues related to multicultural education. What are some of their suggestions as to how these various classroom problems might be solved?

FOR FURTHER READING

Black, R.W. (2009). English-language learners, fan communities, and 21st-century skills. *Journal of Adolescent & Adult Literacy, 52*(8), 688–697. doi: 10.1598/JAAL.52.8.4

Burns, M.K., & Helman, L.A. (2009). Relationship between language skills and acquisition rate of sight words among English language learners. *Literacy Research and Instruction, 48,* 221–232.

Borrero, N. (2009). Top-notched supports for language learners. *Educational Leadership, 66,* 60–61.

Clark, K. (2009). The case for structured English immersion. *Educational Leadership, 66,* 42–46.

Menken, K. (2010). NCLB and English language learners: Challenges and consequences. *Theory into Practice, 49*(2), 121–128, doi: 10.1080/00405841003626619

Exposito, S., & Barillas, M. (2009). Writing their way to success. *Educational Leadership, 66,* 62–63.

Rance-Roney, J. (2010). Jump-starting language and schema for English language learners: Teacher-composed digital jumpstarts for academic reading. *Journal of Adolescent & Adult Literacy, 53*(5), 386–395. doi: 10.1598/JAAL.53.5.4

Hadaway, N.L. A narrow bridge to academic reading. *Educational Leadership, 66,* 38–41.

Moughamian, A.C., Rivera, M.O., & Francis, D.J. (2009). *Instructional models and strategies for teaching English language learners.* Portsmouth, NH: RMC Research Corporation, Center on Instruction.

Ogle, D., & Correa-Kovtun, A. (2010). Supporting English-language learners and struggling readers in content literacy with the "partner reading and content, too" routine. *The Reading Teacher, 63*(7), 532–542. doi: 10.1598/RT.63.7.1

Orosco, M.J., & Klingner, J. (2010). One school's implementation of RTI with English language learners: "Referring into RTI." *Journal of Learning Disabilities, 43*(3), 269–288. doi:

Rivera, M.O., Moughamian, A.C., Lesaux, N.K., & Francis, D.J. (2008). Language and reading interventions for English language learners and English language learners with disabilities. Portsmouth, NH: RMC Research Corporation, Center on Instruction.

Teale, W. (2009). Students learning English and their literacy instruction in urban schools. *The Reading Teacher, 62*(8), 699–703.

Walker-Dalhouse, D., Sanders, V., & Dalhoues, A.D. (2009). A university and middle-school partnership: Preservice teachers' attitudes toward ELL students. *Research and Instruction, 48,* 337–349.

ONLINE RESOURCES

Internet TESL Journal
http://iteslj.org/
TESOL Connections
http://www.tesol.org/s_tesol/tc/index.asp
TESOL Journal
http://www.tesol.org/s_tesol/seccss.asp?CID=1997&DID=12258
TESOL Essential Teacher
http://www.tesol.org/s_tesol/seccss.asp?CID=206&DID=1676
ESL Reading
http://www.eslreading.org/
Reading Rockets (Colorin, Colorado)
http://www.readingrockets.org/

Literacy Coaching

In schools where teachers work with [literacy] coaches regularly, teachers, coaches and administrators report a growth of collaborative teacher culture marked by increased teacher willingness and ability to collaborate, peer accountability, and individual teacher knowledge about other teachers' classrooms.

—Kiley Reynolds (2003)

Because the primary role of reading coaches is to provide support to classroom teachers for classroom reading instruction, it is essential that they be excellent classroom teachers themselves.

—International Reading Association (2004)

The coach's major job is to provide professional development and support to teachers to improve [literacy] instruction.

—Camile Blachowicz et al. (2005)

Leaders are made, not born. They are made by hard effort, which is the price which all of us must pay to achieve any goal that is worthwhile.

—Vince Lombardi

What exactly is a literacy coach? While consensus standards are emerging (e.g., the joint standards for middle school coaches developed by IRA, NCTE, NCTM, NSTA, and NCSS), the most appropriate job descriptions are still evolving, and the current dialogue is rich and varied. However, there seems to be complete agreement on one matter: the primary function of a coach is to facilitate professional development. Most educators would agree that the minimal course requirements at the preservice level fail to adequately prepare beginning teachers for the challenges of effective reading instruction. This means that their continued growth must be fostered once they enter the profession, and it is not enough to assume that the on-the-job training involved in running a classroom will be sufficient. An effective program of professional development can play an important role, and the literacy coach is well situated to make it happen.

Just what can a coach do, specifically, to facilitate the professional growth of teachers in a school? While no exhaustive list exists, a literacy coach can enhance the expertise and practice of classroom teachers in at least the following ways:

- observing and conducting follow-up conferences with individual teachers,
- modeling a particular instructional approach while a teacher observes,
- organizing book study groups,
- interpreting achievement data and meeting with grade-level groups and individual teachers to discuss patterns,
- learning as much as possible about commercial programs in use,

- arranging for sales representatives to visit the school to address implementation issues,
- conducting professional development surveys,
- establishing, monitoring, and contributing to teacher blogs,
- researching the answers to questions posed by teachers,
- arranging for consultants to visit the school to address focused topics identified through surveys or achievement patterns, and
- following-up such presentations by observing individuals or meeting with groups of teachers.

These last two points lead to an important caveat. By far the worst approach to professional development begins with a presentation by a consultant or some other expert and ends with teachers being left to their own devices as to how the ideas presented will be implemented in their classrooms. Typically, they listen politely and then return to business as usual. This system is sometimes disparagingly referred to as "drive-by" professional development or "the seagull approach," in which an expert flies in, drops his load, and flies out again. Such derogatory characterizations capture a long history of dismal research. One-shot presentations, without follow-up, usually do not have the intended effect. The coach, however, is positioned to make such presentations more effective by making follow-up visits to classrooms, meeting with grade-level groups, and so forth.

A coach might also facilitate degree or endorsement programs. These are costly and time consuming, but they meet the needs of recertification and help to build a working community of literacy educators. We make this latter point not just because it sounds good or because the interests of our institutions are served. When a school is staffed by teachers knowledgeable about reading, a climate conducive to growth is created. A good example involves an elementary school in Kansas. All of the teachers attained their state reading endorsement through a district-paid project. Subsequent reading achievement scores rose significantly (Miller & Ellsworth, 1985). Of course, not all degree programs and endorsements are the same. Regrettably, some include fluff and theory while minimizing practical applications. Nevertheless, this route to professional development can be a very effective one, and a literacy coach can organize and promote such a program.

AS YOU READ

Coaching entails a host of practical questions, and these two articles address many of them. McKenna and Walpole describe models of coaching and characterize them on a scale from "soft" to "hard." As you weigh each model, consider your own orientation toward coaching. Were you to accept a position as a coach, and assuming you were free to coach as you wished, how hard or soft would you be? Which of the models appeals to you most? L'Allier, Ellish-Piper, and Bean present seven guiding principles of coaching, and they support them with research and capsule cases. Consider the extent to which you concur with each principle. Are the seven principles compatible with all the seven of the models described by McKenna and Walpole?

REFERENCES

Blachowicz, C. L., Obrochta, C., & Fogelberg, E. (2005). Literacy coaching for change. *Educational Leadership, 62,* 55–58.

International Reading Association. (2004). *The role and qualifications of the reading coach in the United States.* Newark, DE: International Reading Association.

Miller, J. W., & Ellsworth, R. E. (1985). Evaluation of a two-year program to improve teacher effectiveness in reading instruction. *Elementary School Journal, 85,* 485–496.

Reynolds, K. (2003). *Literacy coaching: How school districts can support a long-term strategy in a short-term world.* San Francisco: Bay Area School Reform Collaborative.

Standards for middle and high school literacy coaches. (2005). Joint publication of the Carnegie Corporation, IRA, NCTE, NCTM, NSTA, and NCSS. Available: http://www.reading.org/resources/issues/reports/coaching.html

What Matters for Elementary Literacy Coaching? Guiding Principles for Instructional Improvement and Student Achievement

SUSAN L'ALLIER, LAURIE ELISH-PIPER, AND

RITA M. BEAN

▪ ▪ ▪ ▪ ▪

Although literacy coaching offers promise in terms of improving teacher practice and student achievement, guidance is often needed regarding the qualifications, activities, and roles of literacy coaches.

Amanda Davis (all names are pseudonyms), the literacy coach at Washburn Elementary, arrives at school and checks her e-mail. She responds to a message from her principal about an upcoming staff meeting, and she replies to a third-grade teacher who wants to meet with her. Amanda then reviews her daily calendar. She will be modeling a guided reading lesson in a first-grade classroom, holding a preobservation conference with a second-grade teacher, and meeting with the kindergarten teachers to discuss their students' phonemic awareness assessment scores. Amanda also plans to prepare for an upcoming book study group. Although Amanda has clear plans for her day, she often finds herself faced with unexpected situations, requests, and emergencies. For example, she may be asked to assess a newly enrolled student, or she may find herself researching information about a reading strategy to respond to an inquiry from a grade-level team. At times, Amanda feels overwhelmed and wonders how she can best spend her time so that she is able to support teachers and students in her school.

Whether a reading professional is spending all of her time coaching, dividing time between coaching and working with students, or considering adding coaching to her work as a reading specialist, the tasks that fall to this individual can be daunting. Questions remain about literacy coaching such as: What types of knowledge and preparation does a literacy coach need to be successful in the position? How much time should the literacy coach devote to working directly with teachers as compared with completing other coaching activities? What can a literacy coach do to build collaborative relationships with teachers? Which literacy coaching activities help teachers enhance their instruction and students improve their learning? These types of questions suggest that further guidance is needed regarding the qualifications, activities, and roles of literacy coaches. In this article, we provide such guidance in the form of seven research-based principles for literacy coaching.

Background

Literacy coaching provides job-embedded, ongoing professional development for teachers (International Reading Association [IRA], 2004). This approach to professional development is rooted in cognitive coaching, peer coaching, and mentoring (Costa & Garmston, 1994; Showers, 1984; Toll, 2005, 2006). To date, the available research related to literacy coaching has focused mainly on roles, responsibilities, and relationships (e.g., Bean et al., 2007; Bean, Swan, & Knaub, 2003; Bean & Zigmond, 2007; Deussen, Coskie, Robinson, & Autio, 2007; Dole, 2004; Poglinco et al., 2003; Rainville & Jones, 2008). Some research has examined the relationship between literacy coaching and teacher knowledge, beliefs, and practices (Blachowicz, Obrochta, & Fogelberg, 2005; Gibson, 2006; Neufeld & Roper, 2003). Yet other research has investigated the effects of literacy coaching on student achievement in reading (Bean et al., 2008; Biancarosa, Bryk, & Dexter, 2008; Elish-Piper & L'Allier, 2007; L'Allier & Elish-Piper, 2006, 2009).

We synthesized the findings from our studies (Bean et al., 2007; Bean et al., 2008; Bean et al., 2003; Bean & Zigmond, 2007; Elish-Piper & L'Allier, 2007; L'Allier & Elish-Piper, 2006, 2009) and the related literature to develop seven guiding principles that literacy coaches can use to focus their work on the improvement of literacy teaching and learning in the elementary grades. In addition, a vignette is provided to illustrate each guiding principle in action. We developed the vignettes based on our several years of work with literacy coaches during professional development and research activities.

Guiding Principles for Literacy Coaching

Principle 1: Coaching Requires Specialized Knowledge

The major responsibilities of literacy coaches involve helping classroom teachers improve their instruction through job-embedded, ongoing professional development. These professional development activities may include providing large-group presentations about literacy education, facilitating small teacher-study groups and grade-level team meetings, and supporting individual teachers as they work to develop their instructional and assessment skills (IRA, 2004). All of these activities revolve around knowledge of literacy processes, acquisition, assessment, and instruction; therefore, it is essential that literacy coaches bring a strong knowledge base about the various aspects of literacy education to their coaching (Frost & Bean, 2006). Coaches also need to know how to work effectively with teachers; this requires an understanding of adult learning principles which suggest that adults are most open to learning when they are involved in planning instruction, when experience is the basis for learning, when learning has immediate job-related relevance, and when learning is problem-centered (Flaherty, 2005; Knowles, 1984).

How do coaches develop this expansive knowledge base? Successful classroom teaching experiences must form the foundation of any coach's knowledge base. In addition, their active participation in ongoing professional development builds on the knowledge and skills gained during their initial certification programs. Furthermore, a graduate degree that leads to advanced certification helps them gain in-depth knowledge of literacy and provides opportunities for them to learn about how to work with teachers to improve their practice. Taken together, these experiences enable coaches to meet IRA's (2004) criteria.

Sometimes schools must hire literacy coaches quickly to meet grant requirements or to address district mandates (Frost & Bean, 2006). In other instances, principals want to appoint one of their exemplary teachers as the literacy coach. In such cases, does it really matter if a coach has advanced preparation in reading?

What Can Be Learned from the Research?   Yes, advanced preparation for coaches does matter! L'Allier and Elish-Piper (2006) conducted a study in a diverse, low-income school district that had received a Reading First grant (hereafter referred to as the Valley District Study). The study's participants included 5 literacy coaches, 65 kindergarten through grade 3 classroom teachers, and 1,596 students. The researchers collected students' fall and spring test scores as well as weekly literacy coaching logs that used a structured protocol. Analysis of the data indicated that the highest average student reading gains occurred in classrooms supported by a literacy coach who held a Reading Teacher endorsement (24 credit hours of course work in reading); conversely, the lowest average student gains occurred in classrooms supported by a literacy coach who had neither an advanced degree in reading nor a Reading Teacher endorsement.[3] The results from these two studies indicate that advanced preparation does make a difference for literacy coaching effectiveness related to student reading performance.

In a second study conducted by Elish-Piper and L'Allier (2007), the participants included 12 literacy coaches, 121 kindergarten through grade 3 classroom teachers, and 3,029 students (hereafter referred to as the Metropolitan District Study). The Metropolitan District Study was also conducted in a diverse, low-income school district that had received a Reading First grant.

Teachers in both districts used a core text-book, guided reading instruction, and literacy centers/stations within the framework of an uninterrupted 90-minute reading block. As in the Valley District Study, weekly coaching logs and students' fall and spring test scores were collected. Analysis of the data using hierarchical linear modeling (HLM) suggested that significant reading achievement gains were made by students of teachers who received support from a literacy coach who had either a Reading Teacher endorsement or Reading Specialist certificate (32 credit hours of course work in reading).

While the specific requirements for a master's degree, reading endorsement, or reading certificate may vary from state to state, completion of advanced preparation in literacy education indicates that the coach has acquired a solid knowledge base through an articulated set of courses so that her understanding of literacy is both broad and deep. In summary, the results from these two studies indicate that advanced preparation does make a difference for literacy coaching effectiveness related to student reading performance.

The Guiding Principle in Action.   Amanda Davis, who was introduced at the beginning of this article, is a case in point. She recently earned her master's degree in reading, which enabled her to meet the qualifications for a Reading Teacher endorsement. She finds that she relies on her knowledge on a daily basis in her work as a literacy coach in a large urban district. Her previous experience as an elementary teacher is very helpful in her work with teachers, but she realizes that literacy coaching also requires specialized knowledge across multiple grade levels and at the student, classroom, and school levels. She developed much of that knowledge while completing her master's degree, and she continues to update her knowledge base by reading professional journals and books and by attending conferences. In addition, her graduate course work and ongoing professional development have enabled her to enhance her expertise with assessment, data analysis, Response to Intervention (RTI), and other new initiatives that are essential for her literacy coaching work. When asked about what has contributed to her success as a literacy coach, Amanda responded, "Having the Reading Teacher endorsement and using the in-depth knowledge from my graduate program are key pieces of my literacy coaching success."

Principle 2: Time Working with Teachers Is the Focus of Coaching

To provide ongoing, job-embedded professional development for teachers, coaches spend time with teachers engaged in activities such as observing, modeling, conferencing, co-teaching, and leading book study groups (Casey, 2006; Froelich & Puig, 2010; IRA, 2004). However, many coaches also spend a great deal of time on other activities such as organizing book rooms, administering assessments, and participating in district-level meetings (Bean et al., 2007; Bean & Zigmond, 2007; Knight, 2006; Roller, 2006). In fact, a study of 190 coaches working in school districts funded by Reading First grants (Deussen et al., 2007) indicated that, on average, coaches spent only 28% of their time working with teachers. Using time allocation to categorize the main focus of their coaching, four categories of coaches emerged: teacher-oriented, student-oriented, data-oriented, and managerial. Only one third were classified as teacher-oriented coaches—coaches who spent between 41% and 52% of their time interacting with teachers. In light of the varied ways that coaches spend their time, it seems important to ask, do students benefit when coaches' schedules include a high percentage of time working with teachers?

What Can Be Learned from the Research?   Yes, students do benefit when coaches work with teachers! Results from the Valley District Study (L'Allier & Elish-Piper, 2006) indicated that the highest average student reading gains occurred in classrooms supported by a literacy coach who engaged in the most interactions with teachers; conversely, the lowest average student gains occurred in classrooms supported by a literacy coach who spent the lowest percentage of time with teachers.

In a study of literacy coaching in schools that received Reading First grants, 20 literacy coaches each participated in five in-depth retrospective interviews during which they described exactly what they had been doing during the previous 24-hour period (Bean et al., 2008). The researchers divided the schools where the literacy coaches worked into two groups based on the median amount of time coaches spent working with teachers engaged in group and individual coaching. The researchers found significant differences between the two groups of schools; that is, schools in which coaches spent more time working directly with teachers (i.e., high coaching schools) had a greater percentage of students scoring at the proficient level in first and second grade. Furthermore, in high coaching schools, a lower percentage of first- and second-grade students scored in the at-risk range on standardized assessments. The results of these studies indicate that students benefit when literacy coaches' time is spent working directly with teachers to help them improve their practice.

The Guiding Principle in Action.   Let's listen in as Selena Rodriguez, a literacy coach at Lincoln Elementary School located in a suburban school district, meets with her principal, Marilyn Tobart, to discuss her goal of increasing her coaching time with teachers. Marilyn begins their discussion by saying, "I love the way you've organized the book room and compiled all of the assessment data."

Selena replies, "Yes, I'm pleased with my work in both areas, but they did take a lot of time—reducing the time I spent with teachers. Next year's schedule offers more opportunities for working with teachers; there are different designated times for the primary and intermediate literacy blocks as well as common planning times for each grade level. If someone could catalog and organize new guided reading materials and help me input the assessment data, I could spend more time helping teachers with guided reading and assisting them in designing data-driven instruction."

After further discussion, Marilyn responds, "I can schedule time for one of our teaching assistants to input the assessment data. I also know a retired teacher who wants to volunteer in our school; the book room activities might be perfect for her." Selena leaves the meeting confident that there is a plan in place to help her meet her goal of spending at least 50% of her coaching time with teachers.

Principle 3: Collaborative Relationships Are Essential for Coaching

Although a shared focus on student achievement can provide the foundation for collaborative relationships between coaches and teachers, coaches must build on that foundation by establishing trust, maintaining confidentiality, and communicating effectively with teachers. Coaches establish trust by openly respecting teachers' professional expertise (Knight, 2009) and following through on the commitments they make to teachers. As coaches engage in activities such as making classroom observations and conferencing with teachers about those observations, they must maintain confidentiality by not discussing those activities with other teachers or the principal (Rainville & Jones, 2008). And when coaches focus their discussions on how to address the needs of students—rather than on the strengths or weaknesses of a teacher's instruction (McCombs & Marsh, 2009)—they clearly communicate their intention to be a collaborator with the teacher, not an evaluator (Casey, 2006; Toll, 2005).

What Can Be Learned from the Research?   Insights about building collaborative relationships can be gained from listening to teachers who work with literacy coaches (L'Allier & Elish-Piper, 2009; Vanderberg & Stephens, 2009). Vanderberg and Stephens interviewed 35 teachers, each of whom had worked with a literacy coach for three years. In terms of building trust, interview data indicated that teachers felt coaches respected their abilities to select strategies based on their students' needs. Teachers also noted that their coach was "more like a facilitator of their learning rather than a dictator" (p. 3). The coaches' willingness to answer questions and to offer suggestions, not absolute solutions, was cited as an example of this facilitative communication style.

In another study involving 6 literacy coaches and 19 of the teachers with whom they worked, findings from structured interviews indicated that teachers consistently cited trust and confidentiality as two essential elements of effective literacy coaching (L'Allier & Elish-Piper, 2009). One teacher we interviewed in that study explained, "I know my literacy coach is there to help me and not to judge me. She is professional, and she will keep my questions, no matter how silly I think they may be, private."

Additional insights about building collaborative relationships can be gained from the research about coaches' use of language. Perkins (1998) found that, when compared with novice coaches, experienced coaches' conversations with teachers included more paraphrasing of teacher concerns and comments, more open-ended questions, and more respect for teachers' opinions, indicating that experienced coaches used their language to build collaborative relationships with teachers. Rainville and Jones (2008) concluded that a coach's language is often indicative of the relationship between the coach and the teacher. Thus, they suggest that professional development for coaches include opportunities to analyze the language used by other coaches as well as to reflect on their own use of coaching language through role-playing activities. Such activities will highlight the important role that language plays in the development of collaborative relationships.

The Guiding Principle in Action.   Selena Rodriguez believes that trust is the foundation for all of her coaching work; therefore, she uses a three-pronged approach to build trusting relationships with the teachers in her school. First, she contacts teachers who are new to the building before the start of the school year to introduce herself, to explain what her role is, and to offer help in setting up their classroom libraries. Selena also works hard to establish and maintain trusting relationships with all teachers by clarifying through her words and actions that she is not part of the evaluation process and that her primary goal is to be a person with whom teachers can think and solve problems. She often prefaces conferences with teachers by saying, "Remember, I'm here to be a sounding board and a resource. What we discuss will stay here." Finally, by actively participating in grade-level meetings and attending local conferences and workshops with groups of teachers, Selena positions herself as a colearner with the teachers in her school.

Selena also knows that the way she says something can be as important as what she says. For example, she recently met with Jasmine, a teacher who came to Selena for ideas to improve her guided reading instruction. Selena started the conversation by saying, "So, Jasmine, tell me about your guided reading groups." By using an open-ended prompt, Selena invited Jasmine to share her ideas without creating a tense or negative situation. Jasmine replied, "I think I've grouped the students well, and I'm finding interesting materials that are appropriate for each group. However, I'm really concerned that I'm not providing enough instruction." Selena responded, "Let's talk about what you are doing now and then discuss some ideas you might want to add to ensure that your instruction supports students' learning. Or I can come in to watch you teach a group to get a better idea of what you are doing. Which would be most helpful to you?" By using this type of response, Selena gives the teacher choices while also emphasizing the importance of working together to help Jasmine reach her goal of improving guided reading instruction.

Principle 4: Coaching That Supports Student Reading Achievement Focuses on a Set of Core Activities

Literacy coaches juggle dozens of different activities in a typical week as they work to support teachers (Walpole & Blamey, 2008). For example, Geraldine Martin, a literacy coach in an urban school, facilitates grade-level meetings, coplans lessons, coteaches in classrooms, facilitates professional book clubs, and delivers monthly professional development workshops for teachers. With so many activities that can be done to support teachers, Geraldine wonders which coaching activities she should prioritize, especially because she wants to focus on activities that support student reading achievement.

What Can Be Learned from the Research?   Findings from the HLM analyses of the Metropolitan District Study (Elish-Piper & L'Allier, 2007) suggested that when literacy coaches administer and discuss student assessments with teachers, observe teachers' instruction and offer supportive feedback, conference with teachers about their instruction and students, and model instruction in classrooms, student achievement in reading increases significantly more than in comparable classrooms where these coaching activities are not provided. What is it about these literacy coaching activities that supports student achievement gains?

When a literacy coach administers assessments and shares results with a classroom teacher, she is able to explain results, offer suggestions for grouping, and help develop plans to differentiate instruction. When a literacy coach observes a teacher's instruction and offers supportive feedback, the teacher is able to enhance and fine-tune her implementation of best practices. When a literacy coach conferences with a teacher, she is able to discuss that teacher's instruction, curriculum, and students in an in-depth manner. Finally, when a literacy coach models instruction in a classroom, that teacher is able to see best practices in action with her own students, which provides a foundation to support the teacher with implementing such instruction in the future. By engaging in these activities, a literacy coach is able to provide support that is tailored to each individual teacher's students, needs, and goals (Kise, 2006).

The Guiding Principle in Action.   Let's visit Geraldine Martin, the literacy coach at a large urban elementary school, to see what this principle looks like in her coaching work. Geraldine's belief that assessment should drive instruction (Bernhardt, 2008) is apparent in her recent work with Tyson Davis, a third-grade teacher. At his request, she completed a Developmental Reading Assessment (DRA) for several of the struggling readers in his classroom.

Geraldine shared the results of the DRA with Tyson, and they discussed how Tyson is currently teaching these students. Tyson explained, "I do guided reading with these kids, but I'm not sure they are getting the comprehension instruction they need." Geraldine suggested, "Why don't I come in to observe these students during guided reading? I would then have a better idea about how we can work together to improve their comprehension." Tyson agreed, and Geraldine observed in his classroom the next morning. Later that day, Tyson and Geraldine met to confer about her observations, his questions, and their next steps. When Geraldine asked if he thought the think-aloud approach might help these students, Tyson responded, "I've tried it a few times, but I don't really feel confident using think-alouds." Geraldine asked, "Would you like me to model a guided reading lesson with a think-aloud for comprehension instruction tomorrow?" Tyson agreed, and Geraldine modeled the think-aloud strategy while Tyson observed. By focusing her coaching on the activities of administering and discussing assessments, observing, conferencing, and modeling, Geraldine was able to stay on target with her coaching goals: supporting teachers and promoting student reading achievement gains.

Principle 5: Coaching Must Be Both Intentional and Opportunistic

Effective coaches recognize that intentionality is critical to their successes. In each situation, the coach must have a plan for working with teachers that is deliberate but flexible. For example, a coach working with a novice teacher may decide that modeling is a good first step followed by coteaching and, finally, observing the teacher in action. That same coach may select a different route with an experienced teacher who is hesitant about coaching support. The coach might, for instance, facilitate discussions at grade-level meetings that include the sharing of instructional ideas by all members. The key is that coaches have road maps that guide their work, and they understand the need to modify and readjust, if necessary.

At the same time, effective and efficient coaches take advantage of opportunities. They are available and accessible. They chat with teachers in the hallways, stop in classrooms, and visit the teachers' lounge to say "hello" or to talk briefly with teachers. They have an open-door policy not only for classroom teachers but also for others such as librarians, special educators, and administrators. Most of these encounters are short and spontaneous. They often lead to more intense interactions that can then become intentional.

What Can Be Learned from the Research?   In an interview study of 20 coaches who worked in districts that received Reading First grants, Bean and colleagues (2008) concluded that these coaches had an in-depth understanding of why and how they were working with teachers. Several examples from the interviews illustrated this notion of intentional coaching. In one instance where the coach felt that the teacher would benefit from extended support to implement the literacy framework, the coach worked with that teacher during the entire 90-minute reading block, 3 days a week for 3 weeks. In another instance, the coach provided an experienced third-grade teacher with some supplemental resources for her struggling readers, reviewed their use, and then suggested that the two of them meet at the end of the week to discuss whether the materials were helpful. From past experience, the coach knew that this teacher would be more likely to raise questions and identify possible next steps (e.g., coplanning and modeling) if she first had the opportunity to actually use new strategies or materials with her students.

Eighteen of the 20 coaches also reported opportunistic or on-the-fly coaching. For example, teachers would stop the coaches in the hallways or catch them in the office in the morning. Sometimes, opportunistic coaching occurred when coach and teacher happened to be sitting next to each other at a school meeting. Several coaches noted that these encounters opened the door to intentional coaching.

The Guiding Principle in Action.   Geraldine Martin, in building her schedule for the upcoming week, reserved three 30-minute periods in the morning where she could work with a new second-grade teacher who was experiencing difficulty with guided reading. She had planned with this teacher yesterday, and they had decided how their work would proceed during the three lessons. Geraldine also scheduled a meeting with two kindergarten teachers who, while walking into school with her that morning, had voiced their concerns about the effectiveness of their instruction for several of their students who were English-language learners. Geraldine suggested that they meet to talk about their concerns in more depth.

After scheduling several activities for the upcoming week, Geraldine walked down the hall to coteach a phonics lesson in a first-grade classroom. On the way, Sam, the special education teacher, stopped her to talk about a new student. Specifically, he wanted to know what some of the assessment scores in the student's folder meant. Geraldine took a few minutes to answer Sam's question and indicated her willingness to review the entire folder with him at another time. She then continued down the hallway to the first-grade classroom. It is evident that Geraldine is intentional about her coaching, and also, that by being accessible and receptive, she often has on-the-fly opportunities to coach.

Principle 6: Coaches Must Be Literacy Leaders in the School

Literacy coaches are frequently involved in three practices that are considered essential for successful literacy leadership: setting goals or directions in a school, developing people, and redesigning the organization to facilitate accomplishment of goals (Leithwood, Louis, Anderson, & Wahlstrom, 2004). Many coaches, along with teachers, are involved in setting the direction for the school in the area of literacy. Further, in their role as a developer of people, coaches support teachers' professional growth by working collaboratively with teachers to help them achieve the school's literacy goals, by facilitating study groups about literacy topics, and by working with individual teachers. Through these activities, literacy coaches promote collegiality and teacher leadership in the school.

Coaches also contribute to redesigning the organization in various ways; they can work with principals to create literacy blocks that enable teachers to effectively implement the school's literacy framework and to develop a plan for using paraprofessionals to support small-group, differentiated instruction. Moreover, these coaches often serve as the communication hub for the school; they share information about local, state, and federal literacy initiatives with teachers and administrators, and serve as a link to parents and the community. They also serve as advocates for the school, highlighting its accomplishments to the community (Bean et al., 2008; Quatroche & Wepner, 2008).

What Can Be Learned from the Research?   In-depth interviews of 20 coaches in schools that received Reading First grants (Bean et al., 2008) revealed that these coaches often took leadership roles. Many chaired committees that made decisions about goals for the reading program or the selection of materials; others were involved in writing proposals for funding. Most worked collaboratively with specialized personnel and teachers to make decisions about how to provide effective instruction for all students. All had responsibilities for developing people through facilitating grade-level meetings, providing professional development, and coaching individual teachers. By working closely with the principal, the coaches also had a voice in making decisions about how to modify the organizational structure to facilitate reading instruction.

Coaches in the Bean and colleagues (2008) study were involved in developing and scheduling learning labs for students as an additional period for reading instruction and changing schedules so that teachers at a specific grade level could meet together. As summarized in Leithwood and colleagues (2004), administrators cannot do the job alone; they need the contributions of others, including literacy coaches, to help them conceptualize, implement, and evaluate their literacy programs.

The Guiding Principle in Action.   As Ben Jackman, a literacy coach in a rural elementary school, reviewed the reading test scores of the fifth-grade students, he noted that many of these students were having difficulty with reading comprehension. He also observed differences between their comprehension of narrative text as compared with informational text. Given that the teachers had identified improvement in reading comprehension as one of the key goals for the school year, Ben knew they would want to address these results. Although he had talked informally with individual fifth-grade teachers about teaching comprehension, Ben felt that teachers needed to see the data across classrooms and to begin thinking as a group about reasons for the lack of improvement. This could be an important professional development experience for these teachers.

After the meeting, Ben began to think about the teachers' suggestion that more time be allocated in the reading block for meeting with small groups and for discussions that called for higher levels of thinking. Ben had promised the teachers that he would model such a discussion for them. In addition, he would work with the principal to identify possible modifications to the current schedule that would allow time for meeting with small groups and then discuss those options with the teachers. By helping teachers focus on one of the school's reading goals and by setting into action a series of steps that would build teacher knowledge and modify the schedule to allow for small-group work, Ben certainly demonstrated his role as a literacy leader.

Principle 7: Coaching Evolves Over Time

Some coaches who accept a coaching position do so with a great deal of teaching and collaboratie experience; they enjoy working with adults and have excellent leadership and interpersonal skills in addition to having in-depth knowledge about literacy and instruction. On the other hand, some new coaches begin their role with little experience in working with other adults, even though they may be experienced teachers. Moreover, there may be little structure or direction for them, given the newness of the position. These coaches, faced with an uncertain agenda and some tentativeness about their role, may have a more difficult journey as they learn on the job. But both sets of coaches continue to learn, develop positive relationships with teachers, and modify what they do as they evolve as literacy coaches.

What Can Be Learned from the Research? In a study of coaches from districts in Pennsylvania that received Reading First grants (Bean & Zigmond, 2007), the 30 coaches who completed logs in the first year of Reading First funding and then again in the third year changed significantly in how they allocated their time. There were significant decreases over those years in the percentage of time they allocated to assessing students, entering and analyzing data, and attending professional development sessions. On the other hand, there were significant increases in time spent conferring with teachers, observing in classrooms, and coteaching. The coaches also spent significantly more time providing professional development to groups of teachers in their schools.

Although coaches spent significantly less time planning and organizing, there was a significant increase in the time allocated to administrative tasks, such as scheduling and providing materials for testing, distributing and organizing instructional resources, and copying materials needed by teachers. This increase in administrative duties seemed to be a reflection of the demands of the Reading First grant with its reporting expectations as well as the fact that school leadership often relied on coaches to handle various administrative responsibilities. Overall, however, coaches seemed to allocate more time to working directly to support teachers during the third year than in the first year on the job.

The Guiding Principle in Action. Ben Jackman was looking forward to another busy day of coaching. He had structured his day so that he could be in each third-grade teacher's classroom for 30 minutes. The teacher would be conducting a guided reading group; the reading teacher would also be in the classroom, working with a small group; and Ben's responsibility, as agreed upon by the teachers, would be to observe the teachers' guided reading groups and monitor the students working independently so that he could talk with the teachers about what they thought went well, their concerns, and possible next steps.

The plan to schedule these classroom visits and follow-up conversations with the third-grade team was made by the teachers and Ben after they had reviewed the progress monitoring data last week. In 15 minutes, they had planned and organized the activities. What a difference a year makes! Ben thought back to his initial attempts last year as a new coach. Even after looking at test data, teachers seemed hesitant about his suggestion that he visit their classrooms to get a sense of how the students were doing. It seemed as though it took several months before teachers were willing to trust that he was there to support their efforts. And even then, he reflected, it was not until he had worked closely and successfully with Molly O'Day, the lead teacher in third grade, that the other members of the team seemed to become more comfortable with him. Finally, he was easily able to schedule individual and group coaching activities because the teachers saw them as opportunities to discuss students' needs and the instructional practices that would address those needs. Coaching was so much more effective and rewarding now, he thought.

Discussion and Conclusions

The number of literacy coaches in elementary schools is increasing, and this offers great promise in terms of improving teacher practice and student reading achievement. To fulfill this promise, literacy coaches and administrators who hire them can benefit from guidance regarding the qualifications, activities, and roles of literacy coaches. The guiding principles in this article offer research-based suggestions for literacy coaching.

First and foremost, literacy coaches must have specialized knowledge that goes beyond just knowing how to teach reading well; they must also understand how to work effectively with adults. Additionally, literacy coaches need to spend at least half of their time working directly with teachers because when literacy coaches are working directly with teachers, they are more likely to produce positive growth in teacher practice and in student learning. Furthermore, literacy coaches must develop productive working relationships with the teachers they coach. Such relationships are the foundation for all coaching work; therefore, building trust, maintaining confidentiality, and communicating effectively with teachers must be primary considerations for literacy coaches.

In addition, literacy coaches must prioritize the activities they implement so that they focus on research-based practices associated with student achievement gains. Namely, coaches are more likely to produce student reading achievement gains in the classrooms where they coach when they focus on conferencing with teachers, administering and discussing assessments with teachers, observing classroom instruction and offering supportive feedback, and modeling instruction in classrooms. Literacy coaches also need to balance intentional coaching with opportunistic coaching to make the best use of their time and to support teachers in meaningful and relevant ways. Additionally, literacy coaches must view themselves and be viewed by others in their schools as literacy leaders who set goals and directions for the literacy program, support teachers and other school personnel in providing high quality literacy instruction for all students, and redesigning the school organization to meet literacy goals. Finally, because literacy coaching evolves over time; educators must be patient and mindful of the goals of coaching while providing time for new literacy coaches to lay the foundation for their coaching work.

As the coaching stories about Amanda, Selena, Geraldine, and Ben illustrate, literacy coaching is a complex process. We believe these seven research-based guidelines will help literacy coaches make decisions and enact practices that will have the greatest impact on classroom instruction and student reading achievement.

REFERENCES

Bean, R.M., Belcastro, B., Draper, J., Jackson, V., Jenkins, K., Vandermolen, J., et al. (2008). Literacy coaching in Reading First schools: The blind men and the elephant. Paper presented at the National Reading Conference, Orlando, FL.

Bean, R.M., Jenkins, K., Belcastro, B., Wilson, R.,Turner, G., & Zigmond, N. (2007, December). What reading coaches do and why they do it: A diary study. Paper presented at the National Reading Conference, Austin, TX.

Bean, R.M., Swan, A.L., & Knaub, R. (2003). Reading specialists in schools with exemplary reading programs: Functional, versatile, and prepared. The Reading Teacher, 56(5), 446–455.

Bean, R.M., & Zigmond, N. (2007, March). The work of coaches in Reading First schools and their roles in professional development. Presentation at American Educational Research Association Conference, Chicago, IL.

Bernhardt, V.L. (2008). Data, data everywhere: Bringing all the data together for continuous school improvement. Larchmont, NY: Eye on Education.

Biancarosa, G., Bryk, A., & Dexter, E. (2008, April). Assessing the value-added effects of Literacy Collaborative professional development on student learning. Paper presented at the meeting of the American Educational Research Association, New York, NY.

Blachowicz, C.L.Z., Obrochta, C., & Fogelberg, E. (2005). Literacy coaching for change. Educational Leadership, 62(6), 55–58.

Casey, K. (2006). Literacy coaching: The essentials. Portsmouth, NH: Heinemann.

Costa, A.L., & Garmston, R.J. (1994). Cognitive coaching: A foundation for Renaissance Schools. Norwood, MA: Christopher-Gordon.

Deussen, T., Coskie, T., Robinson, L., & Autio, E. (2007). "Coach" can mean many things: Five categories of literacy coaches in Reading First (Issues & Answers Report, REL 2007-No. 005). Washington, DC: U.S. Department of Education, Institute of Education Sciences, National Center for Education Evaluation and Regional Assistance, Regional Educational Laboratory Northwest. Retrieved July 5, 2007, from ies.ed.gov/ncee/ed-labs/regions/northwest/pdf/REL_2007005.pdf

Dole, J.A. (2004). The changing role of the reading specialist in school reform. The Reading Teacher, 57(5), 462–471. doi:10.1598/RT.57.5.6

Elish-Piper, L.A., & L'Allier, S.K. (2007, December). Does literacy coaching make a difference? The effects of literacy coaching on reading achievement in grades K–3 in a Reading First district. Paper presented at the annual conference of the National Reading Conference, Austin, TX.

Flaherty, J. (2005). Coaching: Evoking excellence in others (2nd ed.). Burlington, MA: Elsevier Butterworth-Heinemann.

Froelich, K.S., & Puig, E.A. (2010). The literacy leadership team: Sustaining and expanding success. Boston: Pearson/Allyn & Bacon.

Frost, S., & Bean, R. (2006, September). Qualifications for literacy coaches: Achieving the gold standard. Retrieved March 20, 2009, from www.literacycoachingonline.org/briefs/LiteracyCoaching.pdf

Gibson, S.A. (2006). Lesson observation and feedback: The practice of an expert reading coach. Reading Research and Instruction, 45(4), 295–318.

International Reading Association. (2004). The role and qualifications of the reading coach in the United States. A position statement of the International Reading Association. Newark, DE: International Reading Association.

Kise, J.A.G. (2006). Differentiated coaching: A framework for helping teachers change. Thousand Oaks, CA: Corwin.

Knight, J. (2006). Instructional coaching: Eight factors for realizing better classroom teaching through support, feedback and intensive, individualized professional learning. School Administrator, 63(4), 36–40.

Knight, J. (2009). What can we do about teacher resistance? Phi Delta Kappan, 90(7), 508–513.

Knowles, M.S. (1984). Andragogy in action: Applying modern principles of adult learning. San Francisco: Jossey Bass.

L'Allier, S.K., & Elish-Piper, L. (2006, December). An initial examination of the effects of literacy coaching on student achievement in reading in grades K–3. Paper presented at the annual conference of the National Reading Conference, Los Angeles, CA.

L'Allier, S.K., & Elish-Piper, L. (2009, May). Literacy coaching in three school districts: Examining the effects of literacy coaching on student reading achievement. Paper presented at the annual conference of the International Reading Association, Minneapolis, MN.

Leithwood, K., Louis, K.S., Anderson, S., & Wahlstrom, K. (2004). Review of research: How leadership influences student learning. Minneapolis: Center for Applied Research and Educational Improvement (University of Minnesota); Toronto: Ontario Institute for Studies in Education at the University of Toronto.

McCombs, J.S., & Marsh, J.A. (2009). Lessons for boosting the effectiveness of reading coaches. Phi Delta Kappan, 90(7), 501–507.

Neufeld, B., & Roper, D. (2003). Coaching: A strategy for developing institutional capacity—Promises and practicalities. Washington, DC: Aspen Institute Program on Education; Providence, RI: Annenberg Institute for School Reform. Retrieved June 28, 2007, from www.annenberginstitute.org/pdf/Coaching.pdf

Perkins, S.J. (1998). On becoming a peer coach: Practices, identities, and beliefs of inexperienced coaches. Journal of Curriculum and Supervision, 13(3), 235–254.

Poglinco, S.M., Bach, A.J., Hovde, K., Rosenblum, S., Saunders, M., & Supovitz, J.A. (2003). The heart of the matter: The coaching model in America's choice schools. Philadelphia: University of Pennsylvania Consortium for Policy Research in Education.

Quatroche, D.J., & Wepner, S.B. (2008). Developing reading specialists as leaders: New directions for program development.

Literacy Research and Instruction, 47(2), 99–115. doi:10.1080/19388070701878816

Rainville, K.N., & Jones, S. (2008). Situated identities: Power and positioning in the work of a literacy coach. The Reading Teacher, 61(6), 440–448. doi:10.1598/RT.61.6.1

Roller, C.M. (2006). Reading and literacy coaches: Report on hiring requirements and duties survey. Newark, DE: International Reading Association.

Showers, B. (1984). Peer coaching: A strategy for facilitating transfer of training. Eugene, OR: Center for Educational Policy and Management.

Toll, C.A. (2005). The literacy coach's survival guide: Essential questions and practical answers. Newark, DE: International Reading Association.

Toll, C.A. (2006). The literacy coach's desk reference: Processes and perspectives for effective coaching. Urbana, IL: National Council of Teachers of English.

Vanderberg, M., & Stephens, D. (2009, January). What teachers say they changed because of their coach and how they think their coach helped them. Retrieved March 31, 2009, from www.literacy-coachingonline.org/briefs/what_teachers_say_about_coaching_1.2.09.pdf

Walpole, S., & Blamey, K.L. (2008). Elementary literacy coaches: The reality of dual roles. The Reading Teacher, 62(3), 222–231. doi:10.1598/RT.62.3.4

L'Allier teaches at Northern Illinois University, DeKalb, USA; e-mail slallier@niu.edu. Elish-Piper teaches at Northern Illinois University; e-mail laurieep@niu.edu. Bean teaches at the University of Pittsburgh, Pennsylvania, USA; e-mail ritabean@pitt.edu.

Models of Coaching

■ ■ ■ ■ ■

There is no doubt that coaching is a hot topic in professional development (Cassidy & Cassidy, 2007). In fact, though *coaching* may be so ubiquitous a term these days that members of the literacy community may not understand one another as they use it. *Coaching* is a strategy for implementing a professional support system for teachers, a system that includes research or theory, demonstration, practice, and feedback (Joyce & Showers, 2002). Such a thing is easier said than done. As we have worked with coaches and with coaching, we have come to realize that we must propose and define multiple models for coaching, and we must support schools in choosing a coaching model even before we assist them in using one. In this first chapter, we compare and contrast several models of coaching. Our goal is to get you thinking about models that currently exist and to provide a strategy for understanding and incorporating new models into your thinking. We are certain of this: There is no one right coaching model for all settings, *and* there are models that would be poor choices. Time spent considering which coaching model to use in a specific setting is time well spent; given the fact that *coaching* is an emerging and evolving term, you may also be well advised to create a coaching model specific to the circumstances of the setting in which it will be implemented.

Coaching Standards

We are surely not the only ones considering flexible definitions of *coaching*. One way to evaluate coaching models is to test them against coaching standards. Standards reflecting the positions of professional organizations are important because they can guide university program development and in-service support for educators. We have been impressed with the evolution of position statements and standards for coaching endorsed by the International Reading Association (IRA); a brief overview follows. You may also want to download and study the standards for yourself. They are all available online (see Figure 1).

Title	Date	Web Address
Excellent reading teachers	2000	www.reading.org/resources/issues/positions_excellent.html
Teaching all children to read: The roles of the reading specialist	2000	www.reading.org/resources/issues/positions_excellent.html
National Staff Development Council's *Standards for Staff Development*	2001	www.nsdcorg/standards/index.cfm
The role and qualifications of the reading coach in the United States	2004	www.reading.org/resources/issues/positions_coach.html
Standards for Middle and High School Literacy Coaches	2006	www.reading.org/resources/issues/reports/coaching.html

FIGURE 1   Standards important to coaching.

As we read the coaching standards, we note how they constitute a snapshot of the evolution of coaching over time. We make this claim by working backward from the two most recent sets of standards: the standards for reading coaches (IRA, 2004) and the standards for middle and high school coaches (IRA, 2006). Both of those documents represent a gradual scale-up from competence in the intact, diverse classroom, to specialized knowledge of the needs of struggling students, to an understanding of the needs of other classroom reading teachers, to an understanding of the needs of content area teachers. For many literacy coaches, this progression actually matches their own professional history; many coaches began their career in the classroom, earned Master's degrees as reading specialists, served struggling readers, and then began to work in leadership roles and in site-based professional development for teachers.

Here is our view of this evolution (see also Walpole & McKenna, 2008): The standards themselves are actually additive. Literacy coaches must begin with the characteristics of excellent classroom reading teachers (IRA, 2000a). They must have taught in a classroom informed by deep knowledge of literacy development, assessment, instruction, and materials. That classroom-based excellence is not enough, though. Literacy coaches must have additional understanding of the needs of struggling students, the more focused skills of reading specialists (IRA, 2000b). These reading specialists must be able to apply this knowledge to support classroom teachers and to assume instructional leadership roles. Finally, reading coaches (IRA, 2004) add an additional area of specialization to those encompassed by reading specialists: they understand how to work with adults, enacting the National Staff Development Council (NSDC, 2001) *Standards for Staff Development*. And those reading coaches who work in middle school and high school settings (IRA, 2006) add to this list a deep understanding of the structure of knowledge in the content areas of English language arts, mathematics, science, and social studies, as well as scaled-up notions of how to evaluate teaching and learning within and across classrooms and disciplines. As we initially considered these standards, we wondered whether they only described individuals with superhuman knowledge and skills (Walpole & McKenna, 2008); as we have worked with excellent coaches, though, we have met individuals who do answer this comprehensive call with wisdom and grace.

To start our own work on understanding multiple coaching models, we had to define what would constitute a coaching model in the first place. Neufeld and Roper (2003) propose two general types of coaches: *change coaches* and *content coaches. Change coaches* work mainly with administrators. They help administrators reorganize resources and build leadership and understanding related to site-based goals; in essence, change coaches set the stage for coaches of teachers. *Content coaches* work once resources are generally well allocated. While they interact with administrators, their focus is more squarely on the teachers. They help teachers to learn new ideas and to implement them during instruction. Then, content coaches provide formative feedback. These broad categories of work with administrators or teachers are important, but they are insufficiently nuanced for us to really describe the choices that individual districts, schools, and coaches make as they define their own models.

We assume that coaches can and should work with both administrators and teachers; influenced by Neufeld and Roper's work, we wanted to get more specific. We listed broad characteristics that would be present in various specific models, but that would constitute real choices. We constructed the criteria listed in Figure 2 to reflect our thinking: A *coaching model* is a set of guidelines for professional developers who provide ongoing formative support for teachers; those professional developers are called *coaches*, and their specific roles in schools vary. A coaching model includes a logistical plan for collaboration with teachers and specific strategies for designing,

- Establishing a role for the coach
- Building knowledge for teachers
- Choosing instructional strategies
- Making instructional plans
- Reflecting on instructional quality
- Assessing student learning

FIGURE 2   Characteristics of a coaching model.

understanding, and reflecting on teacher instruction. It provides for knowledge building, instructional planning, and observation of teaching. It is informed by strategies for assessing student achievement.

All of these features sound very positive in the abstract, but coaching itself assumes an uncomfortable truth; many problems in student achievement are likely related to poor instruction. Increasing the quality of instruction means addressing these problems. Coaches are in schools to do just that, but they do it with specific teachers at different rates and in very different ways.

Selected Models of Coaching

Different models might emphasize some specific criteria over others, but all take the stance that improving student achievement is important and is accomplished by improving instruction. We describe models that stand out for us in the literature, and we also include our own take on the strengths and weaknesses of each model. We have organized the models in an order that corresponds to their relative intrusiveness, a topic to which we return at the close of this chapter.

Mentoring New Teachers

One of the most long-standing (and perhaps ill-defined) forms of coaching is the *mentoring of new teachers*. Given that teachers develop expertise over time, perhaps in stages ranging from the novice who consciously implements rules for teaching and learning, to the expert who can automatically and fluidly adapt to new situations (see Block, Oakar & Hurt, 2002, for a description), it makes sense for districts and schools to establish mentoring or induction programs to link novices and experts in coaching relationships. The realities of such relationships focus attention on the nuts and bolts of teaching in a very situated way; *mentors* simply help novice teachers to keep their heads above water and to integrate themselves within the context in which they are working (see Figure 3). This fact may evidence a general failure of mentoring programs for new teachers; they may tend to simply reproduce the status quo in a school rather than serve as guides into the profession of teaching or agents of instructional improvement and change (Achinstein & Athanases, 2006).

These criticisms of new-teacher mentoring aside, mentoring is a form of coaching that can stimulate thinking about coaching. Mentoring is a one-on-one relationship, planned to link an experienced teacher with a beginner. It is always nonevaluative. Mentoring relationships entail honest, safe opportunities to share confusions and frustrations. They are likely to evolve into coplanning sessions, with the mentor and novice sitting side-by-side, organizing for instruction. In the best mentoring situations, mentors respond to the needs of their partners in flexible ways; they might interpret achievement

Coaching Characteristics	Model-Specific Choices
Establishing a role for the coach	Support and induction to work within a particular school or district
	Knowledgeable, experienced peer support
Building knowledge for teachers	Outside-the-classroom support to understand requirements, procedures, and curriculum
Choosing instructional strategies	Implement what has been chosen
	Benefit from the wisdom of practice
Making instructional plans	Coplanning
Reflecting on instructional quality	Observe and reflect on instruction
Assessing student learning	Critically evaluate student achievement

FIGURE 3   Mentoring new teachers.

data, form instructional groups, observe and provide feedback, model instructional strategies, or create materials for instruction. Overlaying all other mentoring activities, mentors listen. They provide a safe space for novice teachers to share their fears.

Given the fact that induction into teaching is difficult, mentors are well positioned to be received by new teachers. The strength of mentoring (its flexibility and responsiveness) is also its weakness. Mentoring, done well, is very expensive. Mentors are usually classroom teachers who take on additional responsibilities to support their novice partners. They must have release time to provide assistance during the instructional day, and they must have additional time after school to work with their partners. Many districts respond to this expense by naming one district staff member as new teacher mentor, releasing that individual to provide mentoring full-time. That changes the coaching relationship, though, because the mentor is no longer really an expert peer. In general, mentoring establishes a relationship between two individuals, but it does not specify exactly how they will interact.

Cognitive Coaching

The "hows" of coaching are very well specified in *Cognitive Coaching* (Costa & Garmston, 1997, 2002). The "cognitive" in *cognitive coaching* signals its focus: to mediate the invisible thinking that guides a teacher's work. The goal of cognitive coaching is to facilitate the self-directed learning of teachers (see Figure 4). Cognitive coaches do this by learning personal interaction techniques that remind us of the strategies used by counselors. In addition, cognitive coaches engage in three other specific support services: collaboration in both planning and instruction, consulting to build knowledge and skills outside of the classroom, and evaluating to explore the quality of teaching.

At its most intense, cognitive coaching involves a coaching cycle. First, the coach meets with the teacher in a planning conference. The goal of that conference is for the coach to understand and clarify the teacher's goals, collaborate with the teacher to choose evidence that those goals are met, anticipate choices and strategies that might help the teacher to achieve his or her goals, and establish a self-assessment process for the teacher. The next stage in the coaching cycle is monitoring the event, observing teaching. The role of the coach during observation is to gather evidence chosen during planning and to document choices and strategies for the teacher. The final stage in the coaching cycle is a reflection conference, taken after the teacher has had time to reflect personally.

Coaching Characteristics	Model-Specific Choices
Establishing a role for the coach	To assist teachers to move from their current understandings to their desired understandings
Building knowledge for teachers	Consulting with teachers, based on their self-reported needs
Choosing instructional strategies	Collaboration with teachers, based on their individual goals
Making instructional plans	Collaboration with teachers, based on their individual goals
Reflecting on instructional quality	Reflecting conference, with the coach listening to and supporting self-reflection
Assessing student learning	Evidence chosen collaboratively to match the teacher's own goals

FIGURE 4   Cognitive coaching.

The goal of this stage is to provide a setting for self-reflection, to share evidence collected during the lesson, and to connect new learning to future lesson planning.

To us, the strengths of cognitive coaching lie in its specific strategies for building relationships with teachers and for engaging in reflective conversation about teaching. In fact, we think that all coaches would be wise to read Costa and Garmston's work. Another strength of cognitive coaching is that it is flexible with regard to instructional focus. A cognitive coaching cycle could be used to support virtually any teaching goal.

We can also upend those strengths and call them weaknesses. Cognitive coaching encourages relationship building with teachers and reflection on teaching, but it does not specify anything about what or how to teach. It may be inappropriate to implement cognitive coaching when teachers are selecting goals for instruction that are inconsistent with current research; a series of many coaching cycles could move an individual teacher toward setting research-based goals, but that would be a very costly model to adopt for a school.

Peer Coaching

Joyce and Showers (1996) developed this well-articulated coaching model, which has evolved over time; *peer coaching* was designed and redesigned to build a bridge between formal professional development and classroom implementation. The model assumes that an instructional leader (e.g., a principal) has a concern about achievement and identifies an expert outside of the school to select and present a broad-based instructional strategy targeted to address the concern. It then engages the entire school staff to implement the strategy and model it for one another. Like cognitive coaching, peer coaching is also flexible in general about what instructional strategies are targeted, but the model includes choice of a specific schoolwide focus (see Figure 5).

The quality that makes peer coaching unique is the coaching itself. After the instructional strategy has been demonstrated in traditional outside-the-classroom professional development, teachers act as coaches for one another. Here's how it works: The principal ensures that teaching colleagues form groups of two or more. These collaborative coaching teams meet to discuss instructional goals and to develop specific lesson plans. Then, they observe one another as they implement these lesson plans. In fact, Joyce and Showers assert that the "coach" is the teacher teaching the lesson; the observer is being coached by observing, and no feedback is provided from the observer (Joyce & Showers, 1996). This is an interesting change in perspective from other coaching models.

Coaching Characteristics	Model-Specific Choices
Establishing a role for the coach	Peers coach one another
	Demonstrate instructional strategies
Building knowledge for teachers	Outside-the-classroom sessions with an external facilitator
	Observation of teaching
Choosing instructional strategies	Collaborative up-front efforts of the principal and external facilitator
	Schoolwide focus
Making instructional plans	Collaboration within each coaching team
Reflecting on instructional quality	Personal reflection, in private
Assessing student learning	Not specified

FIGURE 5   Peer coaching.

Peer coaching has much to recommend it. It is relatively inexpensive to implement. It is unlikely to be perceived by teachers as threatening. It is likely to build cohesive relationships within the instructional team. Peer coaching is especially appropriate if one very specific instructional strategy (e.g., guided oral reading, reciprocal teaching, concept mapping) has been identified as appropriate for school wide attention. Surely a principal-initiated peer coaching model ensures more consistent implementation than a traditional one-shot in service presentation; however, the downside of peer coaching is that it assumes one concept or strategy implemented across the school will increase achievement, and there are relatively few quality controls on the implementation of that strategy.

Subject-Specific Coaching

Subject-specific coaching nests all instructional decision making within a particular discipline (e.g., math, English language arts, science, social studies). In that way, subject-specific coaching honors the differences inherent in the academic disciplines and is easily linked to local, state, and national standards. That fact makes it much easier to choose a set of instructional strategies that foster academic excellence and achievement of the standards for all students. Like new-teacher mentoring, though, subject-specific coaching is a common district- or state-level strategy that is enacted in many different ways with little guidance (see Figure 6).

As literacy is our field, we tend to focus on that literature, Gabriel (2005) provides a model for subject-specific coaching that evolved from his work as a high school English department chair. We think, though, that this model would work equally well with other disciplines. He argues that teacher leaders must empower other leaders within their team, sharing the helm, but that the boat must always be aimed in the direction of expert implementation of the curriculum.

There is a strong theme about observing teachers in Gabriel's work. He encourages the subject-specific coach to observe teachers on his or her team and to help them reflect on the strengths and weaknesses of the lessons. Although he separates these observations from those of an administrator and reminds the coach not to participate in teacher evaluation or to document observations for the principal, he does suggest that a coach might see some practices that are so inconsistent with the norms of the school or discipline that the coach might have to take very specific action. He recommends that the coach try to resolve these issues personally by sharing them with the teacher and offering

Coaching Characteristics	Model-Specific Choices
Establishing a role for the coach	Ensure implementation of effective practices and monitor student outcomes
Building knowledge for teachers	Linked to deep understanding of curriculum and standards
Choosing instructional strategies	Nested within the discipline
	Vertically articulated
Making instructional plans	Collaboration curriculum development
	Curriculum mapping
Reflecting on instructional quality	Focused observation
Assessing student learning	Teachers-development assessments
	State-mandated assessments

FIGURE 6   Subject-specific coaching.

to help, but that if these efforts are unsuccessful, the next step would be to bring the problem to the attention of the principal. We think that this concept, however unpleasant, is important. As our coaching models become more specific and intrusive, the chance for real conflict increases. Although it does not make conflict easier to manage, it may be helpful simply to anticipate that coaches might fail to achieve their objectives with some teachers. Such is the reality of work with teachers. They are not all equally skilled or committed.

Another theme that Gabriel pursues in his description of subject-specific coaching is the need for careful, evolving curriculum mapping. He describes the map in an interesting way. A map shows various routes to a destination; it is up to the user to choose the exact route. Such curriculum maps allow teams of teachers to ensure horizontal alignment (across sections of the same course) and vertical alignment (across grade levels) so that all students have a path to the final destination. He does anticipate that the curriculum map will evolve to include differentiation within the curriculum to address achievement differences and to provide remediation for those students whose achievement is so far below grade-level expectations that differentiation alone will not provide access to the end goal.

Finally, Gabriel provides specific scenarios about how a subject-specific coach, often working in tandem with a principal, can use data. He suggests that while data analysis alone cannot determine teacher effectiveness, it can open the door to instructional change. In effect, student achievement data (both from teacher-designed tests and from standardized tests) provide a window for discussion of new goals. Data may actually be a less intrusive way for a subject-specific coach to engage teachers to really consider altering their instructional strategies.

Program-Specific Coaching

As we move toward more and more intrusive coaching, instructional strategies become more specific, and the role of the coach changes from facilitator of a teacher reaching his or her own goals to a teacher becoming masterful at a specific set of external goals. This is a controversial topic in literacy education; for instance, Hoffman and Pearson (2000) and Duffy (2004) make a very strong case that "training" teachers to follow a specific program exactly is inconsistent with the professional education of teachers. We think, though, that program-specific coaching can be part of the professional education of teachers, and concepts from program implementation are important.

In fact, *program-specific coaching* is a real coaching model, and it has been effectively applied to very different curricula (Walpole & Meyer, 2007). Program-specific coaching is targeted and outcome-oriented. It is designed to equip an individual to implement a new program with facility. Although we describe two program-specific coaching models, there are many others. In fact, almost all commercial materials available for instruction include offers of program-specific coaching opportunities, controlled by program designers, to help schools in initial implementation.

In the field of literacy, we can compare and contrast two high-profiles, program-specific coaching models: Reading Recovery and Success for All (SFA). Reading Recovery is an approach to tutoring first-grade struggling readers; SFA is a comprehensive school reform for kindergarten through sixth grade. Both curricula have been recently reviewed by the What Works Clearinghouse *(http://ies.ed.gov/ncee.wwc/)* and achieved positive or potentially positive effects on overall reading achievement. The routes that they take to get there include highly program-specific coaching.

Reading Recovery has a specific 30-minute lesson frame that involves diagnostic decision making as children read progressively more difficult books, selected based on the reading strategies the teacher will encourage the child to use. Implementation of this lesson frame entails complex decision making before, during, and after the lesson. Knowledge and skills required by a Reading Recovery teacher are developed in a "train the trainer" model. That means that Reading Recovery trainers participate in extensive, specific academic work, defined by the organization and accomplished through universities. Once certified themselves, these trainers can certify teachers to become Reading Recovery teachers. Their strategies include deep understanding of the "whys" of the program, as well as extended observations with feedback; they tutor children while their trainers watch them from behind a one-way mirror (Reading Recovery Council of North America, 2004). This organized, layered coaching yields high level of consistency in the knowledge and practices of Reading Recovery teachers (Pinnell, 1985; Pinnell, Fried, & Estice, 1990).

Success for All is a comprehensive reading program including instructional materials, grouping plans, periodic assessments, and specific requirements for 90 minutes of reading instruction in a 5-day cycle. Its designers have subjected the program to external evaluation to document its effectiveness (Borman et al., 2005a, 2005b). The program itself is highly specified, but teachers need extensive support to implement it. SFA also employs a layered training model. Like Reading Recovery, SFA is an organized, national movement with national, regional, and site-based coaches (called *facilitators*).

SFA instruction and SFA classrooms have specific characteristics (including materials that must be displayed, instructional procedures that are used every day, and management tools), and SFA facilitators and SFA Foundation coaches use observation checklists to monitor fidelity to the program requirements. SFA coaches have ready-made tools to guide their work, and they can use a variety of strategies to support teachers who are struggling.

The role of an SFA coach is clearly specified to establish fidelity to the SFA model. Coaches do not choose curricula or strategies. Coaches have lesson plan templates specifying the type, amount, and time for instruction, and teachers are required to implement these lesson plans exactly. Coaches also receive observation templates and must conduct specific observations. They have direct support in how to monitor student achievement through specific program-embedded assessments, and also in how to use achievement data to make new grouping decisions.

Program-specific coaching models are likely to be effective in their goal: establishing fidelity to the program model. The choices they require, represented in Figure 7,

Coaching Characteristics	Model-Specific Choices
Establishing a role for the coach	Trainer
Building knowledge for teachers	Deep understanding of how and why to implement the program
Choosing instructional strategies	External, completed by the program designers
Making instructional plans	External, included in the program
	Internal, specified for the setting
Reflecting on instructional quality	Fidelity to the program model
Assessing students learning	Program-embedded assessments
	External assessments

FIGURE 7 Program-specific coaching

make this fact clear. In fact, they are much more effective than simply providing teacher's editions and a few hours of training by company representatives and then having teachers make their own interpretations. Program-specific models go well beyond that, giving teachers ongoing support and opportunities for reflection and problem solving. They also provide coaches with very direct tools to monitor their work, including both student-level assessments and teacher-level observation guidance. This level of direction for the coach is attractive given the debate about what coaches are doing in Reading First initiatives (Deussen, Coskie, Robinson, & Autio, 2007).

Reform-Oriented Coaching

It is to Reading First that we move in order to introduce our most intrusive model, the one that we ourselves have been developing and adapting over time. We call our own model *reform-oriented coaching* for two reasons. First, we have developed it within specific federally funded reform contexts (the Reading Excellence Act Reforms and Reading First initiatives). Both reforms targeted curriculum change in kindergarten through third grade. Both included funding for new materials, new assessments, and professional development for teachers. In the settings where we worked, districts and schools chose to use grant funds to hire site-based literacy coaches. The second reason that we call this model *reform-oriented* (and describe it as most intrusive) is that, in contrast to the program-specific coaching models described earlier, where instructional outcomes are specified in advance and both teachers and coaches know what these outcomes are and move toward them, our reform-oriented model is a moving target. The model itself must evolve and change as student achievement data dictate. In effect, it must be constantly reformed.

Our reform-oriented coaching model (see Figure 8) assumes several up-front decisions. First, the school community recognizes that past practices are not yielding acceptable outcomes. Second, the school has used a comprehensive, thoughtful procedure to select high-quality commercial instructional materials for grade-level instruction and for intensive intervention. Third, district and school leaders have committed to extended instructional time and school wide assessments. And, finally, there is time during and after the school day for the coach to provide professional development for teachers.

In our model, we are asking much of classroom teachers (Walpole & McKenna, 2007). They must be skillful classroom managers, implementing an interactive read-aloud, fast-paced grade-level instruction, and multiple differentiated small groups every day.

Common Characteristics	Implementation Choices
Establishing a role for the coach	Director and/or mentor
Building knowledge for teachers	Understanding of scientifically based reading research
	Implementation of whole-group instruction differentiated small-group instruction and intensive intervention
Choosing instructional strategies	Schools choose commercial materials for whole-group instruction
	Schools choose commercial materials for intensive intervention
	Schools choose instructional strategies for small-group, differentiated instruction
Making instructional plans	Grade-level collaboration, guided by the coach
Reflecting on instructional quality	Walkthroughs
	Observations
Assessing student learning	Valid and reliable assessment systems for screenings, progress monitoring, and outcomes
	Informal assessments to guide differentiated instruction

FIGURE 8   Reform-oriented coaching.

We are also asking much of coaches (Walpole & McKenna, 2004). They must work with each of their grade-level teams to construct classroom schedules to specify how their core program will be implemented, design an assessment system to screen students for potential problems, employ flexible informal strategies to specify exactly what those problems are and how to address them, monitor progress to document the effectiveness of instruction, and understand outcome measures to chart growth over time. They must be able to interpret and represent data for individual children, classrooms, grade levels, and schools, using both cross-sectional and cohort tracking. And, finally, they must design and implement a reflexive professional support system—a system that allows all teachers to develop their knowledge of research and pedagogy through book study and to use walkthroughs and observations to identify targets for professional learning. The fact that these coaches accomplish some of this work in district or regional teams, and with the support of knowledgeable state staff, mediates the difficulties in such a model only slightly.

We highlight only one aspect of this coaching model here; more specifics will be infused in other chapters. We see our reform-oriented coaches adopting one of two roles, which we have termed *director* and *mentor* (Walpole & Blamey, 2008). They are similar to Neufeld and Roper's *change* and *content coaches*. Recall that the change coach worked primarily with the administration to reorganize the school for teaching and learning; our directors tackle that job first, establishing instruction schedules for grade-level instruction and for intensive intervention, organizing materials and assessment systems, and building knowledge about reading and the curriculum. Mentor coaches are like content coaches; they work directly with teachers, because either they or the principal has already organized the school for the difficult work of schoolwide reform.

The strength of our model is its comprehensiveness and its maintenance of choice. We see each individual school as its own project, led by a coach and principal who understand the school context. As our work with this model is ongoing and intensive, we cannot help but address all of the issues of context that arise. However, our relationships with coaches are founded on choice; we will not recommend specific commercial solutions, and we will not choose specific assessments. Rather, we provide ongoing, evolving guidelines in response to data from the field.

The strength of comprehensiveness and choice is also the major weakness of our model. It may be that this model is simply too demanding for the personnel or the institution; it may also be that teachers' resistance to the type or pace of their professional development and the requirements imposed in their classroom yield resistance too difficult to address. As we said at the start, our model is intrusive.

Choosing and Using a Model of Coaching

We continue to grow in our understanding of coaches and coaching; we acknowledge that thoughtful researchers and wise school and district leaders are wrestling with coaching and that they have described viable models with substantive differences. The array of choices of coaching models is larger now than it was when we began, and it is getting larger every day. To say that models abound and that they differ is not to say that all models are equal in ease of implementation or in effectiveness. In fact, there may be an important interaction—models that are easier to implement may be less effective in the long run. Geologists have long used a 1-to-10 scale to describe the hardness of minerals, with 1 being the softest (talc) and 10 the hardest (diamond). We suggest that this is a useful metaphor to describe coaching (see Figure 9). *Soft coaching* is invitational in nature. It engages teachers in nonthreatening, nonconfrontational ways. Teachers' professional expertise is respected and never overtly challenged. Multiple perspectives on teaching are embraced and honored equally. Problems are approached collaboratively and, while compromises are sought, teachers have the last word. *Hard coaching* is based on the assumption that instructional methods vary in their effects on student achievement and that empirical research can identify the best methods. The goal of hard coaching is to support teachers to implement more effective methods and to abandon those that do not work as well. As they work to achieve this goal, coaches may encounter road blocks and resistance. One thing is sure—the harder the model that is chosen for a given site, the more work a coach and principal must do up front to set the stage for success.

We invite you into the rest of this book with this goal: to choose or construct a model for coaching. But don't do it yet. Wait until you have thought through the ideas that we present in each chapter. At the end of your work with this book, come back to this chapter and see whether a particular model is attractive to you and appropriate for your school or whether you should construct your own. That's the stance on coaching that we take ourselves; don't be too sure too early.

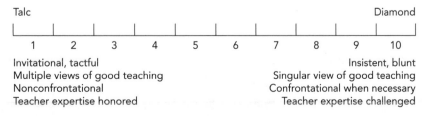

FIGURE 9   A hardness scale for coaching.

REFERENCES

Achinstein, B. & Athanases, S. B. (Eds.). (2006) *Mentors in the making: Developing new leaders for new teachers.* New York: Teachers College Press.

Block, C. C., Oakar, M., & Hurt, N. (2002). The expertise of literacy teachers: A continuum from preschool to grade 5. *Reading Research Quarterly, 37,* 178–206.

Borman, G. D., Slavin, R. E., Cheung, A., Chamberlain, A. M., Madden, N. A., & Chambers, B. (2005a). Success for All: First-year results from the national randomized field trial. *Educational Evaluation and Policy Analysis, 27,* 1–22.

Borman, G. D., Slavin, R. E., Cheung, A., Chamberlain, A. M., Madden, N. A., & Chambers, B. (2005b). The national randomized field trial of Success for All: Second-year outcomes. *American Educational Research Journal, 42,* 673–696.

Costa, A., & Garmston, R. (1997). *Cognitive coaching: A foundation for Renaissance Schools* (3rd ed.). Norwood, MA: Christopher-Gordon.

Deussen. T., Coskie, T., Robinson, L., & Autio, E., (2007). *"Coach" can mean many things: Five categories of literacy coaches in Reading First.* (Issues & Answers Report, REL 2007-No. 005) Washington, DC: U.S. Department of Education, Institute of Education Sciences, National Center for Education Evaluation and Regional Assistance, Regional Educational Laboratory Northwest. Retrieved July 6, 2007, from http://ies.ed.gov/ncee/edlabs

Duffy, G. G. (2004). Teachers who improve reading achievement: What research says about what they do and how to develop them. In D. S. Strickland & M. L. Kamil (Eds.), Improving reading achievement through professional development (pp. 3–22). Norwood, MA: Christopher-Gordon.

Gabriel, J. G. (2005). *How to thrive as a teacher leader.* Alexandria, VA: Association for Supervision and Curriculum Development.

Hoffman, J., & Pearson, P. D. (2000). Reading teachers education in the next millennium: What your grandmother's teacher didn't know that your granddaughter's teacher should. *Reading Research Quarterly, 35,* 28–44.

International Reading Association. (2006). *Standards for middle and high school literacy coaches.* Newark, DE: Author, in collaboration with NCTE, NCTM, NSTA, NCSS, and the Carnegie Corporation of New York.

International Reading Association. (2004). *The role and qualifications of the reading coach in the United States.* Newark, DE: Author. Available: http://www.reading.org/resourcess/issues/positions_coach.html

Joyce, B., & Showers, B. (1996). Staff development as a comprehensive service organization. *Journal of Staff Development, 17(1),* 2–6.

National Staff Development Council. (Revised, 2001). *Standards for staff development.* Oxford, OH: NSDC. Available: http://www.nsdc.org/standards/index.cfm

Walpole, S., & Mckenna, M. C. (2008). Literacy coaches: Their emerging leadership roles. In S. B. Wepner & D. Strickland (Eds.), *Administration and supervision of reading programs* (4th ed., pp. 45–54). New York: Teachers College Press.

CLASSROOM IMPLICATIONS

1. What qualities do you think are important that a coach possess? Are these characteristics likely to vary from one school to another? In what ways?

2. What factors will affect the success or failure of the coaching movement? What is your own prediction concerning this movement? Will we find coaches in schools a decade from now?

Collected online articles about coaching, compiled at the University of Virginia and presented in reverse chronology. http://curry.edschool.virginia.edu/reading/projects/garf/Coaching Articles.htm

International Reading Association. (Posted 2000). Roles of the Reading Specialist. Position Statement. http://www.reading.org/resources/issues/positions_specialist.html

International Reading Association. (Posted 2004). Roles and Qualifications of the Reading Coach in the United States. Position Statement. http://www.reading.org/resources/issues/positions_coach.html

Clair, N. & Adger, C.T. (1999). Professional Development for Teachers in Culturally Diverse Schools. ERIC Digest. http://www.eric.ed.gov/ERICDocs/data/ericdocs2/content_storage_01/0000000b/80/2a/2e/fb.pdf

Ferraro, J. (2000). Reflective Practice and Professional Development. ERIC Digest. http://www.eric.ed.gov/ERICDocs/data/ericdocs2/content_storage_01/0000000b/80/2a/32/84.pdf

Fillmore, L.W., & Snow, C. (2000). What Elementary Teachers Need to Know about Language. ERIC Digest. http://www.eric.ed.gov/ERICDocs/data/ericdocs2/content_storage_01/0000000b/80/2a/31/f0.pdf

Grisham, D.L., Albright, L., Berger, S., Kozub, R., Loughman, P., Sanchez, C., & Sullivan, A. (Posted August 2000). Teacher Voices: Research as Professional Development. [Editorial]. Reading Online. http://www.readingonline.org/editorial/edit_index.asp?HREF=/editorial/august2000/index.html

Huling, L. (2001). Teacher Mentoring as Professional Development. ERIC Digest. http://www.eric.ed.gov/ERICDocs/data/ericdocs2/content_storage_01/0000000b/80/2a/34/e4.pdf

International Reading Association. (Posted 2000). Excellent Reading Teachers. Position Statement. http://www.reading.org/resources/issues/positions_excellent.html

National Staff Development Council. http://www.nsdc.org

Weiss, E.M., & Weiss, S.G. (1999). Beginning Teacher Induction. ERIC Digest. http://www.eric.ed.gov/ERICDocs/data/ericdocs2/content_storage_01/0000000b/80/2a/2f/a7.pdf

FOR FURTHER READING

Bean, R.M., & Eisenberg, E. (2009). Literacy coaching in middle and high school. In K. Wood & W. Blanton (Eds.), *Promoting literacy with adolescent learners: Research based instruction* (pp. 107–124). New York, NY: Guilford Press.

Blachowicz, C.L.Z., Buhle, R., Ogle, D., Frost, S., Correa, A, & Kinner, J.D. (2010). Hit the ground running: Ten ideas for preparing and supporting urban literacy coaches. *The Reading Teacher, 63*(5), 348–359. doi: 10.1598/RT.63.5.1

Elish-Piper, L., & L'Allier, S.K. (2010). Exploring the relationship between literacy coaching and student reading achievement in grades k-1. *Literacy Research and Instruction, 49,* 162–174. doi: 10.1080/19388070902913289

Frost, S., Buhle, R., & Blachowicz, C.L.Z. (2009). *Effective literacy coaching: Building expertise and a culture of literacy.* Alexandria, VA: ASCD.

Peterson, D.S., Taylor, B.M., Burnham, B., & Schock, R. (2009). Reflective coaching conversations: A missing piece. *The Reading Teacher, 62*(6), 500–509. doi: 10.1598/RT.62.6.4

Toll, C. (2009). Literacy coaching: Suggestions for school leaders. *Principal Leadership, 9*(9), 24–28.

ONLINE RESOURCES

The Literacy Coaching Clearinghouse, a site jointly sponsored by IRA and NCTE.
http://www.literacycoachingonline.org/

7

Adolescent Literacy

It is one of the great pleasures of a student's life to buy a heap of books at the beginning of the autumn. Here, he fancies, are all of the secrets.

—Robert Lynd (1923)

The impact of even one good book on a young person's mind is surely an end in itself, a valid experience which helps him form standards of judgment and taste at the time when his mind is most sensitive to impressions of every kind.

—Lillian H. Smith (1953)

Adolescent literacy—the reading and writing of middle and high school students— is critical to student success in all areas of the curriculum.

—Implementing the No Child Left Behind Act:
Using Student Engagement to Improve Adolescent Literacy (2005)

Classroom environments and curricula are not often structured to shape students' lives by engaging them with texts that they find meaningful and significant.

—Alfred Tatum (2008)

Many adolescents do not see reading as an important aspect of their daily lives, and this is a major concern today both to educators and the general public. The results in the recent report of the National Assessment of Educational Progress (*The Nation's Report Card: Reading 2009*) support the seriousness of the situation:

- Thirty-three percent of fourth graders performed below the basic level in reading, which is characterized by "partial mastery of the knowledge and skills that are fundamental for proficient work at a grade level."
- Twenty-five percent of eighth graders performed below the basic level in reading.
- Fifty-three percent of African American and fifty-two percent of Hispanic fourth-grade students scored below the basic level in reading.
- Forty-four percent of African American and 41% of Hispanic eighth-grade students scored below the basic level in reading.

The causes of these dire statistics are complex. To gain a more nuanced perspective, let's examine the situation in middle schools.

The Middle School Problem

A visitor to Oglethorpe Academy in Savannah, Georgia, is not likely to be alarmed. Standardized test scores in reading and content subjects are high, disciplinary referrals are few, and teacher morale is good. Such a visitor might find it difficult to believe that a substantial literacy problem exists in America's middle schools. After all, Oglethorpe Academy is a public school, its physical facilities are modest, and its parents do not pay tuition. The fact is, however, that Oglethorpe is not a typical middle school. Its parents tend to be well educated and, through a state charter, agree to volunteer extensively. Most of its students had strong academic records at the elementary level before entering Oglethorpe and are college bound as they move on to high school. Nearly all of them speak English as their first language, and only thirty percent qualify for free or reduced-price lunches.

To gain an understanding of the problem, let us visit a middle school that is more representative of the nation. Rather than single out a real school, we will create a composite–Jefferson Middle School–based on national data. Jefferson serves 605 students in grades six–eight. Although many of them are good readers, twenty-seven percent of the eighth graders cannot read at even a basic level, as defined by the National Assessment of Educational Progress. Their reading problems did not begin when they entered Jefferson. As fourth graders, a similar percentage was experiencing problems. Poverty levels at Jefferson are moderate; about twenty-seven percent of the students qualify for free or reduced-price lunches. Parents often have limited education and find it difficult to volunteer extensively at the school. Many of these parents do not harbor fond memories of Jefferson and feel uncomfortable when they visit the school. Girls at Jefferson tend to be better readers than boys, and whites, as a group, outperform African Americans and Hispanics. Test scores at Jefferson have allowed the school to demonstrate adequate yearly progress in reading and other areas, but Jefferson is currently flirting with the state's needs-improvement list and is unlikely to make AYP for much longer.

It is easy to see that Jefferson and Oglethorpe are not very similar. In fact, we might joke that the only thing they have in common is the age of the students. Tragically, however, even that is not quite true since the average age of Jefferson students is higher than the students at Oglethorpe because of frequent retentions.

For these reasons, success stories like Oglethorpe's are rarely if ever exportable to struggling schools. The faculty at Jefferson must work for changes that will realistically address the challenges posed by the students they serve. They would do well to begin by studying the factors that led to the literacy crisis in their school.

What Has Caused the Middle School Literacy Problem?

False Causes. Let's start by dispelling two causes that have no direct bearing on middle school literacy achievement. The first is race. Because in the United States, race happens to be *correlated* with reading achievement, it is falsely believed by some educators to be a *cause* of low achievement. But when we account for factors such as income level and parental education, we find that race is a very poor predictor of achievement. For example, children of well-educated, middle-income African American parents are just as likely to succeed in school as children of well-educated, middle-income white parents.

The other false factor is technology. Many educators (particularly language arts teachers) lament the proliferation of video gaming, Internet access, cell phones, and the like, which they perceive to be attractive nuisances that relegate literacy to a lower priority for the nation's youth. Similar charges were leveled at television at the time of its advent during the 1950s and '60s. A displacement theory was proposed, suggesting that the time available for recreational reading was displaced by watching television. While NAEP findings do indeed show that extreme amounts

of televiewing (six or more hours per day) are associat[e]
achievement, it has never been clear that heavy watchers wou[l]
for a book if the plug were pulled. Nor does the displacement [
likely in the case of recent technology applications. This is true fo[r]
First, the percentage of eighth graders who have performed poorly o[n]
test has remained relatively constant over nearly four decades since the
first given–long before microchips began to transform the lives of adolescent[s]
ond, many of these technology applications involve some level of literate activ[ity]
Whether a student is surfing the Internet, reading clues in a video game, or send
ing text messages to friends via cell phone, there is no doubt that technology is
changing what counts as literacy. But these changes can work to the advantage of
middle grades teachers, as we shall see. In the meantime, let's identify the true
causes of the middle school literacy problem.

Education and Culture. Literacy is an attainment that is not universally valued. Its
importance is viewed differently by individuals and groups within the American
population. The value of literacy is reflected in one's level of education and tends
to be acquired from parents and peers. Children who witness literate activity being
modeled and valued tend to acquire those values themselves. Children who are
not exposed to these influences often develop different views.

Poverty. Because individuals of limited education tend to earn less, a vicious cycle
develops from one generation to the next. Parents of limited education find it difficult to foster high levels of literacy in their children, who grow up at risk of school
failure and eventually take jobs for which the literacy demands are low. We believe
that literacy is the key to the cycle of poverty, but it is a key that usually must be
turned from the outside by dedicated educators. We are not suggesting that literacy is perfectly correlated with income. There are many literate people of modest
means. However, extreme poverty makes the attainment of literacy doubtful, for it
frequently goes hand-in-glove with one's level of education.

Text Demands. Jeanne Chall (1983/1996) spoke of a "fourth-grade slump," the
point where she believed reading achievement began to flag. Chall attributed
this decline in part to the failure of many students to attain prerequisite skills,
such as automatic word recognition and fluency. Another factor is the nonfiction text that children encounter. These texts gradually increase in difficulty, but
they are still within the reach of most fluent fourth graders. But their complexity and abstractness do not level off. Robert Calfee, long-time editor of the
Journal of Educational Psychology, concluded, based on data from the Stanford
Achievement Test, that a major slump occurs around grade seven, when the
cumulative demands of vocabulary pose considerable challenges. It is in middle
school that the conceptual demands of content textbooks become truly troublesome, which is why it is imperative that teachers of science and social studies
employ instructional methods that facilitate their students as they wrestle with
assigned materials.

Lack of Instruction. In most middle schools, reading instruction falls in the language arts program, with the exception of remedial and special services. The focus
of language arts teachers is split among competing standards. They must teach
grammar and mechanics, literature, and composition. There is little time left for
what struggling middle schoolers need most: systematic instruction in vocabulary
and comprehension strategies. The frequent result is that no one takes responsibility for these prerequisites of reading success.

School Readers

...riencing reading problems vary considerably, but most of them reflect ...patterns. To understand these patterns, it helps to contrast them with ...g development. Chall (1983/1996) proposed a series of stages through ...s pass on their way to becoming proficient readers. These stages were ...ier, but following chart summarizes them. (We have altered her labels ...djusted the typical grade levels according to present-day instructional

...culated that most striving readers experience difficulties because they do ...y skills at certain stages. Her idea is now strongly supported by research ...pear-Swerling & Sternberg, 1997). According to Chall, normally progressing middle grades children should be able to read grade-appropriate nonfiction with good comprehension. Of course, we know that many cannot. Chall's stages help us understand why. While a very small percentage of middle schoolers exhibit symptoms of developmental dyslexia, most can trace their problems back to a particular stage of development where they went "off track." Let's examine the patterns that result.

Jamal is a fluent reader, who can read textbook passages aloud at reasonable speeds and with natural phrasing. However, he has little understanding of what he reads even when he reads silently and does need not be concerned about his public performance as a reader. He has passed through the fluency stage successfully but has not acquired the vocabulary and comprehension strategies he needs to gain meaning from text.

Joanne reads aloud haltingly. She can decode nearly every word, given enough time, but lacks a large sight vocabulary. She has passed through the decoding stage but has not attained fluency. As a result, her attention is on word identification at the expense of comprehension.

Jack finds reading extremely difficult. He often stops at unfamiliar words and lacks the decoding skills to pronounce them. His instructional reading level is several

Stage	Name	Description	Grades
0[1]	Emergent Literacy	Oral language develops, children learn how print functions; they acquire phonological awareness and knowledge of the alphabet	
1	Decoding	Children grasp the alphabetic principle, learn to decode most unfamiliar words quickly; many words now recognized automatically	K–1
2	Fluency	Oral reading of grade-level text becomes relatively rapid, marked by natural phrasing and intonation	2–3
3	Reading to Learn (Learning the New)	Children can purposefully extract and interpret information from grade-level nonfiction text	3–8
4	Multiple Viewpoints	Students recognize that authors embrace different views; they learn to discern differences in perspective	9–12
5	A World View	Students interpret text in terms of their own perspectives, noting differences among authors and between authors and themselves	College

[1]The emergent literacy stage involves a very gradual approach to literate activity, and it cannot truly be called a stage. For this reason, Chall designated it as "Stage Zero"!

years below his grade placement. He has never successfully passed through the decoding stage.

While precise statistics are not available, striving readers like Jamal are clearly the most numerous, while fortunately there are far fewer readers like Joanne and still fewer like Jack. Determining which of these patterns best fits a particular student is not difficult, and it is a necessary first step towards meeting their instructional needs. These readers cannot attain proficiency unless they progress from their current stage through reading to learn.

Appreciating the nature of these stages and then gaining a notion of the percentage of students at each of them are important if the literacy status of a particular middle school is to be understood. Thinking of achievement in terms of developmental stages gets us past the point of trying to analyze mere test scores and helps us gain a better sense of where we need to go.

How Do We Address the Problem of Adolescent Literacy?

The critical question becomes how to change this current situation in adolescent literacy. A report to the Carnegie Corporation, *Reading next: A vision for action and research in middle and high school literacy* (Biancarosa & Snow, 2004) suggested a number of essentials as to how educators might enhance their adolescent literacy instruction. These included the following points:

1. **Direct, explicit comprehension.** Instruction makes reading comprehension strategies explicit to students through modeling and explanation and gives students ample opportunities for practice.
2. **Effective instructional principles embedded in content.** Instruction is embedded and reinforced across content areas, with attention paid to content-specific texts and tasks.
3. **Motivation and self-directed learning.** Instruction promotes engagement and self-regulated learning for the development of motivated and flexible literacy skills.
4. **Text-based collaborative learning.** Instruction enables students to engage in guided interactions with texts in groups in order to foster learning of new knowledge.
5. **Strategic tutoring.** Individualized instruction is more intense for struggling readers and focuses on instilling independence.
6. **Diverse texts.** Students have access to, and experience with, texts at a variety of difficulty levels that vary in the styles, genres, topics, and content areas they cover.
7. **Intensive writing.** Instruction should integrate writing as a vehicle for learning and as a measure of comprehension and learning across content areas.
8. **A technology component.** Technology is used to leverage instruction time to provide additional support and practice for students as well as prepare students for the ways different technology alters the reading and writing experience.
9. **Ongoing formative assessment of students.** Instruction should be determined by the use of ongoing assessment of students that helps teachers target instruction.
10. **Extended time for literacy:** Reading and writing instruction takes place for longer than a single language arts period and is extended through integration and emphasis across curricula. Extended time may also include additional time devoted to literacy instruction, especially for learners more than two grade levels behind.
11. **Professional development.** Teachers participate in professional development experiences that are systematic, frequent, long-term, and ongoing to improve their ability to teach reading and writing across the curriculum.

12. **Ongoing summative assessment of students and programs.** Students' progress is monitored and tracked over the long term.
13. **Teacher teams.** Infrastructure supports teachers working in small interdisciplinary teams to allow for coloration and more consistent and coordinated instruction and professional development.
14. **Leadership.** Principals and administrators participate in professional development and foster teachers taking leadership roles.
15. **A comprehensive and coordinated literacy program.** Instruction encompasses all aspects of literacy in ways that allow all facets of the program to complement one another and is consistent with professional development as well as the chosen materials and approaches for learning (p. 9).

In a Position Statement titled *Supporting Young Adolescent Literacy Learning* (International Reading Association, 2001), four specific recommendations were made for classroom teachers to help their students with their various literacy activities. They included the following:

- Engage in whole-school planning to implement components of a successful school- or district-wide literacy learning plan that is integrative and interdisciplinary.
- Collaborate with administrators, librarians, guidance counselors, intervention specialists, and other school-based educators to improve reading instruction and achievement.
- Interpret assessment data and make information available to other teachers and school-based educators.
- Provide opportunities for students to read material they choose and to be read to each school day.

AS YOU READ

The two selections in this chapter represent some of the current thinking by literacy educators on this topic. Tom Bean and Helen Harper begin by describing different perspectives on the notion of adolescence. These include defining adolescence by age or grade level (biologically, in other words), defining it by changing literacy needs (developmentally), and reconsidering the concept of adolescence in terms of the emerging implications of the new digital literacies. Each of these perspectives should inform how we conceptualize adolescent literacy, and we encourage you, as you read, to develop your own perspective integrating all three perspectives. Sharon Pitcher and her colleagues describe their investigation of seven adolescent readers experiencing problems with reading. They wanted to determine whether there was an appropriate match between the kind of instruction these adolescents received and the kind they needed. These researchers were also interested in finding out how the students felt about their children's problems. We believe you will find these seven snapshots helpful in developing a broader perspective on the challenges faced by teachers of adolescent literacy.

REFERENCES

Biancarosa, G., & Snow, C. E. (2004). *Reading Next: A vision for action and research in middle and high school literacy*. Washington, DC: Alliance for Excellent Education.
Chall, J. (1983/1996). *Stages of reading development*. New York: McGraw-Hill.

Lynd, R. (1923). *Solomon in all his glory.* New York: G. P. Putnam.

Implementing the No Child Left Behind Act: Using student engagement to improve adolescent literacy. (2005). Naperville, IL: North Central Regional Laboratory.

International Reading Association. (2001). *Supporting young adolescents' literacy learning: A joint position statement of the International Reading Association and the National Middle School Association.* Newark, DE: International Reading Association. Available: http://www.reading.org/downloads/positions/ps1052_supporting.pdf

National Center for Education Statistics (2009). *The Nation's Report Card: Reading 2009* (NCES 2010-458). Institute of Education Sciences, U.S. Department of Education, Washington, DC.

Reading to achieve: A governor's guide to adolescent literacy. (2005). Washington, DC: National Governors Association.

Smith, L. H. (1953). *The unreluctant years: A critical approach to children's literature.* Chicago: American Library Association.

Spear-Swerling, L., & Sternberg, R. J. (1997). *Off track: When poor readers become "learning disabled."* Boulder, CO: Westview.

Strickland, D. S., & Alvermann, D. (2004). Learning and teaching literacy in grades 4–12. In D. S. Strickland & D. Alvermann (Eds.), *Issues and challenges in bridging the literacy achievement gap: Grades 4–12.* New York, NY: Teachers College Press.

The "Adolescent" in Adolescent Literacy

A Preliminary Review

THOMAS W. BEAN AND HELEN HARPER

■ ■ ■ ■ ■

Guiding Questions

1. What has the field of adolescent literacy revealed about adolescents and their current literacy practices?
2. How has the field itself constructed adolescents and their literacy?
3. What does this mean for future research in adolescent literacy?

Students stream into class, oozing an array of emotions ranging from wild enthusiasm to absolute indifference. It is Thursday afternoon, which means it is Ms. Campinello's senior English Literature class. Four new students have recently transferred into Ms. Campinello's class. Rafael, one of these newly transferred students, enters the classroom. He has his black hood pulled up against the winter cold. His iPod earbuds are in and he's listening to an old Bob Marley reggae tune. His touch screen cell phone is on, and he's watching a rough clip of a YouTube video he and other class members are creating to promote recycling and the banning of plastic bags at his school. Alongside Rafael is Tiffany, swinging a large, Hello Kitty bag, which, among an incredibly large assortment of other items, carries her favorite novel (she will carefully tuck it inside the class-assigned text, *The Merchant of Venice,* and read surreptitiously during class, then text her friends about it later). Damian, who trips in behind her, has already read *The Merchant of Venice* in its entirety and loved it. He has set as a secret project to read as many Shakespearean plays as possible this semester. Anna, who struggles to understand English, despite many years in an English language learner (ELL) class, slinks in behind them, hoping to escape the teacher's attention and hide her failure yet again to complete the class reading assignment. She pauses to write her boyfriend's name, along with a heart, on the inside cover of her English/Polish dictionary. She smiles. The heart and name will help distract her from whatever impossible task she'll be asked to do in this class.

Ms. Campinello picks up her own well-marked copy of *The Merchant of Venice* and looks out at the class. This is a large class and, as usual, there are not enough desks, not enough books, not enough help, and not enough time. Moreover, she feels a huge gap between her students and herself. They are worlds apart from each other. She knows so little about them and their lives. Ms. Campinello sighs; she needs time to think about and get to know these students of hers, collectively and individually. But for now, with the sound of the buzzer, she begins the lesson.

The Adolescent and Society

It may seem that Ms. Campinello does not know her students. Certainly she feels this. And in truth she has not had much interaction with them, or at least not as much as she would like, but Ms. Campinello is in many respects already very familiar with "adolescents" and perhaps even with their "adolescent literacies." For following the teacher and the students into the classroom are both individual histories of how the "adolescent" life has been lived out, and the broader social history of how "adolescence" has been named, characterized, and categorized in our society. To some degree the teacher and her students already know each other, or more accurately, know *of* each other through these histories.

Individual and social histories are not unrelated. How society names, organizes, and structures adolescence affects how individuals may live out their lives as teenagers at any given moment. It is society, or more precisely, the state that determines when an adolescent can get a driver's license, quit school, enter the labor market, or be married. Such government policies and common social practices name and separate the adolescent from the adult and the child. These policies and practices, and notions about the adolescent that underwrite them, help at least to some degree to standardize or normalize adolescent life in and out of school. Those adolescents whose lives do not conform to policies or practices and the assumptions that support them must negotiate the problem of being defined as deviant, odd, or strangely exceptional. And they must cope with myriad programmatic remedies concocted by adults to cure them of such labels.

Ms. Campinello wants to know her students to better educate them, and she already knows something about adolescents from her own history, from her previous students, and from what she knows about the social history and organization of adolescents. All of this equips her with what might be deemed "commonsense" or common knowledge about adolescents. Of course, as a high school teacher, she is also educated in the practices, policies, and organization of schooling in America and its history that determine how adolescents are named and understood. Her classroom, the school building itself, and indeed all classrooms and school buildings, with their structure, location, texts, equipment, and artifacts, embody to various degrees what is and what has been thought about the education of high school students. Curricula, class schedules, extracurricular events, and administrative structure all indicate something about how adolescent learners and their education are understood. Both Ms. Campinello and her students enter into a site that is imbued with a history that precedes them, and that organizes and influences their interactions, learning, and teaching experiences.

As is evident in the opening vignette, Ms. Campinello is not just any high school teacher; she is an English teacher. Indeed, she is a literacy specialist working on an advanced degree in adolescent literacy. As will be shown, the field of adolescent literacy itself offers "readings" or particular understandings of adolescence and adolescent literacy practices that also help to construct and organize Ms. Campinello's knowledge of her students and of the kind of literacy education she can and will provide them. Knowing how *adolescence* is defined in society, in school, and in the field of adolescent literacy may be a first step toward the possibility of truly knowing and providing for the students that Ms. Campinello and all of us meet in our literacy classrooms.

In this chapter, we focus on how adolescence is configured in the field of adolescent literacy. The three guiding questions at the beginning of the chapter organize our thinking. We begin by briefly situating these questions in the context of the larger milieu of contemporary America that informs the ways that adolescence has been defined and understood, that is, produced in our classrooms, our schools, and our field.

Defining Adolescence

The vignette that opens this chapter offers a quick sketch of adolescent life, adolescent literacies, and literacies of the adolescents' teacher. It is a representation, perhaps familiar, but not a particularly comprehensive one. However, as described in the work of Nancy Lesko (2001), more all-encompassing constructions of adolescence that are apparent in both popular and academic discourses are indeed quite powerful, serving to name and organized adolescence systematically in many fields of endeavor, including the law, government, psychology, medicine, and education. Lesko defines these constructions as (1) biological or developmental and (2) sociohistorical. According to Lesko, of the two, the view of adolescent life as a biological or development stage of life is the most dominant. From this perspective, adolescence is viewed as a natural biological phenomenon, universal and predictable in its characteristics and onset, and all aspects of adolescent life, including the cognitive, social, and psychological aspects, are affected by it. Because adolescence is not a static state but one that changes over time as the individual matures, teachers working within this perspective focus on teens' developmental achievements, including emotional stability, self-control, rationality, and conformity to adult norms and standards, all of which are seen as sequential and cumulative.

Myriad assumptions arise from this view; for example, that adolescents "come of age"; that adolescents are controlled by raging hormones; that they are peer-oriented, and best understood and represented by age (Lesko, 2001, p. 2). In general, this perspective suggests that teenagers, in comparison with adults, are "unfinished products" whose age-related biological and developmental condition requires particular care and protection to ensure their optimal development.

The sociohistoric view posits adolescence as an invention of the twentieth century, more specifically, not as a product of biology, but of cultural, economic, and educational circumstances. From this perspective, adolescence in North America and Europe is said to have begun in the late 1800s, when child labor laws, industrialization, and union organization limited employment, in particular, the apprenticeships that youth traditionally entered after some modicum of public schooling. Extending compulsory education proved to be one means of dealing with the threat of idle, unemployed youth. Because of their economic dependence, all adolescents were defined through their collective lives as high school students, and they became the "teenagers" of the twentieth and now twenty-first century. Economic, institutional, and social changes allowed for the development of teen-based popular culture that in turn created a generation of youth quite different from those in previous generations.

Because of its emphasis on context, this perspective acknowledges differences rather than universalities among youth. Gender, race, ethnicity, and social class, for example, are seen as dramatically affecting the nature and experience of adolescent life. Moreover, it is possible that some individuals, particularly youth living in places with different economic, social, and cultural practices, might never experience an "adolescence" at all.

These two perspectives have informed, or at least have provided a backdrop, and it stands to reason that adolescence is understood and explained in schools, in the field of adolescent literacy, to which we now turn.

The Field of Adolescent Literacy

Adolescent literacy as a field was developed and formalized in large measure through the efforts of the International Reading Association (IRA) and its creation of the Commission on Adolescent Literacy in the mid-1990s (Richardson, 2008). Although interest in the reading skills of teenagers goes back to the early twentieth century, and research in the content-area literacy of adolescents back to the 1970s, these areas of research and scholarship by the 1990s were largely subsumed by the category of *adolescent literacy* (Vacca, 1998). In an effort to address growing interest in the adolescent learner, the Commission on Adolescent Literacy created a position paper to drive curriculum policy and funding decisions (Moore, Bean, Birdyshaw, & Rycik, 1999). Now, 10 years later, the field of adolescent literacy is on a firmer footing, and in part because of the history of the field it encompasses, multiple views of adolescence, some of which hint at a biological or developmental framing; others, the majority of views, seem to suggest a sociohistorical understanding of both adolescence and adolescent literacy. In general, our preliminary review of the documents and major texts indicates that amid lingering unanswered questions and assumptions about what comprises adolescence, the field is certainly challenging simplistic and universal views, while offering its own particular and bounded reading of teens' lives and their literacies. We all need to be aware of these readings, if we ever hope to know or at least acknowledge the complexity and diversity of the adolescents we teach.

Views of Adolescence and Adolescent Literacy Practices

We examined in this preliminary review the following texts, policies, and position statements:

1. Edited texts, including the first and second editions of *Reconceptualizing the Literacies in Adolescents' Lives* (Alvermann, Hinchman, Moore, Phelps, & Waff, 1998, 2006); *Literacy for the New Millennium: Volume 3. Adolescent Literacy* (Guzzetti, 2007); *Adolescent Literacy Research and Practice* (Jetton & Dole, 2004); and *Adolescent Literacy Instruction: Policies and Promising Practices* (Lewis & Moorman, 2007).
2. Journals and journal articles including an examination of the publishing history and content of the *Journal of Adolescent & Adult Literacy* and selected articles and editorials appearing in general literacy journals, such as *Reading Research Quarterly*, and *English Journal*.
3. Policy documents and position papers, including *Adolescent Literacy: A Position Statement for the Commission on Adolescent Literacy of the International Reading Association* (Moore et al., 1999); a related Carnegie Corporation case study report and book, *Principled Practices for Adolescent Literacy: A Framework for Instruction and Policy* (Sturtevant et al., 2006); two Carnegie-funded reports, *Reading Next* (Biancarosa & Snow, 2006) and *Writing Next* (Graham & Penn, 2007); and the annual report in the IRA's publication *Reading Today* on "What's Hot for 2008" (Cassidy & Cassidy, 2008), as well as a related 10-year analysis of this column, published in the *Journal of Adolescent and Adult Literacy* (Cassidy, Garrett, & Barrera, 2006).

Each of these policy and position papers charts the growing interest in adolescent literacy, often attributed to the extension of the No Child Left Behind legislation to include adolescent learners and related federal funding for striving reader grants (Cassidy et al.,

2006). Based on our reading and interpretive analysis of these and other documents characterizing adolescent learners, we examine four major ways in which adolescence has been configured in the field.

Adolescence as a Grade- or Age-Level Designation

The growing body of work aimed at understanding adolescent literacy practices reveals a rich and complex terrain, but one in which, with rare exception,[1] adolescence is not directly theorized. Instead, adolescence is taken as a given, named, if defined at all, by grade- or age-level designation. This is particularly true in state and federal policy documents, and in position papers by various interest groups. The National Institute of Child Health and Human Development (NICHD), for example, in its literacy initiatives, defines *adolescents* as middle and high school students. This would seem practical, indeed commonsensical, but as Terry Salinger (2007) points out, middle school entry can occur at fifth grade or later. The IRA position statement on adolescent literacy also uses a grade-level designation, defining *adolescents* as "the more than 20,000,000 students currently enrolled in U.S. middle and high schools" (Moore et al., 1999, p. 3). The *Journal of Adolescent & Adult Literacy*, which we edit, has a history of using the designation "age 12 and up" for adolescents. We suspect that this designation has been used to differentiate the journal from *The Reading Teacher,* which focuses on elementary school reading.

The age- or grade-level designation of the adolescent may be in response to government initiatives that have focused exclusively on ensuring that all students can read by grade 3. The use of grade 3 as an endpoint designation is critical. In 1999, Carol Santa, then President of the IRA, stated, "In the United States, most Title 1 budgets are allocated for early intervention—little is left over for the struggling adolescent reader. Even if all children do learn to read by Grade 3, the literacy needs of the adolescent reader are far different from those of primary-grade children" (Moore et al., 1999, p. 1). Santa's statements create a distinct separation of primary grade students from adolescent students of middle and high school, even if basic literacy is attained. This common position is evident in the field. However, it has been challenged by some, including Patricia Alexander (2005/2006) whose work draws on developmental psychology but nonetheless suggests that literacy "evolves and matures over time in ways not governed by grade-level designations" (cited in Salinger, 2007, p. 7). Alexander is troubled by simplistic notions of adolescents and their literacies as fixed by age or grade-level. Other ways that adolescents and their literacies have been defined in the field speak more to literacy needs and practices, irrespective of, or at least with less emphasis on, specific age or grade levels, or the developmental or biological assumptions that underlie these designations.

Adolescence Defined by Literacy Needs

Another way that adolescents are defined in the field is through their literacy needs, which are positioned as separate and distinct from the literacy needs of others. Thus, adolescence is understood as a time when one's literacy needs shift, so that appropriate and particular forms of instruction are required.

---

[1]Although not specific to and about the field of adolescent literacy, the most explicit theorizing about adolescence we reviewed was apparent in *Re/Constructing "the Adolescent": Sign, Symbol, and Body* (Vadeboncoeur & Stevens, 2005).

Early achievement does not guarantee success

Evident in the literature are two major literacy needs of adolescents: (1) teens need more advanced literacy instruction for the increasingly complex materials they face in their classes, and (2) many teens need basic literacy instruction. In the first case, many in the field would agree that literacy is a continuum, and that learning to read and write is just the beginning, or it occurs near the beginning, of an individual's literacy education, certainly not the end. The IRA adolescent literacy position statement reads: "Reading success in the early grades certainly pays off later, but early achievement is not the end of the story. . . . There are developmental stages—reading and [early literacy accomplishments] are only the first steps of growth into full literacy" (cited by Salinger, 2007, p. 3).

Although a developmental or biological perspective is suggested in these statements, in much of what we read, the need for further literacy education, or "full literacy," is not brought about by an individual's cognitive or psychological development per se, but by the academic literacy demands placed on individuals in secondary classrooms (Bean, Readence, & Baldwin, 2008). Context, then, rather than one's internal psychology or biology (i.e., age) is the key factor in understanding the literacy of adolescents. Thus, *adolescence* is not defined in terms of age or grade, but in terms of literacy needs that expand due to the demands of schooling and the individual's expanding interests and abilities. These reading skills include comprehending multiple-content texts laden with technical vocabulary and sometimes arcane text structures. Each content area (e.g., biology, mathematics, history, and English) has its own idiosyncratic ways of conveying information and concepts, of naming evidence, and of assessing validity and quality. Coupled with the vast array of content material on the Internet, often organized according to a particular Web author's logic, a huge array of information in various forms and of varying quality and credibility confronts contemporary students (McNabb, 2006). Moreover, the ideological and political context and foundation of informational and narrative material also require consideration. For many, this suggests a need for critical reading and critical literacy practices, in addition to more standard content-area reading support (Morrell, 2008; King, Hart, & Kozdras, 2007; Stevens & Bean, 2007).

As outlined, many perceived adolescent reading needs are described as being distinct from those of primary school children, shifting from a learning-to-read to a reading-to-learn stance, and a potentially more sophisticated set of skills, knowledge, and attitudes. However, another way in which adolescent needs have been defined in the field is in relation to deficiencies in basic literacy; to adolescents as illiterates or aliterates, or, more euphemistically, as struggling or striving readers. These adolescents are deemed to need specialized or at least appropriate teaching instruction and literacy materials to improve and encourage reading. This is a major area of concern and, indeed, much of the attention toward adolescents and adolescent literacy is centered on the needs of *struggling readers,* often defined as those students performing below grade-level expectations (Biancarosa & Snow, 2006; Jetton & Dole, 2004).

If discussed at all, the ultimate origins of low achievement are not usually attributed to biological conditions. Rather, low achievement is attributed to socioeconomic, cultural, and institutional or pedagogical factors. Whatever the cause, the category of struggling or striving readers is often undifferentiated in policy, with little attention to adolescents as individuals with radically different histories and unique social contexts, with strengths as well as deficiencies. Williams Dee Nichols (2007) notes that "classifying struggling readers as illiterate often overgeneralizes their true reading identity and does not completely acknowledge their literacy capacities" (p. 7). Supportive instructional efforts that recognize local funds of knowledge on which adolescents may draw in their out-of-school lives (writing hip-hop songs, poetry, music, etc.), taps into this resource as a way to engage struggling readers in bridging to content-area material, sometimes through a critique of how diverse cultures are erroneously portrayed in the media (Morrell, 2008).

Whatever their circumstances and strengths, the number of students performing below grade level is a critical factor in the field for teachers, researchers, and policymakers. Various policy documents that now drive funding for adolescent struggling readers sound a note of alarm. The economic well-being of the nation, as well as the individual, is at risk. Widely quoted national reports, including *Reading Next* (Biancarosa & Snow, 2006) and *Writing Next* (Graham & Penn, 2007), suggest a crisis in need of immediate research-based solutions. Recognizing the absence of a fully developed research base in adolescent literacy, the *Reading Next* report uses the best current scientifically based quantitative studies to craft a call to action. Pointing to a lack of reading skills as one of the most commonly cited reasons for adolescents' departure from high school, the authors have developed a reasonably sound series of cognitive instructional recommendations.

Similarly, *Writing Next* (Graham & Penn, 2007) paints a grim picture of adolescent learners, with fully 70 percent described as low-achieving writers who compare poorly to their international peers. Citing research syntheses in much the same fashion as its sister report *Reading Next,* this report points to specific writing strategies (e.g., summarization instruction) that are supported in the research and offer, again, a solid cognitive solution to the perceived problem of a growing population of struggling adolescent writers. In essence, if we can boost adolescents' reading and writing skills, using what we know about strategies that work (e.g., graphic organizers), then the crisis may be solved.

This deficit view of adolescent struggling readers has received considerable attention in the literature, with a number of critiques aimed at deconstructing and countering an exclusively cognitivist view of instruction for adolescent learners. For example, Hall (2006) explored how middle-grade struggling readers coped with metacognitive comprehension and study strategies that their well-meaning social studies, mathematics, and science teachers offered to help them with text reading. These students were well aware of how they were being positioned as struggling readers, and the comprehension strategies simply elevated their visibility as deficient in reading. As an alternative coping strategy that preserved their identity with their peers as "good" students, they chose to listen carefully to text discussions and to use alternative routes to obtain meaning from texts. Rather than adopt a learned helplessness view of adolescent struggling readers, Hall recommended that educators move beyond an obsession with effective methodology and strategies. Rather, teachers should carefully consider students' social and cultural worlds better to fashion whole-school interventions that are useful to all students and unlikely to marginalize struggling readers (Fisher & Ivey, 2006).

With the cautionary statement that adolescent struggling readers are more complex than recent national reports reveal, these prominent reports and their instructional recommendations are not without considerable merit. Indeed, they offer very well grounded research syntheses, pulling together a wide array of instructional studies supporting strategy instruction. However, with respect to struggling adolescent readers, they do represent a particular stance that needs to be tempered with a broader, sociocultural critique. Are adolescents in crisis as learners? The answer may be more complex than those typically offered in policy documents, in grant calls for proposals to benefit "striving readers," and in common wisdom and conversation. For example, Franzak (2006) argues that a deficit medical model that disenfranchises and marginalizes struggling readers persists in policy documents. But many adolescents are well aware of their struggling reader status and take active measures to protect their social identities as learners.

A curriculum that acknowledges and enhances students' feelings of competence and control across reading ability levels is preferable to isolated metacognitive strategy instruction. For example, Franzak (2006) recommends multimedia material as a powerful and engaging vehicle for adolescent readers. Books based on video games such as Halo, as well as popular movies, are natural bridges to contemporary students' interest in visual media. In addition, well-designed sustained silent reading (SSR) programs with self-selected reading materials and contemporary young-adult literature hold promise within a whole-school literacy program for all students (Bean et al., 2008; Fisher & Ivey, 2006). In a carefully crafted study of a high school intervention program in which 35 percent of the students were reading one or more grade levels below grade placement, Fisher and Ivey found that four key elements supported measurable increases in students' achievement and motivation to read. A combination of SSR, using young adult novels in conjunction with content-area learning, offering alternative texts to struggling readers and advanced readers in content classrooms, and buddy reading to elementary school students produced positive results. The point is that simply adopting well-researched cognitive strategy instruction is not enough. Intervention efforts, such as that described by Fisher and Ivey, as well as other notable efforts (e.g., Brozo & Hargis, 2003), hold promise because they adopt a whole-school stance that neither names nor marginalizes struggling readers, nor does it place places high-performing students in an elevated status.

Defining *adolescence* as a time of changing literacy needs that are not being addressed or fully addressed by the educational community has been a key way that the field has named its mission. Certainly, this definition has served to galvanize recent research and government initiatives. Although important, these initiatives and the interventions that result need to be tempered by the complexity of literacy learners, who cannot simply be defined by their "neediness," which then directs our adult "generosity" and "responsibility." The field of adolescent literacy, as represented in the policy documents, texts, and articles we examined, uses and at times complicates the definition of *adolescence* in relation to literacy "needs." In part, this has been done through recognition of literacy strengths, as previously discussed. Receiving perhaps the most attention recently has been adolescents' new literacies practices (i.e., their use of communication technologies). These new practices are viewed not only as strengths but also as unique gifts, if you will, that define a generation. We turn now to this particular construction of adolescence.

Adolescents Defined by Their New and Multiple Literacy Practices: The Millennials

In addition to defining *adolescents* in relation to their literacy needs, another area dominating the field concerns the new literacies of adolescents. The term *new literacies* refers to the practices, skills, and knowledge involved with new and emerging information and communication technologies (ICTs). Here, *adolescence* is defined by one's comfort and expertise with various forms of new and emerging computer-mediated technologies. More specifically, to be an *adolescent* is equated with being a "native" user rather than adult "immigrant" user of technology (Moorman & Horton, 2007). As producers of texts in an Internet-based world, it is argued, today's adolescents read and write more than did previous generations, but the nature of this social interaction is dramatically different for millennials than for previous generations. *Millennials* are defined chronologically and with reference to the evolution of personal computers. Students born between 1982 and 2002 comprise a generation that has never known a world without computers, cell phones, and other forms of ICTs (Moorman & Horton, 2007). This is a generation that is accustomed to writing their views on Weblogs (blogs), text messaging friends, and playing complex, multiplayer video games spanning global boundaries. Each of these distinctly new literacy practices combines elements of older, print-based forms with newer, visual media dimensions in which design and composition are important. Indeed, ethnographic studies and thoughtful analyses of adolescents' literacy practices show that teens occupy a world in which ever-changing text forms coexist with older, print-bound forms of text (Alvermann & Eakle, 2007; Moorman & Horton, 2007; Moje & Hinchman, 2004). However, it has been argued that these out-of-school literacy competencies are not always acknowledged or capitalized upon in the classroom (Moore & Cunningham, 2006; O'Brien, 2006; Smith & Wilhelm, 2002, 2006).

David G. O'Brien has argued that struggling readers often are misperceived based on narrow views of literacy competency that fail to recognize a host of new literacy practices these readers may well engage in outside of school. These practices include creating multimedia music productions in Apple's GarageBand, podcasts for YouTube, and iMovie productions, all of which demand a high tolerance for ambiguity and an aesthetic sensibility for design. Thus, providing opportunities for struggling readers to display competencies in new literacies may be a more powerful way to bridge within-school and out-of-school contexts. For example, engaging in digital media literacy critiques aimed at viewing and evaluating productions (e.g., podcasts and YouTube clips) places struggling readers in a role quite different from that of learned helplessness.

According to this view, today's teachers are seen as needy. They require both the knowledge and the environment (i.e., a technologically rich classroom) that can capitalize on millennial adolescents' so-called "natural affinity" for and competence with new literacies. They also need an open attitude toward change. The attitude is crucial because of the claim that a growing array of multimedia tools are altering the print-based landscape and changing the nature of what it means to be literate, despite the intensification of high-stakes and standardized testing in traditional print literacy (Bean & Wimmer, 2007; Lewis, Leander, & Wang, 2007; Luke & Elkins, 1998).

This construction of adolescence often celebrates not only those whose practices include them in this category but also the new technologies themselves. Although a critical perspective is evident in the field (see, e.g., Wilder & Dressman, 2006), it has been easier to offer more exuberant portrayals of teens and their new literacies that universalize adolescents as the amazing "native" users of technology. Undoubtedly, this exuberance is a response to the ongoing, relentless reinscription of traditional literacies in classrooms despite changing times and changing literacy patterns in these "new times." However, the concern is whether this rendering of adolescence is indeed an accurate portrayal of all youth, locally or globally, and whether the comfort and expertise suggested by the term *native-user* best describes all those who chronologically fit the designation of millennial.

Adolescence as a Diverse and Dynamic Population of Literacy Learners

This final construction of adolescence that is evident in the field names and highlights social difference rather than universality across the population defined conventionally as *adolescents*. Much of this largely ethnographic research examines how gender, race, ethnicity, social class, sexuality, home language, citizenship, and so on, are organized by and organize school and home literacy practices (e.g., Blair, 2007; Lytle, 2006; Smith & Wilhelm, 2002, 2004; Blackburn, 2002, 2003; Gunderson, 2000; Moje, 2006; Finders, 1997).

Drawing strongly on a sociocultural perspective, this research presents a much more complex picture of the lives and literacies of any group of adolescents.

The intense study of individual and group cases emphasizes difference to the extent that even categories of race and ethnicity cannot be assumed to be definitive: Moje (2006) comments that "individual difference is a complex intersection of all of those qualities of difference, so that a third-generation Latina living in Detroit may be more like an African American girl living in Detroit than she is like a Latino living in New Mexico" (p. 123). To extend Moje's comment further, it is possible to consider that, in terms of literacy practices, a third-generation Latina might at times be more like working-class boys in her class or, in some aspects, more like her Latino parents.

Ethnographic work complicates any particular notion of what might constitute *adolescence*. Certainly, it makes any generalization about youth difficult. Also undercutting the category is the idea of identity, which, under the guise of postmodern thought, speaks to a more multiple and fluid sense of self. This self is constructed not by personality, but discursively, that is, through the use of linguistic and material resources that organize and reorganize social scripts, or what James Gee (2000, 2006) calls *identity kits*. These resources also include the discourses on adolescence found in popular culture (Hagood, 2007; Moje & van Helden, 2004). Most important, in much of what we reviewed, literacy practices were deeply implicated in the formation of self. Many of the chapters in Alvermann et al. (2006) demonstrate the ways that identities are formulated with and against literacy texts and literacy practices available in and out of schools (see chapters in Alvermann et al. by Neilsen, Marsh, and Stolle; O'Brien; Moje & Dillion; and Moore). Identity within this perspective is not fixed, stable, or unified for anyone, particularly when new literacy practices emerge.

The emphasis on differences among teens, and the fluid and multiple identity formations–reformations of individual teens (and all of us) threatens to undo entirely the category of adolescence or, at the very least, to complicate any generalization that can be made. This suggests care in forming any absolutes that seem to construct the category of *adolescence*.

Tentative Conclusions and Future Research on Adolescence and Adolescent Literacy

This is a preliminary review, and certainly for future reference, we would like to extend and intensify our reading and analysis of the various texts that make up the field. In particular, we would like to look at more international texts and contexts in relation to adolescent literacy, because much of what we have reviewed is American. Because this is a preliminary review, our observations and conclusions are tentative. Nonetheless, we believe that the four patterns we found are worthy of thought and further inquiry.

What seems apparent is that the various ways in which adolescence and adolescent literacy together are configured in the field create a complex and multifaceted picture of adolescent life and literacy. It seems to us that the four constructions of adolescence act as foils for each other, each naming and limiting the next. We see good reason to remember each of these constructions individually and collectively as the field continues to develop. For example, we suggest that taking a strictly cognitive stance toward understanding struggling or, indeed, any readers and their needs may be seriously limited when the various understandings of *adolescence* are considered.

We want to issue a call for more theorizing about adolescence and adolescent literacy practices in complex and instructionally useful ways. In this effort, we are adding to

Donna Alvermann's initial challenge in 1998 to "question simplistic notions of adolescence and literacy" (cited in Phelps, 2006, p. 3), and to those researchers who have already begun to answer her challenge. What we highlight is the importance of critical self-reflection about the field, from the field, and remaining vigilant to the possibility of universalizing adolescence in a fashion that creates new boundaries that may limit our thinking and our actions, even as we enthusiastically create and embrace new research on adolescents and their literacies.

In relation to the opening vignette with Ms. Campinello and her class, including Rafael, Tiffany, Damian, and Anna, the explicit theorizing about adolescence, and the exposure and critique of the various ways that adolescents and their literacies are defined, may help both teacher and students to know, understand, and define each other with, against, and, most importantly, beyond not only the frames provided to them but also to all of us within and outside the field of adolescent literacy. We consider this to be freedom.

QUESTIONS FOR DISCUSSION

1. How do we hold on to the complexity and individuality of adolescents and their literacies in our teaching and research?

2. When and how does the category of adolescents divide, collide, and meld with the categories of children and adults? When should this occur?

3. Most important, what is the work of these categories (socially, psychologically, pedagogically, institutionally), and whose interest do they service?

FURTHER READING

Alvermann, D. E., Hinchman, K. A., Moore, D. W., Phelps, S. F., & Waif, D. R. (Eds.). (2006). *Reconceptualizing the literacies in adolescents' lives* (2nd ed.). Mahwah, NJ: Erlbaum.

Biancarosa, C., & Snow, C. E. (2006). *Reading next: A vision for action and research in middle and high school literacy: A report to the Carnegie Corporation of New York* (2nd ed.). Washington, DC: Alliance for Excellent Education. Available at *www.all4ed.org/publications/readingnext/readingnext.pdf*.

Cassidy, J., Garrett, D., & Barrera, E. S. (2006). What's hot in adolescent literacy 1997–2006. *Journal of Adolescent and Adult Literacy, 50(1),* 30–36.

Graham, S., & Penn, D. (2007). *Writing next: Effective strategies to improve writing of adolescents in middle and high schools: A report to the Carnegie Corporation of New York.* Washington, DC: Alliance for Excellent Education. Available at *www.all4ed.org/publications/writingnext/writingnext.pdf*.

Guzzetti, B. J. (Ed.). (2007). *Literacy for the new millennium: Vol. 3. Adolescent literacy.* Westport, CT: Praeger.

Jetton, T. L., & Dole, J. A. (Eds.). (2004). *Adolescent literacy research and practice.* New York, NY: Guilford Press.

Lesko, N. (2001). Act your age!: A cultural construction of adolescence. New York, NY: Routledge.

Lewis, J., & Moorman, G. (Eds.). (2007). *Adolescent literacy instruction: Policies and promising practices.* Newark, DE: International Reading Association.

Moore, D. W., Bean, T. W., Birdyshaw, D., & Rycik, J. A. (1999). *Adolescent literacy: A position statement for the Commission on Adolescent Literacy of the International Reading Association.* Newark, DE: International Reading Association.

Sturtevant, E. G., Boyd, F. B., Brozo, W. G., Hinchman, K. A., Moore, D. W., & Alvermann, D. E. (Eds.). (2006). *Principled practices for adolescent literacy: A framework for instruction and policy.* Mahwah, NJ: Eribaum.

Vadeboncoeur, J. A., & Stevens, L. (2005). *Re/constructing "the adolescent": Sign, symbol, and body.* New York, NY: Peter Lang.

WEBSITE

www.reading.org—the Website of the International Reading Association. It contains information on the *Journal of Adolescent & Adult Literacy* and other publications of the International Reading Association.

REFERENCES

Alexander, P. A. (2005/2006). The path to competence: A lifespan developmental perspective on reading. *Journal of Literacy Research, 37(4)*, 413–436.

Alvermanfl, D. E., & Eakie, J. A. (2007). Challenging literacy theories and practices from the outside. In J. Lewis & G. Moorman (Eds.), *Adolescent literacy instruction:Policies and promising practices* (pp. 64–81). Newark, DE: International Reading Association.

Alvermann, D. E., Hinchman, K., Moore, D. W., Phelps, S. W., & Waff, D. (Eds.). (1998). *Reconceptualizing the literacies in adolescents' lives.* Mahwah, NJ: Erlbaum.

Alvermann, D. E., Hinchman, K. A., Moore, D. W., Phelps, S. F., & Waif, D. R. (Eds.). (2006). *Reconceptualizing the literacies in adolescents' lives* (2nd ed.). Mahwah, NJ: Eribaum.

Bean, T. W., Readence, J. E., & Baldwin, R. S. (2008). *Content area literacy: An integrated approach* (9th ed.). Dubuque, IA: Kendall/Hunt.

Bean, T. W., & Wimmer, J. (2007). Resources for adolescent literacy. In B.J. Guzzetti (Ed.), *Literacy for the new millennium: Vol. 3. Adolescent literacy* (pp. 265–278). Westport, CT: Praeger.

Biancarosa, C., & Snow, C. E. (2006). *Reading next: A vision for action and research in middle and high school literacy: A report to Carnegie Corporation of New York* (2nd ed.). Washington, DC: Alliance for Excellent Education. Retrieved January 8, 2007, from, *www.all4ed.org/pubications/readingnext/ Teadingxt.pdf.*

Blackburn, M. (2002). Disrupting the (hetero) normative: Exploring literacy performances and identity work with queer youth. *Journal of Adolescent & Adult Literacy, 46,* 312–324.

Blackburn, M. (2003). Exploring literacy performances and power dynamics at The Loft: Queer youth reading the word and the world. *Research in the Teaching of English, 37,* 467–490.

Blair, H. (2007). I used to treat all the boys and the girls the same: Gender and literacy. In B. Guzzetti (Ed.), *Literacy for the new millennium: Vol. 3. Adolescent literacy* (pp. 189–206). Westport, CT: Praeger.

Brozo, W. G., & Hargis, C. H. (2003). Taking seriously the idea of reform: One high school's efforts to make reading more responsive to all students. *Journal of Adolescent & Adult Literacy, 47,* 14–23.

Cassidy, J., & Cassidy, D. (2008). What's hot for 2008. *Reading Today, 25(4),* 1, 10.

Cassidy, J., Garrett, D., & Barrera, E. S. (2006). What's hot in adolescent literacy 1997–2006. *Journal of Adolescent & Adult Literacy,* 50(1), 30–36.

Finders, M. (1997). *Just girls: Hidden literacies and life in junior high.* New York, NY: Teachers College Press.

Fisher, D., & Ivey, G. (2006). Evaluating the interventions for struggling adolescent readers. *Journal of Adolescent & Adult Literacy, 50(3),* 180–189.

Franzak, J. K. (2006). Zoom: A review of the literature on marginalized adolescent readers, literacy theory, and policy implications. *Review of Educational Research, 76,* 209–248.

Gee,J. P. (2000). Teenagers in new times: A new literacy study perspective. *Journal of Adolescent & Adult Literacy, 43,* 412–420.

Gee, J. P. (2006). Self-fashioning and shape-shifting: Language, identity, and social class. In D. E. Alvermann, K. A. Hinchman, D. W. Moore, S. F. Phelps, & D. R. Waff (Eds.), *Reconceptualizing the literacies in adolescents' lives* (2nd ed., pp. 165—185), Mahwah, NJ: Eribaum.

Graham, S., & Perin, D. (2007). *Writing next: Effective strategies to improve writing of adolescents in middle and high schools: A report to Carnegie Corporation of New York.* Washington, DC: Alliance for Excellent Education. Retrieved February 12, 2007, from *www.all4ed.org/publications/writingnext/ writingnext.pdf.*

Gunderson, L. (2000). Voices of the teenage diasporas. *Journal of Adolescent & Adult Literacies, 43,* 692–706.

Guzzetti, B. J. (Ed.). (2007). *Literacy for the new millennium: Vol. 3. Adolescent literacy.* Westport, CT: Praeger.

Hagood, M. (2007). Linking popular culture to literacy learning and teaching in the twenty-first century. In B. Guzzetti (Ed.), *Literacy for the new millennium: Vol. 3. Adolescent literacy* (pp. 223–238). Westport, CT: Praeger.

Hall, L. A. (2006). Anything but lazy: New understandings about struggling readers, teaching, and text. *Reading Research Quarterly, 41(4),* 424–426.

Jetton, T. L., & Dole, J. A. (2004). Introduction. In T. L. Jetton & J. A. Dole (Eds.), *Adolescent literacy research and practice* (pp. 1–11). New York: Guilford Press.

King, J., Hart, S., & Kozdras, D. (2008). Critical literacy and adolescents. In B. Guzzetti (Ed.) *Literacy for the new millennium: Vol. 3. Adolescent literacy* (pp. 173–188). Westport, CT: Praeger.

Lesko, N. (2001). *Act our age!: A cultural construction of adolescence.* New York: Routledge.

Lewis, C., Leander, K., & Wang, X. (2007). Digital literacies. In B. Guzzetti (Ed.), *Literacy for the new millennium: Vol. 3. Adolescent literacy* (pp. 207–222). Westport, CT: Praeger.

Lewis, J., & Moorman, G. (2007). *Adolescent literacy instruction: Policies and promising practices.* Newark, DE: International Reading Association.

Luke, A., & Elkins, J. (1998). Reinventing literacy in "new times." *Journal of Adolescent & Adult Literacy, 42,* 4–7.

Lytle, S. (2006). The literacies of teaching urban adolescents in these times. In D. E. Alvermann, K. A. Hinchman, D. W. Moore, S. F. Phelps, & D. R. Waif (Eds.), *Reconceptualizing the literacies in adolescents' lives* (2nd ed., pp. 257–278). Mahwah, NJ: Erlbaum

McNabb, M. (2006). *Literacy learning in networked classrooms: Using the Internet with middle-level students.* Newark, DE: International Reading Association.

Moje, E. B. (2006). A scholar's response to Principle 7: Adolescents need opportunities to connect reading with their life and their learning inside and outside of school. In E. G. Sturtevant, F. B. Boyd, W. G. Brozo, K. A. Hinchman, D. W. Moore, & D. E. Alvermann (Eds.), *Principled practices for adolescent literacy: A framework for instruction and policy* (pp. 110–124). Mahwah, NJ: Erlbaum.

Moje, E. B., & Hinchman, K. (2004). Culturally responsive practices for youth literacy learning. In T. L.Jetton, & J. A. Dole (Eds.), *Adolescent literacy research and practices* (pp. 321–350). New York: Guilford Press.

Moje, E. B., & van Helden, C. (2004). Doing popular culture: Troubling discourses about youth. In J. Vadeboncoeur & L. Stevens (Eds.), *Re/constructing "the Adolescent": Sign, symbol, and body* (pp. 211–248). New York: Peter Lang.

Moore, D. W., Bean, T. W., Birdyshaw, D., & Rycik, J. A. (1999). *Adolescent literacy: A position statement for the Commission on Adolescent Literacy of the International Reading Association.* Newark, DE: International Reading Association.

Moore, D. W., & Cunningham, J. W. (2006). Adolescent agency and literacy. In D. E. Alvermann, K. A. Hinchman, D. W. Moore, S. F. Phelps, & D. R. Waif (Eds.), *Reconceptualizing the literacies in adolescents' lives* (2nd ed., pp. 129–146). Mahwah, NJ: Eribaum.

Moorman, G., & Horton, J. (2007). Millenials and how to teach them. In J. Lewis & G. Moorman (Eds.), *Adolescent literacy instruction: Policies and promising practices* (pp. 263–285). Newark, DE: International Reading Association.

Morrell, E. (2008). *Critical literacy and urban youth: Pedagogies of access, dissent, and liberation.* New York, NY: Routledge.

Nichols, W. D. (2007). Introduction to the adolescent reader [Special issue]. *Reading Psychology, 28(1),* 5–10.

O'Brien, D. (2006). "Struggling" adolescents, engagement in multimediating: Countering the institutional construction of incompetence. In D. E. Alvermann, K. A. Hinchman, D. W. Moore, S. F. Phelps, & D. R. Waff (Eds.), *Reconceptualizing the literacies in adolescents' lives* (2nd ed., pp. 29–46). Mahwah, NJ: Erlbaum.

Phelps, S. F. (2006). Introduction to Part I: Situating adolescents' literacies. In D. E. Alvermann, K. A. Hinchman, D. W. Moore, S. F. Phelps, & D. R. Waif (Eds.), *Reconceptualizing the literacies in adolescents' lives* (2nd ed., pp. 3–4). Mahwah, NJ: Erlbaum.

Richardson, J. S. (2008). Content area reading: A 50-year history. In M.J. Fresh (Ed.), *An essential history of current reading practices* (pp. 120–14). Newark, DE: International Reading Association.

Salinger, T. (2007). Setting the agenda for adolescent literacy. In J. Lewis & G. Moorman (Eds.), *Adolescent literacy instruction: Policies and promising practices* (pp. 3–19). Newark, DE: International Reading Association.

Smith, M. W., & Wilhelm, J. D. (2002). *"Reading don't fix no Chevys": Literacy in the lives of young men.* Portsmouth, NH: Heinemann.

Smith, M. W., & Wilhelm, J. D. (2004). "I just like being good at it": The importance of competence in the literate lives of young men. *Journal of Adolescent & Adult Literacy, 47,* 454–461.

Smith, M. W., & Wilhelm, J. D. (2006). *Going with the flow: How to engage boys (and girls) in their literacy learning.* Portsmouth, NH: Heinemann.

Sturtevant, E. G., Boyd, F. B., Brozo, W. G., Hinchman, K. A., Moore, D. W., & Alvermann, D. E. (2006). *Principled practices for adolescent literacy: A framework for instruction and policy.* Mahwah, NJ: Erlbaum.

Vacca, R. T. (1998). Let's not marginalize adolescent literacy. *Journal of Adolescent & Adult Literacy, 41,* 604–609.

Vadeboncoeur, J. A., & Stevens, L. (2005). *Re/constructing "the adolescent": Sign, symbol, and body.* New York, NY: Peter Lang.

Wilder, P., & Dressman, M. (2006). New literacies, enduring challenges?: The influence of capital on adolescent readers' Internet practices. In D. E. Alvermann, K. A. Hinchman, D. W. Moore, S.F. Phelps, & D. R. Waff (Eds.), *Reconceptualizing the literacies in adolescents' lives* (2nd ed., pp. 29–46). Mahwah, NJ: Erlbaum.

The Literacy Needs of Adolescents in Their Own Words

SHARON M. PITCHER, GILDA MARTINEZ,
ELIZABETH A. DICEMBRE, DARLENE FEWSTER,
AND MONTANA K. McCORMICK

■ ■ ■ ■ ■

By featuring the stories of seven students, the authors of this article hope to prompt administrators and teachers to examine the literacy instruction in their schools and make practical changes to meet adolescents' needs.

Over the last few years, we have noted an increase in the amount of adolescents seeking literacy help through our university reading clinic. The majority of these students need comprehension instruction focused on learning to apply strategies when reading, which is a national trend (Alvermann, 2003; Biancarosa & Snow, 2004). Although we are seeing these problems in our assessments, some of the students were achieving proficient or above on state reading assessments. Others are in reading programs focused on phonics instruction. Therefore, we decided to thoroughly examine the reading needs of adolescent students coming to the reading clinic to better understand the problem.

Seeking understanding of this disparity and realizing the far-reaching problems these low literacy levels will cause, we assembled an investigative team with research experience in adolescent literacy, English-language learners (ELLs), special education, secondary education, parent involvement, and curriculum development to look at the data from different perspectives. Together, the team has over 75 years of experience working in different roles in school systems. We sought to reach beyond the boundaries of the university to design research to explore the problem.

Significance of the Problem

Biancarosa and Snow (2004) reported that approximately eight million adolescents struggled with reading. The National Endowment for the Arts (2007) found that "little more than a third of high school seniors now read proficiently" (p. 13). The U.S. Department of Education suggested that "reading ability is a key predictor of achievement in mathematics and science, and the global information economy requires today's American youth to have far more advanced literacy skills than those required by any previous generation" (Kamil et al., 2008, p. 1). Alvermann (2003) suggested resisting the temptation to "fix" learners and instead address the learning conditions to meet their needs. She cautioned against schools focusing on finding a "magic bullet" (p. 2). Researchers have also voiced concerns that external pressures and mandates force teachers to work in classrooms where they have little say in how they are teaching (Alvermann, 2003; Santa, 2006).

In 1999, the International Reading Association's position statement on adolescent literacy suggested that adolescents deserve access to a wide range of materials, instruction that includes both skill development and motivation, assessment that shows their strengths as well as needs, instruction in comprehension strategies, and reading specialists to help struggling readers (Moore, Bean, Birdyshaw, & Rycik, 1999). Ten years later, we see little of these recommendations being met in the schools surrounding our university. Instead, scripted, one-size-fits-all programs are being put in place or students are receiving no intervention at all. Also, reading specialists are either not available or are required to use the assessments and instruction provided with the scripted reading programs.

The study described in this article sought to examine the needs of adolescent readers. To accomplish this and to extend information from previous studies, the researchers examined the contexts that foster adolescents' reading motivation, connections between their current literacies and academic literacies, and their needs as readers as suggested by research (Guthrie & Humenick, 2004; National Governors Association, 2005; Pitcher et al., 2007).

Procedures

Objectives of the Study

Our objectives were to investigate the following research questions: (a) What types of reading instruction are adolescent students receiving? (b) Are the adolescents in this study receiving the type of instruction that they need? and (c) Do parents understand what kind of reading instruction their children need and what role to play in their adolescents' reading education?

To answer these questions, we examined the needs of seven adolescent students who attended the university reading clinic for 12 weeks in the spring of 2008. The students were tested with assessments, including QRI-4 (Leslie & Caldwell, 2006), the Lexia Comprehensive Reading Test (Lexia Learning Systems, 2004), and the Adolescent Motivation to Read Survey-R (Pitcher et al., 2007), and interviewed. Their parents were also interviewed using questions that paralleled the student interview. In addition, we researched the reading programs that the students and parents stated were currently used for instruction to examine the programs' components and determine how the programs met their needs. The students all lived in the Baltimore metropolitan area, attended different types of schools (except one that was homeschooled), were in grades 6 through 8, were all experiencing some reading difficulties, and were from various ethnic, cultural, religious, and socioeconomic backgrounds.

Methodology

This study used a collection of case studies to analyze whether reading/literacy programs are meeting adolescents' individual needs. Seven adolescents were assessed one-on-one to find out what motivated them to read, their word identification levels, their comprehension levels, and which reading strategies they used to comprehend text. Next, members of the research team interviewed both the students and their parents to help establish the answers to the research questions. This follows the recommendations of Conley and Hinchman (2004), who suggested that adolescents "can contribute immeasurably to diagnoses of their literacy-related needs" (p. 44). The curriculum used by the schools was determined through a review of multiple sources, such as Web sites, interviews with parents, and information from teachers in the respective school systems.

Then, the researchers individually analyzed the cases using the constant comparative method to determine recurring themes (Bogdan & Biklen, 2002). Next, the team met to compare themes. Finally, using mutually agreed upon themes, the team developed snapshots of each student to examine similarities and differences, including quotes from the students and their parents. Conclusions about how the reading instruction met the adolescents' literacy needs were determined through data triangulation of the interviews, assessments, and review of curriculum documents. The conclusions across all of the cases were then examined to determine recurring themes crucial to understanding the needs of all the students. All names in the following snapshots are pseudonyms.

The Student Snapshots

■ CASE 1: Tamika

Tamika, originally from South Africa, is in sixth grade in a public school and is an ELL. She participates in a reading intervention class in her school using Language! (Greene, 1996), a scripted program focused on phonics, decoding, and spelling. The method of instruction she encounters in content area classes is assigned readings and answering questions. Tamika enjoys math class best because there is not much reading involved. However, she spends around five hours a day on the computer, reading and writing e-mails, updating her Web site, and playing games. Tamika stated that she did not have any problems reading on the computer. When asked, "What kind of difficulties are you having when you read?" Tamika responded, "Understanding what the topic is about."

Tamika was not receiving comprehension instruction in school. Her mother concurred that her greatest difficulty is reading comprehension: "The difficulties my daughter is having is the comprehension part. She can read, she can spell, but the comprehension part for some reason is hard for her." Her mother stated that she was not invited to a parent conference because Tamika was supposedly doing "okay." She went on to explain that Tamika was placed in the Language! class as a result of one test, and she was notified via mail of this placement. Her mother believed this program was not challenging her daughter, and she would have valued conferencing with the teacher. Therefore, she brought Tamika to the reading clinic, sharing that she struggles with comprehension and is not motivated to read.

From assessments administered in the reading clinic, we determined that Tamika's comprehension is on the second-grade level, whereas her word recognition is at the sixth-grade level, her current grade placement. Her strengths included sight word recognition, word identification, and awareness of her own reading needs. Tamika's needs included vocabulary development and during-reading strategies. Comparing her needs with the school's instruction, there seems to be a disconnect between the two. The school's reading program focuses on decoding strategies, grammar, and spelling, whereas she needs vocabulary development and comprehension.

Tamika's reading clinic instruction focused on using before-, during-, and after-reading strategies while reading and summarizing text. Visual organizers, sticky note strategies, and chunking text were used. She applied all of the techniques she learned to whatever text she read. She also learned to use games to help her learn new vocabulary. This helped her monitor her own understanding of what she read.

■ CASE 2: Karl

Karl is in seventh grade and homeschooled. He was diagnosed with attention deficit disorder when he was in public school and had an individual education plan (IEP). He received pull-out reading support in elementary school. When asked what reading he enjoys, he shared that he enjoys reading on his porch and likes to keep up with current events using Google. Karl indicated that reading and thinking aloud help him understand what he reads. He spends about three hours a day on the computer e-mailing friends, using MySpace, and reading the news. When asked if reading is ever a problem on the computer, his response was simply, "Uh, no."

Karl's father said Karl's mother, not a trained teacher, homeschools him to ensure instruction matches his needs. She uses a homeschool curriculum, consisting of reading and answering questions, and supplements the curriculum with reading and researching online. Karl asserted that self-selected readings and journaling are helpful. His parents enrolled him in the reading clinic to improve his reading comprehension and writing skills. From the assessments, we determined that his word recognition and comprehension were both on the second-grade level. He was motivated to read self-selected texts. His needs included decoding, vocabulary, fluency, and comprehension. He did not use before-, during-, or after-reading strategies.

The clinic instruction focused on teaching him to make connections to improve comprehension. His teacher concentrated on making predictions, thinking aloud, and visualizing strategies. Both the teacher and his parents reported that his understanding of what he was reading improved considerably during this short amount of instruction.

The curriculum his parents use with Karl focuses more on practicing reading than learning strategies. Homeschooling in Maryland receives very little oversight by the Maryland State Department of Education. Students are not required to take state assessments, and parents only meet with the student's zoned public school once a year to show the curriculum used.

■ CASE 3: Kathy

Kathy is an eighth grader in a suburban school system. She enjoys riding horses, playing the piano, playing basketball on a team, and acting in a community theater group. She wants to be a librarian; the library is her favorite place to go, because she can choose any book she wants.

Kathy was diagnosed with autism at a young age and has received special education services throughout her school years. In middle school, she receives small-group, pull-out help in reading daily, provided by a special educator. The school's reading intervention program, Corrective Reading (Engelmann, Carnine, & Johnson, 1999), focuses mostly on auditory phonics development, with comprehension primarily concentrated in answering recall questions. The instruction in this program is mostly teacher centered with little independent application. She does not get any reading support in her content area classes. She maintained that she has the most trouble understanding what she reads in science class but receives no support with that class. She further stated that in elementary school she had opportunities to choose books, but this is not done in her middle school. When asked about what helps her to read, she answered, "When I was in elementary school, I read, like, different kinds of stories in different books."

Kathy uses the computer at home for a variety of activities. She has many pen pals and writes them letters. She enjoys making bookmarks with clip art she finds on the Internet to give to special people as gifts. When she wants to know something, she looks it up on the Internet. She has even learned to shop online, because she really does not like to go to stores. She stated that she seems to understand more of what she reads on the computer than she does in print texts.

Kathy's parents shared their frustration that the school will not recognize that the computer can help Kathy learn. They feel it would distract her and did not include any computer use on her IEP. The times that the parents tried to fight this, their input was ignored. Her father shared, "Here's the window to this child, and no one can take advantage of it. At 3 years old, we sat her down in front of the computer, and now she writes her own stories."

Both of Kathy's parents are very knowledgeable about her educational needs. From the time she was very young, they researched autism, sought professional help, and used many methods to help her at home. Her mother shared that Kathy needs a very visual, kinesthetic learning approach, which is why the computer interaction has been successful. Her mom is also concerned about her limited vocabulary, stating that Kathy needs to make connections with words in context rather than "just reading a definition on paper."

Kathy's parents want to partner with Kathy's school, but they continually receive resistance from the school's faculty. Her father remarked that "they can't answer the hard questions." Since her parents are very conscious of her needs, they have been very frustrated with the scripted reading program being used in Kathy's school. Her father serves on the advocacy group for parents of special education students in their county school system. When he researched the reading program that is being used in the county, he discovered that it is not research based, focuses on word identification with very weak vocabulary and comprehension components, is predominantly auditory based, and has no computer component. When he shared this with teachers, he got "the deer in the headlights stare."

Our findings agreed with Kathy's parents' conclusions. Kathy's word recognition was on the sixth-grade level, but her comprehension was on a first-grade level. When asked about reading strategies, she could not verbalize any. Her strength, though, was writing. She wrote in correct, well-developed sentences with correct capitalization, punctuation, and grammar.

Kathy's reading clinic teacher reported that she made connections when reading strategies were taught using pictures, writing, and story maps. Vocabulary definitely got in her way, but expanding vocabulary by helping her make connections to the words improved her understanding. The success of this instruction demonstrates that she could be taught to comprehend through visual approaches.

The school's reading program not only did not fit Kathy's needs but also was incongruent with her learning style. We concluded that she needs a visual, kinesthetic approach to instruction, with opportunities for independent practice and a focus on reading strategy instruction. Instead the school is using an auditory-based program focused on word identification skills.

■ CASE 4: Stacy

Stacy is enrolled in a sixth-grade class in a private school. She is an avid reader and enjoys trips to the local public library and bookstores. She is actively engaged in many extracurricular activities; for example, she is active in her Girl Scouts troop and enjoys playing softball and basketball.

When asked about the type of reading instruction provided in her school, Stacy responded, "I read chapter books in class." Also, "no one really reads with me, and it's not like a one-on-one thing." She further added, "I like working on the computer." When asked about the kinds of materials she likes to read, her response was, "I like to read in math, because there isn't much to read."

According to her parents, areas that present difficulty for Stacy include "comprehension and motivation." Throughout the parent interview, her parents made numerous references to her difficulty with comprehension. They commented that although

"Stacy has a positive self-concept about her reading," she experiences difficulty with comprehension. In addition, her parents expressed concern that there is a "disconnect between Stacy's reading needs and what she receives." She has been very frustrated with many Ds on her report card, and her parents are at a loss for how to help her. The principal, who is also her language arts teacher, tries to tutor her after school when he has time.

From the assessments administered, we determined that Stacy can read words on the sixth-grade level, but she only comprehends on a first-grade level, having difficulty with any questions except simple recall. She enjoys reading and has a positive self-concept as a reader but does not think the instruction she receives is motivating. When assessed, she applied no strategies consistently. When asked about what reading strategies she has been taught, she shared that she has not been taught strategies.

Her instruction in the reading clinic included a systematic approach teaching one reading strategy at a time. She responded well to visual organizers that she could design and use herself to learn the strategy. Her reading comprehension level improved considerably with only 10 hours of instruction focused on learning one strategy.

In Stacy's school, reading is being used and not taught. There are no reading classes or reading specialists available, and the principal is only giving extra help sporadically when Stacy struggles to read for her assignments. She needs a more systematic approach to how to use strategies to understand what she reads.

■ CASE 5: Sam

Sam is enrolled in a sixth-grade class in an urban public school. He enjoys sports and plays basketball, football, kickball, and baseball. His father describes him as a gifted athlete, to whom basketball comes easily. Sam makes good grades in school, maintaining an 88 percent average across all subjects. However, he received additional one-on-one support from a reading specialist two days a week when he was in the fifth grade.

Sam reported that he does not like to read for pleasure because he lacks understanding of what he reads. He believed that reading was easier when he was 6 years old and there were pictures to help him. He described his reading class as consisting of a drill, talking about something, reading a book, and finally taking tests on the book—"questions and a lot of stuff." He likes reading class best when they get to talk about what they read. He indicated that the reading strategies he uses are reading aloud, rereading, and taking notes. When asked when he likes reading the most, he responded, "When I like the book and it's about what I like . . . like basketball."

Sam's father expressed concern about his son's reading based upon observations made at home. He stated that Sam has always tested on grade level for reading in school, but he believes that Sam has a limited vocabulary, difficulty understanding what he reads, and difficulty retelling important story events. Sam's parents limit his time on the computer at home and allow him to use it mostly for homework. His father explained that when Sam goes on the computer, he downloads music for his iPod or uses it for research for school, but he does not surf the Internet. Sam stated that on weekends, he likes to play Nickelodeon games on the computer. According to his father, Sam has difficulty with comprehension, whether he is reading a print document or reading online. He believes that Sam does not understand the value in working at something that takes time and effort. He would like Sam to understand that when you value something, "you have to put the work behind it in order to become good at it." Although he did not provide any specifics, Sam's father expressed some concern about the reading instruction his son receives in school, stating, "It's not engaging. Learning is not a rote process. It's getting people excited."

From the assessments administered to Sam, we determined that his reading comprehension is at a fifth-grade level. He has strong phonics and decoding skills, uses before-reading strategies effectively, is motivated to succeed, and has a positive attitude toward school and the reading clinic. His needs include vocabulary development and during- and after-reading strategies, as reported by his parents.

The concern with Sam is that he is reading below level but testing on level on the state tests. As a result, he is not receiving specific reading instruction to improve his comprehension but is participating in a reading class where he is just reading, answering questions, and taking tests. The school system that he is in uses tests from the language arts textbooks, which assess knowledge of the story rather than comprehension strategies, and the school system does not have reading specialists in the schools. In this case, assessment aligned with the state standards would help the school understand Sam's needs better. As he progresses to high school, content area reading will present more challenges to him.

Sam's reading clinic instruction focused on making connections and self-questioning to improve his reading comprehension. He learned to use visual organizers and sticky notes to help him comprehend any type of reading selection. Additionally, he learned practical strategies, such as games and webs, to help him learn new vocabulary. His clinic teacher reported that he learned very quickly and was able to use these strategies independently.

■ *CASE 6: Leon*

Leon is enrolled in the seventh grade in an urban school. He has never been retained and has been placed in gifted and talented classes in the past. He has never received extra reading help in school, and the school does not have a reading specialist. On the state reading achievement test, he has always scored in the advanced category. He likes to play football and basketball. He enjoys playing games on the computer but shared that he sometimes struggles with reading the directions of the games; however, he has taught himself to work through this. He also enjoys reading when he can choose what he reads.

Leon shared that he struggles with reading aloud because he had a stuttering problem when he was younger. Unfortunately, reading aloud is often done in his classes. Reading in science class presents the biggest problems for him. He expressed that "before I started the [reading] clinic, I really didn't understand what I read. Yes, I feel like I can understand a lot more than I did before."

Leon's mother related that, although he always scored high on the state assessments, she feels strongly that he has a problem with comprehending what he reads. She worries that the school does not do "a lot of in-depth study and research" and that her son is not learning "higher order thinking." She attributes this to the large class sizes and "new teachers who come and go." She believes her son needs more of a hands-on approach through which he will learn to "synthesize and evaluate all levels of thinking."

Leon's mother also shared a concern that the school does not provide tips on how parents can help or even explain what type of curriculum they are using. She expressed shock that when she applied for her son to go to private school, they recommended that her son repeat seventh grade. Her son's progress in the reading clinic encouraged her because he voluntarily and enthusiastically did the work and "is finally starting to put things together."

In assessing Leon's reading ability in the reading clinic, the teacher found his reading comprehension level was three grades below his grade level on two different assessments. The only strategies he was able to verbalize were sounding out and predicting.

Although his word identification was higher than his comprehension, it was still two grade levels below his actual grade level.

Leon read better orally than silently but is very self-conscious reading aloud because of his early stuttering. His self-concept as a reader was higher than his value of reading when he started working at the reading clinic. He responded best when his interests were considered in selecting reading materials. When comprehension strategy instruction included hands-on activities, such as visual organizers and writing notes while reading, he did well, which his mother predicted.

Leon is in the same school system as Sam. Again, the tests used quarterly in the school were developed by the book publisher and test knowledge of the stories. In many cases this knowledge is very literal, so the school has not actually realized that Leon struggles with comprehension. Like Sam, Leon did well on the state reading assessments though he comprehends below grade level.

■ *CASE 7: Andrew*

Andrew is a 14-year-old boy enrolled in eighth grade in suburban public school who planned to attend a magnet high school the following year. At the time of our interviews, he was participating for the second time in the reading clinic. He is a student athlete, playing both football and basketball. His mother reported that he makes good grades in school but often loses motivation toward the end of the school year. Struggling with reading is not a new phenomenon for Andrew; he worked with a reading specialist from grades 1 through 6 and, in addition to attending the reading clinic, met with a private reading tutor every Saturday.

Andrew loves to discuss sports, read about sports, and buy athletics-themed clothing online. He considers himself an "OK" reader and is able to articulate his main comprehension strategy, which is to go back and reread. He articulated specific difficulty with remembering what he reads, particularly in language arts class. He further elaborated that the teacher picks the stories and books, so students do not have any voice in what they read; he shared that he would prefer to have some choice in reading selections. He related that sometimes the teacher facilitates class discussion, but students mostly answer questions about reading. Overall, he was frustrated with his teachers. When asked what teachers might do to help him become a better reader, he replied, "start teaching and explaining things."

Although Andrew said that he struggled particularly in language arts, his mother reported that he struggled with reading and understanding in science. She expressed frustration with the school and described how she seeks out alternative instruction for Andrew. She enrolled him in a magnet high school for the following year but is concerned that he will struggle because he is behind his peers. She explained that Andrew could only bring home his history and math textbooks, and the teachers rarely communicated with her. "They are just not doing anything, and it is sad. They don't call me. They don't tell me anything. I don't care if you have 50 kids in your class. Ten out of 50 may be doing well. Let me follow up. I don't think they have phone numbers, because they never have called me."

From the assessments administered, we found that Andrew was indeed reading below grade level and was particularly struggling with comprehension. His word recognition was strong. His identified needs include vocabulary, comprehension strategies while he is reading, and writing development.

In the reading clinic, Andrew learned comprehension strategies using sticky notes and visual organizers. His comprehension improved during his first experience in the reading clinic, which he was able to demonstrate when he returned. His mother shared that she was pleased that he was still using strategies from the first reading clinic and could explain them to her.

Andrew is also not in a reading program that teaches comprehension skills in his school. In language arts class, the students use an anthology of literature and respond to questions about the stories. Additionally, strategic instruction of comprehending what is read in the content areas is not being done.

What We Learned

We found that reading comprehension was below level for all students in the study, but none of them were receiving intervention focused on comprehension. Tamika and Kathy received intervention focused on phonics in scripted programs, which were not aligned with their needs or learning strengths. For the other students, the problem was more a lack of any comprehension instruction. The students told us they just read and answered questions in their language arts classes.

The students also all expressed concerns that they had the most problems reading in content area classes and received no help with strategies on how to understand those materials. The students' low comprehension levels were in expository text. Since most of the reading they will do during the rest of their schooling and in future employment will be in this type of text, instruction needs to focus on strategies for understanding its different types. In contrast, the students shared that they were able to understand what they chose to read and what they read on the computer. Giving choices and using online resources may also help improve the understanding of content area reading.

The parents in this study understood the problems their children were experiencing but expressed frustration that the schools communicated very little with them. Some parents also voiced concern that their sons or daughters tested on or above grade level on state reading achievement tests but were struggling to understand what they read. The parents in this study had many excellent perceptions that could help school systems understand how to reach adolescents.

Our research team recommends focusing on the adolescents' needs rather than just putting them in a program. Instruction that focuses on needs requires that funds be spent on hiring qualified reading specialists instead of buying one-size-fits-all programs. The instruction provided by reading specialists should include more self-selected reading to help students see the benefits of improving reading in something they want to read; ways to critically think about text in both language arts and other content areas; more before-, during-, and after-reading comprehension instruction; and, as suggested by the International Reading Association and the National Middle School Association (2002), "well-prepared . . . teachers who integrate individualized reading instruction within their content areas" (p. 2). Finally, ways to use computers to enhance instruction needs to be more thoughtfully included. Our research supports the conclusions of Deshler, Palincsar, Biancarosa, and Nair (2007) that if "adolescents can read the words, comprehension naturally follows" (p. 14) and that technology could be used in many ways to help struggling adolescent readers.

Limitations Provide Opportunities

The investigators realize that from these seven case studies, we cannot generalize beyond these students. We do recognize, though, that these students and their parents have important stories to tell. The parents of these students cannot be considered representative of all parents of adolescents because they actively sought their child's participation in the reading clinic. How many parents do not know where to turn or how to express their concerns?

The student snapshots, therefore, provide the chance to prompt administrators and teachers to examine the literacy instruction in their schools as well as their home-school communication methods. Additionally, the snapshots may help to break down the stereotypes often expressed by secondary educators that parents do not care about being involved with what their students are doing in middle schools.

Suggestions for Future Research

Rampey, Dion, and Donahue (2009) reported that "the average reading score for 17-year-olds was not significantly different from that in 1971" (p. 1). The literacy demands of the workplace today, though, are very different from what they were in 1971. Kamil and colleagues (2008) suggested that "structural barriers at the middle and high school levels" (p. 1) interfere with improving the literacy levels of adolescents. Some of the barriers that they discussed are avoiding reading in the content areas and lack of effective reading instruction to meet the needs of the learners. We would like to add to their concerns the lack of using technology effectively to expand learning, the partnering with parents to meet the needs of the students, and the need for qualified reading specialists in schools who can assess and teach to the needs of students rather than using scripted programs.

We hope that our research will open discussions of how to meet these needs by listening to the voices of the teens in this study and their parents. Additionally, we welcome other researchers and administrators to use our cases to open conversations. Finally, we recommend more research about what changes need to be considered in schools to support adolescents in learning the literacy strategies that they will need to meet the literacy needs of the future.

REFERENCES

Alvermann, D.E. (2003). *Seeing themselves as capable and engaged readers: Adolescents and re/mediated instruction.* Naperville, IL: Learning Point.

Biancarosa, G., & Snow, C.E. (2004). *Reading next—A vision for action and research in middle and high school literacy: A report from Carnegie Corporation of New York.* Washington, DC: Alliance for Excellent Education.

Bogdan, R., & Biklen, S. (2002). *Qualitative research for education: An introduction to theories and methods* (4th ed.). Boston, MA: Allyn & Bacon.

Conley, M.W., & Hinchman, K.A. (2004). No Child Left Behind: What it means for U.S. adolescents and what we can do about it. *Journal of Adolescent & Adult Literacy, 48*(1), 42–50. doi:10.1598/JAAL.48.1.4

Deshler, D.D., Palincsar, A.S., Biancarosa, G., & Nair, M. (2007). *Informed choices for struggling adolescent readers: A research-based guide to instructional programs and practices.* Newark, DE: International Reading Association.

Engelmann, S., Carnine, L., & Johnson, G. (1999). *Corrective reading.* Columbus, OH: SRA/McGraw-Hill.

Greene, J.F. (1996). *Language! The comprehensive literacy curriculum* (3rd ed.). Frederick, CO: Sopris West.

Guthrie, J.T., & Humenick, N.M. (2004). Motivating students to read: Evidence for classroom practices that increase reading motivation and achievement. In P. McCardle & V. Chhabra (Eds.), *The voice of evidence in reading research* (pp. 329–354). Baltimore, MD: Paul H. Brookes.

Note: If you would like to dialogue with the authors about this study, visit our blog, Literacy Needs of Adolescents, at adolescentliteracy.wordpress.com.

International Reading Association & National Middle School Association. (2002). *Supporting young ado-lescents' literacy learning: A joint position statement of the International Reading Association and the National Middle School Association.* Newark, DE; Waterville, OH: Authors.

Kamil, M.L, Borman, G.D., Dole, J., Kral, C.C., Salinger, T., & Torgesen, J. (2008). *Improving adolescent lit-eracy: Effective classroom and intervention practices: A practice guide* (NCEE Publication No. 2008-4027). Washington, DC: National Center for Education Evaluation and Regional Assistance, Institute of Education Sciences, U.S. Department of Education. Retrieved August 12, 2009, from ies.ed.gov/ncee/wwc/pdf/practiceguides/adlit_pg_082608.pdf.

Leslie, L., & Caldwell, J. (2006). *Qualitative reading inventory-4* (4th ed.). Boston, MA: Allyn & Bacon.

Lexia Learning Systems. (2004). *Lexia Comprehensive Reading Test, version 1.3.* Concord, MA: Author.

Moore, D.W., Bean, T.W., Birdyshaw, D., & Rycik, J.A. (1999). *Adolescent literacy: A position statement for the Commission on Adolescent Literacy of the International Reading Association.* Newark, DE: Interna-tional Reading Association.

National Endowment for the Arts. (2007). *To read or not to read: A question of national consequence* (Research Report No. 47). Retrieved August 12, 2009, from www.arts.gov/research/ToRead.pdf.

National Governors Association. (2005). *Reading to achieve: A governor's guide to adolescent literacy.* Retrieved February 19, 2008, from www.nga.org/Files/pdf/0510GOVGUIDELITERACY.PDF.

Pitcher, S.M., Albright, L.K., DeLaney, C.J., Walker, N.T., Seunarinesingh, K., Mogge, S., et al. (2007). Assessing adolescents' motivation to read. *Journal of Adolescent & Adult Literacy, 50*(5), 378–396. doi:10.1598/JAAL.50.5.5

Rampey, B.D., Dion, G.S., & Donahue, P.L. (2009). *NAEP 2008 trends in academic progress* (NCES Report No. 2009-479). Washington, DC: National Center for Education Statistics, U.S. Department of Education.

Santa, C.M. (2006). A vision for adolescent literacy: Ours or theirs? *Journal of Adolescent & Adult Literacy, 49*(6), 466–476. doi:10.1598/JAAL.49.6.2

Pitcher, Martinez, Dicembre, Fewster, and McCormick teach at Towson University, Maryland, USA; e-mail spitcher@towson.edu, gmartinez@towson.edu, edicembre@towson.edu, dfewster@towson.edu, and mkmc-cormick@towson.edu.

CLASSROOM IMPLICATIONS

1. Based on your reading of the materials in this chapter, what do you believe are some specific ways classroom teachers can help adolescents with their reading, both in and out of the classroom?

2. What are some of the major problems related to adolescent literacy that must be faced and overcome before young people realistically consider reading to be an important part of their lives?

FOR FURTHER READING

Benson, S. (2010). "I don't know if that'd be English or not": Third space theory and literacy instruction. *Journal of Adolescent & Adult Literacy, 53*(7), 555–563. doi: 10. 1598/JAAL.53.7.3

Meyer, K. E. (2010). A collaborative approach to reading workshop in the middle years. *The Reading Teacher, 63*(6), 501–507. doi: 10.1598/RT.63.6.7

Sturtevant, E.G., & Kim, G.S. (2010). Literacy motivation and school/non-school literacies among students enrolled in a middle-school ESOL program. *Literacy Research and Instruction, 49,* 68–85. doi: 10.1080/19388070802716907

ONLINE RESOURCES

International Reading Association. (1999). *Adolescent literacy*. Position Statement. **http://www.reading.org/downloads/positions/ps1036_adolescent.pdf**
AdLit.org. Resources for parents and teachers of students from grades 4–12. **http://www.adlit.org/**

CHAPTER

8 Technology

I believe that the motion picture is destined to revolutionize our education system and that in a few years it will supplant largely, if not entirely, the use of textbooks.

—Thomas Edison (1922)

Computers in the future may weigh no more than 1.5 tons.

—Popular Mechanics (1949)

As intuitively appealing as technology may appear, it will be little more than a sophisticated novelty unless teachers are equipped with the skills needed to use it effectively in support of literacy instruction.

—Linda Gambrell (2006)

Change is good. You go first.

—Scott Adams, Dilbert cartoon

Technology in schools is here to stay. At least two powerful arguments suggest that literacy teachers must find effective means of integrating computers into their instruction. The first argument is that the world itself, and particularly the business world, is increasingly driven by technology. Educators at all levels must contend with the question of what sort of future they are preparing their students for. A wired world outside of school necessitates, to some degree, technology-based literacy instruction. The second argument is that computer technology has created reading and writing skills that do not have print counterparts. That is, students must now be able to navigate hypermedia and to compose using not only word processing software but desktop publishing systems capable of integrating multimedia. The times, they are a-changin'.

Schools, however, are often resistant to embracing technology. Seymour Papert (1994), in his book, *The Children's Machine*, compares a school's reaction to computers to the body's reaction to an invading virus. Computers are often relegated to labs or ignored and isolated by classroom teachers. Some teachers are obviously more enthusiastic about technology applications than others, and these technophilic teachers sometimes form a subcommunity within the school or district.

Technology applications raise practical financial questions, such as the turnover of obsolete hardware and the funds needed to purchase quality software. But there are also important pedagogical questions to be addressed by anyone responsible for overseeing a comprehensive reading program.

Perhaps the biggest question is whether to invest time and resources in an integrated learning system (ILS). Like a basal reading program, an ILS embodies a scope and sequence of activities and assessments. Children make their way through a sequence of activities, usually constructed with appealing art and self-competition formats. All the while, their progress is monitored automatically and reports are generated for use by teachers. Objective studies on particular commercial ILSs are hard to come by. One exception is IBM's Writing to Read, an expensive ILS that was effectively killed by the lack of positive research findings (Slavin, 1990). Another is the Waterford Early Reading Program. A recent study showed that it offered no advantages over traditional instruction (Patterson et al., 2003), though a second study indicated its usefulness with struggling readers (Cassady & Smith, 2005). Coiro and her colleagues (2003) concluded that an ILS typically offers early gains, perhaps due to novelty, but that the advantage rapidly disappears.

Another important question is what stand-alone software to purchase. Once again, publishers' in-house studies may be all the research that's available, which is why it is essential to have a working knowledge of effective non-technology-based reading instruction. The degree to which software can embody such techniques is likely to be a good indicator of its effectiveness. In our view, two good sources for exploring new software are the Center for Applied Special Technology (www.cast.org) and the Florida Center for Reading Research (www.fcrr.org). The two Websites are well worth a visit.

Studies conducted at the National Reading Research Center (NRRC) have repeatedly validated the value of e-books. These are electronic versions of print trade books, equipped with digitized pronunciations accessible on a point-and-click basis. When young children read such books, they can independently tackle material near their frustration level and they also acquire new sight words incidentally in the process. For middle schoolers, teachers can use software such as Write Out Loud (Don Johnston) to make digitized pronunciations available with materials for students who still struggle with decoding.

Perhaps the most notable success story involving technology applications to literacy instruction is word processing. Numerous studies confirm that the use of word processing software to teach writing leads to better results (both affective and cognitive) than conventional "paper-and-pencil" approaches. The engaging qualities of computers can probably be thanked for this, together with the ease with which children can form words and letters and revise and edit their work. Of course, as David Reinking (1995) points out, the fact that word processing leads to better writers and writing is almost beside the point. The fact is, students will enter a world of work in which word processing is the expectation. The questions that should concern educators are not whether to embrace word processing but which software best meets our instructional goals.

Internet access in schools, together with its host of ethical issues (ranging from equity of access to plagiarism to child safeguards) has now taken center stage. In 1994, 3 percent of schools had internet access, while 94 percent had access by 2005 (Wells & Lewis, 2006). The primary challenge is to find ways to successfully integrate these technology applications with the instructional objectives that make up the curriculum. This task is more difficult than it sounds and teachers find it tempting to use computer stations as a means of motivating students or occupying them so that they can work with other children without giving adequate thought to the alignment of computer activities with the literacy curriculum.

AS YOU READ

The two selections that follow were chosen to provide an understanding of how digital environments have changed the nature of literacy and should change our teaching. Coiro explains how the internet requires an additional skill set that could lead to erroneous conclusions if comprehension is assessed online. Her discussion of these new skills makes this article especially informative. We encourage you to think about the five differences she identifies and to form a judgment as to whether the differences are truly substantive. The NCTE Policy Research Brief presents key facts that frame the rising trend toward technology use. Its authors then address frequent myths associated with twenty-first-century literacies. See if you agree that these are actually myths. The brief concludes with specific recommendations for teachers, schools, and policymakers. In your judgment, how realistic are these recommendations?

REFERENCES

Cassady, J. C., & Smith, L. L. (2005). The impact of a structured integrated learning system on first-grade students' reading gains. *Reading and Writing Quarterly, 21,* 361–376.

Coiro, J., Leu, D.J., Jr., Kinzer, C.K., Labbo, L., Teale, W., Bergman, L., Sulzen, J., & Sheng, D. (2003, December). *A review of research on literacy and technology: Replicating and extending the NRP subcommittee report on computer technology and reading instruction.* Paper presented at the 53rd annual meeting of the National Reading Conference, Scottsdale, AZ.

Gambrell, L. (2006). Technology and the engaged literacy learner. In M.C. McKenna, L. D. Labbo, R. Kieffer, & D. Reinking (Eds.), *International handbook of literacy and technology* (Vol. 2, pp. 289–294). Mahwah, NJ: Lawrence Erlbaum.

Papert, S. (1994). *The children's machine: Rethinking school in the age of the computer.* New York: Basic Books.

Paterson, W.A., Henry, J. J., O'Quin, K., Ceprano, M.A., & Blue, E.V. (2003). Investigating the effectiveness of an integrated learning system on early emergent readers. *Reading Research Quarterly, 38,* 172–207.

Reinking, D. (1995). Reading and writing with computers: Literacy research in a post-typographic world. In K. A. Hinchman, D. J. Leu, & C. K. Kinzer (Eds.), *Perspectives on literacy research and practice: Forty-fourth yearbook of the National Reading Conference* (pp. 17–33). Chicago, IL: NRC.

Slavin, R. E. (1990). "IBM's Writing to Read: Is it right for reading?" *Phi Delta Kappan, 72,* 214–216.

21st-Century Literacies

A Policy Research Brief produced by the National Council of Teachers of English

■ ■ ■ ■ ■

National Council of Teachers of English

This publication of the James R. Squire Office of Policy Research offers updates on research with implications for policy decisions that affect teaching and learning. Each issue addresses a different topic. To download this policy brief, visit the NCTE Website at www. ncte.org and search for "21st-Century Literacies." For more on this topic, search for "Research Clips on 21st-Century Literacy."

A Changing World for Literacy Teachers

Global economies, new technologies, and exponential growth in information are transforming our society. Today's employees engage with a technology-driven, diverse, and quickly changing "flat world."[1] English/language arts teachers need to prepare students for this world with problem solving, collaboration, and analysis—as well as skills with word processing, hyper-text, LCDs, Web cams, digital streaming podcasts, smartboards, and social networking software—central to individual and community success.[2] New literacies are already becoming part of the educational landscape, as the following "fast facts" suggest:

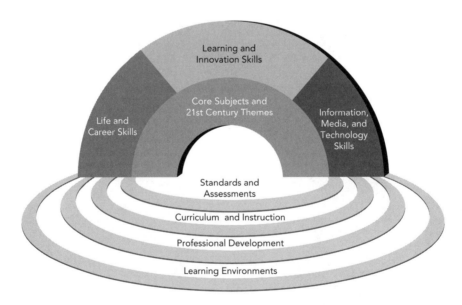

Other tech terms for teachers can be found at the National Education Technology Standards (NETS) Website: http://cnets.iste.Org/teachers/t_glossary.html#t

- In 2011, the writing test of the National Assessment of Educational Progress will require 8th and 11th graders to compose on computers; 4th graders will compose at the keyboard in 2019.
- Thirty-three states have adopted National Educational Technology Standards for K–12 students.
- Approximately 50 percent of four-year colleges and 30 percent of community colleges use electronic course management tools.
- The United States ranks 15th worldwide in the percentage of households subscribed to a broadband Internet service.
- Over 80 percent of kindergarteners use computers, and over 50 percent of children under age 9 use the Internet.[3]
- At least 61 virtual colleges/universities (VCUs) currently educate students in the United States.
- In 2006, 158.6 billion text messages were sent in the U.S.
- Over 106 million individuals are registered on MySpace.
- There are at least 91 million Google searches per day.
- The European Institute for E-Learning aims to enhance Europe's position in the knowledge economy by achieving the goal "e-Portfolio for all" by 2010.

As new technologies shape literacies, they bring opportunities for teachers at all levels to foster reading and writing in more diverse and participatory contexts. Sites like literature's Voice of the Shuttle (http://vos.ucsb.edu), online fan-fiction (http://www.fan-fiction.net), and the Internet Public Library for children (http://www.ipl.org/youth) expand both the range of available texts and the social dimension of literacy. Research on electronic reading workshops shows that they contribute to the emergence of new literacies.[4]

Research also shows that digital technology enhances writing and interaction in several ways. K–12 students who write with computers produce compositions of greater length and higher quality and are more engaged with and motivated toward writing than their peers.[5] College students who keep e-portfolios have a higher rate of academic achievement and a higher overall retention rate than their peers. They also demonstrate greater capacity for metacognition, reflection, and audience awareness.[6] Both typical and atypical students who receive online response to writing revise better than those participating in traditional collaboration.[7]

Common Myths about 21st-Century Literacies

Myth: 21st-century literacy is about technology only

Reality: Although technology is important to literacy in the new century, other dimensions of learning are essential. Studies of workforce readiness show that employers rate written and oral communication skills very highly, and collaboration, work ethic, critical thinking, and leadership all rank higher than proficiency in information technology. The Partnership for 21st-Century Skills (http://www.21stcenturyskills.org) advocates for core academic subjects, learning and innovation skill, and life and career skills, along with technology skills. Even a standardized measure like the iSkills Information and Communication Technology Literacy Test gives significant attention to organization, evaluation, critical thinking, and problem solving.[8]

Myth: The digital divide is closed because schools provide computer and Internet access

Reality: The digital divide—the gap in access to and quality of technology—still exists. In 2005, nearly 100 percent of public schools in the United States had access to the Internet, but student-to-computer ratios and access to broadband service vary widely across socio-economic levels. Furthermore, available computers are often not used effectively or fully; the national average of students' school use of computers is 12 minutes per week.[9]

Myth: Teachers who use technology in their personal lives will use it in their classes

Reality: Research shows that teachers who use word processing, spreadsheets, presentation software, and Internet browsers at home do not bring that knowledge into the classroom. Furthermore, two-thirds of all teachers report feeling under-prepared to use technology in teaching, even if they use computers to plan lessons, access model lesson plans, and create activities.[10]

Myth: Teachers need to be experts in technology in order to use it effectively in instruction

Reality: Research shows that effective teachers collaborate with students to understand the information landscape and think about its use. Since success with technology depends largely upon critical thinking and reflection, even teachers with relatively little technological skill can provide useful instruction.[11]

Myth: Automatic Essay Scoring (AES) systems will soon replace human readers of student writing

Reality: Systems like ETS's Criterion, Pearson's Intelligent Essay Assessor (IEA), the College Board's ACCUPLACER and WritePlacerPlus, and ACT's Compass are all being used to provide immediate feedback or evaluate students' writing. However, the feedback they provide is generic and relatively limited, and these systems are confined to a narrow range of modes and topics.[12]

Key Terms

Affinity Groups: Groups or communities that unite individuals with common interests. Electronic spaces extend the range of possibilities for such groups.[13]

Blogs: Web logs ("blogs" for short) are interactive Websites, often open to the public, that serve as journals and can include Web links and photographs as well as audio and video elements. Some 60 million blogs have been published on the Internet over the past five years.[14]

E-portfolio: Student work that is generated, selected, organized, stored, and revised digitally. Often electronic portfolios are accessible to multiple audiences, and some models can be moved from one site to another easily. E-portfolios can document the process of learning, promote integrative thinking, display polished work, and/or provide a space for reflecting on learning.[15]

Hypertext: Electronic texts that provide multiple links, allowing users to trace ideas in immediate and idiosyncratic directions. Hypermedia adds sound, video, animation, and/or virtual reality environments to the user's choices.[16]

ICT (Information and Communication Technology): ICT refers to the use of computers and computer software to convert, store, process, transmit, and retrieve information.

Podcasts: Digitalized audio files that are stored on the Internet and downloaded to listeners' computers or MP3 players. Although other file formats may be used, audio files are usually saved in the MP3 format. The term "podcast" comes from iPod™, the popular MP3 player.[17]

Web 2.0: This term does not refer to an update in the Web's technical specifications; it refers to a second generation of Web-based communities that demonstrate the participatory literacies students need for the 21st-century. Some examples include:

Myspace (http://www.Myspace.com) is a social networking website offering an interactive, user-submitted network of friends, personal profiles, blogs, groups, photos, music, and videos internationally. Students rate professors, discuss books, and connect with high school and college classmates here. *Myspace* receives nearly 80 percent of visits to online social networking websites; other similar sites include *Facebook* and *Xanga*.[18]

Second Life (http://www.secondlife.com) is an Internet-based 3D virtual world. This simulation's nine million participants use their avatars (digital representations of themselves) to explore, socialize, participate in individual and group activities, and create and trade items (virtual property) and services. Over 160 schools and colleges from all over the world have a presence on *Second Life*, and a number of the 140 colleges and universities represented have distance-learning programs based within it.[19]

SemanticWeb is an extension of the current Web that puts data into a common format so that instead of humans working with individual search engines (e.g., Google, Ask Jeeves) to locate information, the search engines themselves feed into a single mechanism that provides this searching on its own. Sometimes called Web 3.0, this technology will enable integration of virtually all kinds of information for more efficient and comprehensive retrieval.[20]

Webkinz (http://www.webkinz.com) is an Internet simulation where children learn pet care and other skills.[21]

Wiki refers to software that fosters collaboration and communication online. Wikis enable students to create, comment upon, and revise collaborative projects. One of the most prominent is Wikipedia (http://www.wikipedia.org), the online multilingual free-content encyclopedia, which currently has 7.9 million articles in 253 languages.[22]

Youtube (http://www.Youtube.com) is a popular video sharing Website where users can upload, view, and share video footage, including movie clips, TV clips, music videos, as well as amateur content such as student-produced videos.[23]

Research-Based Recommendations for Effective Instruction in 21st-Century Literacies

For teachers . . .

Research shows that effective instruction in 21st-century literacies takes an integrated approach, helping students understand how to access, evaluate, synthesize, and contribute to information. Furthermore, as Web 2.0 demonstrates, participation is key, and effective teachers will find ways to encourage interaction with and among students. Recommendations include:

- Encourage students to reflect regularly about the role of technology in their learning.
- Create a website and invite students to use it to continue class discussions and bring in outside voices.
- Give students strategies for evaluating the quality of information they find on the Internet.
- Be open about your own strengths and limitations with technology and invite students to help you.
- Explore technologies students are using outside of class and find ways to incorporate them into your teaching.
- Use a wiki to develop a multimodal reader's guide to a class text.
- Include a broad variety of media and genres in class texts.
- Ask students to create a podcast to share with an authentic audience.
- Give students explicit instruction about how to avoid plagiarism in a digital environment.
- Consult the resources on the Partnership for 21st-Century Skills Website at http://www.21stcenturyskills.org.

For schools and policymakers . . .

Teachers need both intellectual and material support for effective 21st-century literacy instruction. Accordingly, schools need to provide continuing opportunities for professional development as well as up-to-date technologies for use in literacy classrooms.

- Address the digital divide by lowering the number of students per computer and by providing high quality access (broadband speed and multiple locations) to technology and multiple software packages.
- Ensure that students in literacy classes have regular access to technology.
- Provide regular literacy-specific professional development in technology for teachers and administrators at all levels, including higher education.
- Require teacher preparation programs to include training in integrating technology into instruction.
- Protect online learners and ensure their privacy.
- Affirm the importance of literacy teachers in helping students develop technological proficiency.
- Adopt and regularly review standards for instruction in technology.

This report is produced by NCTE's James R. Squire Office of Policy Research, directed by Anne Ruggles Gere with assistance from Laura Aull, Hannah Dickinson, Melinda McBee Orzulak, and Ebony Elizabeth Thomas, all students in the Joint Ph.D. Program in English and Education at the University of Michigan.

ENDNOTES

1. Friedman, T.L. (2007). *The world is flat. A brief history of the 21st-century.* New York: Picador.
2. Kist, W. (2005). *New literacies in action: Teaching and learning in multiple media.* New York: Teachers College Press.
3. Olson, L. (2007). NAEP writing exams going digital in 2011. *Education Week,* 26(27): p.23.

International Society for Technology in Education. (2007). National Educational Technology Standards for Students: The Next Generation. Retrieved on August 17, 2007, from http://www.iste.org/inhouse/nets/cnets/index.html.

Green, K.C. (2007). Icons of the Internet. The Campus Computing Project. Retrieved on August 17, 2007, from http://www.itpb.ucla.edu/documents/documents/Green-Icons-UCLA-Apr07.pdf.

European Institute for E-Learning. (2007). Retrieved on August 20, 2007, from www.elearning 2006.fi/main.site?action=binary/ file&id=6&fid=72.

Epper, R.M., & Garn, M.(2004). Virtual universities: Real possibilities. *Educause Review*, 39(2): 28-39. Retrieved on August 18, 2007, from http://www.educause.edu/ir/library/pdf/erm0422.pdf.

Lenhardt, A., & Madden, M. (2005). Teen content creators and consumers. Washington, DC: Pew Internet and American Life Project. Retrieved on August 20, 2007, from http://www.pewm-ternet.org/PPF/r/166/report_display.asp.

Briggs, T.W. (2007). 15 years after birth, book's not closed on texting. *USA Today*. Retrieved on September 9, 2007, from http://www.usatoday.com/tech/news/2007-09-03-texting-language_N.htm?csp=34.

National School Board Association. (2007). Creating & connecting: Research and guidelines on online social—and educational—networking. Retrieved on September 12, 2007, from http://www.nsba.org/site/docs/41400/41340.pdf.

Shift Happens. (2007). Retrieved on August 17, 2007, from http://www.youtube.com/shifthappens.

4. Larson, E.L.C.(2007). A case study exploring the "new literacies" during a fifth-grade electronic reading workshop. Retrieved on August 20, 2007, from dle/2097/352.

   Waldman, J.A. (2007). Acknowledging criteria: A look at research and reality of children's digital libraries. Retrieved on August 20, 2007, from http://etd.ils.unc.edu:8080/dspace/handle/1901/398?mode=simple.

5. Goldberg, A., Russell, M., & Cook, A. (2003). The effect of computers on student writing: A meta-analysis of studies from 1992 to 2002. *Journal of Technology, Learning, and Assessment, 2(1)*. Available from http://www.jtla.org.

6. Desmet, C., Griffin, J., Miller, D.C., Balthazor, R., & Cummings, R. (forthcoming). Revisioning revision with e-Portfolios in the University of Georgia First-year composition program. In D. Cambridge, B. Cambridge, and K. Yancey (Eds.), *Electronic Portfolios 2.0: Emergent Findings and Shared Questions*. Washington, DC: Stylus Publishing.

   Eynon, B. (forthcoming).The LaGuardia ePortfolio. In D. Cambridge, B. Cambridge, and K. Yancey (Eds.), *Electronic Portfolios 2.0: Emergent Findings and Shared Questions*. Washington, DC: Stylus Publishing.

7. Carmichael, S., & Alden, P. (2006). The advantages of using electronic processes for commenting on and exchanging the written work of students with learning disabilities and/or AD/HD. *Composition Studies, 34(2): 43–57*.

   Goldberg, A., Russell, M., & Cook (2003). The effect of computers on student writing: A meta-analysis of studies from 1992–2000. *Journal of Technology, Learning & Assessment*, 2(1): 1-51.

   Hertz-Lazarowitz, R., & Bar-Natan, I.(2002). Writing development of Arab and Jewish students using cooperative learning (CL) and computer-mediated communication (CMC). *Computers and Education, 39*(1): 19–36.

   Hewett, B. (2000). Characteristics of interactive oral and computer-mediated peer group talk and its influence on revision. *Computers and Composition, 17*(3): 265–288.

   Koehler, M. Yadar , A., & Phillips, M. (2005). What is video good for? Examining how media and story genre intersect. *Journal of Educational Multimedia and Hypermedia, 14*(3): 249–272.

   Lundell, D. (2000). Developing writers, developing professionals: Graduate students bridging theory and practice in basic writing. *Research and Teaching in Developmental Education, 16*(2): 43–53.

8. Partnership for 21st-Century Skills (2006). Are they really ready to work? Employers' perspectives on the basic knowledge and applied skills of new entrants to the 21st-Century U.S. workforce.

   Retrieved on August 12, 2007, from http://www.21stcenturyskills.org/Final_Report_PDF09-29-06. Partnership for 21st-Century Skills (2007). Framework for 21st-Century Learning. Retrieved on August 13, 2007, from http://www.21stcenturyskills.org/documents/frame-workflyer_072307.pdf.

   ETS iSkills.(2007). Retrieved on August 12, 2007, from http://www.ets.org/portal/site/ets/menuitem.435c0b5cc7bd0ae7015d9510c 3921509/?vgnext.

9. Wells, J., & Lewis, L. (2006). Fast/Facts: Internet Access in U.S. Public Schools and Classrooms: 1994–2005 (NCES 2007-020). U.S. Department of Education. Washington, DC: National Center for

Education Statistics. Retrieved on July 30, 2007, from http://nces.ed.gov/fastfacts/display.asp7idM6Wells.

National Telecommunications and Information Administration. (1999). Falling through the Net: Defining the digital divide. Washington, DC: U.S. Department of Commerce. Retrieved on July 18, 2007, from http://www.ntia.doc.gov/ntiahome/fttn99/appendix. html#e.

Norris, C., Sullivan, T., Poirot, J., & Soloway, E. (2003). No access, no use, no impact: Snapshot surveys of educational technology in K–12. *Journal of Research on Computing in Education,* 36(1): 15–28.

Grunwald Associates (2003). Connected to the future: A report on children's Internet use from the Corporation for Public Broadcasting. Retrieved on July 18, 2007, from http://www.cpb.org/stations/reports/connected/connected_report.pdf.

Wells, J., and Lewis, L. (2006). Internet access in U.S. public schools and classrooms: 1994–2005 (NCES 2007-020). U.S. Department of Education. Washington, DC: National Center for Education Statistics. Retrieved on August 3,2007, from http://nces.ed.gov/pubs2007/2007020.pdf.

10. Kajder, S. (2005). Not quite teaching for real: Preservice secondary English teachers' use of technology in the field following completion of an instructional technology methods course. *Journal of Computers in Teacher Education,* 22(1): 15–33.

Web-based Education Commission (2000). The power of the internet for learning: Moving from promise to practice. Retrieved on August 18, 2007, from http://www.hpcnet.org/webcommission.

11. Edwards, S., & Bruce, C.(2000). Reflective Internet searching, an action research model. In Ortrun Zuber-Skerrit (Ed.). *Action learning, action research and process management. Theory, practice,* praxis. Action Research Unit, Griffith University, 5th World Congress of Action Learning, Action Research, and Process Management, University of Ballarat,Victoria, September, pp. 141–152.

Fitzgerald, M., & Galloway, C. (2001). Helping students use digital libraries effectively. *Teacher Librarian,* 29(1): 8–14.

12. Whithaus, C. (2005). *Teaching and evaluating writing in the age of computers and high-stakes testing.* Mahwah, NJ: Erlbaum.

13. Keddie, A. (2004). Research with young children: The use of an affinity group approach to explore the social dynamics of peer culture. *British Journal of Sociology of Education,* 25(1): 35–51.

14. Borja, R.R. (2005). 'Blogs' catching on as tool for instruction. *Education Week,* 25(15): 1,17.

Heath, M. (2002). Electronic portfolios for reflective self-assessment. *Teacher Librarian,*30(1): 19.

15. Wright, V.H., Stallworth, B.J., & Ray, B.(2002). Challenges of electronic portfolios: Student perceptions and experiences. *Journal of Technology and Teacher Education,* 20(1): 49–61.

16. Bangert-Drowns, R., & Swan, K. (1997). Electronic texts and literacy for the 21st century. *English Update: A Newsletter from the Center on English Learning and Achievement,* 6–8. Retrieved from ERIC Database, August 1, 2007.

17. Siegle, D. (2007). Podcasts and blogs: Learning opportunities on the information highway. *Gifted Child Today, 30(3):* 14–19.

18. "MySpace gainstop ranking of US Web sites" Reuters, July 11, 2006. Retrieved on August 9, 2006.

19. Second Life (2007) Education. Retrieved on August 18, 2007, from http://secondlife.com/businesseducation/education.php.

Foster, A.L. (2007) Professor Avatar. *Chronicle of Higher Education.* Retrieved on September 17, 2007, from http://chronicle. com/weekly/v54/i04/04a02401.htm?=attn.

20. Semantic Web Education and Outreach Interest Group. (2007). W3C semantic Web frequently-asked questions. Retrieved on August 13, 2007, from http://www.w3.org/2001/sw/SW-FAQ #swgoals.

21. Waldman, J.L (2007).

22. Borja, R.R. (2006, April). Educators experiment with student-written 'wikis'. Education Week, 25(30): 10.

23. "Google closes $2B YouTube deal," Reuters. Retrieved on November 14, 2006.

Rethinking Online Reading Assessment

■ ■ ■ ■ ■

Online and offline reading tap different skills. Assessment techniques must take those differences into account.

—Julie Coiro

Although the No Child Left Behind legislation makes it virtually impossible for schools to avoid thinking about how to measure reading comprehension, few educators or policymakers have considered how Internet technologies affect conventional thinking about reading assessment. Even fewer have tackled the issue of how schools might reliably measure the new skills required to comprehend online text.

Over the last seven years, as a member of the New Literacies Research Team (see www.newliteracies.uconn.edu/team.html), I have analyzed recordings of hundreds of adolescents engaged in reading for information on the Internet. Preliminary evidence from these analyses reveals that reading comprehension on the Internet differs from traditional reading comprehension in at least five important ways. Let's examine these differences and consider how teachers might expand their range of reading assessment practices to capture the skills and strategies students need to comprehend information in the digital age.

Difference 1. Students need new skills

A typical book-based reading assignment asks students to read a common text, answer questions about the main ideas, and respond to these ideas through writing, art, or class discussion. In contrast, a typical Internet-based reading assignment requires students to generate appropriate search requests, sift through disparate sources to locate their own texts, synthesize the most reliable and relevant information within those texts, and respond with online communication tools such as an e-mail message or blog post. Sifting through a vast field of information to find the best sources becomes integral to the reading task.

To complete online reading assignments well, students need new skills beyond those currently measured by standardized tests of offline reading comprehension (Coiro, 2007). In addition to using conventional knowledge of vocabulary and informational text structures, skilled online readers can efficiently use search engines, navigate multilayered Website, and monitor the appropriateness of their pathway through a complex network of connected text (Coiro & Dobler, 2007). Moreover, high scores on some online reading tasks correlate weakly with high scores on a standardized test of traditional reading comprehension skills (see Leu et al., 2008). Cases are emerging in which a high-achieving offline reader appears to be a low-achieving online reader and vice versa. In other words, we can no longer assume that a standardized assessment of a student's offline reading comprehension ability will adequately measure important skills that influence online reading performance.

Julie Coiro is Assistant Professor of Reading at the University of Rhode Island; jcoiro@snet.net.

So, how might teachers determine which students are proficient in online reading and which students require more support? One suggestion is to incorporate curriculum-based measures of online reading ability into classroom assessment practices. These measures, called *online reading comprehension assessments* (or ORCAs) are more than compilations of static reading passages and multiple-choice questions transferred into a Web-based environment. A curriculum-based ORCA is designed to capture "real-time" online reading skills and strategies.

My colleagues and I piloted a series of six ORCAs with hundreds of U.S. seventh graders in language arts and science classrooms. We found these assessments collected valid, reliable scores of online reading comprehension performance (Coiro, Castek, Henry, & Malloy, 2007).

What does a curriculum-based online reading comprehension assessment look like? Generally, an ORCA engages individual students in a series of three to four related information requests posted in an online quiz interface. Students toggle between the online quiz and the open Internet, where they locate, critically evaluate, and synthesize the requested information or share ideas using such tools as e-mail, blogs, or wikis.

Figure 1 shows a series of online reading tasks integrated into "ORCA-Iditarod," an online reading comprehension assessment that might be used during a middle-school unit on the Iditarod sled dog races in Alaska. You can explore the online version of this assessment at www.surveymonkey.com/s.aspx?sm=nA_2bGnBO2W8OlNmaQQWo0sA_3d_3d.

Teachers can use software like Camtasia (www.techsmith.com/camtasia.asp) or I Show U (http://store.shinywhitebox.com/home/home.html) to create a video recording of students' actions and voices while they complete the ORCA, just as if the teacher were watching over their shoulders. An online tool such as Quia (www.quia.com) or Survey Monkey (www.surveymonkey.com) can automatically compile student responses. Teachers can play back the video recordings to better understand how students accomplish or struggle with online reading comprehension tasks.

To develop this kind of assessment, teachers should begin with a curriculum-based unit of study, such as homelessness or human body systems. Construct short challenges within the online quiz interface that direct students to locate, evaluate, synthesize, and communicate information online (for example, "Use the Internet to locate the record time for the Iditarod dog sled race and who set it. Report your answer, tell where you found it, and explain how you know the information is accurate").

To complete this task, students must (1) locate relevant information using a search engine, (2) verify information with at least one other source, (3) efficiently communicate electronic Web addresses so the receiver can quickly return to the appropriate location, and (4) critically evaluate the information's accuracy.

Other fruitful tasks are to explore a Website to determine the author's purpose and how that purpose might influence the site's claims. Asking questions like, Does the site provide factual information? or Does the site try to sell you something? helps students gauge author intent. (See www.ascd.org/ASCD/pdf/journals/ed_lead/el200903_coiro_author_intent.pdf for a sample activity investigating a Website's purpose.) You might have students read and respond to posts representing multiple viewpoints on a simulated online discussion board.

Difference 2. Dispositions toward the Internet affect online reading abilities

Positive attitudes about reading on the Internet are key to learning in a digital age. Certain attitudes, self-judgments, and beliefs about the Internet are positively related to effective strategy use when reading challenging online texts. For instance, higher-performing online readers display persistence, flexibility, a healthy sense of skepticism, and confidence as they navigate rapidly changing Internet texts. Lower-performing online readers give up easily and are less open to alternative strategies, less apt to question information they encounter, and less confident in their ability to use the Internet without help (Coiro, 2008; Tsai & Tsai, 2003).

Web 2.0 technologies (such as open-source and social networking sites) and emerging learning standards demand that online readers be personally productive, socially responsible, and able to collaborate with diverse team members both face-to-face and online (American Association of School Librarians, 2007; Partnership for 21st Century Skills, 2007). Accomplished Internet readers are expected to not only gain new knowledge from their reading, but also confidently generate and share knowledge with other members of a globally networked community.

To better understand students' instructional needs in this area, consider having students complete a short survey of their online reading dispositions at various points in the year. Survey items might ask students to rate the value of the Internet for research or its potential—relative to printed information sources—to pique their interest in reading tasks. (See www.ascd.org/ASCD/pdf/journals/ed_lead/el200903_coiro_survey. pdf for a sample survey of online reading dispositions.) Ask students to elaborate on circumstances under which they view themselves as capable Internet readers, as opposed to circumstances that cause anxiety or frustration.

By analyzing responses to these surveys, teachers can identify students who might benefit from guided online reading experiences that will build their confidence or increase their capacity to work collaboratively within electronic communities. For example, a teacher might explicitly show a student who lacks confidence in judging Website authors' expertise how to locate the "About Us" button on Websites and scan the information provided for relevant details about each author's past work experiences. Later, the teacher could designate this student as one of the class experts in online critical evaluation skills and encourage classmates having similar difficulties to seek help from the student. Over time, taking on an "expert" role will foster the student's self-efficacy as a competent online reader.

Difference 3. Students often seek answers on the Internet collaboratively

Anyone who watches a group of students engaged in online research will notice that they often work collaboratively or seek help from others online. Adolescents, in particular, might use instant messaging to quickly share or solicit a Website address or post their question on a blog to learn what others think about the issue before composing a response.

Unfortunately, students' skills at collaborative online inquiry are rarely captured with traditional assessments that evaluate reading performance individually and without online assistance. Teachers need new assessments that capture such 21st-century abilities as strong interpersonal communication skills, an understanding of what kind of team dynamics foster high-quality outcomes, an appreciation of differences in cultural practices and work patterns, and the ability to respond appropriately to peer feedback (Afflerbach, 2007; Partnership for 21st Century Skills, 2007).

Although there are few existing models to guide future efforts in this area, schools should at least begin to consider alternative measures that evaluate group collaboration and productivity and readers' ability to seek help from a globally networked community. School leaders might benefit, for example, from discussing the theoretical and practical issues involved in designing, using, and interpreting scores on assessments of group collaboration (see Webb, 1995). In addition, members of New Zealand's University of Teaching Development Centre (2004) provide a useful list of critical questions and guidelines to consider before finalizing a program assessing student group work.

Difference 4. Reading processes should inform reading instruction

Among skilled online readers, a typical product from a reading session includes a synthesis of relevant and reliable information gleaned from two or three Websites as well as a set of Website addresses (URLs) that accurately refer to the information's sources—in other words, a trail of effective processes. However, the process trails of students who have difficulty reading online are more often an uninformative sentence like, "I couldn't find anything about that."

A useful alternative strategy is to play back certain students' online video recordings to access real-time data about what they were doing (for example, generating keywords or navigating among Websites) when their online reading comprehension began to break down. View examples of online reading videos at www.newliteracies.uconn.edu/reading.html and www.newliteracies.uconn.edu/coirodissertation.

A quick review of these online recordings, for instance, highlights the fact that many adolescents do not actually use a search engine or type in keywords to launch an online query. Instead, they use a ".com strategy"; they type a whole question or phrase into the address bar at the top of an Internet browser, add ".com" to the end, and hope for the best. Similarly, process data reveals three disturbing trends: (1) many students don't look down the page of search engine results; they just click on the first link; (2) although students sometimes attempt to locate information about a Website's authors to evaluate their level of authority, they often give up when they can't find such information easily; and (3) some students—apparently unaware of simple copy/paste strategies for transferring Website addresses from one location to another—retype lengthy URLs letter by letter, which often leads to mistakes.

When teachers spot such processing errors, they get key information that helps them better understand which online reading skills and strategies their students struggle with. This information provides a specific reference point for where in the online reading process a group of students, or one reader in particular, needs the most support. In an age of data-informed instruction, we do a disservice to our students by not using readily available technologies to help determine how we can best prepare them for the challenges of Internet reading.

Difference 5. The nature of reading comprehension is changing because of digital technology

The ultimate challenge in assessing online reading comprehension is that online texts, tools, and reading contexts will continue to change rapidly as new technologies emerge. Until recently, definitions of reading comprehension were grounded in at least 20 years of theory and research that informed educators' thinking about how to measure reading comprehension. Although new comprehension theories and practices have certainly emerged over the years, few have altered the nature of literacy as quickly as the Internet and other digital communication technologies are doing. To help students realize their potential as citizens in a digital age, we need to continually reconsider and expand what it means to be a skilled online reader. Subsequent revision and reconfiguration of online reading comprehension measures will need to realistically keep pace.

Obviously, changes in online texts and their associated reading comprehension practices will make it extremely difficult to establish the reliability of scores over time or the validity of scores from one online reading context to the next. But rapidly changing technological innovations will make it easier for teachers to collect, score, and interpret data in practical ways that inform classroom instruction. For example, a computer-based assessment program might soon be able to process electronic scores from an ORCA to generate graphical maps showing how a student's performance in each dimension of online reading comprehension evolves over the year.

So, how should educators move forward with attempts to measure online reading comprehension in a climate of constant change? One idea might be to consider new types of adaptive assessment designs that enable teachers to easily revise portions of assessments of online reading like the ORCA described here rather than design an entirely new measure. A second strategy might be to encourage policy-makers and measurement specialists to grapple more deeply with issues of reliable and valid assessments of reading in a digital age.

But, while we're waiting for test designers and policymakers to pay attention, I recommend that we accept the inevitability of change and think more creatively about how to measure literacy and learning with online reading as part of the picture. Yes, this type of thinking is difficult. But as teachers tackle these new challenges, we should model the kind of flexible, collaborative problem solving we hope students will adopt to help them tackle a rapidly changing digital world.

REFERENCES

Afflerbach, P. (2007). *Understanding and using reading assessment.* Newark, DE: International Reading Association.

American Association of School Librarians. (2007). *AASL standards for the 21st century learner.* Chicago: Author. Available: www.ala.org/ala/mgrps/divs/aasl/aasl-proftools/learningstandards/standards.cfm

Coiro, J. (2007). *Exploring changes to reading comprehension on the Internet: Paradoxes and possibilities for diverse adolescent readers.* Unpublished doctoral dissertation. University of Connecticut, Storrs. Available: www.newliteracies.uconn.edu/coirodissertation

Coiro, J. (2008, December). *Exploring the relationship between online reading comprehension, frequency of Internet use, and adolescents' dispositions toward reading online.* Paper presented at the annual meeting of the National Reading Conference, Orlando, FL.

Coiro, J., Castek, J., Henry, L., & Malloy, J. (2007, December). A closer look at measures of online reading achievement and school engagement with seventh graders in economically challenged school districts. In D. Reinking (Chair), *Developing Internet comprehension strategies among adolescent students at risk to become dropouts: A three-year IES research grant.* A symposium presented at the annual meeting of the National Reading Conference, Austin, TX. Available: www.new literacies.uconn.edu/iesproject/documents/NRC2007AssessmentPaper.doc

Coiro, J., & Dobler, E. (2007). Exploring the comprehension strategies used by sixth-grade skilled readers as they search for and locate information on the Internet. *Reading Research Quarterly, 42,* 214–257.

Leu, D. J., Zawilinski, L., Castek, J., Banerjee, M., Housand, B., Liu, Y., et al. (2008). What is new about the new literacies of online reading comprehension? In A. Berger, L. Rush, & J. Eakle (Eds.), *Secondary school literacy: What research reveals for classroom practices* (pp. 37–68). Chicago, IL: National Council of Teachers of English.

Partnership for 21st Century Skills. (2007). Life and career skills. *Route 21.* Tucson, AZ: Author. Available: www.21stcenturyskills.org/route21/index.php?option=com_content&view=article&id=11&Itemid =11

Tsai, M-J., & Tsai, C-C. (2003). Information searching strategies in Web-based science learning: The role of Internet self-efficacy. *Innovations in Education and Teaching International, 40,* 43–50.

University of Teaching Development Centre. (2004). *Group work and group assessment: UTDC guidelines.* Victoria, New Zealand: University of Wellington. Available: www.utdc.vuw.ac.nz/resources/guidelines/GroupWork.pdf

Webb, N. M. (1995). Group collaboration in assessment: Multiple objectives, processes, and outcomes. *Educational Evaluation and Policy Analysis, 17,* 239–261.

CLASSROOM IMPLICATIONS

1. To what extent do you agree or disagree with the differences between online and traditional reading comprehension that Coiro outlined? Which seems most important to you? Why?

2. What do you think about the idea that we often seek answers collaboratively in online settings (her difference #3)?

3. What might an alternative assessment that evaluates the group's collaboration and productivity and ability to seek help from a "globally networked community" look like?

4. Consider the myths and realities presented in the NCTE Policy Research Brief: do any surprise you? The brief acknowledges a rise in technology use, both in school and at home, while also pointing out that most teachers do not bring their computer knowledge into the classroom (and that two-thirds of teachers feel unprepared for using technology in teaching). What is needed in order for teachers to feel more prepared? Develop some practical solutions schools could implement.

FOR FURTHER READING

Anderson, R., & Balajathy, E. (2009). Stories about struggling readers and technology. *The Reading Teacher, 62*(6), 540–542. doi: 10.1598/RT.62.6.9

Brozo, W. G., & Puckett, K. (2008). *Supporting content area literacy with technology: Meeting the needs of diverse learners.* Boston, MA: Allyn & Bacon.

Coiro, J. (2009). Promising practices for supporting adolescents' online literacy development. In K.D. Wood and W.E. Blanton (Eds.), *Promoting literacy with adolescent learners: Research-based instruction* (pp. 442–471). New York, NY: Guilford Press.

Considine, D., Horton, J., & Moorman, G. (2009). Teaching and reading the millennial generation through media literacy. *Journal of Adolescent & Adult Literacy, 52*(6), 471–481. doi:10.1598/JAAL.52.6.2

Drouin, M., & Davis, C. (2009). R u texting? Is the use of text speak hurting your literacy? *Journal of Literacy Research, 41,* 46–67. doi: 10.1080/10862960802695131

Larson, L.C. (2009). Reader response meets new literacies: Empowering readers in online learning communities. *The Reading Teacher, 62*(8), 638–648. doi: 10.1598/RT.62.8.2

Lawrence, S.A., McNeal, K., & Yildiz, M.N. (2009). Summer program helps merge technology, popular culture, reading, and writing for academic purposes. *Journal of Adolescent & Adult Literacy, 52*(6), 483–494. doi: 10.1598/JAAL.52.6.3

Meyer, B.J.F., Wijekumar, K., Middlemiss, W., Higley, K., Lei, P., Meier, C., & Spielvogel, J. (2010). Web-based tutoring of the structure strategy with or without elaborated feedback or choice for fifth- and seventh-grade readers. *Reading Research Quarterly, 45*(1), 62–92. doi: 10.1598/RRQ.45.1.4

O'Brien, D., & Scharber, C. (2010). Teaching old dogs new tricks: The luxury of digital abundance. *Journal of Adolescent & Adult Literacy, 53*(7), 600–603. doi: 10.1598/JAAL.53.7.7

Tarasiuk, T.J. (2010). Combining traditional and contemporary texts: Moving my English class to the computer lab. *Journal of Adolescent & Adult Literacy, 53*(7), 543–552.

Turner, K.H. (2009). Flipping the switch: Code-switching from text speak to standard English. *English Journal, 98*(5), 60–65.

Wells, J., & Lewis, L. (2006). Internet Access in U.S. Public Schools and Classrooms: 1994–2005 (NCES 2007-020). U.S. Department of Education. Washington, DC: National Center for Education Statistics.

ONLINE RESOURCES

IRA's Technology in Literacy Education Special Interest Group (TILE)
http://www.reading.org/General/AdvocacyandOutreach/SIGS/TechnologySIG.aspx

IRA Position Statement on New Literacies and 21st-Century Technologies
http://www.reading.org/General/AboutIRA/PositionStatements/21stCenturyLiteracies.aspx

9 Writing

By the usual method of teaching to write, the art of writing is totally distinct from reading or spelling. On the new plan, spelling and writing are connected and equally blended with reading.

—Joseph Lancaster (1808)

Children's early written products resemble spoken language, but the complexity of the written productions increases steadily through the elementary school years.

—Albert J. Harris and Edward R. Sipay (1990)

. . . writing is a powerful ally and aid to reading. From the very beginning, students need to engage frequently in activities in which reading and writing are paired....

—Michael Graves, Connie Juel, and Bonnie Graves (2007)

Research on Writing Instruction

Unlike reading, for which an abundance of research evidence is available, writing suffers from a dearth of research; some would say neglect. However, a report of the Carnegie Corporation (Graham & Perin, 2007) identifies eleven elements of instruction for teaching children in the upper elementary grades and higher. These are:

1. **Writing Strategies**, which involves teaching students strategies for planning, revising, and editing their compositions.
2. **Summarization**, which involves explicitly and systematically teaching students how to summarize texts.
3. **Collaborative Writing,** which uses instructional arrangements in which adolescents work together to plan, draft, revise, and edit their compositions.
4. **Specific Product Goals**, which assigns students specific, reachable goals for the writing they are to complete.
5. **Word Processing**, which uses computers and word processors as instructional supports for writing assignments.
6. **Sentence Combining**, which involves teaching students to construct more complex, sophisticated sentences.
7. **Prewriting**, which engages students in activities designed to help them generate or organize ideas for their composition.
8. **Inquiry Activities**, which engages students in analyzing immediate, concrete data to help them develop ideas and content for a particular writing task.
9. **Process Writing Approach**, which interweaves a number of writing instructional activities in a workshop environment that stresses extended writing opportunities, writing for authentic audiences, personalized instruction, and cycles of writing.

10. **Study of Models**, which provides students with opportunities to read, analyze, and emulate models of good writing.
11. **Writing for Content Learning**, which uses writing as a tool for learning content material. (Graham & Perin, 2007, pp. 4–5)

The Carnegie Report may be downloaded free of charge. See the Online Resources section of this chapter for details.

AS YOU READ

Michael Moore, Editor of NCTE's journal, *English Education*, is a national authority on approaches to writing instruction and assessment. He wrote this article at our request, and it captures the chronology of how these approaches have evolved. We think readers will appreciate not only his insights, but also his personal experiences and honest admissions about his own teaching. In addition, we include an article discussing current issues in writing instruction. In their article, Applebee and Langer review data and trends from the National Assessment of Educational Progress (NAEP) and highlight both positive and negative trends and statistics over the course of the last two decades. They conclude with a call for teachers to teach beyond the type of writing required for success on high-stakes assessments, and instead to engage in discussions about the writing demands their students will need for success beyond the classroom. As you read, aim for an integrated perspective on how the trends in writing instruction have evolved and how and why they have championed different approaches to instruction.

REFERENCES

Adams, M. J. (1990). *Beginning to read: Thinking and learning about print.* Cambridge, MA: MIT Press.

Cunningham, P. M., & Allington, R. L. (2007). *Classrooms that work: They can all read and write* (3rd ed.). Boston, MA: Pearson, Allyn & Bacon.

Graves, M. F., Juel, C., & Graves, B. (2007). *Teaching reading in the 21st century* (4th ed.). Boston, MA: Allyn & Bacon.

Harris, A. J., & Sipay, E. R. (1990). *How to increase reading ability: A guide to developmental & remedial methods* (9th ed.). New York, NY: Longman.

Kear, D. J., Coffman, G. A., & McKenna, M. C. (1997, December). *Students' attitudes toward writing: A national survey.* Paper presented at the meeting of the National Reading Conference, Scottsdale, AZ.

Lancaster, J. (1808). *Improvements in education.* London: J. Lancaster.

What Is Happening in the Teaching of Writing?

ARTHUR N. APPLEBEE AND JUDITH A. LANGER
University at Albany, State University of New York

■ ■ ■ ■ ■

It has been almost 30 years since the last systematic look at writing instruction in middle schools and high schools in the United States (Applebee, *Writing*). Since that report, there have been a number of significant changes in the contexts in which we teach and in which our students learn to write. In the larger culture, the technologies for creating written text have changed from electric typewriters to word processors and a plethora of related tools. In a related development, Internet search engines and the resources to which they lead have become a primary source for information from the mundane to the exotic. The context of schooling has also changed, with programs and practices affected most directly by an emphasis on standards and assessments as part of a growing concern with accountability. Given a focus on reading, rather than writing or literacy more generally, by the No Child Left Behind Act (NCLB), this movement has had an impact on teaching and learning at all levels of public education. It has also led to reemphasis of the importance of professional "capacity"—and on the continuing development of teachers' knowledge and expertise to be sure that such capacity exists.

Amid all of these changes, it is time for those of us concerned about the teaching of English to take stock of the state of writing instruction and to ask, What has been happening to the teaching and learning of writing in American schools? How have these changes, particularly the emphasis on reading rather than literacy more broadly, influenced the ways in which writing instruction is offered by teachers and experienced by students, across the curriculum? Fully answering these questions will require a new national study of writing instruction, a project that is currently underway as part of a collaboration between the Center on English Learning and Achievement and the National Writing Project. Check our website (http://www.albany.edu/cela) for updates as that study progresses.

Before gathering new data, we began by examining information available from the National Assessment of Educational Progress (NAEP; Applebee and Langer). During the spring of 2007, the U.S. Department of Education released the latest results from its periodic assessments of the writing achievement of American school children. Stretching back to the 1969–1970 school year, NAEP, also known as the Nation's Report Card, gathers background data about teachers' and students' perceptions of curriculum and instruction as well as measuring student performance. It thus provides some interesting perspectives on changes over time in writing instruction as well as in writing achievement.

How Well Do Students Write?

NAEP assesses students' writing achievement with an extensive set of on-demand writing tasks developed through a consensus process involving teachers, administrators, and scholars from around the country. Assessments may include 20 to 25 different tasks at each grade level, designed to assess students' abilities to write imaginatively, persuasively, and informatively, including the ability to analyze and synthesize. In emphasis, the NAEP tasks parallel the writing components of many state assessments, but the national sampling plan allows more tasks to be assessed each year than any state or district is able to include in their assessments. Each student response is scored using a focused holistic rubric that includes components for purpose, audience, idea development/support, organization/structure, sentence structure, word choice, voice, and mechanics. Results across students are pooled statistically to provide estimates of group performance on a standardized writing scale (ranging initially from 0–500), which NAEP uses to estimate performance levels. Aware that on-demand assessment might differ from classroom-based performance, NAEP has also systematically assessed classroom-based writing, with quite similar results (Gentile, Martin-Rehrmann, and Kennedy).

In 2007, between 80% and 90% of middle school and high school students had achieved what NAEP identifies as "basic" writing skills appropriate to their grade level, but only 31% at Grade 8 and 23% at Grade 12 were rated as "proficient." In the NAEP framework, being proficient at Grade 12 means a student is "able to produce an effectively organized and fully developed response within the time allowed [the specific amount of allotted time has varied in recent years from 15 to 50 minutes] that uses analytical, evaluative, or creative thinking. Their writing should include details that support and develop the main idea of the piece, and it should show that these students are able to use precise language and variety in sentence structure to engage the audience they are expected to address" (Loomis and Bourque, 10). Gaps in achievement in 2007 were large, with only 8% of Black twelfth-grade students and 11% of Hispanic twelfth-grade students rated as proficient, compared with 29% of their White peers.

Looking more broadly at NAEP data makes it clear both how deeply ingrained this pattern is and how widespread are the inequities in achievement. Figure 1 summarizes long-term trends in literacy achievement on a 0–500 scale that allows comparisons over time and across grades. The most complete data are for reading achievement across the period 1971–2004 (the last long-term trend reading assessment for which data are available); results for a similar set of measures of writing achievement for the 12-year period from 1984 to 1996 are superimposed on those for reading. Although some year-to-year fluctuations in both reading and writing achievement are statistically significant, the most striking aspect of the chart is how slow changes in performance have been. The youngest students (9-year-olds/Grade 4) showed the greatest gain; 11 points on the 500-point scale over thirty-three years; the oldest students (17-year-olds/Grade 12) showed no change at all, with 13-year-olds in between, with a 4-point gain across this 33-year span of time.

The relatively modest gains for students as a whole mask some significant improvements for historically underachieving subgroups. Across the 29-year span for which data can be disaggregated, the gaps between White students and their Hispanic and Black peers narrowed at all three ages assessed (see Figure 2), although not significantly so for Hispanic 13-year-olds. In general, the progress was greatest at the older ages, with students making better progress than their Hispanic classmates. It is discomforting to note, however, that the gaps that remain are larger than the gains that have been achieved. In the case of Hispanic 13-year-olds, the gap is still some four times as large as the 29-year gain (a 6-point gain with a 24-point gap remaining).

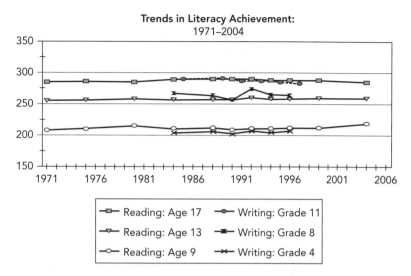

FIGURE 1   Trends in Literacy Achievement: 1971–2004

Source: U.S. Department of Education, Institute of Education Sciences, National Center for Education Statistics, National Assessment of Educational Progress, Long-Term Trend Assessment in Reading; writing results from Campbell, Voelkl, and Donahue.

		White Average	Black Gap	Hispanic Gap
Age 9	1975	216.6	−35.4	−33.8
	2004	*226.4*	*−26.0*	*−21.1*
	Difference		*9*	*6*
Age 13	1975	262.1	−36.3	−29.6
	2004	*266.0*	*−21.6*	−23.5
	Difference		*15*	*6*
Age 17	1975	293.0	−52.3	−40.5
	2004	292.8	*−29.0*	*−29.2*
	Difference		*23*	*11*

FIGURE 2   Differences in Average Reading Achievement, NAEP Long-Term Trend Results, 1975–2004

Source: U.S. Department of Education, Institute of Education Sciences, National Center for Education Statistics, National Assessment of Educational Progress, Long-Term Trend Assessment in Reading. Figures in italics are statistically significantly different from 1975.

The attempt to maintain a long-term trend line in writing was abandoned after 1996 because there were too few items in the trend assessment to yield accurate results. Because of this, results from the writing assessments after 1996 were reported on a different scale (0–300) that allows comparisons across years but not across grades. Using this scale, shorter-term trends, over the nine years from 1998 to 2007, show significant gains in writing achievement at Grades 8 (6 points) and 12 (4 points), for the nation and for specific subgroups. (Grade 4, which was not included in the 2007 assessment, showed a 5-point gain from 1998 to 2002.) These gains in overall achievement in writing were not matched by reductions in the gaps for Black and Hispanic students or for those eligible for free or reduced-price lunch. The inequities in achievement remain large.

Surprisingly, given the typically high correlation between reading and writing achievement—reflected in the nearly parallel lines in Figure 1—reading achievement has not shown a similar improvement at eighth or twelfth grade during this period, in spite of the focus on reading generated by NCLB. Grade 4 reading, however, does show parallel growth between 1998 and 2002, and continued growth through 2007.

How Much Writing Do Students Do?

In 2002, the College Board established a high-profile National Commission on Writing, which took as one of its premises that the quality of writing must be improved if students are to succeed in college and in life. In their major policy statement, *The Neglected "R": The Need for a Writing Revolution*, the Commission emphasized the importance of devoting more time to writing instruction, recommending that the amount of time that students spend on writing should be at least doubled, and that writing should be assigned across the curriculum. NAEP provides some interesting data related to this issue, including some indication of trends over time.

One set of questions in NAEP long-term trend data asked students about the kinds of writing that they had done for English class during the previous week (see Figures 3 and 4). In 1988, 42% of 13-year-old students (typically Grade 8) reported having written at least one essay, composition, or theme for English; by 2004, this had increased to 62%. Other types of writing also showed significant increases over this 16-year period, including the percentage of students who had written another kind of report, a letter, a

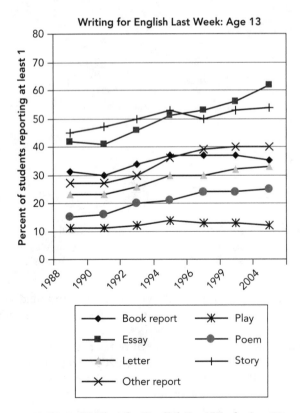

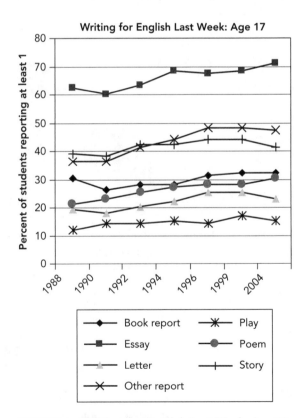

FIGURE 3   Writing for English Last Week: Age 13   FIGURE 4   Writing for English Last Week: Age 17

Source: U.S. Department of Education, Institute of Education Sciences, National Center for Education Statistics, National Assessment of Educational Progress, Long-Term Trend Assessment in Reading.

poem, or a story. At age 17 (Grade 12), 62% of the students in 1988 reported having written an essay, composition, or theme in the past week, which increased to 71% by 2004. Reports for other types of writing also tended to show an increase for 17-year-olds, but the changes were significant only for other reports (which rose from 36% to 47%), plays (from 12% to 15%), and poems (from 21% to 30%).

These results suggest that at least through the 1990s, English teachers were gradually increasing the amount of writing that they were asking students to do. The results also suggest that both expository and imaginative writing benefited to some degree from this increase in emphasis, though by the end of high school, instruction was focused much more narrowly on essay writing.

During this period, teachers also seemed to be raising the stakes a bit on the writing that students were asked to do. Between 1988 and 1998, both teachers and students reported an increase in requirements for longer writing—papers of one or two pages and papers of three pages or more—particularly at Grade 12. This increase seems to have occurred by 1992 and leveled off after that. Even in 1998, however, some 40% of twelfth-grade students reported *never* or *hardly ever* writing papers of three pages or more for their English language arts classes, and 14% were not writing papers of even one or two pages.

Thus, although over the longer term there has been some increase in the writing students are doing, many students seem not to be given assignments requiring writing of any significant length or complexity. This is of particular concern for the college-bound students who will be expected to write even longer papers when they begin their college coursework, as well as for those entering better-paying jobs with higher literacy demands in the workforce (American Diploma Project).

More recent results, however, suggest that these gains may be eroding in the face of an increased emphasis on reading skills, and perhaps also on high-stakes tests in which writing may have little place. Student reports of the types of writing they do "for school" between 2002 and 2007 show a small but significant drop at Grade 8 in the frequency of every type of writing about which students were asked: essays that interpret or analyze (4 percentage points lower for reports of "at least monthly"), letters or essays to persuade others (1 point), a story about personal or imagined experience (3 points), summaries of something read (5 points), observations in a log or journal (3 points), and business writing (e.g., résumé or letter to a company; 2 points).

Over the same five-year period, students in Grade 12 reported far fewer changes: persuasive writing and summaries of readings dropped slightly (2 points), while persuasive writing (3 points) and use of logs or journals (2 points) increased slightly.

These reports from students are reinforced by teachers' reports of their instructional emphases at Grade 8. In both 2002 and 2007, eighth-grade teachers were asked to estimate the percent of time in which their primary instructional focus was on writing, on literary analysis, or on reading skills. Their responses are summarized in Figure 5 and show a small but significant drop in the degree of emphasis on writing, with concomitant increases in the emphasis on the development of reading skills and on literary analysis. (Teacher reports are not available at Grade 12.)

Is There Any Evidence of Writing Across the Curriculum?

Studies of instruction in the early 1980s suggested that while English language arts classes are the most likely to focus on writing, students write more for their other subjects combined than they do for English (Applebee, *Contexts*). This in turn has a significant effect on their development as writers.

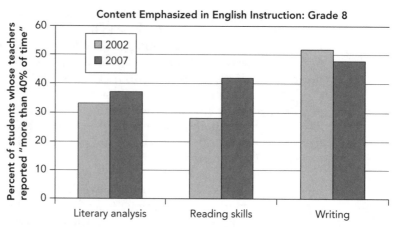

FIGURE 5   Content Emphasized in English Instruction: Grade 8

Source: U.S. Department of Education, Institute of Education Sciences, National Center for Education Statistics, National Assessment of Educational Progress, 2002 and 2007 Writing Assessments.

Student reports on NAEP items suggest that their writing for other subjects continues to represent a substantial part of their total writing experiences. In 2007, 69% of eighth-grade students reported writing of at least paragraph length at least once a week for English, together with 44% for social studies, 30% for science, and 13% for math. Twelfth-grade students reported somewhat more writing for English (77%) and somewhat less for each of the other content areas: 42% for social studies, 21% for science, and 8% for math.

These results on writing in the content areas also show small but significant declines of 2 percentage points in emphasis at Grade 8 between 2002 and 2007 for English, social studies, and science. Twelfth grade again shows a different pattern, with small but significant increases for English (3 percentage points) and social studies (2 points) over this five-year period.

Is Technology Used to Support Writing Instruction?

One of the biggest changes to affect the teaching of writing in the past two decades has been the spread of technology, and with it the development of powerful word-processing software and Internet resources. The National Commission on Writing was enthusiastic about the potential benefits of technology for writing instruction, and reviews of research on the effect of word processing on students' writing achievement support that enthusiasm (Bangert-Drowns; Graham and Perin). In general the use of word-processing software has a positive effect on the development of writing abilities, and particularly so for underachieving students.

The spread of technology is readily apparent in NAEP data. In 1984, 20% or fewer of middle school and high school students reported using computers in their writing; by 1994, over 90% reported doing so (Campbell, Voelkl, and Donahue 191).

After 1996, NAEP began to ask more specific questions about the ways in which computers were being used. Figure 6 summarizes student responses in 2002 and 2007. The majority of eighth- and twelfth-grade students report that they "almost always" use the Internet to look for information to use in a paper or report, with twelfth-grade

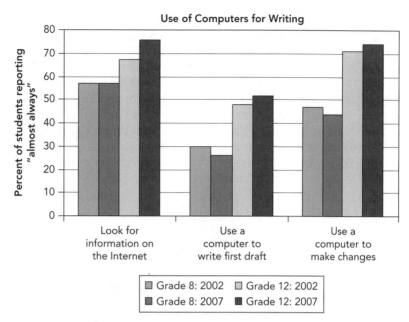

FIGURE 6   Use of Computers for Writing

Source: U.S. Department of Education, Institute of Education Sciences, National Center for Education Statistics, National Assessment of Educational Progress, 2002 and 2007 Writing Assessments.

students being even more likely to do so than eighth-grade students. Interestingly, Internet use to gather information is consistently reported more frequently than is the use of word processing for writing and editing a draft. In fact, in 2007, only 26% of eighth-grade students reported that they "almost always" use a computer from the beginning to write their first draft, though 44% reported using a computer for such editing functions as spell-checking or cutting and pasting. Twelfth-grade students showed a similar pattern, though with more frequent use of the computer for both drafting and revising.

The two grade levels also show quite distinct patterns of change between 2002 and 2007. While twelfth-grade students were more likely to use computers for all three tasks in 2007 than in 2002, eighth-grade students reported slightly but significantly less use of computers for writing drafts and for revising.

There are several different factors contributing to these results. One is certainly the continued spread of computer technology and the increasing availability of computers both in school and at home, which has led to greater use of computer-based tools of all sorts. At the same time, many classrooms do not have computers available at all times for all students, so that much of the time students begin assignments by hand in class, moving their work to a computer after they have already gotten started.

There is still another factor that may be limiting the use of computers at Grade 8: Many high-stakes exams are still given with paper and pencil rather than from a computer-based platform. (NAEP data indicate that even in 2002 some 92% of seventh- or eighth-grade students faced a state exam in English language arts.) This makes some teachers, and indeed some districts, reluctant to allow their students to make regular use of word processing, in case students might find it difficult to make the transition back to paper and pencil in the exam context. Michael Russell and Lisa Abrams, for example, found in a 2001 survey that nationally some 30% of teachers report that they do not use computers when teaching writing because it does not match the format of the state assessment, and 4.4 percent report that school or district policy actually prohibited computer use for the teaching of writing.

Although the impetus for these policies is understandable, they have the perverse effect of limiting students' ability to use the tools that will be required for success in higher education and the world of work, where word processing and computer use are now taken for granted. This problem may be ameliorated in the relatively near future, as large-scale testing, including NAEP, migrates toward computer-based delivery. The framework for the 2011 NAEP writing assessment, for example, calls for eighth-and twelfth-grade students to be assessed with word processors, with access to a variety of commonly available editing tools (Act, Inc., "Writing").

What about Instruction?

Time and attention to writing instruction are not all that is necessary to improve the teaching of writing. What students are taught also matters.

For at least the last twenty-five years, the improvement of writing instruction has emphasized teaching students the skills and strategies needed to write effectively in a variety of contexts and disciplines. Such instruction has typically been called process-oriented and has tended to emphasize extensive prewriting activities, multiple drafts, sharing of work with partners or small groups, and careful attention to writing conventions before sharing with others.

By 1992, process-oriented instruction had become the conventional wisdom, with over 71% of the students at Grade 8 in classrooms where the teacher reported that it was a *central* part of instruction, and another 26% in classrooms using it as a *supplemental* part; results in 1998 were essentially identical. (Comparable data are not available for Grade 12 or for later years.) By 1998, the reported emphasis on process instruction was consistent across subgroups of students defined by race/ethnicity and by eligibility for free or reduced-price lunch.

Although later assessments did not ask teachers about their emphasis on process-oriented instruction, they do include reports from students on how they approached school writing tasks. Overall patterns are quite similar at Grades 8 and 12 in 2007, with more than 60% reporting that they almost always make changes to fix mistakes, and 30% to 40% reporting almost always writing more than one draft. Strategies requiring interaction with others were somewhat less frequent at both grades (brainstorming, 15%; working with others in pairs or small groups, 25% to 28%).

In spite of the overall similarity between Grades 8 and 12, the two groups moved in opposite directions between 2002 and 2007. Eighth-grade students showed small but significant reductions in each of these strategies, reducing their use from 1 to 3 percentage points. The twelfth-grade students reported small increases, again ranging from 1 to 3 percentage points. (The increases were statistically significant for making changes to fix mistakes and for organizing before beginning to write, and trend toward significance for brainstorming with others.) Again, the grade-level differences over time may be related to the greater demands of high-stakes testing facing eighth-grade students, leading to a focus on the production of first and final drafts with less scope for an elaborated writing process.

The changes at Grade 8 in students' reports between 2002 and 2007 are paralleled by changes in the responses from their teachers. The teacher reports showed similar small but significant reductions in asking students to write more than one draft, to plan before they write, and to check proper spelling and grammar.

What students say they do and what they actually do are not always the same. On some of the writing assessments, students were encouraged to use an extra blank page

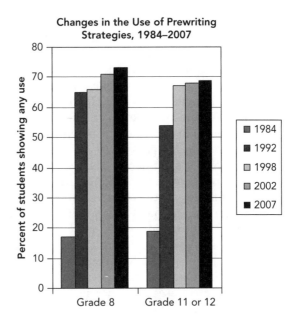

FIGURE 7   Changes in the Use of Prewriting Strategies, 1984–2007

Source: U.S. Department of Education, Institute of Education Sciences, National Center for Education Statistics, National Assessment of Educational Progress, 2002 and 2007 Writing Assessments. Data for 1984 from Applebee, Langer, and Mullis (70); for 1992 from Applebee et al. (181); for 1998 from Greenwald et al. (95).

for planning before they began to write, and these pages were scored for the number of different activities students demonstrated. Over time, the use of this prewriting space for NAEP tasks has changed dramatically (see Figure 7). In 1984, a few of the assignments in the assessment left a blank page for the students to make notes or outlines, but fewer than 20% of Grade 8 or Grade 11 students made use of the space. Since 1992, every task has provided room for prewriting. (From 1998 on, students were also given a separate brochure that emphasized the importance of selected planning and revising strategies.) In these later assessments, many more students made at least some use of the space provided. Even with the differences in test administration, students' tendency to do some overt planning before they begin to write seems to have increased across this 23-year time span.

Are Teachers Engaging in Appropriate Professional Development?

The past twenty years of educational reform have placed a special emphasis on professional development as a way to build instructional "capacity" in schools and districts. This has been accompanied by a movement away from one-shot inservice programs toward longer-term engagement in the development of new strategies and approaches to curriculum and instruction. The National Writing Project, which is cosponsoring our current study of writing instruction, was one of the earliest and has been one of the most successful of these new approaches to professional development.

In 2002, 78% of Grade 8 students and 69% of Grade 12 students were in schools that reported providing professional development experiences to their teachers emphasizing reading and writing processes. Similar proportions (76% at Grade 8 and 72% at Grade 12) were in schools that reported professional development experiences that emphasized language arts across the curriculum. Results in Grade 8 in 2007 show a slight shift, with 4% more reporting professional development was "to a large extent" focused on reading and writing, and 4% fewer reporting it focused to "a large extent" on language arts across the curriculum. Grade 12 responses followed a similar pattern, but the differences were not statistically significant.

Another question asked Grade 8 teachers about the characteristics of the professional development experience that had most influenced their teaching. Interestingly, 78% of the students had teachers who cited an experience that emphasized reading or writing processes. This is testimony to how important understanding of underlying literacy processes is to teachers of English language arts.

At both Grades 8 and 12, the great majority of students in 2002 were in schools in which professional development focused on linking instruction to standards, with slightly greater emphasis at Grade 12 than at Grade 8 (81% versus 88%).

In 2002, the majority (83%) of Grade 8 students had teachers who also agreed that their state's language arts standards support good teaching, although only 50% had teachers who believed that the accompanying state assessments were good measures of their students' language arts achievement, and 62% felt that preparing for and taking the state assessment uses too much instructional time. (These questions were not asked of teachers at Grade 12.)

These data suggest that teachers of English language arts are by and large aware of the potential usefulness of standards and respond positively to professional development experiences that help them support their students' reading and writing processes. However, such learning experiences were not made available to 20%–30% of the teachers surveyed, and the extent and usefulness of the experiences that were provided is unclear. Further, fully half of teachers seem to have perceived a mismatch between their statewide tests and their professional notions of good performance.

This first look at the state of writing instruction through the lens of the National Assessment of Educational Progress leads to a number of conclusions and a great many more questions. Long-term trend data for both writing and reading show a remarkable stability in levels of achievement over time. Despite small ups and downs, by and large, student writing proficiency has remained steady. Gaps between more-advantaged and less-advantaged students also continue, even with the noticeable upturn in writing achievement between 1998 and 2007 at Grade 8, and between 2002 and 2007 at Grade 12. The twelfth-grade upturn may in fact be a cohort effect, with earlier gains at Grade 8 showing up a few years later at Grade 12.

Although a fuller picture using more than one indicator of students' literacy abilities is critical for making decisions about individual students, the NAEP results point to a real and pervasive problem, one that, despite small ups and downs, has remained relatively persistent since NAEP was authorized by Congress in 1969. It is certainly true that the assessment emphasis on on-demand writing is out of alignment with curriculum and instruction that emphasizes an extended process of writing and revision, taps only a subset of the academic skills and knowledge students need, and leaves no room for the technological tools that students increasingly use both in and outside of school. However, it is also true that even given these failings, a consistent message from the NAEP results points to a need for improvement—in the ways in which curriculum and instruction are conceived as well as in how achievement is tested.

Data over time also suggest that there has been some increase in emphasis on writing and the teaching of writing, both in English language arts classrooms and across the curriculum, although this may have begun to decline from its high. Process-oriented writing instruction has dominated teachers' reports at least since 1992, but what teachers mean by this and how it is implemented in their classrooms remains unclear. The consistent emphasis that emerges in teachers' reports may mask considerable variation in actual patterns of instruction (see Langer and Applebee).

What is clear is that even with some increases over time, many students are not writing a great deal for any of their academic subjects, including English, and most are not writing at any length. Some 40% of twelfth-grade students, for example, report never or hardly ever being asked to write a paper of three pages or more. Although short, focused writing is also important, extended writing is necessary to explore ideas or develop arguments in depth. It also reflects the demands that they will face in post-secondary education.

The NAEP data also highlight some external forces that are affecting the teaching of writing, in particular the spread of state standards and accompanying high-stakes tests. In some cases, these may be shifting attention away from a broad program of writing instruction toward a much narrower focus on how best to answer particular types of test questions. Both students and teachers at Grade 8, for example, report small but significant declines in emphasis on a variety of writing processes, which may reflect the importance of short, on-demand writing on high-stakes tests. Teachers at Grade 8 also report a shift in overall emphasis in their use of instructional time away from writing toward reading.

Advances in technology have made word-processing tools and Internet resources widely available, and students report making extensive use of them in their writing. At the same time, new genres and forms of publication have emerged that integrate a variety of media and capitalize on the flexibility of hypertext. From instant messages to Web pages to blogs to embedded graphics and videos, these changes are certainly having an impact on students' writing experiences, although they do not yet appear in NAEP. We do not know the extent to which students have opportunities to engage with the wealth of data available through technology as input for their writing nor the frequency with which they use various unimodal or multimodal technologies to carry out school tasks. Even the use of word processors for drafting and revising may be less prevalent in schools than might be expected, as a byproduct of limited availability of the necessary technology as well as in response to testing programs that emphasize paper-and-pencil assessments.

Education has been high on the nation's agenda since at least the mid-1990s with the national standards movement, followed by NCLB. But where has this taken us? We are living in an educational era in which reading is often considered content-free, where mathematics and science skills and content knowledge rather than ways to think about that content still predominate (although the standards in both subjects call for a broader focus on problem solving and communication skills), and where writing seems to have evaporated from public concern. In an article in *Education Week*, Kathleen Kennedy Manzo reported that high school students who aspire to attend college will likely be unprepared to tackle the complex reading and writing tasks they will encounter. A large part of the article was based on a 2006 ACT report that only 51% of the ACT test takers who wished to attend colleges met ACT's college benchmarks in reading (Act, Inc., *Reading*). Along with interview comments by experts across the country, Manzo concludes that although there is a rush to bolster math and science, there is reason for concern that reading and writing (and their role in content learning) will be "left out of the mix" (1). Despite national concern for overall student achievement, the analyses of NAEP data reported here suggest that writing may already be dropping from attention.

English teachers can take these results as both a warning and a call. They warn us that one major aspect of the English curriculum has unwittingly been given short shrift, and that one aspect of our mission may be receding without our notice. The findings also provide a call. While aligning instruction with standards has become an ongoing activity in many schools, this needs to be done with a special eye to what is happening in writing, including awareness of the frequency, length, and types of writing students are asked to do, as well as the various technologies they employ when doing so. Knowing that our assessments do not test all that students need to know and be able to do, NAEP results can be seen as a call for English teachers across the country to enter into professional discussions about the writing skills and knowledge students will need to do well at school, in higher education, and on the job. Although it is important for students to do well on high-stakes tests, it is our professional obligation to ensure they become the writers they will need to be as they leave our secondary schools at the cusp of lives as adults and citizens.

NOTE

The preparation of this article has been funded by the National Writing Project, the College Board, and the Spencer Foundation as part of the National Study of Writing Instruction.

Except as otherwise noted, the data in this article are drawn from NAEP's online data analysis system, the NAEP Data Explorer (http://nces.ed.gov/nationsreportcard/naep-data/). This system generates customized tables based on a variety of background variables generated at student, teacher, school, and community levels, including tests of the statistical significance of differences between groups or over time. Two different sets of NAEP data are available. For the long-term trend assessment, students respond to exactly the same items over time in targeted subject areas at ages 9, 13, and 17. Cross-sectional assessments provide point-in-time data with a shifting pool of items for both achievement and background variables. Results cited in the present article focus on public schools in the nation as a whole.

WORKS CITED

ACT, Inc. *Reading between the Lines: What the ACT Reveals about College Readiness in Reading.* Iowa City: ACT, 2006. 6 January 2009 <http://www.act.org/research/policymakers/pdf/reading_report.pdf>

———. "Writing Framework for the 2011 National Assessment of Educational Progress (Pre-Publication Edition)." Washington: National Assessment Governing Board, 2007. 6 January 2009 <http://www.nagb.org/publications/frameworks.htm>

American Diploma Project. *Ready or Not: Creating a High School Diploma That Counts.* Washington: Achieve, Inc., 2004. 6 January 2009 <http://www.achieve.org/files/ADPreport_7.pdf>.

Applebee, Arthur N. *Contexts for Learning to Write: Studies of Secondary School Instruction.* Norwood: Ablex, 1984.

———. *Writing in the Secondary School: English and the Content Areas.* Urbana, IL: NCTE, 1981.

Applebee, Arthur N., and Judith A. Langer. *The State of Writing Instruction in America's Schools: What Existing Data Tell Us.* Albany, NY: Center on English Learning & Achievement, University at Albany, 2006.

Applebee, Arthur N., Judith A. Langer, and I. V. S. Mullis. *Writing Trends across the Decade, 1974–1984.* Princeton, NJ: NAEP, 1986.

Applebee, Arthur N., et al. *NAEP 1992 Writing Report Card.* Washington, DC: U.S. Government Printing Office for the National Center for Education Statistics, U.S. Department of Education, 1994.

Bangert-Drowns, Robert L. "The Word Processor as an Instructional Tool: A Meta-Analysis of Word Processing in Writing Instruction." *Review of Educational Research* 63.1 (1993): 69–93.

Campbell, Jay R., Kristin E. Voelkl, and Patricia L. Donahue. *NAEP 1996 Trends in Academic Progress.* Washington: National Center for Education Statistics, 1997. 6 Jan. 2009 <http://www.eric.ed.gov/ERICDocs/data/ericdocs2sql/content_storage_01/0000019b/80/14/f4/66.pdf>

Gentile, Claudia, James Martin-Rehrmann, and John H. Kennedy. *Windows into the Classroom: NAEP's 1992 Writing Portfolio Study* (No. 23-FR-06). Washington, DC: U.S. Department of Education, 1995.

Graham, Steve, and Dolores Perin. *Writing Next: Effective Strategies to Improve Writing of Adolescents in Middle and High Schools.* Washington: Alliance for Excellent Education, 2007. 6 January 2009 <http://www.all4ed.org/files/WritingNext.pdf>

Greenwald, Elissa A., et al. *NAEP 1998 Writing Report Card for the Nation and the States.* Washington: U.S. Department of Education, National Center for Education Statistics, 1999.

Langer, Judith A., and Arthur N. Applebee. *How Writing Shapes Thinking: A Study of Teaching and Learning.* Research Monograph Series No. 22. Urbana, IL: NCTE, 1987.

Loomis, S. C., and M. L. Bourque. *National Assessment of Educational Progress Achievement Levels, 1992–1998 for Writing.* Washington: National Assessment Governing Board, 2001.

Manzo, Kathleen Kennedy. "Graduates Can't Master College Text." *Education Week* 25.25 (2006): 1/16.

National Commission on Writing in America's Schools and Colleges. *The Neglected "R": The Need for a Writing Revolution.* New York, NY: College Entrance Examination Board, 2003. 6 January 2009 <http://www.writingcommission.org/prod_downloads/writingcom/neglectedr.pdf>

Russell, Michael, and Lisa Abrams. "Instructional Use of Computers for Writing: The Effect of State Testing Programs." *Teachers College Record* 106.6 (2004): 1332–357.

Arthur N. Applebee is Distinguished Professor at the University at Albany, State University of New York, and director of the Center on English Learning and Achievement. He has published widely on the teaching and learning of English, and co-chaired the planning committee which developed a new, computer-based framework for the 2011 NAEP writing assessment. Applebee is a past recipient of NCTE's David H. Russell Award for distinguished research in the teaching of English. Email him at AApplebee@uamail.albany.edu. **Judith A. Langer** is an internationally known scholar in literacy education. She is Distinguished Professor at the University at Albany, State University of New York, founder and director of the Albany Institute for Research in Education, and director of the Center on English Learning and Achievement. Her research focuses on how students become highly literate and on what teachers and schools can do to ensure effective learning for all. She may be reached at JLanger@uamail.albany.edu.

Issues and Trends in Writing

MICHAEL T. MOORE

■ ■ ■ ■ ■

In his seminal essay, *A thousand writers writing: Seeking change through the radical practice of writing as a way of being,* Yagelski (2009) imagines a thousand writers in one place, all diligently writing. He asks his reader to imagine being part of this group and to think about the experience of writing as separate from the text produced. It is the experience itself that is transformative.

> Writing in schools should be more like those 1,000 writers writing together in that ballroom. When it is, writing's transformative power is more likely to be realized, and it ceases to be merely a matter of procedure, a tool for communication, an exercise in control, and a means of sorting and norming, as writing tends to being formal schooling. Instead, writing becomes a way of being in the world. (p. 7)

The point of his essay lies in asking teachers to shift focus from both process and product to the transformative power of writing, and to make this the center of teachers' work. Over thirty years ago when I started teaching, I would have laughed aloud at such a notion. Maybe Saul Bellow and Ernest Hemmingway were transformed when they wrote, but not my sixth graders at the Highland Middle School. But such a concept was over thirty years from even being suggested.

Those of us who lived through the days when writing process/composition theory was still developing all have our own particular stories. Each of us sees this history in a unique way, through the lens of personal and professional context. It is my hope that sharing my own story will help crystallize key issues and trends in the teaching of writing, and bring us to Yagelski's paradigm change.

As an English and reading teacher in the early seventies, I am still amazed at how inadequately prepared I was to teach writing. I can think of no college course that even mentioned the teaching of writing in my undergraduate teacher preparation. In retrospect, I intuited how to teach writing from my personal experiences, first as a student in public school and later in college. These experiences were remarkably similar. They involved writing reams of compositions, submitting them to be graded, and receiving each one back, hideously scarred with red ink that eerily resembled war wounds. A cycle of subsequent rewrites then began (when rewrites were allowed), and with each revision there seemed to be less "blood." I was a journeyman, or apprentice, at what seemed a highly technical craft governed by arcane rules. I learned about comma splices and fused sentences by committing these errors (first as a high school writer and later as a college freshman), having my transgressions pointed out to me, and then doing the appropriate penance. As I grew more adept at anticipating what was expected, I became a better academic writer. I intuited what each teacher wanted through the inevitable cycle of revisions.

The lessons I learned in red were the lessons that I passed along to my own students when I became a teacher. As a beginning classroom teacher, I had no idea that I would live through a paradigm shift that would substantially change the way we conceptualize and teach writing. When I now reflect, I am amazed at what we did not know as a field when I started teaching, and what we now take for granted and that is, in fact, part of every teacher education program. I didn't know about process, free writing, journals and writing logs, topic choice, multiple perspectives, multiple drafts, the effect of audience, the many ways writing could be assessed (holistic evaluation, primary trait scoring, the effect of audience on writing, peer editing, and portfolio assessment), the effect of topic on writing, or even the many kinds of writing that could exist in school much less transformative writing. I could not have predicted the trends that I would see develop from this shift in emphasis. The study of process over product would spawn the writing process movement, the Bay Area and National Writing Projects, workshop approaches to teaching writing, a reappraisal of revision in writing, and a new focus on writing assessment.

The first inkling I had that change was in the wind for writing instruction was when I joined the National Council of Teachers of English in 1973 and read an article in *English Journal* by Toby Fulwiler on the subject of journal writing and its implications for multiple drafts. This was the first time I had ever considered a form of writing other than a formal essay. During this time, I became a writing teacher at the middle school, high school, and college levels, as well as a writing researcher.

A Brief History of Writing Research

It is difficult to separate writing from rhetoric since composition/writing grew out of the nineteenth-century topic of rhetoric. In fact, this tradition has returned, as indicated by a quick review of the tables of contents in such leading writing journals as *College Composition and Communication* and *Written Communication*. Further evidence is in the number of university departments that have broken from literature studies to form new departments or programs often named Rhetoric and Composition Studies or variations of these terms. This division has implications for both elementary and secondary schools, where composition has always played a subordinate role to literature study, and where writing is typically viewed as supporting reading or English. At the postsecondary level, more fragmentation exists; composition and rhetoric are often found in a separate department offering support courses for all majors and including minors in writing, creative writing, technical writing, and so on. Before 1830, the notion of writing as composing did not really exist, and writing instruction focused on penmanship and transcription (Monaghan, 2003). This instruction occurred in grammar schools. Eventually, reformers influenced schooling to the extent that students were permitted to self-actualize their experiences through writing (Woods, 1985). Continued reform moved the notion of writing as a matter of mental gymnastics involving grammar toward a model of practice-while-doing. Ironically perhaps, schools were much more innovative than universities in this movement (Shultz, 1999). This is no doubt due to the rise of the normal schools during this era.

The acknowledged view from the late 1930s until recently stemmed from a "formalist" view of literature instruction that originated with the "New Critics." This group included Robert Penn Warren, John Crowe Ransom, Allen Tate, and others who advocated that the meaning of a text could only be determined by a close reading. It was the text alone that counted—not the writer or the circumstances that surrounded the creation of the text. In other words, any text should stand-alone. Everything we needed to construct meaning was in any given text. This view wended its way from literary critics to college classrooms and soon to public school English curricula. Thus, writing for students meant that their written products were subject to the same kind of close reading used to read published texts. Accordingly, texts were subject to rigid structural guidelines in the four traditional modes of discourse: description, narration, exposition, and argument (Young, 1978).

This model entailed a close study of grammar. This "classical" model held that the importance of an education was to train one's memory and one's reasoning ability (Applebee, 1974). English itself held little interest as a subject, but grammar had two things going for it. Students had to learn rules and how to apply them—tasks that lent themselves to explicit curricula and concrete assessments. Grammar instruction became great preparation for college but was not necessarily a college subject.

Interestingly enough, 1874 marked the first time that composition became a prescribed course at a university (Harvard). English study as a discipline in our public schools traces its own beginnings to 1958, when funding from the Ford Foundation coincided with righteous curricular squabbling involving both the Modern Language Association and the National Council of Teachers of English (Applebee, 1974). Although I think most teachers probably trace the emergence of composition as a subject/tradition to private, east coast, Eurocentric, pedagogically situated institutions, recent scholarship (Fitzgerald, 2009) actually traces composition as a discipline emerging from the social, economic, cultural, and ideological contexts set out in normal schools. Unlike the Harvards and Yales, normal schools emerged from German systems of pedagogy and teacher training. Theirs was more a merging of composition and pedagogy or theory and practice as synthesis. Primary sources, teachers, journals, lesson plans, accounts from professional meetings show teachers at normal schools distancing themselves from the textbooks produced by elite institutions. As a field matures, a worldview emerges from the accumulation of research, and this view becomes dominant. Paradigm shifts occur when the previous stance is no longer tenable. A paradigm shift in the teaching of writing began in the early sixties. In 1963, Braddock, Lloyd-Jones, and Schoer, writing in *Research in Written Composition*, identified a list of 504 studies, and the "worldview" became evident. Only two of these studies dealt with the process of writing; the rest were grounded in a very different perspective. Specifically, what existed prior to 1962 was what Young (1978) called a concern with the composed product, the analysis of discourse, and a general preoccupation with the essay form and the term paper. The studies reviewed by Braddock et al. in 1963 focused on curricula, textbook making, rhetoric, teaching by television, writing vocabulary, handwriting, typewriting, among others. Thus, North (1987) dates the birth of modern Composition (with a capital "C"), to 1963 and the seminal review by Braddock et al. of written composition research to that time. Over the next ten years, a distinct shift in stance would be very apparent in Janet Emig's book, *The Composing Process of Twelfth Graders*, James Moffett's *Teaching the Universe of Discourse*, Donald Murray's *A Writer Teaches Writing*, Peter Elbow's *Writing without Teachers*, and Ken Macrorie's *Telling Writing*. Also during this period, NCTE began plans for a bulletin soon to become the journal, *Research in the Teaching of English*, first edited by Richard Braddock and N. S. Blount. This new journal became a forum for composition research (Gere, 1985). Cooper and Odell (1978) in *Research on Composing: Points of Departure*, their sequel to *Research in Written Composition*, challenged researchers to examine the nature of writing competence, successful writing practices, characteristics of competent writing teachers, and to develop new methods or procedures suited to studying these questions.

Kuhn (1964) calls a "paradigm" a system of widely held beliefs, values, and supporting elements that form a discipline or a worldview. In his influential book, *The Structure of Scientific Revolutions*, Kuhn (1964) called into question the standard view of science. He critically examined previous approaches and encouraged new interpretations of previous research and new research embracing new approaches. By 1973, writing research therefore had the theoretical underpinnings to explode in several new directions, most notably into questions of process and assessment. Cooper and Odell's challenge clearly signaled the end of the previous paradigm and the ushering in of a new paradigm in the teaching of writing. However, a word of caution. Although our conceptions of writing were about to irrevocably change, writing in schools was still subject to the same fragmentation as standards and curricula. Bohm and Peat (2000) note that fragmentation is an aspect of science and the Cartesian–Newtonian paradigm and valued by scientists because they hope "that this will enable them to extend their powers indefinitely to predict and control things" (Bohm & Peat, 2000, pp. 10–11). Composition research initially focused on separate actions, which were isolated, analyzed as discrete actions. Early composition research studied just about any aspect of writing that could be observed and counted.

Writing as a Process

The birth of the process writing approach arguably occurred in 1971 with the publication of Janet Emig's dissertation, *The Composing Processes of Twelfth Graders*. North (1987) called it "the single most influential piece of Researcher inquiry–and maybe *any* kind of inquiry–in Composition's short history" (p. 197). Emig's study was a venture away from product examination, and it focused on how writers actually wrote. Her study spawned a plethora of similar investigations that looked at college writers, children learning to write, the causes of writing failure, the role of the teacher, and other issues. Emig's study also served to condemn public school writing instruction, which she called "a neurotic activity" (p. 99). She wittily observed:

> A species of extensive writing that recurs so frequently in student accounts that it deserves special mention is the five-paragraph theme, consisting of one paragraph of introduction...three of expansion and example...and one of conclusion. This mode is so indigenously American that it might be called the Fifty-Star Theme. In fact, the reader might imagine behind this and the next three paragraphs Kate Smith singing "God Bless America" or the piccolo obligato from "The Stars and Stripes Forever." (p. 97)
>
> I encountered Emig's work in 1973 as a graduate student and first-year middle grades teacher. She described the writing process as both "laminated and recursive" and claimed that there was a "blending" of identifiable writing behaviors she had observed, such as "planning, starting, stopping," and so on. Over the next thirty years, composition research on process would flourish to the extent that most universities now support composition studies as a distinct discipline. Writing research is published regularly in both liberal arts and education venues. The Bay Area Writing Project and later the National Writing Project continue to be partially funded by the federal government. Writing Across the Curriculum as a movement has been with us almost as long as research on composing. Growing scholarship on writing assessment and technology has identified new areas of research on writing. However, old habits die hard, and although most teachers know "process" a regular observer of schools might note that a wide gulf continues to exist between research and practice (Burhans, 1983). One does not have to travel far to find that the five-paragraph theme is alive and well, and indeed flourishing, in our nation's schools.

One of the earliest process-writing proponents was Donald Murray and especially influential was his 1968 book, *A Writer Teaches Writing*. Although this book has undergone several editions, I have always found that his first edition most clearly conceptualizes what we mean by process. Murray later crystallized his view of this process as "Collect, Plan, Develop" (Murray, 1985), but it is in his description of the writer's "seven skills" that I began to understand what Emig was referring to as a "recursive process." Murray's seven skills were simply these: A writer "discovers a subject, senses an audience, searches for specifics, creates a design, writes, develops a critical eye, and rewrites" (pp. 2–12). Although missing from subsequent editions, these seven skills became the way I understood process to work and what it might mean for a new teacher. The term *recursive* means that we are not quite sure when a particular process is happening. That is to say, writing is not a lock-step affair; while there is a general order, the steps are occasionally repeated and feed back to each other. A writer might be developing a topic at any time, including when he/she is developing a critical eye or editing. Editing itself might be occurring as the writer is discovering a topic or sensing an audience.

The purpose of instruction shifted from teacher to student. The implications for instruction were that writing was about student choice. Students wrote to clarify and understand their own thinking. Writing was no longer only formal; personal, and narrative forms of writing were encouraged. Multiple drafts became part of the process and we kept student writing in writing portfolios, a device borrowed from artists.

The first real challenge to tradition that would make its way from research to practice was the Dartmouth Conference held as a joint Anglo-American Seminar in September 1976. Put forward by the British were two things that were to have a lasting effect on the way writing should be taught: "One, there is little room for grammar; direct systematic teaching of knowledge about language is virtually excluded from the curriculum. Two, writing is learned by doing it and sharing it with real audiences, not by studying and applying abstract rhetorical principles in exercises which the teacher alone will read and judge" (Parker, 1979, p. 320).

Clearly influenced by the Dartmouth conference, James Moffett published *Teaching the Universe of Discourse* in 1968 as a companion to his *Student Centered Language Arts Curriculum, Grades K 13: A Handbook for Teachers* (1983). He proposed a highly interactive curriculum that stressed drama, writing for different audiences, peer review, and editing and adaptation over formal writing assessment. Moffett also wrote about the reading-writing connection in *Active Voice: A Writing Program Across the Curriculum* (1992). The "role of the teacher, then," wrote Moffett, "is to teach the students to teach each other" (p. 196). Moffett put his theory into practice by publishing the highly controversial "Interaction" series through Houghton Mifflin. This series was an integrative curriculum that promoted trade books containing real literature and students' responding to literature through a process approach. This series actually led to rioting in Kanawha County, West Virginia. This account is chronicled by Moffett (1989) in *Storm in the Mountains: A Case Study of Censorship, Conflict, and Consciousness*.

Today, writing process is seen to comprise a number of events (not always agreed upon). They include talking, reading, planning, idea generating, detail generating, collaborating, drafting, editing, reenvisioning, proofing, sharing, publishing, responding and revisiting. These events are recursive in nature. Imagine a circle and being able to jump on or off at different points. This means that something like editing can jump in or out of the circle anywhere, and the same is true with the rest of the events. Students choose their own subjects, they become part of a community of writers, they write to explore, they have something to say to each other, and us, and they publish what they write. Standard Five in the *IRA/NCTE Standards for the English Language Arts* (1996) reads: "Students employ a wide range of strategies as they write and use different writing process elements appropriately to communicate with different audiences for a variety of purposes." Unfortunately, in too many writing classrooms the emphasis is still on the product, and the primary goal is that students learn to write academically acceptable exposition. Traditions die hard.

Process and the Writing Development of Children

As a new college professor, I became a consultant to a local school system interested in implementing a writing process approach. We decided to begin our program with kindergarten. During the summer, the kindergarten teachers and I discussed process writing and the approaches they might use. We decided we would implement journals and guided writing assignments at the beginning of the school year. On the first day of school, students found nicely bound journals on their desks, colorfully decorated and embossed with each student's name. Children were invited to write in their journals with their teacher as part of each morning's routine. I then observed what I had only read about in research journals (Dyson, 1982; Graves, 1981; Gundlach, 1981). Given a brief daily prompt to write about their families, pets, school, or favorite things to do, children proceeded to write or imitate behaviors they'd observed to be associated with writing. In other words they opened their journals and began to write, moving from left to right and top to bottom. Most of what we observed were squiggly lines that imitated writing. Along with the "writing" were drawings, the beginning of letters and other curious symbols. There were a very few children who could actually write some words. However, most could only vaguely imitate writers; thus, they attempted to produce something that they thought resembled a text. When children were invited to sit in the "Author's Chair" and share their writing, they then imitated readers reading a text. When interrupted and asked exactly where certain words occurred in their writing, the children were able to point without hesitation to certain lines confidently. If stopped early on, they pointed to "words" near the top of the page. If asked to stop later, they pointed to words correspondingly farther down. This behavior reflects the complex and hierarchical nature of the symbol system of written language. Children appear to have an almost intuitive grasp of written syntax in much the same way that they quickly assimilate spoken syntax and often feel free to experiment with it. As students wrote daily in their journals, with their teachers, and shared every day, we noticed that students soon became frustrated by what they couldn't produce. We began to see more attempts at letters and comments like, "That's a *T* and it goes in Brittany, but I don't know how to make that." As children learned the symbol system, the alphabetic nature of writing, journals became much harder for them to write, but the production of written language began to grow.

We also noted a greater concern for accuracy when children wrote cards or other such work destined to go home—to a different audience. We began to see closer attention to real text production. We noticed that most of the children learned the letters of their names first and that connections started to build between these letters and other words with the same letters. Dyson and Freedman (2003) suggest that teachers listen closely to children's talk at this stage to gain insight and to help them reflect further on all aspects of thinking and writing. We also noticed that children's knowledge of narrative structure was more advanced than we thought it would be. Children knew how to tell stories and knew enough about basic plot, character, and action to wish to reproduce these in their writing.

Children in this project engaged in all aspects of the writing process, as we knew it at the time. We focused on making writing a daily activity, we sought to encourage the recursive aspect of the process and not promote the process as linear. We had children writing for real audiences and we gave them opportunities to share their writing. Our aim was to continue with these same students from grade to grade so that they would have the benefit of a consistent model.

Outgrowths of the Writing Process Movement: The Bay Area Writing Project and the National Writing Project

Tracing its roots directly to the outgrowth of writing/composition theory was the 1974 inception of the Bay Area Writing Project (Bay Area Writing Project Website) in the Graduate School of the University of California at Berkeley. The Bay Area Writing Project would later become the flagship site of the National Writing Project. Writing projects abound and are firmly entrenched as summer institutes in most states. A teacher-teaching-teachers model is used, in collaboration with a university writing program. The Bay Area Writing Project's stated goals are:

- To improve student writing abilities by improving the teaching and learning of writing in Bay Area schools.
- To provide professional development programs for classroom teachers;
- To expand the professional roles of teachers;
- To increase the academic achievement of the Bay Area's diverse student population (Bay Area Writing Project Website).

The Bay Area Project like the National Writing Project embraces the following principles:

- writing is fundamental to learning in all disciplines;
- writing deserves constant attention from kindergarten through university;
- teachers are the key to educational change;
- the best teacher of teachers is another teacher;
- effective literacy programs are inclusive, reaching all teachers in order to reach all students;
- universities and schools accomplish more in partnership;
- exemplary teachers of writing write and use writing themselves;
- excellent professional development is an ongoing process (Bay Area Writing Project Website).

Each year, close to 4,000 teachers participate in the Bay Area Project alone. Different sites set their own programs, but among the areas of focus are: process, theory, workshop approaches, writing across the curriculum, emergent writing, publishing student writing, coaching models for teaching writing, among other strategies. At each project, teachers learn to teach writing by first becoming writers themselves. Teachers become immersed in all aspects of the process and become convinced (as they will soon convince their own students) that they are real writers with all the rights and privileges thereof.

Writing Across the Curriculum/Writing in the Disciplines

The WAC/WID movement is a broadly based pedagogical practice that grew from the process movement. Most WAC/WID programs stemmed from faculty workshops in 1970 as an outgrowth of the writing process movement and were started on university campuses across the country. This became a progressive reform movement over the next thirty years. Although not as widely based in public schools, WAC/WID programs hold the premise that writing is important in all academic areas, not just composition classes. Administrators have long favored the sound-bite aphorism that all teachers should be teachers of writing. In actuality, writing is the low rung on the academic ladder in most colleges and universities, relegated to the freshman year and taught by an army of temporary faculty. In public schools, writing was stuck on the margins between discourse communities. The National Assessment of Educational Progress reports from the early seventies fueled a public outcry about the lack of effective writers in schools. It was additionally thought that students use writing as a bridge from what is known to what one expects to learn, and writing is a means of making sense of a discipline. Most sites urge that all courses include a writing component, but a popular model is one in which a number of courses are deemed by the university as writing-intensive courses. Thus, students know in advance that writing will be an important aspect of the course. Often, writing-intensive courses are listed as such on student transcripts. For a number of years at Georgia Southern University, all new faculty underwent writing across the curriculum training and some courses were earmarked in the course catalog as being writing intensive. However, like Dewey himself, impetus could not be sustained although vestiges remain in several other movements.

Workshop Approach

An outgrowth of both writing projects and of the whole language movement in the early eighties was the implementation of the Writers' Workshop approach. Since writing projects saw it as their job to convince teachers that they were real writers, teachers next had to convince their students that they also were real writers. Writing and reading workshops grew out of the concept of writing retreats, where writers worked on their own materials and came together to share, discuss, criticize, and edit. The person who captured teachers' imaginations about how writing workshops could be organized for instruction was Nancie Atwell (Atwell, 1987). Atwell showed teachers that workshops could be highly organized and could function smoothly. Atwell describes her approach to the workshop as having principles that serve to inform both teaching and learning:

1. Writers need regular chunks of time—time to think, write, confer, read, change their minds, and write some more.
2. Writers need their own topics. Right from the first day of kindergarten, students should use writing as a way to think about and give shape to their own ideas and concerns.
3. Writers need response. Helpful response comes during—not after—the composing. It comes from the writer's peers and from the teacher, who consistently models the kinds of restatements and questions that help writers reflect on the content of their own writing.
4. Writers learn mechanics from context, from teachers who address errors as they occur within individual pieces of writing, where these rules and forms will have meaning.
5. Children need to know adults who write. We need to write, share our writing with our students, and demonstrate what experienced writers do in the process of composing, letting our students see our own drafts in all their messiness and tentativeness.
6. Writers need to read. They need access to a wide-ranging variety of texts, prose and poetry, fiction and nonfiction.

7. Writing teachers need to take responsibility for their writing and teaching. We must seek out professional resources that reflect the far-reaching conclusions of recent research into children's writing. And we must become writers and researchers, observing and learning from our own and our students' writing. (Atwell, 1987, pp. 17–18).

Atwell showed teachers how to respond to student writing in a workshop format, how to negotiate grading, and how to implement instruction through "writing mini-lessons." She clearly articulated the roles of teacher and student. As a student, you knew what you were supposed to do on a daily basis and how to go about doing it. Teachers also let students know what they themselves were responsible for and allowed students to hold teachers responsible for their obligations in the workshop. Atwell's book, now in its second edition, remains very popular with whole language teachers and graduates of writing projects.

Whole Language

Although more thought of as a reading movement, Goodman (1989) does trace the theoretical underpinnings of whole language to composition theorists such as Alvina Burrows, Donald Graves, James Britton, and the National Writing Project. A decade later, Daniels, Zemelman, and Bizar (1999) analyzed 60 years of research to conclude that support exists for wholistic, literature-based approaches to writing. Curiously, the reform movement of the early part of the century brought on by No Child Left Behind kept a good deal of focus on writing. Programs like America's Choice, an approved program for schools not achieving Annual Yearly Progress, adopted a writing workshop approach. However, the skills were not thought of recursively as they had been in whole language but in a linear, stepwise, skills-based approach.

Trends in Writing Assessment

Writing assessment has largely followed the same trends as reading assessment. As reading assessment shifted from a focus solely on the text to a focus on how students read, much the same has happened in writing. Previously, writing assessment was purely textual analysis. Teachers focused on errors, how many and how often. Writing assessment has shifted to interpretation and process. One element of this shift has been from sentence-level correctness to revision as reformulation (Hull, 1985). In *Errors and Expectations: A Guide for the Teacher of Basic Writing*, Mina Shaughnessy (1977) wrote: "Errors count but not as much as most English teachers think" (p. 120). Error analysis now serves as an analytical tool that helps teachers to understand student thinking and to help students develop strategies that lead to better writing. Unfortunately, errors still count. Formal assessment in all aspects of education is growing, and writing assessment in many states focuses solely on grammatical accountability. For writing, this debate focuses on direct and indirect assessment. Proponents of indirect assessment view writing as a means of communicating ideas while proponents of direct assessment view writing as the construction of meaning (Williamson, 1993). In fact, it is only in recent years that formal testing of writing has moved from a multiple-choice examination to a holistic evaluation of students' actual writing.

Holistic Assessment

Perhaps the most common form of informal assessment is holistic scoring. Many state competency tests and college placement tests in writing favor an open topic structure (these tend to produce more errors in student papers (see Smith et al., 1985) and thus tend to make it easier for evaluators to place students. Basically, in holistic evaluation, two readers rate each paper on a four- or five-point scale (most use a four-point scale because differences are easier to resolve). If the raters are in agreement, then a third rater is not needed. If raters are not in agreement, then a third rater is used to resolve disagreements. Another way of conducting holistic evaluation is to have three readers read each student essay and then average their ratings. In a holistic evaluation, where readers have been trained, error is one of several factors that influence raters. Other factors might include, format, content, vocabulary, and spelling. However, since the mid-seventies, holistic evaluation has attempted—through carefully posed topics, scoring guides, and sample papers for raters to use for uniformity and attention to reliability and validity—to rate student papers for placement and minimum competency as accurately as possible. The downside of holistic evaluation is its prohibitive cost both in time and money, especially in large-scale assessment.

Portfolio Assessment

Portfolio advocates make a strong case for using portfolios in large-scale assessment. They argue that a portfolio is much more reliable as a measure of growth and ability. It really is not quite accurate to call portfolios a means of assessment, however. Portfolios are a means of collection. Some sort of holistic evaluation would need to be conducted in order to judge the content of the portfolios. Questions must be decided about what to include in portfolios as well as the purpose of the portfolio in the first place.

Primary Trait Guides

Another form of writing assessment is the use of primary trait scoring guides. A primary trait guide focuses specifically on a few key aspects of student writing. A primary trait guide might focus on errors, especially particular types of errors. Another guide might focus on paragraph patterns or topic sentences. Although generally viewed as unsuitable for large-scale assessment, primary trait guides are very useful in classroom settings, especially those advocating a workshop format.

Issues in Writing Assessment

The current political climate for assessment means that large-scale writing assessment is likely to continue. The shift from using multiple-choice measures to evaluating student-produced essays has turned the corner, however. As of this writing, even the venerable SAT not includes a writing sample scored by rubrics. However, issues of reliability and validity will continue to persist. Work by Smith (1993) has questioned exactly what the difference is between a 3 and a 4 on a 4-point scale and especially between a 2 and 3, since the rater is likely to realize that the rating given might affect a student being placed in a remedial program or, in extreme circumstances, not graduating from high school.

Technology and Writing

Most would readily agree that technology has greatly affected the teaching of writing. Students routinely use classroom computer stations for much of their writing, and these tools now have their own applications for error study and analysis, fluency, and organization. Information and Communication Technology (ICT) has expanded the notion of writing instruction, but it has decidedly not replaced or supplanted it. Cutting-edge research in writing might focus today on multimodal literacies and digital technologies. Some researchers are beginning to distance themselves from these new technologies in order to study their impact on us (Swenson et al., 2006). Leu (2005) reflected that the Internet as well as evolving technologies are not technological issues but literacy issues. While digital texts can take forms similar to their print counterparts, we also see how profoundly different these can be. "Many digital texts are dynamic, their content updated and revised continuously. Such content is typically multimodal, incorporating visual, auditory, and other non-verbal elements" (Swenson et al., 2006, p. 354). These new digital arrays, collectively called *hypermedia*, change the ways we read and how we connect texts to texts. Of course, this affects how students then produce writing—and what counts as writing (see Bromley, this volume). As Postman (1992) warns us, it is "a mistake to suppose that any technological innovation has a one-sided effect" (p. 4).

However, it is not as if we educators are blazing a technology trail for our classes since our media-saturated students spend an average of 6.5 hours per day with media (Roberts, Fehr, & Rideout, 2005). Interestingly enough, while our students are text messaging, blogging, using multiple forms of digital texts on MySpace or Facebook, the national emphasis on accountability, standardized tests, and the writing prompt on the SAT have had an ironically reductionist effect on the teaching of writing, as evidenced by such programs as 6+1 Writing Traits (2003) and America's Choice Writer's Advantage, both programs that encourage formulaic approaches to student composing. Heilker (1996) cautions that such formulaic approaches encourage students not to think critically or innovatively. Curiously, students' written communication in school may consequently prove to be vastly different from written communication in non-school settings.

Writing in the Post-Process Era

Ironically, process writing isn't even fully entrenched in schools after almost thirty years of hype and we are now into post-process writing. Post-process writing is a text-based focus that appears to come from Critical Discourse Analysis (Luke, 2009). Texts are analyzed through social, cultural, linguistic lenses and through economies of schooling. The idea is that all texts exist in a political and social framework and students first understand how these forces influence readers. Writers create new social identities that encompass multiple new texts and hybrid forms of text. These social identities form and reform continually. Student writers are encouraged to understand audience from multiple perspectives. Post-process writing is not necessarily seen as a paradigm change but as an extension of the writing process. Atkinson (1999) refers to post-process as the "rich, multifocal nature of the field–our need and ability, in our current and future work to go beyond now traditional views of L2 writing research and teaching and focus on issues such as drafting, teacher-feedback, peer review, editing, grammar correction, and the like" (p. 1539). Yagelski (2009) observed, "Whatever else it may be (and it is many other things, too) writing is an ontological act: When we write, we enact a sense of ourselves as beings in the world. In this regard, writing both shapes and reflects our sense of who we are in relation to each other and the world around us" (pp. 7–8). Yagelski reminds us that it is in the experience of writing where the real value of writing lies and in its transformative power to connect us to the world.

Conclusion

Nothing these days is more a political hot button than literacy in general and "'readin' and 'ritin'" in particular. Interest in writing is not likely to flag any time soon. To be sure, the focus on the product and on students' ability to produce academic writing will remain in the forefront of educational reform. Clearly, process is part of this reform, as is writing for real audiences and writing for personal understanding. How process and product will play out in this era of high-stakes assessment is anyone's guess. We are currently entering an era of common (national) standards reform. Already, at this writing, endorsed by forty-eight states, more emphasis is placed on writing as the aim of schools decidedly becomes focused on college preparation. Common standards nationally will eventually mean common forms of writing assessment. Since the common standards are being written by a panel with more than its fair share of members from Educational Testing Services and the SAT, I expect to see writing assessment moving toward primary trait scoring guided assessment. More importantly, though, the lessons learned over the last thirty years are that writers get better at writing by writing. Good teachers find ways of motivating students to produce their best writing by paying careful attention to *both* process and product. Surprisingly, technology has not had the effect one would have imagined on writing. Surely, computers have made writing easier to edit and revise. Teachers can take far less time to edit student's papers, and publishing no longer relies on justifiers and professional publishers. It is the rare school where students do not have access to word processors for at least final drafts. So, while the nature and applications of writing are evolving, and while instructional approaches continue to mature over time, the future of writing instruction is far from certain.

REFERENCES

Applebee, A. N. (1974). *Tradition and reform in the teaching of English: A history*. Urbana, IL: NCTE.

Atkinson, D. (2009). Writing in the post-process era: Introduction. In S. Miller (Ed.), *The Norton book of composition studies* (pp. 1532–1543). London: W.W. Norton.

Atwell, N. (1987). *In the Middle: Writing, reading, and learning with adolescents*. Portsmouth, NH: Boynton Cook/Heinemann.

Bohm, D., & Peat, F.D. (2000) *Science, order, and creativity* (2nd ed.) New York, NY: Routledge.

Braddock, R., Lloyd-Jones, R., & Schoer, L. (1963). *Research in written composition*. Champaign, IL: NCTE.

Bay Area Writing Project. Retrieved on June 24, 2002, from http://bawpblogs.org/

Burhans, C. S. (1983). The teaching of writing and the knowledge gap. *College English, 45*, 639–656.

Cooper, C. R., & Odell, L. (1978). *Research on composing: Points of departure*. Urbana, IL: NCTE.

Daniels, H., Zemelman, S., & Bizar, M. (1999). Whole language works: Sixty years of research. *Educational Leadership, 57*(2), 32-37.

Dyson, A. H. (1981). Oral language: The rooting system for learning to write. *Language Arts, 58*, 776–784.

Dyson, A.H., & Freedman, S. W. (2003). Writing. In J. Flood, D. Lapp, J.R. Squire, & J. M. Jensen (Eds.), *Handbook of research on teaching the English language arts* (2nd ed.). Mahwah, NJ: Lawrence Erlbaum Associates.

Elbow, P. (1973). *Writing without teachers*. New York, NY: Oxford University Press.

Emig, J. (1971). *The composing processes of twelfth graders*. Urbana, IL: NCTE.

Fitzgerald, K. (2009). A rediscovered tradition: European pedagogy and composition in nineteenth-century Midwestern normal schools. In S. Miller (Ed.), *The Norton book of composition studies* (pp. 171–192). London: W.W. Norton.

Gere, A. (1985). Empirical research in composition. In B. W. McClelland & T. R. Donovan (Eds.), *Perspectives on research and scholarship in composition* (pp. 116–124). New York: MLA.

Goodman, Y. M. (1989). Roots of the Whole Language Movement. *Elementary School Journal, 90*, 113–127.

Graves, D. (1981). *A case study observing the development of primary children's composing, spelling, and motor behaviors during the writing process* (Final report to the National Institute of education). Durham: University of New Hampshire.

Gundlach, R. (1981). On the nature and development of children's writing. In C. Fredericksen & J. Dominic (Eds.), *Writing: The nature, development, and teaching of written communication: Vol. 2. Writing, process, development and communication* (pp. 133–152). Hillsdale, NJ: Lawrence Erlbaum associates.

Heilker, P. (1996). *The essay: Theory and pedagogy for an active form.* Urbana, IL: National Council of Teachers of English.

Kuhn, T. S. (1964) *Structure of scientific revolutions.* Chicago, IL: University of Chicago Press.

Leu, D. J., Jr. (November 2005). *New literacies, reading research, and the challenge of change: A deictic perspective.* Invited presidential address to the National Reading Conference, Miami, FL. Retrieved on September 6, 2006, from http://www.newliteracies.uconn.edu/nrc/don_leu_2005.html

Luke, A. (2009). Theory and practice in critical discourse analysis. In S. Miller (Ed.), *The Norton book of composition studies* (pp. 1339–1350). London: W.W. Norton.

Macrorie, K. (1970). *Telling writing.* Rochelle Park, NJ: Hayden.

Moffett, J. (1992). *Active voice: A writing program across the curriculum.* Portsmouth, NH: Boynton/Cook.

Moffett, J. (1989). *Storm in the mountains: A case study of censorship, conflict, and consciousness.* Carbondale, IL: Southern Illinois University Press.

Moffett, J. (1968). *Teaching the universe of discourse: A theory of discourse: A rationale for English teaching used in student-centered language arts curriculum.* Boston: Houghton Mifflin.

Moffett, J. & Wagner, B.J. (1983). *Student-centered language arts and reading, K-13: A handbook for teachers.* (3rd ed.). Boston, MA: Houghton Mifflin.

Monaghan, J. (2003). The uses of literacy by girls in colonial America. In J. E. Greer (Ed.), *Girls and literacy in America: Historical perspectives to the present* (pp. 53–80). Santa Barbara, CA: ABC Clio.

Murray, D. M. (1975). *A writer teaches writing.* (2nd ed.). Boston, MA: Houghton Mifflin.

Murray, D. M. (1968). *A writer teaches writing: A practical method of teaching composition.* Boston, MA: Houghton Mifflin.

North, S. M. (1987). *The making of knowledge in composition: Portrait of an emerging field.* Upper Montclair, NJ: Boynton/Cook.

Parker, R. P. (1979). From Sputnik to Dartmouth: Trends in the teaching of composition. In S. Miller (Ed.), *The Norton book of composition studies* (pp. 171–192). London: W.W. Norton.

Postman, N. (1992). *Technopoly.* New York, NY: Knopf.

Roberts, D. F., Foehr, U. G., and Rideout, V. (2005). *Generation M: Media in the lives of 8–18 year olds.* Menlo Park, CA: Kaiser Family Foundation.

Shaughnessy, M. (1977). *Errors and expectations: A guide for the teacher of basic writing.* New York, NY: Oxford University Press.

Schultz, L.M. (1999). *The young composers: Composition's beginnings in 19th century schools.* Carbondale, IL: Southern Illinois University Press.

Smith, W. L., Hull, G. A., Land, R. E., Moore, M. T., Ball, C., Dunham, D. E., Hickey, L. S., & Ruzich, C. W. (1985). Some effects of varying the structure of the topic on college students' writing. *Written Communication, 2*, 73–89.

Smith, W. L. (1993). Assessing the reliability and adequacy of using holistic scoring of essays as a college composition placement technique. In M. M. Williamson & B. A. Huot (Eds.), *Validating holistic scoring for writing assessment* (pp. 142–205). Cresskill, NJ: Hampton Press.

Standards for the English language arts. (1996). Urbana, IL: IRA/NCTE.

Swenson, J., Young, C., McGrail, E., Rozema, R., & Whitin, P. (2006). Extending the conversation: New technologies, new literacies, and English education. *English Education, 38*, 351–369.

Williamson, M. M. (1993). An introduction to holistic scoring: The social, historical, and theoretical context for writing assessment. In M. M. Williamson & B. A. Huot (Eds.), *Validating holistic scoring for writing assessment* (pp. 1–44). Cresskill, NJ: Hampton Press.

Woords, W. F. (1985). The cultural tradition of nineteenth-century "traditional" grammar teaching. *Rhetoric Society Quarterly, 15*(1–2), 3–12.

Yagelski, R. (2009). A thousand writers writing: Seeking change through the radical practice of writing as a way of being. *English Education, 42*, 6–28.

Young, R. E. (1978). Paradigms and problems: Needed research in rhetorical invention. In C. R. Cooper & L. Odell (Eds.), *Research on composing: Points of departure* (pp. 29–48). Urbana, IL: NCTE.

CLASSROOM IMPLICATIONS

1. How can *both* process and product concerns best be addressed in your instructional setting?

2. How can you contend with the time required for the process approach?

3. Why is writing the perennial stepchild of literacy instruction? Should it receive more attention than it does?

4. What are the major trends in writing research, writing instruction, and writing assessment?

5. What future projections seem likely in these areas, especially given the advent of technology?

6. Are high-stakes assessments causing a pendulum swing back to the product mentality, or will process and product remain merged?

FOR FURTHER READING

Ellis, R. A. (2006). Investigating the quality of student approaches to using technology in experiences of learning through writing. *Computers and Education, 47,* 371–390.

Engle, T., & Streich, R. (2006). Yes, there "Is" room for soup in the curriculum: Achieving accountability in a collaboratively planned writing program. *The Reading Teacher, 59,* 660–679.

Fisher, D., & Ivey, G. (2005). Literacy and language as learning in content-area classes: A departure from "Every teacher a teacher of reading." *Action in Teacher Education, 27,* 3–11.

Levy, G. A., Gong, Z., Hessels, S., Evans, M. A., & Jared, D. (2006). Understanding print: Early reading development and the contributions of home literacy experiences. *Journal of Experimental Child Psychology, 93,* 63–93.

Manning, M. (2006). Celebrations in reading and writing: Be true to yourself. *Teaching Pre K-8,* 68–69.

Mason, L.H., Benedek-Wood, E., & Valasa, L. (2009–2010). Teaching low-achieving students to self-regulate persuasive quick write responses. *Journal of Adolescent & Adult Literacy, 53.* doi: 10.1598/JAAL.53.4.4

McDonald, N. L., & Fisher, D. (2006). *Teaching literacy through the arts. Tools for teaching literacy series.* New York, NY: Guildford Publications.

Ostrosky, M. M., & Gaffney, J. S., & Thomas, D. V. (2006). The interplay between literacy and relationships in early childhood settings. *Reading and Writing Quarterly, 22,* 173–191.

Peterson, S. S., & Kennedy, K. (2006). Sixth-grade teachers' written comments on student writing: Genre and gender influences. *Written Communication, 23,* 36–62.

Reynolds, G.A., & Perin, D. (2009). A comparison of text structure and self-regulated writing strategies for composing from sources by middle school students. *Reading Psychology, 30*(3), 265-300. doi:10.1080/02702710802411547

Scheuer, N., de la Cruz., M., Pozo, J. I., Huate, M. F., & Sola, G. (2006). The mind is not a black box: Children's ideas about the writing process. *Learning and Instruction, 16,* 72–85.

Simmons, J. (2009). Writing instruction in the secondary classroom: Surviving school reform. In S.R. Parris, D. Fisher, & K. Headley (Eds.), *Adolescent literacy, field tested: Effective solutions for every classroom* (pp. 21–33). Newark, DE: International Reading Association.

Smith, L. A. (2006). Think-aloud mysteries: Using structured, sentence-by-sentence text passages to teach comprehension strategies. *The Reading Teacher, 59,* 690–697.

Vincent, J. (2006). Children writing: Multimodality and assessment in the writing classroom. *Literacy, 40,* 51–57.

Zenkov, K., & Harmon, J. (2009). Picturing a writing process: Photovoice and teaching writing to urban youth. *Journal of Adolescent & Adult Literacy, 52,* 575–584.

ONLINE RESOURCES

Graham, S., & Perin, D. (2007).
Writing Next: Effective strategies to improve writing of adolescents in middle and high schools—A report to the Carnegie Corporation of New York. Washington: Alliance for Excellent Education. Available:
http://www.all4ed.org/publications/ReadingNext/

The Literacy Hub: Connecting Reading and Writing. Don Leu's site at the University of Connecticut.
http://www.literacy.uconn.edu/writing.htm

The Nation's Report Card: Writing. Results of the National Assessment of Educational Progress.
http://nces.ed.gov/nationsreportcard/writing/

10 Response to Intervention

The goal of the RTI legislation is to reduce the number of students who are referred for special education services. The hope is that by providing instructionally needy students with intensive reading interventions, they will be able to demonstrate the ability to catch up with their achieving peers.

—Richard L. Allington, 2008

The Commission embraces the concept of RTI and seeks to clarify it with regard to issues related to language and literacy. The Commission finds it productive to think of RTI as a comprehensive, systemic approach to teaching and learning designed to address language and literacy problems for all students through increasingly differentiated and intensified language and literacy assessment and instruction.

—IRA Commission on Response to Intervention, 2010

The problem of how best to serve struggling readers has persisted for decades. There has always been consensus that intervention in the form of special education should be a last resort, but concern has arisen that some students are prematurely categorized as having a specific learning disability. Conventional thinking has been that in cases of true learning disability, (1) neurological difficulties prevent children of normal intelligence from reading as well as they should; and (2) because these difficulties are constitutional in origin, they can only be accommodated rather than eliminated through instruction. Following this logic has meant assessing cognitive capacity to rule out an intellectual deficit. Although this approach has doubtless succeeded in identifying many children who actually suffer from a specific learning disability (SLD) (let's call them true positives), the concern has been that many children without neurological impairment may inadvertently be grouped in the same category (false positives).

The consequences of identifying a child falsely as learning disabled can include years of special education, not to mention the possibility of stigma. Not only are instructional resources wasted, but harm may actually result. The question is how to avoid the identification of false positives. A promising approach is to systematically employ various research-based instructional methods with a child who is struggling and keep track of how successfully they help the child learn. In other words, the classroom teacher, and in some cases a reading specialist or special educator, will maintain records of how responsive the child is to various interventions. This process has spawned the acronym, RTI. In cases where a history of lack of responsiveness is documented, the possibility of an SLD is considered but not before.

The appeal of this policy has been strong. Of the "very hot" topics, RTI is definitely the "hottest" of the "very hot" (Cassidy & Cassidy, 2009/2010). However, like so many innovations, the devil is in the details. Many questions remain about how best to implement RTI. It is a trend involving a host of issues!

AS YOU READ

We have selected these two articles with the aim of providing a quick but thorough grounding in the nature of RTI and the issues that surround it. Eric and Heidi Anne Mesmer succinctly present the history and rational of RTI together with its legal basis. In the second article, Lynn and Doug Fuchs and Donald Compton explore issues that relate to RTI in the middle and high school. They suggest that the nature of the readers served at these grades makes the assumptions common at the elementary level problematic.

Your reading should focus first on understanding the basics of RTI: its rationale and procedures. We suggest that you then consider the issues that now occupy the national conversation. Does RTI work better than the discrepancy model? What are the key problems of assessment and logistics? Is the merger of regular and special education that RTI assumes really feasible? How should RTI be implemented differently in the middle and high school?

REFERENCE

Cassidy, J., & Cassidy, D. (2009/2010). What's hot for 2010. *Reading Today*, 27(3), 1, 8, 9.

Response to Intervention (RTI): What Teachers of Reading Need to Know

ERIC M. MESMER AND HEIDI ANNE E. MESMER

■ ■ ■ ■ ■

Clear definitions, details of relevant legislation, and examples of RTI in action help explain this approach to identifying and supporting learners who may be struggling.

In the most recent "What's hot, what's not for 2008?" *Reading Today* survey, 75% of prominent literacy researchers believed that Response to Intervention (RTI) was "very hot" and the same percentage believed that it should be "hot" (Cassidy & Cassidy, 2008). RTI is a new approach to identifying students with specific learning disabilities and represents a major change in special education law, the Individuals with Disabilities Act (IDEA). This change shifts the emphasis of the identification process toward providing support and intervention to struggling students early and is similarly reflected in the Reading First provisions of No Child Left Behind, which calls for proven methods of instruction to reduce the incidence of reading difficulties. RTI will alter the work of reading teachers because more than 80% of students identified for special education struggle with literacy (Lyon, 1995), and the law names "reading teachers" as qualified participants in the RTI process because of the International Reading Association's (IRA, 2007) lobbying efforts. However, RTI has only recently attracted the attention of the reading community (Bell, 2007), despite having roots in approaches such as prereferral intervention (Flugum & Reschly, 1994; Fuchs, Fuchs, & Bahr, 1990), curriculum-based measurement (Shinn, 1989), and Reading Recovery (Clay, 1987; Lyons & Beaver, 1995).

RTI in Theory

Background and Rationale

RTI was developed because of the many problems with the discrepancy model for identifying students with learning disabilities (e.g., Francis et al., 2005; O'Malley, Francis, Foorman, Fletcher, & Swank, 2002; Stanovich, 2005; Vellutino, Scanlon, & Lyon, 2000; Walmsley & Allington, 2007). In 1977, a learning disability was defined as "a severe discrepancy between achievement and intellectual ability" (U.S. Department of Education, 1977, p. G1082). In practice, this involves schools administering IQ tests and achievement tests and then examining scores for discrepancies between intellect and achievement to identify a learning disability (see Table 1). The discrepancy model has drawn four major criticisms. First, it requires that a learning problem becomes considerably acute in terms of an IQ/achievement discrepancy before a learner can receive additional support, a problem called "waiting to fail" (Vaughn & Fuchs, 2003, p. 139). Second, establishing a discrepancy is not necessary to improve outcomes for struggling readers, as students both with and without a discrepancy are qualitatively the same in their

Table 1   Definitions of RTI Terms

Term	Definition
Discrepancy model	The standard for identifying students with learning disabilities based on the 1977 federal regulations. This process required that a significant difference be documented between a student's ability (IQ) and achievement in order for a learning disability to be identified. RTI models respond to the many problems identified with the discrepancy model.
Intervention	Targeted instruction provided in addition to the regular classroom program that addresses a student's documented instructional needs. Instruction that intends to prevent students who are struggling from falling farther behind their peers and intends to improve their future educational trajectory.
Level data	Information that reflects how students are performing in comparison to peers at a specific point in time.
Slope data	Information that reflects how a student is learning across time in comparison to his or her previous learning. These data capture rate of learning and can also be called growth rates. Slopes that are steeper show more growth over a smaller period of time than slopes that are flatter. Slope data are obtained by repeatedly measuring student performance in a particular area. They are displayed using a line graph.
Student progress monitoring	An assessment technique required by RTI regulations. Teachers administer quick assessments (1–5 minutes) frequently (weekly) to gauge the improvement of a student. The assessments provide information about the student's rate of learning and the effectiveness of a particular intervention (National Center on Student Progress Monitoring, 2007).
Literacy screening	The process of assessing the most basic and predictive literacy skills for all students in a school. The goal of screenings is to select learners whose reading achievement is significantly below standards. Literacy screenings are intended to identify students who require additional help so that further slippage and literacy failure can be prevented.

literacy instructional needs (Fuchs, Mock, Morgan, & Young, 2003; Vellutino et al., 2000). Third, the IQ/achievement discrepancy has shifted focus away from understanding the impact of other possible factors, such as opportunities to learn (Walmsley & Allington, 2007). These factors need to be considered prior to determining that a learning disability exists. Fourth, under the discrepancy model, many districts and states have seen skyrocketing percentages of students identified as learning disabled, particularly minorities (IRA, 2007; Walmsley & Allington, 2007).

The Law

In 2004, IDEA, Public Law 108-446, introduced RTI language (U.S. Department of Education, 2006). In Table 2, the section titled "Specific learning disabilities" (§ 300.307) asserts that states cannot be required to use the discrepancy model for identifying learning disabilities but may "permit the use of a process based on the child's response to scientific, research-based intervention." This is RTI, a process measuring whether a learner's academic performance improves when provided with well-defined, scientifically based interventions. In an RTI model, the "tests" of whether students possess learning disabilities are not standardized measures but students' measured responses to interventions. Within RTI, student potential (IQ) is replaced by a goal that allows for the evaluation of a performance relative to a defined academic standard (e.g., performance of other students in the class or grade level). Students responding quickly and significantly to interventions are less likely to possess a disability than students responding

Table 2   Additional Procedures for Identifying Children with Specific Learning Disabilities

IDEA terminology	IDEA definition
§ 300.307 Specific learning disabilities.	A State must adopt, consistent with 34 CFR 300.309, criteria for determining whether a child has a specific learning disability as defined in 34 CFR 300.8(c)(10). In addition, the criteria adopted by the State: ■ Must not require the use of a severe discrepancy between intellectual ability and achievement for determining whether a child has a specific learning disability, as defined in 34 CFR 300.8(c)(10); ■ Must permit the use of a process based on the child's response to scientific, research-based intervention; and ■ May permit the use of other alternative research-based procedures for determining whether a child has a specific learning disability, as defined in 34 CFR 300.8(c)(10). A public agency must use the State criteria adopted pursuant to 34 CFR 300.307(a) in determining whether a child has a specific learning disability. [34 CFR 300.307] [20 U.S.C. 1221e-3; 1401(30); 1414(b)(6)]

§ 300.309 Determining the existence of a specific learning disability.	The group described in 34 CFR 300.306 may determine that a child has a specific learning disability, as defined in 34 CFR 300.8(c)(10), if:
	■ The child does not achieve adequately for the child's age or to meet State-approved grade-level standards in one or more of the following areas, when provided with learning experiences and instruction appropriate for the child's age or State-approved grade-level standards:
	
	  ■ Oral expression.
	  ■ Listening comprehension.
	  ■ Written expression.
	  ■ Basic reading skills.
	  ■ Reading fluency skills.
	  ■ Reading comprehension.
	  ■ Mathematics calculation.
	  ■ Mathematics problem solving.
	
	■ The child does not make sufficient progress to meet age or State-approved grade-level standards in one or more of the areas identified in 34 CFR 300.309(a)(1) when using a process based on the child's response to scientific, research-based intervention; or the child exhibits a pattern of strengths and weaknesses in performance, achievement, or both, relative to age, State-approved grade-level standards, or intellectual development, that is determined by the group to be relevant to the identification of a specific learning disability, using appropriate assessments, consistent with 34 CFR 300.304 and 300.305; and the group determines that its findings under 34 CFR 300.309(a)(1) and (2) are not primarily the result of:
	
	  ■ A visual, hearing, or motor disability;
	  ■ Mental retardation;
	  ■ Emotional disturbance;
	  ■ Cultural factors;
	  ■ Environmental or economic disadvantage; or
	  ■ Limited English proficiency.
	
	To ensure that underachievement in a child suspected of having a specific learning disability is not due to lack of appropriate instruction in reading or math, the group must consider, as part of the evaluation described in 34 CFR 300.304 through 300.306:
	
	  ■ Data that demonstrate that prior to, or as a part of, the referral process, the child was provided appropriate instruction in regular education settings, delivered by qualified personnel; and
	  ■ Data-based documentation of repeated assessments of achievement at reasonable intervals, reflecting formal assessment of student progress during instruction, which was provided to the child's parents.

Note: From U.S. Department of Education. (2006). *Assistance to states for the education of children with disabilities and preschool grants for children with disabilities* (Federal register 34 CFR Parts 300 and 301). Washington, D.C: Author.

more slowly or not at all. However, data showing a student's response to an intervention serves as only one source of information for determining whether a learning disability is present. Learning disabilities cannot be diagnosed when appropriate instruction, socioeconomic status, culture, sensory issues, emotional issues, or English as a second language may be of concern.

In the section titled "Determining the existence of a specific learning disability" (§ 300.309), the law states that a learning disability may be present when a student's performance is not adequate to meet grade-level standards when provided with appropriate instruction and research-based interventions. The term *appropriate* refers to instruction in the classroom that matches a student's skill level. The descriptors *scientific* or *research-based* indicate that interventions should be based on practices that have produced verifiable results through research studies.

RTI Processes

The processes undergirding RTI have been used for evaluating the success of school-wide supports, individualized interventions, and special education (O'Connor, Fulmre, Harty, & Bell, 2005; Powell-Smith & Ball, 2002; Taylor-Greene et al., 1997). However, in this article we focus on RTI as an initial referral and identification process for students suspected of having learning disabilities.

Step 1

Universal literacy practices are established. Prevention begins with universal literacy screenings to identify students who could be at risk (see Table 3). Any state receiving Reading First monies has identified a literacy screening in grades K–3. All students are screened on basic literacy skills approximately three times per year. Typically, student performance is compared with minimal benchmark scores and students not meeting benchmarks receive help.

Step 2

Scientifically valid interventions are implemented. When students do not meet benchmarks, they need additional instruction. Within most RTI models, interventions are first delivered to a small group and are intended to assist students in developing skills that will allow them to improve their reading skills.

Table 3   Examples of Literacy Screening Assessments

Screener	Authors
Dynamic Indicators of Basic Early Literacy Skills (DIBELS)	Good & Kaminski, 2002
Phonological Awareness Literacy Screening (PALS)	Invernizzi, Juel, Swank, & Meier, 2005
Texas Primary Reading Inventory (TPRI)	Texas Education Agency & University of Texas System, 2006
Illinois Snapshots of Early Literacy (ISEL)	Illinois State Board of Education, 2004

Step 3

Progress of students receiving intervention instruction is monitored. RTI requires that progress-monitoring data are continuously collected as students receive interventions. Progress-monitoring assessments should address the skills that are being targeted for intervention and should indicate if the intervention is changing the student's reading. Also, the assessments should be administered repeatedly (weekly or biweekly) without introducing test-wise bias, which occurs when the results of an assessment reflect the test taker's acquired knowledge about a test rather than true performance. In addition, the assessments should be sufficiently sensitive to small changes in the student's reading performance (i.e., those that might occur within a few days) because if students are showing growth on the more sensitive, microlevel progress-monitoring measures, they will also be showing growth in the more comprehensive measures (Deno, Mirkin, & Chiang, 1982; Fuchs & Deno, 1981; Riedel, 2007). Finally, progress-monitoring measures must be reliable, valid, and brief (National Center on Student Progress Monitoring, 2007). For a list of tools for progress monitoring, see the National Center on Student Progress Monitoring Website at www.student-progress.org/chart/chart.asp.

Step 4

Individualize interventions for students who continue to struggle. Students who continue to struggle despite receiving initial intervention instruction will require more intense, targeted interventions. These interventions may require additional assessments to clarify the nature of the difficulty. The data generated from these additional assessments should be used collaboratively by teachers, reading specialists, school psychologists, and parents to develop more intensive intervention strategies. Upon implementation, the student's progress continues to be monitored.

Step 5

A decision-making process to determine eligibility for special education services occurs when necessary. In the last step, a team of school-based professionals and the student's parents review all data to determine whether the student is eligible for special education services. Special services may be indicated when the student has not responded to interventions that have been well implemented for a sufficient period of time. If the team suspects that the student's lack of response may be explained by some other factor (i.e., not explained by a learning disability), then it should request additional assessment of the student's social, behavioral, emotional, intellectual, and adaptive functioning.

RTI in Real Life: Making a Difference for Mark

To illustrate RTI processes, we use a vignette (with pseudonyms) based on our experiences in schools. This vignette shows how a team including Donisha, a reading teacher; Julie, a special educator; Carol, a second-grade teacher; and Sandra, a school psychologist; worked collaboratively (and sometimes painstakingly) within an RTI model to assist a student named Mark.

Step 1: Universal Literacy Practices Are Established

In September, Mark was administered the Phonological Awareness and Literacy Screening (PALS; Invernizzi, Juel, Swank, & Meier, 2005), an assessment that begins with two screening measures, the first-grade word list, given in the fall of grade 2, and a spelling assessment. From these measures, an entry benchmark score is formed. If the benchmark score does not meet the grade-level minimum, then additional diagnostics are administered (preprimer and primer lists, letter naming, letter sounds, concept of word, blending, and sound-to-letter). Students also read passages through which accuracy, reading rate, phrasing (a 3-point subjective scale), and comprehension scores are collected.

In the fall, Mark received a benchmark score of 22 (7/20 on the first-grade word list) and 15/20 on the spelling assessment. An expected benchmark score of 35, based on 15 words on the first-grade list, and 20 spelling feature points is expected for the beginning of second grade. Mark read instructionally at the primer level (1.1) with moderate phrasing and expression and answered five-sixths of the questions correctly. He read the 120 words in the primer story in 4 minutes and 20 seconds, a rate of about 28 words correct per minute (WCPM) and 20 words below the 50th percentile for second graders in the fall (Parker, Hasbrouck, & Tindal, 1992). When diagnostic assessments were administered, data showed that Mark had mastered alphabetic skills, such as phonemic awareness and letters. Carol described her initial analysis: "Mark seemed to have the basic building blocks for reading but needed more practice at his level." Initially, Mark received small-group classroom instruction, including reading daily in on-level materials and working with Carol on comprehension and decoding. In September, October, and November, Carol took running records on the books that Mark and the other students had been reading. Although the accuracy and book levels of other students were steadily increasing, Mark's accuracy was averaging 90% in less difficult books. Carol explained, "I felt like Mark needed more help, and we needed to act because I was concerned that he would continue to fall behind."

Step 2: Scientifically Valid Interventions Are Implemented

RTI requires that instructional interventions be scientifically valid, public, implemented with integrity, and systematically evaluated. Julie, who had recently attended the district's RTI workshop, explained, "The who, what, when, where, and how of interventions must be clear." The content of the intervention should be designated, the teacher responsible for implementing it identified, and the assessments determined. Often different team members plan, implement, or assess the intervention based on availability and expertise. For this reason, educators must collaborate and share information.

The team discussed Mark's needs and designed an intervention. Based upon its review of the data, the team determined that accurate, fluent reading in connected text seemed to be the problem. Mark could easily understand books above his reading level, but his progress was being impeded by word recognition. The group decided that an intervention increasing the amount of reading practice for Mark would build up his reading level. The designed intervention comprised the following components: modeling of fluent reading, repeated readings, error correction, comprehension questions, and self-monitoring. They decided that Donisha would implement the intervention with three other students in the classroom in 20-minute sessions, three times per week. In addition, Carol continued to work with Mark in the classroom during small-group instruction. Specifically, she had Mark read from the same materials used by Donisha to further increase practice opportunities, and she set a daily goal for Mark on comprehension questions. Mark checked his answers each day and provided the results to his teacher at the end of the reading block.

Step 3: Progress of Students Receiving Intervention Instruction Is Monitored

As the intervention was implemented, Sandra tracked Mark's accuracy and fluency in reading passages at the primer and second-grade levels, because the goal was to understand Mark's progress toward grade-level norms. She used a PDA device loaded with passages at different levels. As Mark read these passages weekly, Sandra kept track of his accuracy (percentage of words correct) and reading rate (WCPM). Figure 1 shows Mark's accuracy and Figure 2 shows his reading rate before and after implementing the intervention for six weeks. Mark demonstrated some gains in accuracy and fluency, but his progress was not increasing at a rate that would allow him to meet established second-grade goals.

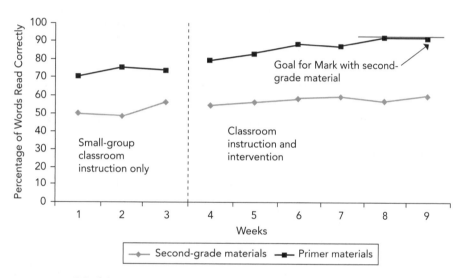

FIGURE 1   **Mark's Accuracy During Intervention Instruction**

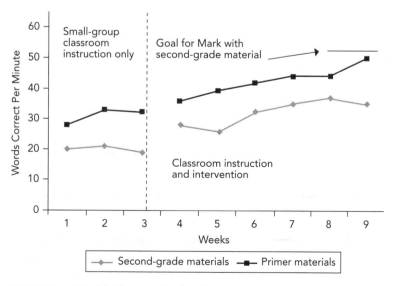

FIGURE 2   **Mark's Fluency During Intervention Instruction**

As we have described RTI to this point, it sounds smooth and trouble free. But it was anything but that for the professionals involved. Donisha's first reaction to RTI was strong:

> At first, I felt like this group was shrinking reading down to something very simplistic. I had to advocate for comprehension questions to be included in the intervention. Even though Mark's comprehension was fine, we did not want him to believe that comprehension didn't matter. We also clarified that interventions are *additive* and by nature narrower because their power lies in solving specific problems. The comprehensive reading program is broad and multifaceted, and it keeps going on while a child is receiving an intervention. So Carol wasn't going to stop guided reading or doing the rest of her program.

We liken the intervention and the reading program to a balanced diet. The intervention is like an extra serving of milk, but it doesn't replace meat, fruits, or vegetables.

Donisha was also concerned that the intervention would be scripted. Scripts are directions to teachers that are read verbatim during instruction. Interventions are specific and systematic, but nothing in the law requires them to be scripted.

Carol also had concerns. "I was not used to people asking me specific questions about exactly what I was doing, and how often, and what my results were. At first, it felt invasive and suspicious." Given the frequency with which blame is placed on classroom teachers, Carol's reaction was understandable. However, the team members pointed out that the instruction was working well for almost all of the other students and acknowledged the time limitations and demands placed on Carol as a classroom teacher. Although she had felt it in the past, Carol did not feel as though fingers were being pointed at her. Sandra had faced equal frustration before:

> I come in because a teacher has a concern and when I start asking questions, I get tight responses and defensiveness. It's like asking questions is stepping on toes. I can't help others further understand the problem or contribute to a useful intervention if we can't talk nitty-gritty. Once I had a teacher tell me, "You're not a teacher. You won't be able to help." While I am not a teacher, I can contribute to the development of interventions, and I have particular skill in measuring effects.

In addition to reviewing Mark's progress during the six weeks of intervention instruction, Mark's mid-year PALS scores were evaluated by the team. He was independent at the primer (1.1) level and barely instructional at the first-grade level with 14 errors and a reading rate of 42 WCPM. Despite his increase in instructional level and fluency, the team remained concerned about the lack of reduction in the number of errors that Mark was making. The team decided that these errors would ultimately become detrimental to Mark's fluency and comprehension, particularly as text increased in difficulty. The team determined that individualized intervention was warranted.

Step 4: Individualize Interventions for Students Who Continue to Struggle

Because they had no measure of decoding, the team decided to assess Mark using the Word Attack Test from the Woodcock Reading Mastery Test. Results from this assessment revealed that Mark was having difficulty decoding words with more than one syllable or those that contained difficult vowel patterns. This resulted in reduced accuracy and fluency. The team enhanced the intervention by adding practice with problem words. Mark practiced incorrectly read words, received instruction in how to analyze word parts, extended analytic skills to similar words, and practiced through word sorts.

Following word sorts, Mark read each word within a sentence. Donisha implemented this individualized intervention for 10 minutes each day following the reading practice intervention (discussed earlier in the article).

Mark's reading accuracy and fluency continued to be monitored weekly by Sandra. The team determined that the intervention would be implemented for a minimum of 6 weeks, as this time frame would correspond with the end of the school year. However, the team recognized that interventions in early literacy often need to run longer, between 10 and 20 weeks, depending on factors such as the needs of the student and the intensity of the intervention (University of Texas Center for Reading and Language Arts, 2003; Wanzek & Vaughn, 2008). Moreover, Mark's progress was measured each week so that the intervention could be modified if he failed to make adequate gains. His response to the individualized reading intervention is provided in Figures 3 and 4. Figure 3 shows that Mark quickly responded to the word attack intervention. Data were

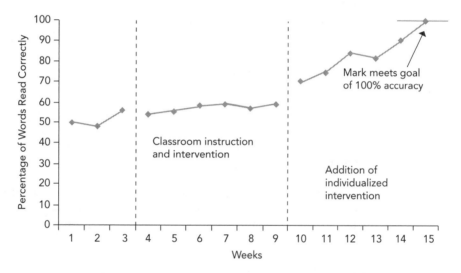

FIGURE 3 Mark's Accuracy During Individualized Intervention

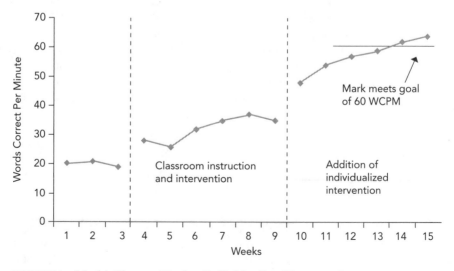

FIGURE 4 Mark's Fluency During Individualized Intervention

collected once per week on the percentage of words read correctly from second-grade passages. Mark's response to the intervention contrasted dramatically with his performance reading unknown words prior to the intervention. By the sixth week, Mark correctly read 100% of words presented when prior to intervention he was only reading 55% to 60% accurately. Figure 4 shows that Mark improved in reading fluency as well. Prior to word attack intervention, the effects of the fluency intervention had leveled off. With the addition of the word attack intervention, Mark's fluency steadily improved until he met the second-grade goal. By the end of May, Mark met the PALS summed score benchmark. His end-of-the-year PALS (58 summer score) showed him meeting the benchmark, reading instructionally at second-grade level with comprehension, and reading at a rate of about 60 WCPM.

Step 5: Decision-Making Process to Determine Eligibility for Special Education Services

Despite falling below the second-grade benchmark in September, Mark demonstrated growth on accuracy, fluency, and decoding as a result of the efforts of school personnel. The team reviewed Mark's intervention data and determined that special education services were not necessary. However, Julie voiced concerns about Mark and the continued need for support:

> I could see that Mark had made great progress, but I knew that summer could potentially influence his starting point in the fall and that his progress was the result of substantive instruction *in addition* to the regular classroom. So I insisted that a meeting be scheduled for him in the fall to be proactive about his needs.

Mark's progress was significant relative to where his skills were at the beginning of the year. If the interventions had not met Mark's needs, the team would have been charged with determining whether the lack of response was indicative of a learning disability.

Why RTI?

As illustrated, RTI is a process that incorporates both assessment and intervention so that immediate benefits come to the student. Assessment data are used to inform interventions and determine the effectiveness of them. As a result of the intervention-focused nature of RTI, eligibility services shift toward a supportive rather than sorting function. A testing model that identifies and sorts students into programs or services is predicated upon the effectiveness of those services. Unfortunately, the effectiveness of special education, particularly placement of students in separate classrooms, has been variable at best (Bentum & Aaron, 2003; Kavale, 1990), even as an increasing percentage of students have been identified as learning disabled over the past 30 years (Gresham, 2002). Within the RTI model, instruction can at last be addressed.

Queries, Concerns, and Future Research

We have worked with state departments of education, school districts, schools, and teachers long enough to have questions about RTI. The first issue is that definitions of scientific research privilege experimental and quasi-experimental research (Eisenhart & Towne, 2003; Pressley, 2003). Experiments occur when subjects are randomly assigned to different conditions and the results measured, and they are the best way to know if a practice is causing a certain learning outcome. However, they depend on delivering an instructional treatment in a standardized way, often with study personnel. When teachers do participate in experiments, they often receive intensive support that may not be available when the strategy is widely implemented. The artifices of experiments can limit the degree to which the instructional treatment can be implemented in the real world (Pressley, 2003).

Second, if scientifically based interventions are to be implemented, then research findings must get to schools. We are concerned that the label *scientifically based* will be misused and will proliferate as publishers and companies slap it on everything they market to schools. The final issue is that diverse ways to screen in literacy are still emerging (Gersten & Dimino, 2006). Researchers note that phonologically based competencies, such as phoneme awareness, letter/sound knowledge, and decoding, contribute to part of what makes a student a successful reader (Gersten & Dimino, 2006; Paris, 2005; Scarborough, 2005). Readers must also have a deep knowledge of word meanings and be able to comprehend text. We know oral reading fluency is a good predictor of grade 1 comprehension (Riedel, 2007), but powerful, direct screenings in the areas of vocabulary and comprehension have yet to be developed for elementary learners. Nonetheless, intervening in these areas is important despite the fact that few screening tools exist.

Despite the challenges with RTI, we have seen this approach increase the quantity and quality of instruction for struggling readers. RTI is an initial attempt to provide an alternative to the dominant and damaging discrepancy model in which so much time is spent admiring the student's reading problem. By this we mean people discuss the problem, collect data on it, and write about it, months before they *do* anything about it. IDEA 2004 provides school districts with a choice to opt out of the discrepancy model.

REFERENCES

Bell, M. (2007). *Reading teachers play key role in successful response to intervention approaches*. Retrieved May 31, 2007, from www.reading.org/downloads/resources/IDEA_RTI_teachers_role.pdf

Bentum, K.E., & Aaron, P.G. (2003). Does reading instruction in learning disability resource rooms really work?: A longitudinal study. *Reading Psychology*, 24(3–4), 361–382. doi:10.1080/02702710390227387

Cassidy, J., & Cassidy, D. (2008). What's hot, what's not for 2008? *Reading Today*, 25(4), 1, 10–11.

Clay, M.M. (1987). Learning to be learning disabled. *New Zealand Journal of Educational Studies*, 22(2), 155–173.

Deno, S.L., Mirkin, P.K., & Chiang, B. (1982). Identifying valid measures of reading. *Exceptional Children*, 49(1), 36–45.

Eisenhart, M., & Towne, L. (2003). Contestation and change in national policy on "scientifically based" education research. *Educational Researcher*, 32(7), 31–38. doi:10.3102/001 3189X032007031

Flugum, K., & Reschly, D. (1994). Prereferral interventions: Quality indices and outcomes. *Journal of School Psychology*, 32(1), 1–14. doi:10.1016/0022-4405(94)90025-6

Francis, D.J., Fletcher, J.M., Stuebing, K.K., Lyon, G.R., Shaywitz, B.A., & Shaywitz, S.E. (2005). Psychometric approaches to the identification of LD: IQ and achievement scores are not sufficient. *Journal of Learning Disabilities*, 38(2), 98–108. doi:10.1 177/00222194050380020101

Fuchs, D., Fuchs, L., & Bahr, M. (1990). Mainstream assistance teams: A scientific basis for the art of consultation. *Exceptional Children*, 57(2) 128–139.

Fuchs, D., Mock, D., Morgan, P.L., & Young, C.L. (2003). Responsiveness-to-intervention: Definitions, evidence, and implications for the learning disabilities construct. *Learning Disabilities: Research & Practice*, 18(3), 157–171. doi:10.1111/15 40-5826.00072

Fuchs, L.S., & Deno, S.L. (1981). *The relationship between curriculum-based mastery measures and standardized achievement tests in reading* (Research Report No. 57). Minneapolis: University of Minnesota Institute for Research on Learning Disabilities. (ERIC Document Reproduction Service No. ED212662)

Gersten, R., & Dimino, J.A. (2006). RTI (Response to Intervention): Rethinking special education for students with reading difficulties (again). *Reading Research Quarterly, 41*(1), 99–108. doi:10.1598/RRQ.41.1.5

Good, R., & Kaminski, R. (2002). *DIBELS oral reading fluency passages for first through third grades* (Technical Report 10). Eugene: University of Oregon.

Gresham, F. (2002). Responsiveness to intervention: An alternative approach to the identification of learning disabilities. In R. Bradley, L. Danielson, & D. Hallahan (Eds.), *Identification of learning disabilities: Research to practice* (pp. 467–519). Mahwah, NJ: Erlbaum.

Illinois State Board of Education. (2008). *Illinois Snapshots of Early Literacy*. Retrieved June 5, 2007, from www.isbe.state.il.us/curriculum/reading/html/isel.htm

International Reading Association. (2007). *Implications for reading teachers in Response to Intervention (RTI)*. Retrieved May 31, 2007, from www.reading.org/downloads/resources/rti0707_implications.pdf

Invernizzi, M., Juel, C., Swank, L., & Meier, J. (2005). *Phonological awareness literacy screening*. Virginia: The Rector and The Board of Visitors of the University of Virginia.

Kavale, K. (1990). Effectiveness of special education. In T.B. Gutkin & C.R. Reynolds (Eds.), *Handbook of school psychology* (2nd ed., pp. 868–898). New York, NY: Wiley.

Lyon, G.R. (1995). Research initiatives in learning disabilities: Contributions from scientists supported by the National Institute of Child Health and Human Development. *Journal of Child Neurology, 10* (Suppl. 1), S120–S126.

Lyons, C., & Beaver, J. (1995). Reducing retention and learning disability placement through reading recovery: An educationally sound cost-effective choice. In R. Allington & S. Walmsley (Eds.), *No quick fix: Rethinking literacy programs in America's elementary schools* (pp. 116–136). New York: Teachers College Press.

National Center on Student Progress Monitoring. (2007). Common questions for progress monitoring. Retrieved May 20, 2007, from www.studentprogress.org/progresmon.asp#2

O'Connor, R.E., Fulmer, D., Harty, K.R., & Bell, K.M. (2005). Layers of reading intervention in kindergarten through third grade: Changes in teaching and student outcomes. *Journal of Learning Disabilities, 38*(5), 440–455. doi:10.1177/00222194050380050701

O'Malley, K., Francis, D.J., Foorman, B.R., Fletcher, J.M., & Swank, P.R. (2002). Growth in precursor and reading-related skills: Do low-achieving and IQ-discrepant readers develop differently? *Learning Disabilities Research & Practice, 17*(1), 19–34. doi:10.1111/1540-5826.00029

Paris, S.G. (2005). Reinterpreting the development of reading skills. *Reading Research Quarterly, 40*(2), 184–202. doi:10.1598/RRQ.40.2.3

Parker, R., Hasbrouck, J., & Tindal, G. (1992). Greater validity for oral reading fluency: Can miscues help? *The Journal of Special Education, 25*(4), 492–503.

Powell-Smith, K., & Ball, P. (2002). Best practices in reintegration and special education exit decisions. In A. Thomas & J. Grimes (Eds.), *Best practices in school psychology-IV* (pp. 541–557). Bethesda, MD: National Association of School Psychologists.

Pressley, M. (2003). A few things reading educators should know about instructional experiments. *The Reading Teacher, 57*(1), 64–71.

Riedel, B. (2007). The relation between DIBELS, reading comprehension, and vocabulary in urban first grade students. *Reading Research Quarterly, 42*(4), 546–567. doi:10.1598/RRQ.42.4.5

Scarborough, H. (2005). Developmental relationships between language and reading: Reconciling a beautiful hypothesis with some ugly facts. In H.W. Catts & A.G. Kamhi (Eds.), *The connections between language and reading disabilities* (pp. 3–24). Mahwah, NJ: Erlbaum.

Shinn, M. (1989). *Curriculum-based measurement: Assessing special children*. New York, NY: Guilford.

Stanovich, K. (2005). The future of a mistake: Will discrepancy measurement continue to make the learning disabilities field a pseudoscience? *Learning Disability Quarterly, 28*(2), 103–106. doi:10.2307/1593604

Taylor-Greene, S., Brown, D., Nelson, L., Longton, J., Cohen, J., Swartz, J., et al. (1997). School-wide behavioral support: Starting the year off right. *Journal of Behavioral Education, 7*(1), 99–112. doi:10.1023/A:1022849722465

Texas Education Agency & University of Texas System. (2006). *Texas Primary Reading Inventory.* Retrieved from www.tpri.org/products/

University of Texas Center for Reading and Language Arts. (2003). *Three-tier reading model: Reducing reading difficulties for kindergarten through third grade students.* Austin, TX: Author.

U.S. Department of Education. (1977). *1977 code of federal regulations.* Washington, DC: Author.

U.S. Department of Education. (2006). *Assistance to states for the education of children with disabilities and preschools grants for children with disabilities, final rule.* Retrieved May 17, 2007, from eric.ed.gov/ERICDocs/data/ericdocs2sql/content_storage_01/0000019b/80/1b/e9/95.pdf

Vaughn, S., & Fuchs, L.S. (2003). Redefining learning disabilities as inadequate response to instruction: The promise and potential problems. *Learning Disabilities Research & Practice, 18*(3), 137–146. doi:10.1111/1540-5826.00070

Vellutino, F.R., Scanlon, D.M., & Lyon, G.R. (2000). Differentiating between difficult-to-remediate and readily remediated poor readers: More evidence against the IQ-discrepancy definition of reading disability. *Journal of Learning Disabilities, 33*(3), 223–238. doi:10.1177/002221940003300302

Walmsley, S., & Allington, R. (2007). *No quick fix, the RTI edition: Rethinking literacy programs in America's elementary schools.* Newark, DE: International Reading Association.

Wanzek, J., & Vaughn, S. (2008). Response to varying amounts of time in reading intervention for students with low response to intervention. *Journal of Learning Disabilities, 41*(2), 126–142. doi:10.1177/0022219407313426

E. Mesmer teaches at Radford University, Radford, Virginia, USA; e-mail: emesmer@radford.edu. H. Mesmer teaches at Virginia Polytechnic Institute and State University, Blacksburg, USA; hamesmer@vt.edu.

Rethinking Response to Intervention (RTI) at Middle and High School

LYNN S. FUCHS, DOUGLAS FUCHS, AND DONALD L. COMPTON

Vanderbilt University

■ ■ ■ ■ ■

In "Response to Intervention for Middle School Students With Reading Difficulties: Effects of a Primary and Secondary Intervention," Sharon Vaughn and colleagues (2010) described a study in which they provided professional development to content area teachers, with the goal of integrating vocabulary and reading comprehension instruction throughout the school day in Tier 1 (i.e., in the general education classrooms). Against this enhanced instructional backdrop, the researchers randomly assigned at-risk students whom they identified based on inadequate performance on the previous year's high-stakes state reading assessment, to two conditions: business-as-usual school services or a researcher-designed, 32- to 36-week Tier 2 reading intervention focused on decoding, fluency, vocabulary, and comprehension. The researchers delivered this Tier 2 intervention in large groups (i.e., 10–15 students per group) to reflect a logistically feasible model for implementation in real schools. The instruction was conducted for nearly 100 hr per student ($SD = 23.1$) at one site and 111 hr ($SD = 11.6$) at a second site. With this ambitious randomized control trial, they examined the efficacy of a RTI Tier 2 intervention at sixth grade.

Few researchers have focused on an older school-age population when studying RTI with such a well-conceptualized, comprehensive intervention. Many researchers avoid middle and high schools entirely because of the scheduling problems and compliance issues often encountered when working with adolescents. These complexities associated with middle and high school may help explain Vaughn et al.'s (2010) disappointing findings. On word-level skills, significant effects for two measures were moderated by students' incoming performance: On decoding, treatment effects were revealed only for students above the pretest mean; on spelling, only for students below the covariate mean. For fluency and comprehension measures, there were no statistically significant effects, and the Tier 2 intervention did not improve the chances of passing the high-stakes state assessment. Across measures, the median effect size was 0.16.

Vaughn et al. (2010) do an admirable job of discussing and contextualizing these findings, and they clarify another factor possibly contributing to their modest results: A disproportionate number of students in the business-as-usual condition received a second level of prevention activities designed and implemented by their own schools (i.e., 49% of controls but only 23% of experimental students). Nevertheless, the results of the researchers' more

Correspondence regarding this article should be addressed to Lynn S. Fuchs. 228 Peabody, Vanderbilt University, Nashville, TN 37203; E-mail: lynn.fuchs@vanderbilt.edu substantial and more carefully designed Tier 2 intervention are sobering and, in this commentary, we consider why differences between elementary versus middle and high school settings may require an alternative conceptualization of RTI at the higher grades.

The RTI Prevention Framework at the Elementary Grades

Children enter kindergarten with differing degrees of preparedness for academic learning. To address these inequities, schools must allocate resources early, as formal academic instruction begins. RTI is a framework for organizing such prevention activities. Before considering RTI at middle and high school, we summarize the typical RTI process at the elementary grades. This Elementary RTI Framework incorporates three levels of prevention services. We use the word level instead of tier to avoid widespread confusion over the term tier. The number of tiers in RTI systems ranges from 1 to 7 (Berkeley, Bender, Gregg Peaster, & Saunders, 2009), with tier referring to the sequence in which interventions are introduced. One school's Tier 2, for example, may be identical in intensity and instructional design to another school's Tier 5. For this reason, the term fails to communicate meaningfully about the intensity of instruction. By contrast, in our Elementary RTI Framework, every intervention (which represents a tier) is categorized within one of the prevention system's three levels, and each level is distinctive in terms of instructional intensity.

Primary prevention comprises the instructional practices that general educators conduct: the core instructional program; classroom routines that provide opportunities for instructional differentiation; accommodations that permit access to the primary prevention program for all students; and problem-solving strategies to address motivational problems that cause some students to fail to perform the academic skills they possess. Most core programs are designed using instructional principles derived from research, but few are validated because of the challenges associated with conducting experimental studies of complex, multicomponent programs.

Secondary prevention (not to be confused with the secondary grades in middle and high schools) usually occurs as small-group tutoring, with the tutor using a validated instructional program. Secondary prevention is reserved for students at risk for serious long-term academic difficulties. Risk is identified via screening. Brief tests are administered to all students to eliminate true negatives from consideration; students who fail that universal screen receive a second stage of testing to discriminate true positives from false positives (e.g., Compton et al., in press). Conducting a second stage of screening is efficient in that schools avoid providing secondary prevention to false positive students (who would develop nicely without intervention). Secondary prevention differs from primary prevention because secondary prevention is empirically validated (whereas primary prevention is research principled) and because it relies on adult-led tutoring in groups of 2–5 students (whereas primary prevention relies primarily on whole-class instruction and sometimes peer tutoring). Secondary prevention can involve only one tier of validated tutoring program, but it can also incorporate a series of validated tutoring programs.

When validated tutoring at the secondary prevention level is implemented with fidelity, a large majority of students are expected to benefit, based on the validation research associated with the small-group tutoring program. However, approximately 5% of the general population is not expected to respond and, for these students, most intensive intervention is required at the tertiary prevention level. In using the term most intensive intervention, we refer to two kinds of practices. The first involves tutoring programs that have been validated as successful for this 5% of the population. Tertiary tutoring programs rely on complex, multicomponent instructional routines and more hours of teaching over longer periods of time with lower (often 2:1; sometimes 1:1) tutor-student ratios. A second type of most intensive intervention involves individualized instruction, whereby teachers systematically experiment with different instructional components, using ongoing progress-monitoring data as the dependent variable to decide which components enhance progress. With this process, teachers inductively tailor an individualized program. In a series of randomized control trials (see Stecker, Fuchs, & Fuchs, 2005), such inductive, data-based individualization has been shown to be effective for students with learning disabilities. The greatest potential for accelerating the academic progress of most difficult- to-teach learners at the tertiary level, however, may exist for a combination of the two approaches. That is, the teacher begins with a more intensive validated tutoring program, while conducting frequent progress monitoring to tailor that program for maximal effectiveness.

Distinctions Between Elementary Versus Middle and High School

In these ways, the Elementary RTI Framework reflects three assumptions that may not apply at middle and high school. The first assumption is that *screening is required to identify risk before academic deficits materialize*. In the early grades, a major challenge for screening is that many scores cluster near the bottom range of the scale, creating a floor effect. This makes it difficult to distinguish between false and true positives. Consider, for example, quantity discrimination as an index of numerosity for predicting student success in learning formal school mathematics. When measured at the start of first grade, quantity discrimination accounts for 25%–63% of the variance in year-end math outcomes (e.g., Chard et al., 2005; Clarke & Shinn, 2004; Lembke & Foegen, 2006). Even so, such measures produce large percentages of false positives: children who fail the quantity discrimination screen but develop adequately without secondary prevention (e.g., Fuchs, Fuchs, Compton, Bryant, Hamlett, & Seethaler, 2007; Seethaler & Fuchs, in press). This is problematic for Elementary RTI because serving large numbers of false positives in secondary prevention, when these students would do fine without those services, not only stresses the resources available in schools to serve students who truly need secondary prevention but also requires students who do not require secondary prevention to miss portions of the primary prevention program. Given the false positive problems, a second stage of more indepth testing is required for students who fail the universal screen.

At middle and high school, however, academic deficits are well established. Moreover, because a greater range of performance in the academic domain can be sampled than in the elementary grades, it is easier to design middle and high school tests whereby students do not cluster near the bottom of the scale, creating meaningful distinctions among students with deficits of larger and smaller magnitudes. For these reasons, at middle and high school, it no longer makes sense to allocate scarce resources to screening for the purpose of identifying students at risk for academic failure. It makes more sense to rely on teacher nomination or existing assessment data to identify students with manifest academic difficulties, which is what Vaughn et al. (2010) did when they relied on the existing high-stakes reading assessment scores to identify students who required intervention beyond the primary prevention program. In contrast to the Vaughn et al. approach, however, it may make sense to gather additional assessment data or scrutinize available data to create functional tutoring groupings with similar instructional needs and, perhaps more important, to distinguish (a) students whose academic deficits are so serious that they warrant immediate tertiary prevention from (b) students likely to succeed with secondary prevention. It is possible that the Vaughn et al. distinction between students at the benchmark "bubble" versus those who scored reliably below the benchmark score might have been useful for such purposes.

This brings us to the second Elementary RTI assumption that may not apply at middle and high school: *Determining responsiveness to less intensive levels of the prevention system is required to identify students who need more intensive services.* Academic deficits accumulate and become more dramatic and severe as students advance through school. As the Vaughn et al. (2010) study reminds us, whereas research demonstrates that validated small-group tutoring delivered in the early grades can alter the course of academic development for many children, the more serious academic deficits associated with middle and high school make large numbers of students resistant to the remedial intensity offered at secondary prevention. Torgesen et al. (2001) illustrated this with 8- to 10-year-olds with learning disabilities who already experienced severe reading deficits. Effecting meaningfully important reading improvement required much greater intensity than what is offered at secondary prevention: two 50-min sessions each day of one-to-one tutoring. And separate from the larger academic discrepancies, adolescents with longstanding serious academic problems frequently demonstrate low motivation and poor academic self-confidence (e.g., LeCompte, 1987; Phelan, Yu, & Davidson, 1994), further complicating and compromising the success of secondary prevention tutoring. Therefore, compared to the elementary grades, many more middle and high school students will be unresponsive to secondary prevention and instead will immediately require the instructional intensity available at tertiary prevention.

In this vein, it is unfortunate that middle and high school resources for secondary prevention require large instructional groupings of 10–15 students—the group size used not only by Vaughn et al. (2010) but also by the participating middle schools as they designed their own versions of secondary prevention. If the students who qualified for the Vaughn et al. study could have been served in groups approximating the typical size in elementary-grade RTI research (i.e., 2–5 students), tutors might have been able to address more effectively student motivation and academic self-confidence issues to circumvent the attendance problems Vaughn et al. encountered, thereby enhancing outcomes. In a more direct way, tutors might have been able to provide greater opportunity for responding, more meaningful corrective feedback, and a greater emphasis on student needs within smaller instructional groups.

Even with the intensity created with groups of 2–5 students, secondary prevention may be appropriate for only a subset of students, perhaps Vaughn et al.'s "bubble" students. Restricting participation in secondary prevention to students for whom the likelihood of success is good creates a better opportunity to serve this population more effectively, which in turn enhances schools' opportunity to provide appropriately intensive tertiary prevention. This is the case because when secondary prevention is offered to a mix of students, some of whom seem likely to respond and others of whom have such large deficits that secondary prevention's intensity is manifestly insufficient, a higher proportion of both subsets of students may fail to respond, thereby flooding tertiary prevention and watering down the intensity required at the tertiary level. This parallels the need for high-quality primary prevention to avoid overwhelming secondary prevention with inappropriate students and thereby decreasing the intensity available at secondary prevention. For these reasons, moving students with the greatest academic deficits directly to a well-conceptualized, most intensive tertiary prevention level may produce more reliable and substantial outcomes for both subpopulations of students.

The third questionable assumption is that *the nature of effective intervention is the same across the grades.* It is instead likely that adolescents require different instructional emphases and strategies. Consider reading. Although the word-reading difficulties associated with phonological processing deficits characterize the behavioral phenotype of children with early reading problems, adolescents with reading difficulties present a more complicated array of weaknesses, ranging from word recognition to higher-order language and metacognitive skills. Shortfalls in any of these areas have been implicated as a significant contributor to comprehension failure, appreciably decreasing students' ability to use text to acquire new vocabulary, information, and knowledge. Even when concentrating specifically on reading comprehension, the traditional focus on strategy use and question answering may be inappropriate for adolescents with substantial knowledge and vocabulary deficits. Innovation is required to address the academic needs of adolescents with serious, accumulated deficits across a range of subcomponent skills within any given academic domain. Moreover, effective intervention must be contextualized within a delivery model that motivates the adolescent, creatively engaging the peer group to support effectiveness. Without peers endorsing the importance of academic intervention, even the most sophisticated programs may prove effective. We are not simply suggesting the use of conventional peer-mediated approaches to intervention; instead, it may be necessary to rethink how intervention materials and procedures are fundamentally engineered and packaged to enlist the peer group's endorsement.

A Modified RTI Model at Middle and High School

This leads us to propose a modified RTI model at middle and high school. In this model, the Elementary RTI Framework is turned upside down in some critical ways. At the elementary grades, the RTI model encourages practitioners to move students to increasingly intensive levels of the prevention system when those students reveal a failure to respond to more normal or standard forms of instruction. By contrast, in the middle and high school RTI model, we believe that practitioners must place severely discrepant students immediately in the most intensive level of the RTI framework (even as they continue to participate in primary prevention to further acquire content knowledge).

In a related way, in terms of accountability for student outcomes, the measurement of "response to intervention" is critical to RTI at all grades, but in differing ways. Elementary RTI increases accountability for outcomes for the purpose of identifying and circumventing risk for academic failure. The focus, therefore, is on monitoring RTI for the purpose of introducing greater intensity only as needed, working hard to avoid that need. By contrast, the goal of accountability and intensity within RTI at middle and high school is to ensure that teachers view their mission as reducing and eliminating already existing, sizable academic deficits. Here, the focus is therefore on monitoring RTI to determine when important academic benchmarks have been achieved for the purpose of transitioning students down the RTI pyramid in the direction of less intensive and more standard or normalized levels of the prevention system.

Conceptualizing RTI at middle and high school in this way introduces new opportunities to improve outcomes for students to overcome sizable academic deficits and restructures existing opportunities. (Although some students are already identified and served by remedial and special education services, the instructional intensity of these services often fails to meet the standards of tertiary prevention. Our argument applies to all students with academic deficits, whether or not they are served through general, remedial, or special education.) Given the limited time remaining in these students' school careers, many older students, including those with and without identified special needs, deserve these new or restructured opportunities for decreasing academic deficiencies, with the goal of eliminating this major obstacle toward successful adult life. The outcomes of students with large academic deficits are, after all, far from satisfactory. According to the National Longitudinal Transition Study-2 (Wagner et al., 2003), one-quarter of students with learning disabilities, who by the time they reach high school are more than 3 years below grade level in reading and math, drop out of school; in 2007, only 46% had regular paid employment within 2 years after leaving school. These sobering data should be viewed as indicating a public health crisis; it should create a sense of urgency to enhance resources at middle and high school for meaningfully intensive RTI secondary and tertiary prevention services.

Research to Support a Modified RTI Model at Middle and High School

A modified RTI model at middle and high school raises important questions that need to be addressed with programmatic research. In terms of assessment, questions include the following: Is teacher nomination an accurate means of identifying students who require services beyond primary prevention? What forms of existing data sources, such as performance on high-stakes testing or schools' benchmark assessments, might be used instead of or in combination with teacher nomination to enhance decision making? What is an accurate means for distinguishing students who require immediate tertiary prevention from those who are likely to succeed with secondary prevention? Which assessments and benchmark scores provide a reliable means for deciding when to move students from tertiary to secondary prevention and sometimes back again? Important questions concerning intervention include the following: What is the optimal group size for secondary and for tertiary prevention to balance effectiveness and efficiency? What are effective strategies for engaging students who have experienced long histories of school failure? What are the critical academic targets for increasing the probability of successful adult life outcomes? How does the nature of effective intervention change for adolescents?

REFERENCES

Berkeley, S., Bender, W. N., Gregg Peaster, L., & Saunders, L. (2009). Implementation of response to intervention: A snapshot of progress. *Journal of Learning Disabilities, 42,* 85–95.

Chard, D. J., Clarke, B., Baker, S., Otterstedt, J., Braun, D., & Katz, R. (2005). Using measures of number sense to screen for difficulties in mathematics: Preliminary findings. *Assessment for Effective Intervention, 30(2),* 3–14.

Clarke, B., & Shinn, M. R. (2004). A preliminary investigation into the identification and development of early mathematics curriculum-based measurement. *School Psychology Review, 33,* 234–248.

Compton, D. C., Fuchs, D., Fuchs, L. S., Bouton, B., Gilbert, J. K., Barquero, L. A., et al. (in press). Selecting at-risk first-grade readers for early intervention: Eliminating false positives and exploring the promise of a two-stage gated screening process. *Journal of Educational Psychology.*

LeCompte, M. D. (1987). The cultural context of dropping out: What remedial programs fail to solve the problems. *Education and Urban Society, 4,* 317–345.

Lembke, E., & Foegen, A. (2006, February). Monitoring student progress in early math. Paper presented at the 14th annual meeting of the Pacific Coast Research Conference, San Diego.

Phelan, P., Yu, H. C., & Davidson, A. L. (1994). Navigating the psychological pressures of adolescence: The voices and experiences of high school youth. *American Educational Research Journal, 31,* 415–447.

Seethaler, P. M., & Fuchs, L. S. (in press). The predictive utility of kindergarten screening for math difficulty: How, when, and with respect to what outcomes should it occur? *Exceptional Children.*

Stecker, P. M., Fuchs, L. S., & Fuchs, D. (2005). Using curriculum-based measurement to improve student achievement: Review of research. *Psychology in the Schools, 42,* 795–820.

Torgesen, T. K., Alexander, A. W., Wagner, R. K., Rashotte, C. A., Voeller, K. K. S., & Conway, T. (2001). Intensive remedial instruction for children with severe reading disabilities. *Journal of Learning Disabilities, 34,* 33–58.

Vaughn, S., Cirino, P. T., Wanzek, J., Wexler, J., Fletcher, J. M., Denton, C. D., et al. (2010). Response to intervention for middle school students with reading difficulties: Effects of a primary and secondary intervention. *School Psychology Review*, *39*, 3–21.

Wagner, M., Marder, C., Blackorby, J., Cameto, R., Newman, L., Levine, P., et al. (2003). *The achievements of youth with disabilities during secondary school*. A report from the National Longitudinal Transition Study-2 (NLTS2). Menlo Park, CA: SRI International. Available at www.nlts2.org/reports/2003_11/nlts2_report_2003_11_complete.pdf

Lynn S. Fuchs is Nicholas Hobbs Professor of Special Education and Human Development at Vanderbilt University. Her research focuses on the effects of instructional and classroom assessment practices on mathematics and reading learning among students at risk for or with learning disabilities, and on the cognitive determinants of mathematics and reading difficulty.

Donald L. Compton is Associate Professor of Special Education at Vanderbilt University. His research focuses on screening for identifying students at risk for poor reading outcomes, progress-monitoring methods for modeling reading development, and the early identification, treatment, and cognitive precursors of students with late-emerging reading comprehension difficulty.

CLASSROOM IMPLICATIONS

1. RTI requires differentiated instruction. What problems do you foresee (perhaps you have already witnessed them) in implementing such instruction?

2. How do you envision the role of special educators changing as a result of RTI?

3. Should special educators work directly with classroom teachers, on a push-in basis, to help plan, guide, and monitor RTI efforts?

4. Should RTI in the middle and high school be structured differently than at the elementary level? If so, in what ways?

FOR FUTURE READING

Chapman, L., Greenfield, R., & Rinaldi, C. (2010). "Drawing is a frame of mind: " An evaluation of students' perceptions about reading instruction within a response to intervention model. *Literacy Research and Instruction, 49*, 113–128. doi:10.1090/19388070902842694

Council for Exceptional Children. (2008). *CEC's position on response to intervention (RTI): The unique role of special education and special educators.* Arlington, VA: Author.

Fuchs, D., & Fuchs, L.S. (2009). Responsiveness to intervention: Multilevel assessment and instruction as early intervention and disability identification. *The Reading Teacher, 63*(3), 250–252. doi:10.1598/RT.63.3.10

Fuchs, L.S., Fuchs, D., & Compton, D.L. (2010). Rethinking response to intervention at middle and high school. *School Psychology Review, 39*(1), 22–28.

Gersten, R., Compton, D., Connor, C.M., Dimino, J., Santoro, L., Linan-Thompson, S., & Tilly, W.D. (2008). Assisting students struggling with reading: Response to intervention and multi-tier intervention for reading in the primary grades. A practice guide. (NCEE 2009-4045). Washington, DC: National Center for Education Evaluation and Regional Assistance, Institute of Education Sciences, U.S. Department of Education.

Johnston, P. (2010). An instructional frame for RTI. *The Reading Teacher, 63*(7), 602–604. doi:10.1598/RT.63.7.8

Vaughn, S., Cirino, P.T., Wanzek, J., Wexler, J., Fletcher, J.M., Denton, C.D., Francis, D.J. (2010). Response to intervention for middle school students with reading difficulties: Effects of a primary and secondary intervention. *School Psychology, 39*(1), 3–21.

Vaughn, S., Wanzek, J., Murray, C.S., Scammacca, N., Linan-Thompson, S., & Woodruff, A.L. (2009). Response to early reading intervention: Examining higher and lower responders. *Exceptional Children, 75*(2), 165–183.

Walpole, S., & McKenna, M. C. (2009). *How to plan differentiated reading instruction: Resources for grades K–3.* New York, NY: Guilford.

ONLINE RESOURCES

International Reading Association
http://www.reading.org/Resources/ResourcesByTopic/ResponseToIntervention/Overview.aspx

What Works Clearinghouse
http://ies.ed.gov/ncee/wwc/

Best Evidence Encyclopedia
http://www.bestevidence.org/

Wright's Law
http://www.wrightslaw.com/info/rti.index.htm

NAME INDEX

Aaron, P.G., 284
Achinstein, B., 177
Adams, M.J., 14, 25
Adams, S., 223
Adler, C.R., 119
Adolescent Literacy Commission, 199
Afflerbach, P., 235
Akhtar, N., 119
Alao, S., 81–83
Alexander, P., 200
Alexander, P. A., 83, 85
Allen, S., 99
Allen, S.A., 114–123
Allington, R., 10, 16, 275, 276
Allington, R. L., 1, 56, 62, 273
Allsopp, D.H., 120
Alvermann, D. E., 199, 204, 206
American Association of School
    Librarians, 235
American Diploma Project, 247
American Educational Research Association,
    51
American Psychological Association, 51
Anderson, R. C., 12, 83, 118, 119
Anderson, S., 169
Anholt, L., 108
Applebee, A. N., 243–254, 258
Armbruster, B.B., 119
Ash, E.A., 28
Ash, G.E., 102
Asimov, I., 76
Athanases, S. B., 177
Atkinson, D., 266
Atwell, N., 263, 264
August, D., 136, 138
Aull, L., 230
Autio, E., 163, 182

Bahr, M., 275
Baker, S., 73
Baldwin, R. S., 83, 201
Ball, P., 278
Bangert-Drowns, R.L., 248
Barber, J., 82
Baron, J., 74
Barrera, E. S., 199
Bauer, E., 132
Bauer, E.B., 153–155
Baumann, J.F., 102
Bauserman, K. L., 89
Bay Area Writing Project, 259, 262
Bean, R., 163
Bean, R.M., 160, 162–172
Bean, T. W., 194, 196–206, 211
Bear, D.R., 15
Beaver, J., 275
Bechtel, L., 115
Beck, I., 142
Beck, I. L., 72–78, 88, 98, 99, 101, 106, 107,
    109, 111, 116–120, 125, 126
Beery, A., 6
Bell, K.M., 278

Bell, M., 275
Bender, W. N., 289
Bennett, S., 45
Bennett-Armistead, V. S., 84, 89
Bentum, K.E., 284
Bereiter, C., 11
Berkeley, S., 289
Bernhardt, V.L., 168
Bialystock, E., 140
Biancarosa, C., 199, 201, 202
Biancarosa, G., 163, 193, 210, 218
Biemiller, A., 97, 101, 102, 110, 117
Biggs, M., 23, 37, 44
Biggs, M. C., 45
Biklen, S., 212
Binder, C., 50
Birdyshaw, D., 199, 211
Bizar, M., 264
Blachowicz, C., 22, 159
Blachowicz, C. L. Z., 116, 125, 126, 163
Blackburn, M., 204
Blair, H., 204
Blake, R. G. K., 72–78
Blake, W., 63
Blamey, K.L., 167, 184
Blewitt, P., 102
Bliss, J., 103
Block, C.C., 177
Bloom, L., 101
Blount, N. S., 258
Bogdan, R., 212
Bohm, D., 259
Bond, G., 9
Boote, C., 101, 102, 110, 117
Borman, G. D., 182
Bourque, M. L., 244
Braddock, R., 258
Bransford, J. D., 74
Braten, I., 83
Braun, C., 9
Bravo, M. A., 82, 101, 102
Brett, A., 102
Britton, J., 264
Brock, C.H., 130
Broek, C., 67
Brown, A. L., 74
Brown, K. J., 73
Browne, A., 69
Brozo, W. G., 203
Bryant, P., 14
Bryk, A., 163
Buehl, M. M., 81
Buhr, J., 119
Burhans, C. S., 259
Burns, M. S., 15, 72, 74
Burrows, A., 264
Butler, Y. G., 126

Calderon, M., 146
Caldwell, J., 49, 55, 211
Calfee, R., 191
Callanan, M.A., 119

Campbell, J.R., 248
Campione, J. C., 74
Carey, S., 102
Cariglia-Bull, T., 74
Carlo, M., 126
Carlo, M. S., 142, 144, 145
Carlson, C., 148
Carnine, L., 213
Carspecken, P.F., 103
Carver, R. P., 73
Casey, A., 71
Casey, K., 165, 166
Cassady, J. C., 224
Cassidy, D., 175, 199, 273, 275
Cassidy, J., 175, 199–200, 273, 275
Castek, J., 234
Celano, D., 81, 82
Center for Research on Education,
    Diversity and Excellence
    (CREDE), 136–137, 140–142,
    147–150
Cervetti, G., 82, 89
Cervetti, G. N., 64, 80–91
Chall, J., 4, 6, 9, 10, 25, 26, 191, 192
Chall, J. S., 82
Chamberlin, D., 87
Chamberlin, N., 87
Chapman, J.W., 15
Chard, D. J., 25, 48, 50, 290
Cheung, A., 138
Chiang, B., 279
Chomsky, N., 9
CIERA School Change study, 85, 185
Clarke, B., 290
Clay, M.M., 13, 275
Coiro, J., 224, 233–235
Cole, C.L., 117
Collier, V., 145
Collins, M., 143
Combs, M.C., 145
Compton, D.L., 117, 288–293
Conley, M.W., 211
Cook, C., 132, 153–155
Cooper, C. R., 258, 259
Coskie, T., 163, 182
Costa, A., 178, 179
Costa, A.L., 163
Cox, K.E., 56
Coxhead, A., 126
Coyne, M.D., 117, 118, 122
Craig, S.A., 16
Crawford, J., 136
Creech, S., 57
Crew, D., 69
Cronin, D., 106, 108
Cunningham, A. E., 72, 97
Cunningham, J. W., 83, 204
Cunningham, P.M., 1, 15, 62

Dahl, R., 106
Dale, E., 102, 117
Daniels, H., 264

Dartmouth conference, 260
David, J., 99
Davidson, A. L., 291
Davies, N., 66
Davis, F.B., 116
Deeney, T., 23
Defee, M., 15
de Maupassant, G., 48
Deno, S.L., 51, 52, 279
Deshler, D.D., 218
Deussen, T., 163, 165, 182
Dexter, E., 163
Diamond, L., 117
Dicembre, E. A., 210–228
Dickinson, D., 102
Dickinson, H., 230
Dimino, J.A., 285
Dion, G.S., 219
Dobler, E., 233
Dochy, F., 81
Dole, J., 13, 104
Dole, J. A., 163, 199, 201
Donahue, P.L., 219, 248
Donley, J., 92
Dorph, R., 80
Dreher, M. J., 84, 88
Dressman, M., 204
Drought, E., 87
Duffy, G. G., 64, 181
Duffy-Hester, A.M., 14
Duke, N. K., 38, 82–85, 89
Dykstra, R., 9
Dyson, A. H., 261

Eakle, J. A., 204
Echevarria, J., 131, 153
Edison, T., 223
Edmunds, K. M., 89
Ehri, L., 14
Eisele, M.R., 120
Eisenhart, M., 284
Elbow, P., 258
Elish-Piper, L.A., 160, 162–172
Elkins, J., 204
Elkonin, D., 13
Elleman, A.M., 117
Ellsworth, R. E., 160
Emig, J., 258, 259
Emig's study, 259
Engelmann, S., 11, 213
Espin, C., 52

Fairbanks, M., 125
Felton, K., 16
Felton, R.H., 49
Ferrara, R. A., 74
Fewster, D., 210–228
Fielding, L., 73
Finders, M., 204
Fisher, C.W., 56
Fisher, D., 101, 202, 203
Fisher, P. J. L., 116, 125
Fitzgerald, J., 130, 131
Fitzgerald, K., 258
Flaherty, J., 163
Flesch, R., 1, 7
Fletcher, J.M., 275
Flood, J., 87, 101
Florida Center for Reading Research, 224
Flugum, K., 275

Foegen, A., 290
Foehr, U. G., 266
Fogelberg, E., 163
Foorman, B., 148
Foorman, B.R., 275
Ford Foundation, 258
Francis, D.J., 275
Franzak, J. K., 202, 203
Freedman, S. W., 261
Frey, N., 101
Fries, C.C., 8
Froelich, K.S., 165
Frost, S., 163
Fuchs, D., 275, 276, 288–293
Fuchs, L., 73, 275
Fuchs, L. S., 52, 275, 279, 288–293
Fulmer, D., 278
Fulwiler, T., 257
Fung, I., 145

Gabriel, J. G., 180, 181
Gagne, R., 10
Gambrell, L., 84, 223
Gandara, P., 140
Garmston, R., 178, 179
Garmston, R.J., 163
Garner, R., 82, 84
Garrett, D., 199
Gaskins, I.W., 15
Gaskins, J.C., 15
Gaskins, R.W., 15
Gates, A.I., 7
Gee, J.P., 204
Genesee, F., 136, 142, 147, 149
Gentile, C., 244
Gere, A., 258
Gere, A.R., 230
Gersten, R., 73, 126, 285
Gibson, E.J., 9, 10
Gibson, S.A., 163
Gillingham, M. G., 82, 84
Glass, G., 138
Golan, S., 85
Goldenberg, C., 131, 133–151
Good, R., 49, 278
Goodlad, J. I., 86
Goodman, K., 2
Goodman, K.S., 9, 12
Goodman, Y. M., 264
Goodman and Goodman (1980), 12
Goswami, U., 14, 15
Goudvis, A., 82
Gough, P., 4
Graesser, A. G., 74
Graham, S., 69, 85, 199, 202, 241, 242, 248
Graves, A., 131
Graves, B., 241
Graves, D., 261, 264
Graves, M., 241
Graves, M. F., 116, 118, 119, 130, 131
Gray, W. S., 1, 7, 88
Greaney, K.T., 15
Green Brabham, E., 102
Greene, J., 138
Greene, J.F., 212
Gregg Peaster, L., 289
Gregory, J. F., 83
Gresham, F., 284
Griffin, P., 15, 72, 74
Griffith, L. W., 44

Gunderson, L., 204
Gundlach, R., 261
Guthrie, J. T., 56, 81–86, 90, 211
Guthrie study, 86
Gutlohn, L., 117
Guzzetti, B. J., 199

Hagood, M., 204
Hailikari, T., 81
Hakuta, K., 126
Hall, D.P., 15
Hall, L. A., 202
Hammond, M., 10
Hare, V. C., 83
Hargis, C. H., 203
Harper, H., 194, 196–206
Harris, A. J., 22, 241
Harris, S. R., 125
Harris, T.L., 47, 49
Hart, B., 72, 97, 116
Hart, S., 201
Harty, K.R., 278
Harvey, S., 82
Hasbrouck, J., 54, 280
Hastings, C. N., 75
Haubner, J. P., 66–71
Hebard, H., 66–71
Heilker, P., 266
Henry, L., 234
Herman, P.A., 104, 119
Heubach, K. M., 43, 44
Hidi, S., 84, 88
Hiebert, E., 64, 82
Hiebert, E.H., 12, 56, 80–91, 101, 117
Hilden, K., 38
Hildyard, A., 84, 88
Hillocks, G., Jr., 69
Hinchman, K., 199, 204
Hinchman, K. A., 199, 211
Hodges, R.E., 47, 49
Hoffman, J., 30, 181
Hoffman, J. V., 38–40
Hoidren, J., 88
Holmes, J., 9
Homan, S., 23, 37, 44
Homan, S. P., 45
Honeycutt, R. L., 69
Honig, B., 117
Hook, C., 75
Horton, J., 203, 204
Hudson, R.F., 22
Hull, G. A., 264
Humenick, N.M., 211
Hurley, M., 102
Hurt, N., 177

Illinois State Board of Education, 278
In-Depth Expanded Application of Science (IDEAS), 90
International Reading Association (IRA), 9, 13, 101, 159, 163, 175, 176, 194, 199, 211, 218, 275
Invernizzi, M., 15, 278, 280
IRA Commission on Response to Intervention, 273
Irby, B., 147
Ivey, G., 202, 203

Jaynes, C. A., 80–91
Jenkins, J.R., 52

Jetton, T. L., 83, 85, 199, 201
Jiménez, R., 138
Jipson, J., 119
Johnson, G., 213
Johnston, D., 224
Johnston, F., 15
Jones, S., 163, 166
Jordan, L., 120
Joyce, B., 175, 179
Juel, C., 66–71, 241, 278, 280
Justice, L.M., 102

Kame'enui, E.J., 102, 118
Kamil, M.L., 116, 117, 219
Kaminski, R., 49, 278
Kato, T., 83
Katzir-Cohen, T., 50
Kavale, K., 284
Kavanagh, J.F., 9
Kennedy, J.H., 244
Kindle, K., 99
King, J., 201
King, M., 136
Kintsch, E., 83, 84
Kintsch, W., 74, 83, 84
Knapp, M. S., 84
Knaub, R., 163
Knight, J., 165, 166
Knowles, M.S., 163
Komulainen, E., 81
Kossan, P., 151
Kozdras, D., 201
Kriete, R., 115
Kubina, R.M., Jr., 50
Kucan, L., 74, 98, 99, 101, 116, 142
Kuhn, M., 23–36
Kuhn, M. R., 22, 23, 25, 27, 28, 38, 49, 56, 57
Kuhn, T. S., 258
Kulikowich, J. M., 83
Kwok, O., 147

LaBerge, D., 26, 48
L'Allier, S.K., 160, 162–172
Lancaster, J., 241
Lane, H., 99
Lane, H. B., 22, 114–123
Langer, J.A., 243–254
Lapp, D., 67, 87, 101
Lara-Alecio, R., 147
Leander, K., 204
LeCompte, M. D., 291
Lederman, N. G., 87, 88
Lehr, F., 119
Leithwood, K., 169, 170
Lembke, E., 290
Lesko, N., 198
Leslie, L., 49, 55, 83, 211
Leu, D. J., 233
Leu, D. J., Jr., 266
Levin, H., 10
Lewis, C., 204
Lewis, J., 199
Lewis, L., 224
Linderholm, T., 74
Lindo, E.J., 117
Linek, W. L., 42
Lloyd-Jones, R., 258
Lombardi, V., 159
Loomis, S. C., 244
Louis, K.S., 169

Luke, A., 204, 266
Lynch-Brown, C., 102
Lynd, R., 189
Lyon, G.R., 275
Lyons, C., 275
Lytle, S., 204

MacLachlan, P., 106
Macrorie, K., 258
Mahoney, K., 138
Malloy, J., 234
Mann, H., 1
Manning, M., 83
Manyak, P., 132
Manyak, P.C., 153–155
Manzo, A.V., 118
Manzo, K. K., 253
Manzo, U.C., 118
Marsh, J.A., 166
Martin, J., 70
Martineau, J. A., 85
Martinez, G., 210–228
Martin-Rehrmann, J., 244
Marzano, R. J., 82, 98
Marzano, R. R., 126
Mathes, P., 147
Mathes, P.G., 57
McClintock, A. H., 83
McCombs, J.S., 166
Mccormick, M.K., 210–228
McDill, E., 136
McGee, L. M., 84, 88, 102
McGuffey, W. H., 22
McKenna, M. C., 22, 160, 176, 183
McKeown, M., 142
McKeown, M. G., 72–78, 88, 98, 99, 101, 106, 116–119, 125, 126
McMurrer, J., 80
McNabb, M., 201
McNamara, D. S., 83
Meier, J., 102, 278, 280
Meisinger, E.B., 22
Mercer, C.D., 120
Merriam, S.B., 103
Mesmer, E.M., 275–285
Mesmer, H.A.E., 275–285
Metropolitan District Study, 164, 167
Metsala, J.L., 56
Meyer, M.S., 49
Mifflin, H., 260
Miller, J., 49, 50
Miller, J. W., 160
Minick, V., 45
Mirkin, P.K., 279
Mock, D., 276
Modern Language Association, 258
Moffett, J., 258, 260
Mohr, K. A. J., 89
Moje, E. B., 204
Monaghan, J., 257
Monk, M., 103
Moore, D., 145
Moore, D. W., 87, 88, 199, 200, 204, 211
Moore, M. T., 256–267
Moorman, G., 199, 203, 204
Moran, M., 66–71
Morgan, P.L., 276
Morphy, P., 117
Morrell, E., 201, 202
Morrow, L. M., 87

Moskal, M.K., 22
Murray, D., 258, 259

Nagy, W.E., 97–99, 118, 119, 122
Nair, M., 218
Nash, R., 146
National Assessment of Educational Progress (NAEP), 54, 55, 135, 153, 189, 190, 227, 242, 243, 245, 246, 248, 249, 251, 252, 263
National Association for the Education of Young Children, 101
National Center for Education Statistics, 245, 246, 248, 249, 251
National Center on Student Progress Monitoring, 276, 279
National Commission on Writing, 246, 248
National Committee on Reading, 87
National Council of Teachers of English, 226, 232, 238, 257, 258
National Council on Measurement in Education, 51
National Governors Association, 211
National Institute of Child Health and Human Development (NICHHD), 1, 9, 47, 64, 116, 119, 200
National Literacy Panel (NLP), 130, 136–137, 139, 140
National Longitudinal Transition Study-2 (NLTS2), 292
National Middle School Association, 218
National Reading Panel (NRP), 1, 22, 25, 26, 30, 38, 39, 47, 64, 72, 119, 139, 150
National Reading Research Center (NRRC), 224
National Research Council (NRC), 15, 72
National School Board Association, 231
National Staff Development Council (NSDC), 176
National Study of Writing Instruction, 254
National Writing Project, 243, 251, 254, 257, 259, 262, 264
Natriello, G., 136
NCTE Policy Research, 225
Neal, H., 141, 143
Nelson-LeGall, S., 67
Ness, M., 22
Neufeld, B., 163, 176, 184
Neuman, S. B., 81, 82
Nevgi, A., 81
Newton, E., 101, 105, 109
Nichols, W. D., 201
Niess, M. L., 87, 88
Norris, J., 147
North, S. M., 258, 259

Oakar, M., 177
O'Brien, D., 204
Obrochta, C., 163
O'Connor, R.E., 278
Odell, L., 258, 259
Oetting, J.B., 119
Ogborn, J., 103
Ogle, D., 116, 125
O'Malley, K., 275
Omanson, R.C., 117
Opitz, M.F., 40
Ortega, L., 147
Orzulak, M.M., 230
Osborn, J., 119
Osser, H., 10

Ouellette, G.P., 116
Ovando, C., 145

Padak, N. D., 38, 42, 101
Palincsar, A. S., 74, 82, 218
Pallas, A., 136
Palmer, R. G., 88, 89
Papert, S., 223
Paris, S.G., 285
Parker, F. W., 86
Parker, R., 280
Paterson, W.A., 224
Pearson, P. D., 9, 12–14, 73, 82, 83, 85, 101, 181
Peat, F.D., 259
Peleg-Bruckner, Z., 83
Penn, D., 199, 202
Perencevich, K. C., 84, 90
Perfetti, C.A., 119
Perin, D., 241, 242, 248
Perkins, S.J., 166
Peterson, D. S., 85
Phelan, P., 291
Phelps, S. F., 199, 206
Phelps, S. W., 199
Pick, A., 10
Pickering, D. J, 126
Pikulski, J.J., 25, 50
Pinnell, G., 49
Pinnock, W., 62
Pitcher, S., 194
Pitcher, S.M., 210–228
Poglinco, S.M., 163
Pollard, R. S., 1
Porche, M. V., 125
Postman, N., 266
Powell-Smith, K., 278
Prado, M., 146
Pressley, M., 38, 64, 74, 82, 284, 285
Pritchard, R., 69
Puig, E.A., 165
Pullen, P.C., 22
Purcell-Gates, V., 84
Putnam, L.R., 68

Quatroche, D.J., 170

Rainville, K.N., 163, 166
Rampey, B.D., 219
RAND Reading Study Group, 89
Ransom, J.C., 257
Raphael, T.E., 130
Rasinski, T., 23, 30, 37, 42, 44, 48
Rasinski, T. V., 30, 31, 38–40, 42, 44, 101
Readance, J. E., 87, 201
Reading Recovery Council of North America, 182
Recht, D. R., 83
Reinking, D., 224
Reschly, D., 275
Restrick, L., 67
Reynolds, K., 159
Reynolds, R., 73
Rice, M.L., 119
Richardson, J. S., 199
Rickelman, R. J., 87
Rideout, V., 266
Riedel, B., 279, 285

Risley, T., 72
Risley, T.R., 97, 116
Roberts, D. F., 266
Roberts, T., 141, 143
Roberts, T.A., 102
Robinson, L., 163, 182
Rodriguez, M. C., 85
Roller, C.M., 165
Rolstad, K., 138
Romance, N. R., 90
Roper, D., 163, 176, 184
Rothlein, L., 102
Royer, J. M., 75
Ruddell, R., 9
Rudolph, M., 8
Rumberger, R., 140
Russell, D., 62
Rycik, J. A., 199, 211

Saiz, A., 140
Salas, R., 67
Salinger, T., 200, 201
Samuel, J., 38
Samuels, S.J., 26, 48, 50
Samuelstuen, M. S., 83
Sandora, C., 74
Santa, C.M., 210
Saunders, L., 289
Saunders, W., 148
Scanlon, D.M., 275
Scarborough, H., 285
Scarcella, R., 134
Schickedanz, J.A., 102
Schoer, L., 258
Schultz, L.M., 257
Schulze, S. K., 83
Schwanenflugel, P.J., 22, 49, 50
Scott, J.A., 12, 122
Scott, W. E., 87
Secco, T., 74
Segars, M., 81
Shanahan, T., 29, 64, 136, 138
Shaughnessy, M., 264
Shinn, M., 275
Shinn, M. R., 54, 290
Shinn, M.M., 54
Short, D., 153
Showers, B., 163, 175, 179
Simmons, D.C., 118
Sinatra, G. M., 73
Sinatra, R., 83
Singer, H., 9
Singer, M., 74
Sipay, E. R., 241
Skinner, B.F., 9
Slater, W.H., 116
Slavin, R., 138, 151
Slavin, R. E., 224
Smiley, S. S., 74
Smith, F., 2
Smith, L. H., 189
Smith, L. L., 224
Smith, M. W., 69, 102, 204
Smith, M.L., 6, 16
Smith, N. B., 6
Smith, W. L., 265
Snow, C., 99
Snow, C. E., 15, 72, 74, 82, 125, 193, 199, 201, 202, 210

Snyder, B. L., 74
Songer, N., 83
Soto, G., 68, 69, 77
Spear-Swerling, L., 192
Spencer Foundation, 254
Spires, H., 92
Squire, J.R., 230
Stahl, K.A.D., 14, 22
Stahl, S., 125
Stahl, S.A., 14, 16, 25, 27, 38, 43, 44, 49, 57, 83, 84, 97, 98
Stanovich, K., 275
Stanovich, K. E., 72, 80, 97, 101, 153
State Board of Education, California, 150
Stauffer, R.G., 11
Stecker, P. M., 290
Stephens, D., 12, 13, 166
Sternberg, R. J., 74, 102, 192
Stevens, L., 200
Stevenson, B., 42
Stewart, R. A., 88, 89
Stoolmiller, M., 118
Stotsky, S., 87
Sturtevant, E., 42
Sturtevant, E. G., 199
Su, Z., 86
Swan, A.L., 163
Swank, L., 278, 280
Swank, L.K., 119
Swank, P.R., 275
Swenson, J., 266
Symons, S., 74

Tabors, P. O., 125
Tate, A., 257
Tatum, A., 189
Taylor, B. M., 85
Taylor-Greene, S., 278
Teaching Development Centre, 236
Templeton, S., 15
Texas Education Agency, 278
Thomas, E.E., 230
Thome, C., 51
Thorndike, E. L., 63, 116
Thorne-Thomsen, G., 86
Tierney, R.J., 51, 83
Tindal, G., 280
Tindal, G.A., 54
Toll, C.A., 163, 166
Tong, F., 147
Torgesen, J.K., 22, 49
Torgesen, T. K., 291
Towne, L., 284
Townsend, D., 67
Trabasso, T., 74
Truss, L., 27
Tsai, C-C., 235
Tsai, M-J., 235
Tunmer, W.E., 15
Tyler, B.J., 48
Tzeng, Y., 74

U.S. Department of Education, 80, 130, 134, 135, 210, 232, 243, 245, 246, 248, 249, 251, 275–277

Vacca, R. T., 199
Vadeboncoeur, J. A., 200

Valley District Study, 164, 165
Van Allen, R., 11
van den Broek, P., 52, 74
van den Broek, P. W., 74
Vanderberg, M., 166
van Dijk, T. A., 74
van Helden, C., 204
Vaughn, S., 48, 141, 275, 283, 288, 290, 291
Vellutino, F.R., 275, 276
Vitale, M. R., 90
Voelkl, K.E., 248
Vogt, M., 153

Waff, D., 199
Wagner, M., 292
Wahlstrom, K., 169
Waif, D. R., 199
Walker, B., 16
Walker, B.J., 5–17
Walmsley, S., 275, 276
Walpole, S., 102, 160, 167, 176, 183, 184
Walsh, B.A., 102
Walsh, K., 87, 126

Walton, L.M., 16
Walton, P.D., 15, 16
Wang, X., 204
Wanzek, J., 283
Warren, R.P., 257
Washington, B. T., 97
Watts-Taffe, S., 116, 125
Watts-Taffe, S.M., 118, 119
Webb, N. M., 236
Wells, J., 224
Wepner, S.B., 170
Whipple, G. M., 87
White, T.G., 116
Wigfield, A., 56, 84, 90
Wilder, P., 204
Wilhelm, J. D., 204
Wilkinson, I., 145
Wilkinson, I.A.G., 12
Williams, J., 10
Williams, J. P., 73
Williamson, M. M., 264
Willig, A., 138
Wilson, R., 8

Wimmer, J., 204
Wineburg, S., 70
Wineburg, S. S., 70
Wolf, M., 50
Woods, W. F., 257
Worthy, J., 74

Yagelski, R., 256, 266, 267
Yolen, J., 69
Yopp, H. K., 25, 84
Yopp, R. H., 25, 84
Young, C.L., 276
Young, M., 74
Young, R. E., 258
Yu, H. C., 291

Zehler, A. M., 134, 135
Zehr, M., 134, 136
Zemelman, S., 264
Zigmond, N., 163, 171
Zirbes, L., 86
Zoido, E., 140
Zutell, J.B., 38

SUBJECT INDEX

Academic language, 99
Accuracy and fluency, 26
Adolescence
  defined by literacy needs, 200–203
  defining, 198
  as diverse and dynamic population
    of literacy learners, 204–205
  future research on, 205–206
  as grade -or age-level designation, 200
  literacy needs, 210–219
  millennials, 203–204
Adolescent literacy, 189, 196
  and adolescence, 199–200
  adolescent literacy instruction, enhancing,
    193–194
  approaches to, 193–194
  culture and, 191
  field, 199
  future research on, 205–206
  lack of instruction and, 191
  middle school problem, 189–193
  needs of, 210–219
  poverty and, 191
  race and, 190
  and society, 197–198
  striving reader profiles and, 192–193
  technologies and, 190–191
  text demands and, 191
Adult mediation in read-alouds, 102
Analogy-based approaches, in phonics, 15
  rime analogies, using, 15–16
  word detectives, 15
Analytic phonics, 8–10
Assessment, of writing, 264–265
Assisted reading, engaging in, 40
Automatic essay scoring (AES) systems, 228
Automaticity and fluency, 26–27, 56

Bottom-up model, of reading process, 3

Center for Research on Education, Diversity
    and Excellence (CREDE), 136–137
Change coaches, 176
Children with specific learning disabilities,
    identifying, 277
Child's reading development, fluency in,
    24–25
Choral reading, 33
Coaching models, 175–185. See also Literacy
    coaching
  characteristics, 177
  cognitive coaching, 178–179
  new-teacher mentoring, 177–178
  peer coaching, 179–180
  program-specific coaching, 181–183
  reform-oriented coaching, 183–185
  selection and usage, 185
  subject-specific coaching, 180–181
Cognitive coaching, 178–179
Collaborative relationships, building,
    166–167
Combat reading, 30

Comprehension, 62
  authenticity and knowledge, building,
    84–86
  as construction vs. reconstruction of
    meaning, 62–63
  content-area reading instruction, 88
  discussion, 76–78
  historian, thinking like, 69–71
  integrated instruction that foregrounds
    knowledge, 89–91
  knowledge, developing, 80, 81–82
  levels of, 63
  measures and outcomes, 75–76
  nonfiction/informational texts, use of, 89
  progressive movement, origin in, 86–87
  reading and content, evolving relationship
    of, 86
  scientist, thinking like, 66–67
  strategies and content approaches, 72, 202
  supporting comprehension with
    knowledge, 82–84
  teaching of skills vs. strategies and, 63–64
  text features and, 67–68
  thematic instruction, 87–88
  writer, thinking like, 68–69
Concept-Oriented Reading Instruction
    (CORI), 90
Content, 5
  -area reading instruction, 88
  coaches, 176
  learning support, for English learners,
    153–155
  objectives, having, 153–154
Context
  development of literacy strategies and, 201
  proficient reading and, 3–4

Decoding, 4–5
Definition, providing, 106
Developmental Reading Assessment (DRA),
    168
Digital technology, reading comprehension
    and, 236–237
Discrepancy model, of RTI, 276
Dysfluent students, 51

Echo reading, 32
Elementary vs. middle and high school,
    distinctions between, 290–292
Emergent literacy, 4
English language development and other
    considerations, 147–149
English-language learners (ELLs), 196, 210
  good instruction and curriculum in general
    holds for, 140–142
English learners, 130
  beginning English speakers in the learning
    process, 154–155
  English language development and other
    considerations, 147–149
  good instruction and curriculum in general
    holds for ELLs, 140–142

implications for improving instruction,
    149–150
improving achievement for English,
    133–151
language and content objectives, having,
    153–154
modifications using only English,
    146–147
modifications using students' primary
    language, 144–146
requiring instructional modifications,
    142–144
studies agreeing on key findings, 136–137
supporting content learning for, 153
teaching students to read in the first
    language, 138–140
using small-group work to maximize
    involvement, 154
Examples, providing, 107

Fast Start, 42–43
Fluency, 5, 22
  accuracy, role of, 26, 47–48
  assessment
  assisted reading, engaging in, 40
  automaticity, 26–27, 56
  choral reading, 22, 33
  deeper view of, 50
  dysfluent students, 51
  echo reading, 22, 32
  effective instruction, 31
  and endurance, instructing, 55–56
  expectations, increasing, 57
  Fast Start, 42–43
  fluency coach, acting as, 39–40
  Fluency Development Lesson (FDL), 42
  Fluency-Oriented Reading Instruction
    (FORI), 43–44
  importance, 25
  in child's reading development, 24–25
  interesting texts, reading, 56
  materials, collecting, 40
  model fluent reading, 39
  one-minute measures, 47, 53–54, 57
  oral reading, 22, 28, 30
  parents and caregivers, engaging, 57
  partner reading, 22, 34–35
  performance and celebration, provide
    for, 41
  prosody, 27–28, 48–49
  rate, 48
  readability levels, decreasing, 56
  readers theater, 44
  reading fluency, 38–45, 47
  reading volume, increasing, 56–57
  rereading, 57
  round-robin reading, 28–30
  singing as reading, 44–45
  time, effects of, 51–53
Fluency Development Lesson (FDL), 42
Fluency-Oriented Reading Instruction (FORI),
    43–44

Hierarchical linear modeling (HLM), 164
High schools, response to intervention (RTI) at, 288–293
Historian, thinking like, 69–71
Holistic scoring, in writing assessment, 265

Incidental learning, 122
Incidental word learning through read-alouds, 102
In-Depth Expanded Application of Science (IDEAS) project, 90
Informational texts, use of, 89
Instructional focus and read-alouds, 103–105
Instructional strategies and read-alouds, 105–109
    clarification and correction, 107–108
    definition, providing, 106
    examples, providing, 107
    extension, 108
    imagery, 108–109
    labeling, 108
    morphemic analysis, 109
    questioning, 105–106
    synonym, providing, 106–107
Integrated learning system (ILS), 223–224
Interest, adolescent literacy and, 203
Interesting texts, reading, 56
Internet reading, 234–236
Intervention, definition of, 276

Knowledge
    building authenticity with, 84–86
    content-area reading instruction, 88
    developing, 80, 81–82
    integrated instruction foregrounding, 89–91
    nonfiction/informational texts, use of, 89
    progressive movement, origin in, 86–87
    reading and content, evolving relationship of, 86–91
    supporting comprehension with, 82–84
    thematic instruction, 87–88

Language and content objectives, having, 153–154
Learning process, beginning English speakers in, 154–155
Letter–sound relationships, 11
    writing, 14
Level data, 276
Literacies, in 21st century, 226–230
    schools and policymakers, research-based recommendations for, 230
    teachers, research-based recommendations for, 229–230
Literacy coaching, 159–160, 172, 175–185
    activities, focuses on, 167–168
    coaches as literacy leaders, 169–170
    coaching standards, 175–177
    cognitive coaching, 178–179
    collaborative relationships, essential of, 166–167
    instructional improvement and student achievement, guiding principles for, 163–171
    intentional and opportunistic, 168–169
    models of, 175–185
    new-teacher mentoring, 177–178
    over time, evolving, 170–171
    peer coaching, 179–180
    professional development program, 159

program-specific coaching, 181–183
    reform-oriented coaching, 183–185
    specialized knowledge, requirement of, 163–165
    subject-specific coaching, 180–181
    time working with teachers, 165–166
Literacy problem, in middle schools, 189–190
    adolescent literacy instruction, enhancing, 193–194
    causes, 190–191
    reading problems, 192–193
Literacy screening, 276
    assessments, examples of, 278
Literacy teachers, changing world for, 226–227

Middle schools, response to intervention (RTI) at, 288–293
Middle school literacy problem, 189–190
    adolescent literacy instruction, enhancing, 193–194
    causes, 190–191
    reading problems, 192–193
Millennials, 203–204
Model fluent reading, 39
Multiple literacies, 203–204

National Assessment of Educational Progress (NAEP), 189, 190
    oral reading fluency scale, 54, 55t
National Literacy Panel (NLP) report, 136–137
Need new skills, needs of, 233–234
No Child Left Behind (NCLB) Act of 2001, 16
Nonfiction/informational texts, use of, 89

One-minute fluency measures, 47, 53–54, 57
    accuracy, 47–48
    assessment choices, 49–50
    assessment, deeper approaches to, 53–55
    automaticity, increasing, 56
    and deeper view of fluency, 50–51
    dysfluent students, 51
    endurance, assessing, 55
    expectations, increasing, 57
    fluency and endurance, instructing, 55–56
    interesting texts, reading, 56
    moving beyond, 57
    parents and caregivers, engaging, 57
    prosody, 48–49
    rate, 48
    readability levels, decreasing, 56
    reading fluency, 47
    reading volume, increasing, 56–57
    rereading, 57
    time, effects of, 51–53
Online reading assessment, 233–237
Oral reading, 28
    changing role of, 30
Oral vocabulary, 117

Partner reading, 34–35
Peer coaching, 179–180
Phonemes, 5
Phonics
    word recognition and, 1–2
    decoding, 4–5
Phonics instruction
    analogy-based approaches, 15–16
    analytic phonics, 8–10
    in early 21st century, 16

letter–sound relationships, 11
    multiple pathways, 13–14
    sound–symbol relationships, 10–11
    spelling-based approaches, 14–15
    whole-language movement, 12–13
    word-by-word reading, 7–8
    writing, 14
Policymakers, research-based recommendations for, 230
Popcorn reading, 29–30
Popsicle reading, 30
Portfolio assessment, in writing assessment, 265
Primary trait guides, in writing assessment, 265
Print vocabulary, 117
Productive vocabulary, 117
Program-specific coaching, 181–183
Progressive movement, origin in, 86–87
Prosody, 48–49
    and fluency, 27–28
Public Law 108-446, 276

Questioning, 105–106

Readability levels, decreasing, 56
Read-alouds and vocabulary, 101–102
    adult mediation in, 102
    discussion, 109–110
    final thoughts, 111
    incidental word learning through, 102
    instructional focus, 103–105
    instructional strategies, 105–109
    recommendations for practice, 110–111
    vocabulary instruction during read-alouds, 103
Readers theater, 44
Reading and content, evolving relationship of, 86
    content-area reading instruction, 88
    integrated instruction foregrounding knowledge, 89–91
    nonfiction/informational texts, use of, 89
    progressive movement, origin in, 86–87
    thematic instruction, 87–88
Reading-and-writing informational text genres, 85
Reading comprehension, changes in, 236–237
Reading development, stages of
    and word recognition, 4–5
Reading fluency, 47
    assisted reading, engaging in, 40
    Fast Start, 42–43
    fluency coach, acting as, 39–40
    Fluency Development Lesson (FDL), 42
    fluency materials, collecting, 40–41
    fluency-Oriented Reading Instruction (FORI), 43–44
    model fluent reading, 39
    performance and celebration, 41
    readers theater, 44
    singing lyrics to songs as reading, 44–45
Reading instruction, 211–212
Reading process
    bottom-up model of, 3
    simple view of, 4
    top-down model of, 2–3
Reading Recovery coaching, 182
Reading Teacher endorsement, 164, 165
Reading volume, increasing, 56–57

Receptive vocabulary, 117
Reform-oriented coaching, 183–185
Rereading, 57
Response to intervention (RTI), 273
    elementary vs. middle and high school,
        distinctions between, 290–292
    importance of, 284
    individualization, 282–284
    law, 276–278
    literacy screening assessments, 278
    at middle and high school, 288–293
    modified RTI model, 292–293
    prevention framework, at elementary
        grades, 289–290
    processes, 278–279
    queries, concerns, and future research,
        284–285
    in real life, 279–284
    scientifically valid interventions,
        implementing, 280
    special education services, determining
        eligibility for, 284
    students progress, monitoring, 281–282
    terminology and definitions, 277
    terms, definitions of, 276
    in theory, 275–276
    universal literacy practices, establishing,
        280
Rime analogies, using, 15–16
Round-robin reading, 28–30

Scaffolding, 31
Schools, research-based recommendations
    for, 230
Scientifically valid interventions,
    implementing, 280
Scientist, thinking like, 66–67
Scoring, holistic
    in writing assessment, 265
Singing lyrics to songs as reading, 44–45
Slope data, 276
Sophisticated vocabulary use, modeling,
    119–121
Sound–symbol relationships, 10–11
Special education services, determining
    eligibility for, 284
Specific learning disabilities, 277
Spelling-based approaches, in phonics,
    14–15
    making words, 15
    word study, 15
Standards for Staff Development, 176
Strategies and content approaches, 72
    comparison of, 74–75
    discussion, 76–78

measures and outcomes, 75–76
    roots and current status of, 73–74
Student-generated definition, extending, 108
    imagery, 108–109
    labeling, 108
    morphemic analysis, 109
Student progress monitoring, 276
Students' primary language, modifications
    using, 144–146
Students progress, monitoring, 281–282
Students response, clarifying and correcting,
    107–108
Subject-specific coaching, 180–181
Success for All (SFA), 182
Synonym, providing, 106–107
Systematic phonics, 1

Teachers
    adolescent literacy and, 194
    research-based recommendations for,
        229–230
Technology, 223–224
    automatic essay scoring (AES) systems, 228
    literacy teachers, changing world for,
        226–227
    online reading assessment, 233–237
    21st-century literacies, 226–230
    writing and, 266
Thematic instruction, 87–88
Time, effects of
    on students' reading, 51–53
Top-down model, of reading process, 2–3
21st-century literacies, 226–230

Universal literacy practices, establishing, 280

Vocabulary, 97
    adult mediation in read-alouds, 102
    affable Annie, 115–116
    clarification and correction, 107–108
    definition, providing, 106
    discussion, 109–110
    examples, providing, 107
    extension, 108
    final thoughts, 111
    imagery, 108–109
    incidental word learning through read-
        alouds, 102
    instruction during read-alouds, 103
    instructional focus, 103–105
    instructional strategies, 105–109
    labeling, 108
    morphemic analysis, 109
    observations and interviews, 103
    oral, 117

print, 117
    productive, 117
    questioning, 105–106
    and read-alouds, 101–102
    receptive, 117
    recommendations for practice, 110–111
    setting for the study, 102–103
    sophisticated vocabulary use, modeling,
        119–121
    synonym, providing, 106–107
    types of, 117
    vocabulary gap, closing, 125–127
    vocabulary learning, role of, 116–117
    weather watcher activity, 114–115
    word consciousness, promoting, 118–119
    word-conscious teacher, being, 122–123
    words selection to teach, 118

Whole language, 264
Whole-language movement, 12–13
Word-by-word reading, 7–8
Word consciousness, promoting, 118–119
Word-conscious teacher, being, 122–123
    vocabulary gap, closing, 125–127
Word processing, writing and, 241
Word recognition. *See also* Phonics; Phonics
        instruction
    bottom-up model, 3
    context and, 3–4
    phonics and, 1–2
    simple view of reading, 4
    stages of reading development and, 4–5
    top-down model, 2–3
Words selection to teach, 118
Writer, thinking like, 68–69
Writing, 241
    assessment issues, 265
    across the curriculum, 247–248
    holistic assessment, 265
    issues and trends in, 256–267
    portfolio assessment, 265
    in the post-process era, 266–267
    primary trait guides, 265
    as process, 259–260
    research on history of, 257–259
    research on instruction in, 241–242
    teaching of, 243–253
    technology and, 266
    trends in assessment, 264
    whole language and, 264
    word processing and, 241
    workshop approach, 263–264
Writing Across the Curriculum/Writing
        in the Disciplines (WAC/WID),
        262–263